keys to Success

Second Canadian Edition

how to

achieve

your

goals

Carol Carter

Joyce Bishop

Sarah Lyman Kravits

Peter J. Maurin

Editorial Consultant:
Richard D. Bucher
Professor of Sociology
Baltimore City Community College

Prentice
Hall

Toronto

Canadian Cataloguing in Publication Data

Keys to success : how to achieve your goals

2nd Canadian ed.
Includes index.
ISBN 0-13-018254-0

1. College student orientation — Canada — Handbooks, manuals, etc. 2. Study skills — Handbooks, manuals, etc. 3. College students — Canada — Life skills guides. I. Carter, Carol. II. Title: How to achieve your goals.

LB2343.34.C3K48 2001   378.1'98   C99-933040-3

ISBN 0-13-018254-0

Vice President, Editorial Director: Michael Young
Executive Editor: David Stover
Senior Marketing Manager: Sophia Fortier
Developmental Editor: Madhu Ranadive
Production Editor: Joe Zingrone
Copy Editor: Lu Cormier
Production Coordinator: Wendy Moran
Page Layout: Hermia Chung
Permissions/Photo Research: Susan Wallace-Cox
Art Director: Mary Opper
Interior Design: Carole Knox
Cover Design: Sarah Battersby
Cover Image: Allan Davey/Masterfile

4 5   05 04 03 02

Printed and bound in the U.S.A.

PHOTO CREDITS:

Chapter Opening Photos

Chapter	Source
1	The Slide Farm/Al Harvey
2	First Light/P. Coll
3	Dick Hemingway
4	Dick Hemingway
5	Dick Hemingway
6	Dick Hemingway
7	Image Network/Stanley Rowin
8	The Slide Farm/Al Harvey
9	Stone/Lori Adamski Peek
10	First Light/J.L. Pelaez
11	Bob Carroll

Interior Photos

Page	Source
10	Bob Daemmrich/Stock Boston
23	Kopstein/Monkmeyer Press
43	Frank Stewart
60	Rick Singer
74	Image Network/Richmond
92	Arnold Zann/Black Star
126	Beryl Goldberg
137	Peter Menzel Photography
167	The Slide Farm/Al Harvey
184	Frank Siteman
193	Unicorn Stock Photos/B.W. Hoffmann
219	Peter Menzel Photography
230	Image Network/Stewart Cohen
247	Stephen Collins/Photo Researchers, Inc.
277	Jeff Greenberg/Picture Cube, Inc.
289	Shackman/Monkmeyer Press
310	Image Network
327	Charles Ness/Gamma Liaison, Inc.
342	First Light/J.L. Perez
353	Toronto Sun
358	Dick Hemingway
376	Bob Carroll
382	Alan Klehr/Churchill & Klehr Photography
391	Michael P. Gadomsky/Photo Researchers, Inc.

CONTENTS

Part 1 Defining Yourself and Your Goals

Part 2 Developing Your Learning Skills

Part 3 Creating Life Success

PREFACE

Keys to Success, Second Canadian Edition Owner's Manual: Please Read Before Operating

When you spend money on a coffeemaker, electric drill, television, car, tape deck, or anything else, getting your money's worth means knowing how to operate your purchase so that it delivers what you want (good coffee, perhaps, or clear channel reception, or high-speed dubbing). When you bring the item home, you generally look over the manual or pamphlet that comes with it before you do anything else. The manual describes the parts, how they operate, and what should result if everything is functioning properly. With that in mind, think of this preface as your owner's manual for this book. Reading it might be one of the most helpful actions you take all year.

As your authors, we have talked to students across Canada. We've learned that you are concerned about your future, you want your education to serve a purpose, you are adjusting to constant life changes, and you want honest and direct guidance on how to achieve your goals. We designed the features of *Keys to Success, Second Canadian Edition* to meet what you have told us about your needs. Knowing how to use the features in this book—and make the most from your work in this class—will help you make the most of the time, effort, and money you are putting into your education.

Following are descriptions of the different pieces of this book and how to use them to your advantage.

The Contents of the Package: What's Included

We chose the topics in this book based on what you need to make the most of your educational experience. You need to *believe in yourself* just to believe that you are worth educating. You need a strong sense of *self, learning style,* and *goals* in order to discover and pursue the best course of study. You need good *study skills* to take in and retain what you learn both in and out of class. You need to know how to *stay healthy* so that you are in class and awake every time you need to be. You need to *manage your time, money,* and *relationships* so you can handle the changes life hands you. *Keys to Success* can guide you in all of these areas and more.

The Parts: Useful Features

The features (distinguishing characteristics and sections) of this book are designed to make your life easier by helping you take in and understand the material you read.

Lifelong learning. If what you study in this course helped you only to read textbooks and to pass tests, its usefulness would end at graduation, and you would have to start all over to learn how to deal with the real world. The ideas and strategies you learn that will help you succeed in school are the same ones that will bring you success in your career and in your personal life. Therefore, this book focuses on success strategies as they apply to *school, work,* and *life,* not just to the classroom.

Thinking skills. Being able to remember facts and figures won't do you much good at school or beyond unless you can put that information to work through clear and competent thinking. This book has a chapter on *critical and creative thinking* that will help you explore your mind's seven primary actions—the building blocks to competent thinking. You will also see how to combine those actions in order to perform thinking processes such as problem solving, decision making, and strategic planning.

Skill-building exercises. Today's graduates need to be effective thinkers, team players, writers, and strategic planners. The exercises at the end of the chapters will encourage you to develop these valuable career skills and to apply thinking processes to any topic or situation.

 Key into Your Life: the first set of exercises at the end of every chapter, a series that encourages you to ask questions and apply critical thinking to your own life.

 Key to Cooperative Learning: an exercise that gives you a chance to interact and learn in a group setting, building your teamwork and leadership skills in the process.

 Key to Self-Expression: a journal-writing exercise that provides an opportunity for you to express your thoughts and develop your writing ability.

 Key to Your Personal Portfolio: an exercise that enables you to gather, create, and maintain concrete evidence of your qualifications and progress, eventually resulting in a packet of information useful in school and in the workplace.

Diversity of voice. Canada is becoming increasingly diverse in ethnicity, perspective, culture, lifestyle, race, choices, abilities, needs, and more. Every student, instructor, course, and school is unique. One point of view can't possibly apply to everyone. Therefore, many voices will speak to you from these pages. What you read will speak to your needs, offer ideas, and treat you with respect.

- *Real World Perspectives,* a question-and-answer feature, will appear once per chapter. In it, one person will present a question about an issue in his or her life, and another person who has had similar experiences will give advice in response.

- *Examples* throughout the text deal with the different situations that different students face—working while in school, parenting, dealing with different financial needs, supporting various lifestyles and schedules, and so on.

- Each chapter's *summary* will introduce to you a word or phrase from a language other than English, and will discuss how you might apply the meaning of that word or phrase to your own life.

- The *exercises* throughout the book recognize and reinforce your uniqueness; they are designed so that you apply what you learn to the particulars of your own life.

Using the Parts: Helpful Hints for Operation

We've worked to make this book as user-friendly as possible. The following features will make your life easier in small but significant ways.

- **Perforations.** Each page of this book is perforated so that you can tear out exercises to hand in, should your instructor ask you to do so. You can also tear out sections if you like, perhaps to take with you somewhere or to keep in your date book as a reference.

- **Exercises.** The exercises are together at the ends of the chapters, so if you want to hand them all in you can do so without removing much of the text. There is a space at the beginning of the exercises where you can write your name.

- **Definitions.** Selected words are defined in the margins of the text. If you don't know these words, the definitions save you a trip to the dictionary; if you do know them, the definitions offer a quick and easy refresher.

- **Weblinks.** Selected Canadian Web addresses are given in the margins. Visit a site for current Canadian news, references, and facts.

- **Layout and style.** The book is divided into parts. Each part has a theme and contains chapters that relate to one another within that theme. Full-colour photos, graphics, and cartoons will illustrate key points as well as spice up your reading. At the end of Parts 1 and 2, a crossword puzzle will offer an entertaining way to review material.

- **Long-term usefulness.** Yes, many people sell back some of the textbooks they use. If you take a good look at the material in *Keys to Success*, however, you may want to keep this book around. We know that you are concerned about the competitiveness of the job market, your future careers, and your quality of life. *Keys to Success* is a reference that you can return to over and over again as you work toward your goals. Measure the few dollars you would earn back against the worth of having helpful information around when you need it.

Take Action: Read

You are responsible for your education, your growth, your knowledge, and your future. If you know yourself, choose the right paths, and follow them with determination, you will earn the success that you deserve in school, the workplace, and your personal life. The best we can do is offer some great suggestions, strategies, ideas, and systems that can help. Ultimately, it's up to you to use them. So take whatever fits your particular self with all of its particular situations, needs, and wants, and make it your own. You've made a terrific start by choosing to pursue an education—take advantage of all it has to give you.

ACKNOWLEDGMENTS

While I am the Canadian author for this, the second Canadian edition of *Keys to Success*, the contents of the book are really the product of years of teaching at several institutions. I would like to thank the following people:

- The students: Whether it was communications or criminology, sociology or stress management, as your lecturer or as your seminar leader, you always taught me something in the process.

- At Mohawk College: Mike Dwyer, Barb Reavley, and Rick Holmes for letting me hear their ideas about teaching and for listening to mine. I always appreciated your support and guidance. A special thanks to Shelagh Gill and Tammy Capone for their support through my early years at the college.

- At Brock University: Bohdan Szuchewycz, Jeanette Sloniowski, Walt Watson, Caroline Stikkellbroeck, and Jim Leach.

- At Pearson Education Canada: Thanks to David Stover and Madhu Ranadive for their support and incredible patience.

- At home: To Kim, Sonja, and Joshua: You are my "keys to success."

Peter J. Maurin

SUPPLEMENTS

Supplements for Instructors

Instructor's Resource Kit

This extensive kit is designed to help you successfully teach student orientation and student success courses. Organized according to the objectives and lessons of each chapter, the kit includes transparency masters, Test Item File questions, pre- and post-class evaluations, lecture guides, and innovative tips to motivate all kinds of students. *Free to instructors using the textbook.*

Overhead Transparencies

Full-colour acetates that relate directly to the course lecture material and help focus students on key objectives. *Free to instructors using the textbook.*

Student Key Advice Video

Contains a selection of motivational tips and advice by beginning post-secondary students, students in their third and fourth years, and professionals in varying career areas. These tapes are in manageable segments designed so that they can be shown individually or all at once. *Free to adopters of the textbook.*

ABC News Video Library

Contains segments that appeared on such award-winning shows as *World News Tonight*, *Nightline*, and *20/20*. These segments are on topics relevant to student success and have been collected into a video library. *Free to adopters of the textbook.* (0-13-746306-5)

Faculty Development/School In-Service Programs

Pearson Education Canada sponsors a variety of faculty workshops on campuses and in specific cities throughout the year. Workshops can be cross-disciplinary or discipline-specific. Contact your local Pearson representative for details.

Teacher Training Video

This library of teaching tips on student success and career development, for first-time instructors as well as those who have taught for years, provides information on how to teach multiple intelligences and critical thinking and supplies school-to-work transition tips.

Also Available:

Ten Ways to Fight Hate (0-13-028146-8)

Lassi—Learning Skills Inventory (0-13-010376-4)

Supplements Available for Students

NCS Career Testing Program

The Enhanced Version of the Career Assessment Inventory. This test compares occupational interests and personality preferences with individuals in hundreds of careers. Contact your local representative for details.

New York Times Spring 2000

These are discipline-specific newspapers geared toward student success and career development. Each contains articles published in *The New York Times. Free when using the textbook.*

Student Success Supersite

Explore different majors that you can take in university, and get advice on study skills, money matters, career goals, fitness and personal well being, and other information essential to a happy and productive student life. www.prenhall.com/success

The Student Planner

Comprising daily and monthly planners, calendars through the year 2001, an address book, course and class planners, and other organizing materials, the Student Planner is designed to help students organize and manage their time more effectively. (0-13-649120-0)

The Student Journal

A book that helps students get the most out of the course by encouraging them to keep track of their progress over time. (0-13-672826-X)

Also avilable:

The Student Organizer CD-ROM (0-13-026427-X)

Study Skills Video (0-13-096095-0)

Canadian Supplements

Instructor's Manual
(0-13-019668-1)

Test Item File
(0-13-019669-X)

Computerized Test Item File
(0-13-019660-6)

Companion Web Site
www.pearsoned.ca/carter

The Pearson Education Canada

companion Website . . .

Your Internet companion to the most exciting, state-of-the-art educational tools on the Web!

The Pearson Education Canada Companion Web site is easy to navigate and is organized to correspond to the chapters in this textbook. The Companion Web site is comprised of four distinct, functional features:

1) **Customized Online Resources**

2) **Online Study Guide**

3) **Reference Material**

4) **Communication**

Explore the four areas in this Companion Web site. Students and distance learners will discover resources for indepth study, research and communication, empowering them in their quest for greater knowledge and maximizing their potential for success in the course.

A NEW WAY TO DELIVER EDUCATIONAL CONTENT

1) Customized Online Resources

Our Companion Web sites provide instructors and students with a range of options to access, view, and exchange content.

- **Syllabus Builder** provides *instructors* with the option to create online classes and construct an online syllabus linked to specific modules in the Companion Web site.

- **Mailing lists** enable *instructors* and *students* to receive customized promotional literature.

- **Preferences** enable *students* to customize the sending of results to various recipients, and also to customize how the material is sent, e.g., as html, text, or as an attachment.

- **Help** includes an evaluation of the user's system and a tune-up area that makes updating browsers and plug-ins easier. This new feature will enhance the user's experience with Companion Web sites.

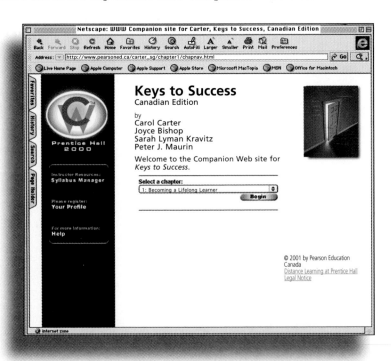

www.pearsoned.ca/carter

Pearson Education

COMPANION
WEB SITE

2) Online Study Guide

Interactive Study Guide modules form the core of the student learning experience in the Companion Web site. These modules are categorized according to their functionality:

- Objectives
- Multiple Choice
- Essay questions

The **objectives** module lists the key topics in each chapter, so students can have an overview of the chapter and plan how they will study. The Multiple Choice modules provides students with the ability to send answers to our grader and receive instant feedback on their progress through our Results Reporter. Coaching comments and references back to the textbook ensure that students take advantage of all resources available to enhance their learning experience.

3) Reference Material

Reference material broadens text coverage with up-to-date resources for learning. **Web Destinations** provides a directory of Web sites relevant to the subject matter in each chapter. **Articles** are selected by the authors with relevant to student life. **Intelligent Essay Assessor** is an interactive assessment tool. Students can respond directly on-screen to an essay question, submit it for marking, and receive an evaluation of their paper. Students are given a word limit and the opportunity to make chances to the essay before it is submitted for making.

4) Communication

Companion Web sites contain the communication tools necessary to deliver courses in a **Distance Learning** environment. **Message Board** allows users to post messages and check back periodically for responses.

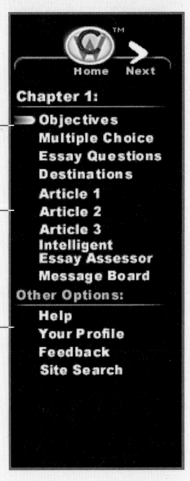

Home Next

Chapter 1:
- Objectives
- Multiple Choice
- Essay Questions
- Destinations
- Article 1
- Article 2
- Article 3
- Intelligent Essay Assessor
- Message Board

Other Options:
- Help
- Your Profile
- Feedback
- Site Search

Note: Companion Web site content will vary slightly from site to site depending on discipline requirements.

The Companion Web sites can be found at:

www.pearsoned.ca/carter

**PEARSON EDUCATION
CANADA**

26 Prince Andrew Place
Don Mills, Ontario M3C 2T8

To order:
Call: 1-800-567-3800
Fax: 1-800-263-7733

For samples:
Call: 1-800-850-5813
Fax: (416) 447-7755
E-mail: cdn.order@pearsoned.com

ABOUT THE AUTHORS

Carol Carter is Vice President and Director of Student Programs and Faculty Development at Prentice Hall. She has written *Majoring in the Rest of Your Life: Career Secrets for College Students* and *Majoring in High School*. She has also co-authored *Graduating Into the Nineties, The Career Tool Kit, Keys to Career Success, Keys to Effective Learning*, and the first edition of *Keys to Success*. In 1992 Carol and other business people co-founded a nonprofit organization called LifeSkills, Inc., to help high school students explore their goals, their career options, and the real world through part-time employment and internships. LifeSkills is now part of the Tucson Unified School District and is featured in seventeen high schools in Tucson, Arizona.

Joyce Bishop holds a Ph.D. in psychology and has taught for more than twenty years, receiving a number of honours, including Teacher of the Year. For the past four years she has been voted "favourite teacher" by the student body and Honor Society at Golden West College, Huntington Beach, CA, where she has taught since 1986 and is a tenured professor. She is currently working with a federal grant to establish Learning Communities and Workplace Learning in her district, and has developed workshops and trained faculty in cooperative learning, active learning, multiple intelligences, workplace relevancy, learning styles, authentic assessment, team building, and the development of learning communities. She also co-authored *Keys to Effective Learning*.

Sarah Lyman Kravits comes from a family of educators and has long cultivated an interest in educational development. She co-authored *The Career Tool Kit, Keys to Effective Learning*, and the first edition of *Keys to Success*, and has served as Program Director for LifeSkills, Inc., a nonprofit organization that aims to further the career and personal development of high school students. In that capacity she helped to formulate both curricular and organizational elements of the program, working closely with instructors as well as members of the business community. Sarah holds a B.A. in English and drama from the University of Virginia, where she was a Jefferson Scholar, and an M.F.A. from Catholic University.

Peter J. Maurin received his Master's degree in sociology from McMaster University in 1992. He is currently teaching in the Media Studies Department at Mohawk College in Hamilton, Ontario. In the past, he has been a student adviser for the General Arts and Science Program at Mohawk. He has taught at Seneca and Niagara College and at Brock University. The second Canadian edition of *Key to Success* is Peter's fourth book for Prentice Hall. Besides teaching, Peter is a professional communicator: He is a freelance business writer and broadcaster, logging more than eighteen years on the air for several radio stations in Ontario.

PART 1

Defining Yourself and your Goals

1 Becoming a Lifelong Learner:
Opening Doors

In this chapter, you will explore answers to the following questions:

- Who is pursuing an education in Canada today?

- How does education promote success in Canada?

- What resources are available at your school?

- How can you strive for success?

- What is your role in a diverse world?

- What skills are Canadian employers looking for?

Welcome—or welcome back—to your education. Whether you are right out of high school, returning to student life after working for some years, or continuing on a current educational path, you are facing new challenges and changes. Whatever you feel—excitement, hesitation, worry, anticipation, or any combination of emotions—you have made an important choice. Every Canadian has a right to seek the self-improvement, knowledge, and opportunity that an education can provide. You have already taken the first step just by being here. By choosing to pursue an education you have given yourself a strong vote of confidence and the chance to improve your future.

This book will help you fulfill your potential as a learner by giving you keys—ideas, strategies, and skills in a variety of areas—that can lead to success in school, on the job, and in life. These keys will help to create opportunities where there were once closed doors. Chapter 1 will give you an overview of the educational world. It will start by looking at today's students—who they are and how they've changed—and at the connection between education and success. The chapter will also show you that you aren't alone in school. There are resources all around to help you deal with issues and problems that may arise. Finally, you will discover in this chapter that the road to success involves a partnership between your school and yourself.

Thinking It Through

Check those statements that apply to you right now:

- ☐ I think that the typical Canadian post-secondary student is an 18-year-old right out of high school.

- ☐ Sometimes school feels like a detour that's just keeping me from moving ahead in my life.

- ☐ When I need help with school or personal issues, I know that there are places I can go but I have no idea how to find them.

- ☐ One moment I believe in myself, and then I turn around and I've lost all my drive for success.

- ☐ I don't really see the point of learning about other cultures; they don't concern me anyway.

Who Is Pursuing An Education in Canada Today?

In various forms, structured learning took place in the ancient civilizations of Rome, Greece, Byzantium, and Islam. Learning institutions became formalized as universities, similar to those we have today, in medieval Europe as early as the eleventh century. In the early life of the university, students and scholars were men, mostly white, seeking religious and intellectual pursuits. Since their inception, universities have evolved, becoming centres for cultural and social inspiration, intellectual growth, and scientific advancements and research.

Because of government support and a universal understanding that a formal education should be the right of all Canadians regardless of race, creed, colour, age, or gender, colleges and universities have become extremely diverse, serving over 1.43 million people per year in Canada. As you enter, or re-enter, your post-secondary education, one thing is clear: The face of post-secondary education is changing. According to the Association of Canadian Community Colleges, as Canada enters the twenty-first century, 175 community colleges—sometimes referred to as technical institutes, CEGEP (in Quebec), or agricultural colleges—offer diplomas, certificates, and training in specialized fields.[1] Seventy-seven universities across Canada offer baccalaureate and advanced (M.A. or Ph.D.) degrees. Some post-secondary institutions report student populations as large as 35 000; others have enrollments of less than 1 000. You can even take virtual classes—particularly business and applied science courses—online. And with Canadian Learning Television, you can earn credits toward your degree or diploma from your television at home.

Today's students are more diverse than at any time in history. Although many students still enter a post-secondary institution directly after high school, the old standard of the student finishing a college or university education at the age of 22 is a standard no longer. Some students take longer than four years to finish. Some students complete part of their education, pursue other paths for a while, and return to finish later in life. Some go right into the work force after high school and decide to pursue a degree after many years. The old rules no longer apply.

The Diverse Student Body

Statistics Canada paints an interesting picture of the Canadian post-secondary student population as we head into the twenty-first century.[2]

- 578 000 students attend universities full time; 288 000 attend part time.
- 410 000 students attend colleges; almost one-quarter of them are transfer students from universities. Another 164 000 attend college on a part-time basis.
- Women now make up the majority of post-secondary students.
- The most popular programs for women are business and the social sciences.

- Men tend to take courses in business, engineering, and the applied sciences.
- 88 000 foreign students study in Canada; over half come from Asia, and about one-fifth come from Europe.

These changes have brought with them a new educational experience defined by the varying needs of an increasingly diverse student body. Not so long ago, if you were female, a minority, or a person with a disability, you had limited opportunity to attend college or university. Even twenty years ago, you might have given up on a post-secondary education if you had limited financial resources, were unable to attend classes during the day, or hadn't enrolled immediately after high school and then felt it was too late to return.

Now, however, an education is available to a wide range of potential students, regardless of their circumstances. You are likely to find a program that's right for you, even if you have financial needs, child-care needs, an unusual work schedule, or a specific learning style. Businesses, educational institutions, and the general public are becoming aware that education benefits the whole society as much as it does the individual.

To reflect the changing nature of students, many post-secondary institutions are now offering credit for prior learning. Lurline Langbell, Director of the Canadian Learning Bank,[3] offers these examples of prior learning credit:

- Credits from other post-secondary institutions are often transferable, even between colleges and universities.
- Training supplied by private training schools can often be used toward a diploma or degree.
- If you are returning to school after a few years in the workplace, you may be able to use professional development activities for credit.
- Many schools also assess the skills you acquired in the "real world" and may grant you credit toward your degree or diploma.

Education isn't an automatic guarantee of a higher-level, better-paying job. Statistically, however, a better-educated population means a more efficient work force, more career fulfillment, and better-paid workers. Statistics Canada reports that education is a key factor not only in helping Canadians find work, but also in finding the kind of work they enjoy.[4] Quality of life can improve when people make the most of their abilities through education.

The decision to take advantage of an education is in your hands. No school can force you to learn. You are responsible for seeking out opportunities and weaving school into the fabric of your life. You may face some of these challenges:

- Handling the responsibilities and stress of parenting children alone, without a spouse
- Returning to school as an older student and feeling out of place
- Learning to adjust to the cultural and communication differences in the diverse student population

Association of Canadian
Community Colleges
www.accc.ca

This group of colleges all across Canada was formed in 1972. The Web site contains links to colleges and industry.

Association of Universities
and Colleges of Canada
www.aucc.ca

This site offers news and information about post-secondary education, student awards, and opportunities for continuing your education around the world through exchange programs.

- Having a physical disability that presents challenges
- Having a learning disability such as dyslexia or Attention Deficit Disorder (ADD)
- Balancing a school schedule with part-time or even full-time work
- Handling the enormous financial commitment that advanced education requires

Your school can help you work through these and other problems if you actively seek out solutions and help from available support systems around you. Explore some reasons why the hard work is worthwhile.

How Does Education Promote Success in Canada?

Education—the process of developing and training the mind—should be far more than the accumulation of credit hours. If you take advantage of all education has to offer, you will develop the skills and talents you need to succeed in your career—and in life.

This book will frequently refer to a profile developed by the Corporate Council on Education, a program of the Conference Board of Canada. The Council is a research organization whose members include Canadian corporations and government. "Employability skills" are defined as the "generic skills, attitudes, and behaviours that employers look for in new recruits and employees."[5] Companies such as Air Canada, Bank of Montreal, CP Rail, Dofasco, General Motors, IBM, and Teleglobe Canada helped determine which generic skills were preferred by Canadian businesses. These were broken down into three categories: Academic Skills, Personal Management Skills, and Teamwork Skills (see Figure 1–1).

Education can help you develop these kinds of generic skills. In *Canada Prospects: Canada's Guide to Career Planning*,[6] Human Resources Development Canada provides a list of how work skills are built in school. For example, communications skills are developed by reading your text, writing essays, and giving oral presentations. Time management skills are built by doing your homework and simply getting to class on time. And learning skills are acquired by asking questions, reading, and joining clubs on campus.

How else can education help you succeed? Here are some of the ways.

Education gives you tools for lifelong learning. You learn facts while you are in school, but, more importantly, you learn how to think. While some of the facts and figures you learn today may not apply to the world of tomorrow, your ability to think will be useful always, in everything you do.

Education expands your self-concept. As you rise to the challenges of education, you will discover that your capacity for knowledge and personal growth is greater than you imagined. As your abilities grow, so do opportunities to learn and do more in class, on the job, and in your community.

Conference Board of Canada
www.conferenceboard.ca

This extensive site contains information about their Employability Skills Profile and some of their pilot projects with Canadian universities and colleges.

Career Tips
www.careertips.com/

Human Resources Development Canada administers this excellent site. It lists career prospects according to skill levels and growth opportunities into the twenty-first century. It also offers a look at what you can expect to be paid in your chosen field.

Figure 1-1   Employability Skills Profile

Academic Skills

Those skills which provide the basic foundation to get, keep and progress on a job and to achieve the best results

Canadian employers need a person who can:

Communicate

- Understand and speak the languages in which business is conducted
- Listen to, understand and learn
- Read, comprehend and use written materials, including graphs, charts and displays
- Write effectively in the languages in which business is conducted

Think

- Think critically and act logically to evaluate situations, solve problems and make decisions
- Understand and solve problems involving mathematics and use the results
- Use technology, instruments, tools and information systems effectively
- Access and apply specialized knowledge from various fields (e.g., skilled trades, technology, physical sciences, arts and social sciences)

Learn

- Continue to learn for life

Personal Management Skills

The combination of skills, attitudes and behaviours required to get, keep and progress on a job and to achieve the best results

Canadian employers need a person who can demonstrate:

Positive Attitudes and Behaviours

- Self-esteem and confidence
- Honesty, integrity and personal ethics
- A positive attitude toward learning, growth and personal health
- Initiative, energy and persistence to get the job done

Responsibility

- The ability to set goals and priorities in work and personal life
- The ability to plan and manage time, money and other resources to achieve goals
- Accountability for actions taken

Adaptability

- A positive attitude toward change
- Recognition of and respect for people's diversity and individual differences
- The ability to identify and suggest new ideas to get the job done— creativity

Teamwork Skills

Those skills needed to work with others on a job and to achieve the best results

Canadian employers need a person who can:

Work with Others

- Understand and contribute to the organization's goals
- Understand and work within the culture of the group
- Plan and make decisions with others and support the outcomes
- Respect the thoughts and opinions of others in the group
- Exercise "give and take" to achieve group results
- Seek a team approach as appropriate
- Lead when appropriate, mobilizing the group for high performance

Source: Reproduced with permission of the Conference Board of Canada.

Education enlarges your possibilities. Education gives you a *base of choices* and *increased power*, as shown in Figure 1–2. First, through different courses of study, it introduces you to *more choices* of career and life goals. Second, through the training you receive, it gives you *more power* to achieve the goals you choose. For example, while taking a writing class, you may learn about careers in journalism. This experience may lead you to take a class in journalistic writing that teaches you about reporting. Down the road, you may

Figure 1-2   Education Increases Choices and Power

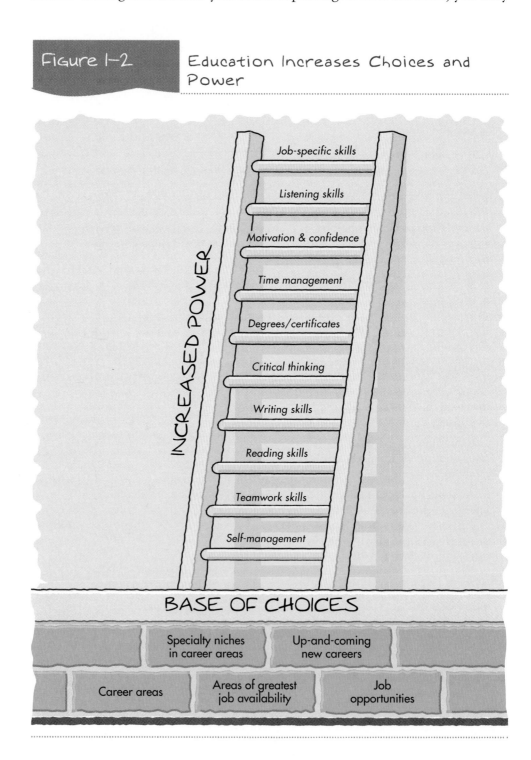

INCREASED POWER

Job-specific skills

Listening skills

Motivation & confidence

Time management

Degrees/certificates

Critical thinking

Writing skills

Reading skills

Teamwork skills

Self-management

BASE OF CHOICES

Specialty niches in career areas

Up-and-coming new careers

Career areas

Areas of greatest job availability

Job opportunities

decide to work on a newspaper and to make journalism your career. Looking back, you realize that two classes you took in college changed the course of your life.

Need more evidence that education improves your chances by increasing your choices and power? In *Boom, Bust and Echo 2000*, David Foot and Daniel Stoffman claim that jobs for Canadians without college or university education continue to disappear. In 1997, for example, 167 000 jobs were created for people with a high school diploma or less, while 431 000 jobs were created for post-secondary graduates. This is a continuation of a trend that started in the early 1990s. In Canada it is easier to find a job if you are a post-secondary graduate, although you may not necessarily find work within your discipline.[7] As outlined earlier in the Conference Board of Canada data, companies like to hire people who have the kinds of skills learned in college and university. Many "manual" jobs now require reading, writing, and analytical skills. Human Resources Development Canada echoes this finding: They maintain that 50 per cent of all jobs created in the 1990s required at least sixteen years of formal education.[8] A post-secondary education will dramatically improve your chances of getting a job you want. The research, writing, computer, interpersonal, and analytical skills you learn while continuing your education are exactly the kinds of skills that Canadian employers demand.

Education improves your employability and earning potential. Learning additional skills raises your competency so you can fulfill the requirements of higher-level jobs. In addition, having a diploma and/or a degree makes an impression on potential employers and makes you eligible for higher-salaried positions. According to Statistics Canada, the average income for a person with a high school diploma is $23 763. Canadians with a college diploma or certificate earn on average a little over $26 395, while a university graduate can expect on average to make $36 650 per year.[9]

Education makes you a well-rounded person. As it widens your understanding about what is possible in the world, education increases your awareness and appreciation of areas that affect and enrich human lives, such as music, art, literature, science, politics, and economics.

Education affects both community involvement and personal health. Education helps to prepare individuals for community activism by helping them understand political, economic, and social conditions. Education also increases knowledge about health behaviours and preventive care. The more education you have, the more likely you are to practise healthy habits in your daily life and to make informed decisions.

Education is more than the process of going to school and earning a degree or certificate. It is a choice to improve your mind and your skills. Any program, no matter the length or the focus, is an opportunity to set and strive for goals. Education is what you make of it. A dedicated, goal-oriented learner will benefit more from school than a student who doesn't focus. If you make the most of your mind, your time, and your educational opportunities, you will realize your potential. Using available resources is part of that process.

What Resources Are Available at Your School?

resources

People, organizations, or services that supply help and support for different aspects of college or university life.

Resources help you make the most of your education. As a student, you are investing money and time. Whether you complete your studies over the course of six months or sixty years, resources can help you get where you want to go.

Like any company that makes products or provides services, your school is a business. The goal of this particular business is the successful education of all who come through its doors. At the same time that it works to provide resources for you, an institution must also hire hundreds of employees, people who maintain buildings and grounds, serve meals, provide financial aid, and support campus organizations. In all that activity, the people at your school may seem unaware of your needs at times, no matter how much they want to help. Don't let that happen. Be vocal in requesting services and resources.

On page 14 you will find Table 1–1, a general summary of resources, most or all of which can be found at your school. Most schools offer a student orientation near the beginning of your first semester that will explain resources and other important information. Even if your school does not, you can orient yourself. The following sections will describe helpful resources—people, student services, organizations, course calendars, and student handbooks.

People

Your school has an array of people who can help you make the most of your educational experience: instructors, administrative personnel, advisers and counsellors, and teaching assistants. They're often busy with numerous responsibilities, but their assistance is provided as a standard part of your educational package. Take the opportunity to get to know them, and to let them get to know you. Together you can explore how they can help you achieve your goals.

Instructors are more than just sources of information during scheduled class time. They can also be valuable resources for you to consult. You might ask them to clarify course material or explain homework assignments. They can advise you on course selection in their department, give educational and career advice, and may even be able to introduce you to professionals in your chosen field. Although this book uses the term "instructor" for simplicity's sake, instructors have official titles that show their rank. From lowest to highest, these include lecturer, instructor, assistant professor, associate professor, and full professor (often just called professor).

Instructors have many time-draining responsibilities outside of teaching. They work to stay on the cutting edge of their fields, and higher-ranked instructors are often expected to publish articles and books. They prepare lectures and class plans and read stacks of student work. Sometimes they are students themselves with their own study commitments. However, you can gain access to your instructors while still respecting the demands on their time. Most instructors keep office hours, and they will tell you the location and times. You are responsible for seeking out your instructor during office hours. If your schedule makes this impossible, let your instructor know. Perhaps you and your instructor can get together at another time. If your school has an electronic mail (e-mail) system that allows you to send messages via computer, you may be able to communicate with your instructor using e-mail.

Teaching assistants are people who help an instructor with a course. You may or may not have teaching assistants in your courses. Often they are studying to be instructors themselves. Sometimes they teach the smaller discussion sections that accompany a large group lecture. They can be a great resource when your instructor is too swamped to talk to you.

Your school's administrative personnel have the responsibility of delivering to you—the student consumer—a first-rate product. That product is the sum total of your education, comprising facilities, instructors, materials, and courses. Schedule a meeting with your dean, the chair of a particular department, or other school administrator if you have an issue to discuss, such as a conflict with an instructor, an inability to get into a class you need, or a school regulation that causes a problem for you. Although administrators don't interact with students as often as instructors do, it is their business to know how the school is serving you. When you ask administrators and their staff members for assistance, you may also gain the assistance and support of someone who is in a position to help you.

Advisers and counsellors can help with both the educational and personal sides of being a student. They provide information, advice, referrals, and other sources of help. Generally, students are assigned academic advisers with whom they meet at least once a semester. Your academic adviser will help you find out about classes, choose a schedule, explore and select a major or design your own when the time comes, and plan out the big picture of your academic life. Visit your academic adviser more than once a semester if you have questions or want to make changes. If you're in university, feel free to visit the chair of your department or program for academic advice.

Counsellors, although not usually assigned, are available to you at any time, usually through student services. Don't hesitate to seek a counsellor's help if you have something on your mind. The ups and downs of your personal life greatly influence the quality of your work in school. If you put some effort into working through personal problems, you will be more able to do your work well and hand it in on time. Occasionally, an illness or family difficulty may interfere with your schoolwork enough to call for special provisions for the completion of your classes. Most institutions are more than happy to assist you during challenging times. Drop by your school's Registrar's Office for information on how to make an appointment with a counsellor.

Student Services

Your school has a variety of services aimed at helping students. Basic services offered by almost every school include the following: academic advising and personal counselling, student health/wellness, career planning and placement, tutoring, fitness/physical education, and financial aid. Depending on your school, you may also find other services: child care, housing and transportation, adult education services (for adults returning to school), disabled student services, academic centres (reading centre, writing centre, math centre, etc.—for help with these specific subjects), various support groups, school publications, and campus radio that help keep you informed of developments that affect you.

Often a school will have special services for specific populations. For example, at a school where most of the students commute, there may be a transportation office that helps students locate bus schedules and routes, find parking and sign up for permits, or track down car pools. Similarly, at a school where many students are parents, a child-care centre may provide day care during class time and also refer students to outside baby-sitters. You will find additional details about school services in Table 1–1 on page 14. They can help you earn the maximum benefit from your educational experience.

Organizations

No matter what your needs or interests, your school probably has an organization for you. Some organizations are sponsored by the school (academic clubs), some are independent but have a branch at the school (political parties), and some are student-run organizations (International Student Association). Some organizations focus on courses of study (Nursing Club), some are primarily social (fraternities and sororities), some are artistic (Film Society), and some are geared toward a hobby or activity (Runner's Club). Some you join in order to help others (Big Brothers or Big Sisters), and some offer help to you (Overeaters Anonymous).

When you consider adding a new activity to your life, weigh the positive effects against the negative effects. Positive effects could be new friends, fun activities, help, a break from schoolwork, stress relief, improved academic performance, increased teamwork and leadership skills, aid to others, and experience that can broaden your horizons. On the negative side there may be a heavy time commitment, dues, inconvenient location or meeting times, or too much responsibility. Explore a club carefully to see if it makes sense for you. As you make your decision, consider this: Studies have shown that students who join organizations tend to persist in their educational goals more than those who don't.

To find out about organizations at your school, consult your student handbook, ask friends and instructors, or check the activities office or centre if your school has one. Some schools, on registration days, have an area where organizations set up tables and make themselves available to talk to interested students. Some organizations seek you out based on your academic achievements. Find out as much as you can. Ask what is expected in terms of time, responsibility, and any necessary financial commitment. Talk to students who are currently involved. Perhaps give an organization a test run to see if you like it.

If you try out an organization, make a commitment that you will stay for the right reasons. Don't be afraid of being labelled a "drop-out"; if something becomes more than you can handle, bow out gracefully. In the best of all possible worlds, your involvement in organizations will enrich your life, expand your network of acquaintances, boost your time-management skills, and help you achieve goals.

University and College Calendars and Student Handbooks

Navigating through your school's course offerings, the departments and resource offices, and even the layout of the campus can seem overwhelming. There are two publications that can help you find your way—university and college calendars and the student handbook. Most schools provide these materials as a standard part of their enrollment information.

The *calendar* is your school's academic directory. It lists every department and course available at the school. Each course name will generally have two parts—"SS108" or "Comm3F60," for example. The first part is one or more letters indicating department and subject matter, and the second part is a number indicating course level (lower numbers for introductory courses and higher numbers for more advanced ones). The calendar groups courses according to subject matter and lists them from the lowest-level courses up to the most advanced, indicating the number of credits earned for each class. (See Figure 1–3 for a segment of an actual college calendar from Mohawk College.) A registration guide released prior to each semester will indicate details such as the instructor, the days and times the course meets, the location (building and room), and the maximum number of students who can take the course.

University and college calendars contain a wealth of other information. They may provide general school policies such as admissions requirements, the registration process, and withdrawal procedures. They may list the departments to show the range of subjects you may study. They may outline instructional programs, detailing core requirements as well as requirements for various majors, degrees, and certificates. They may also list administrative personnel as well as faculty and staff

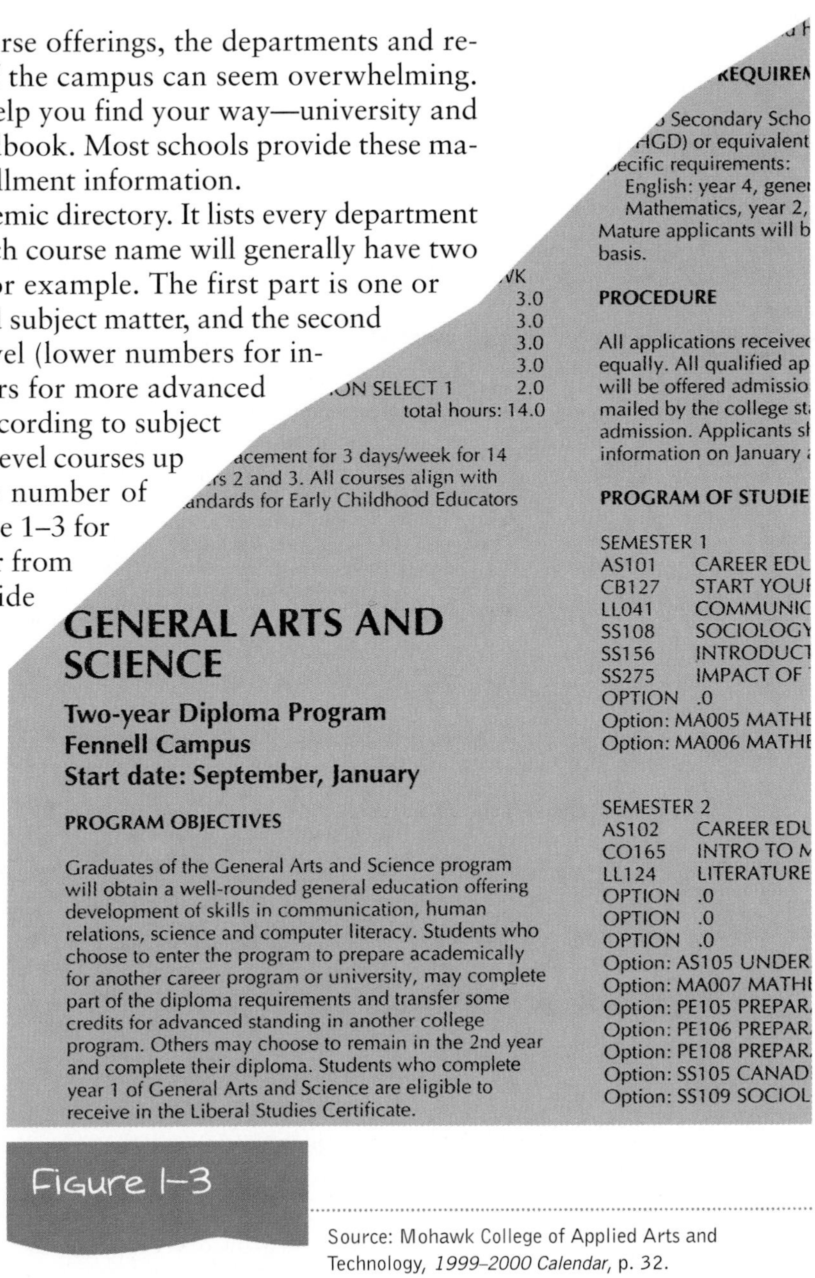

REQUIREM

o Secondary Scho
HGD) or equivalent
ecific requirements:
  English: year 4, gener
  Mathematics, year 2,
Mature applicants will b
basis.

PROCEDURE

All applications received
equally. All qualified ap
will be offered admissio
mailed by the college st
admission. Applicants sh
information on January

PROGRAM OF STUDIE

SEMESTER 1
AS101   CAREER EDU
CB127   START YOUF
LL041   COMMUNIC
SS108   SOCIOLOGY
SS156   INTRODUCT
SS275   IMPACT OF
OPTION .0
Option: MA005 MATHE
Option: MA006 MATHE

SEMESTER 2
AS102   CAREER EDU
CO165   INTRO TO M
LL124   LITERATURE
OPTION .0
OPTION .0
OPTION .0
Option: AS105 UNDER
Option: MA007 MATHI
Option: PE105 PREPAR.
Option: PE106 PREPAR.
Option: PE108 PREPAR.
Option: SS105 CANAD
Option: SS109 SOCIOL

VK
3.0
3.0
3.0
3.0
ON SELECT 1 2.0
total hours: 14.0

acement for 3 days/week for 14
rs 2 and 3. All courses align with
andards for Early Childhood Educators

GENERAL ARTS AND SCIENCE

Two-year Diploma Program
Fennell Campus
Start date: September, January

PROGRAM OBJECTIVES

Graduates of the General Arts and Science program will obtain a well-rounded general education offering development of skills in communication, human relations, science and computer literacy. Students who choose to enter the program to prepare academically for another career program or university, may complete part of the diploma requirements and transfer some credits for advanced standing in another college program. Others may choose to remain in the 2nd year and complete their diploma. Students who complete year 1 of General Arts and Science are eligible to receive in the Liberal Studies Certificate.

Figure 1–3

Source: Mohawk College of Applied Arts and Technology, *1999–2000 Calendar*, p. 32.

Table 1-1   How Resources Can Help You

Resource	Academic Assistance	Financial Assistance	Job/Career Assistance	Personal Assistance
Instructors	Choosing classes, clarifying course material, helping with assignments, dealing with study issues		Can tell you about their fields, may be a source of networking contacts	During office hours, are available to talk to you
Administrators	Academic problems, educational focus, problems with school services		Can be a source of valuable contacts	Can help you sort through personal problems with instructors or other school employees
Academic Advisers	Choosing, changing, or dropping courses; getting over academic hurdles; selecting/changing a major		Can advise you on what job opportunities may go along with your major or academic focus	
Personal Counsellors	Can help when personal problems get in the way of academic success	Services are usually free for students; there may be a nominal charge for workshops or tutorials		Help with all kinds of personal problems
Financial Aid Office		Information and counselling on loans, grants, scholarships, financial planning, work-study programs	Information on job opportunities within your school environment (work/study and others)	
Academic Centres	Help with what the centre specializes in (reading, writing, math)		Perhaps an opportunity to work at the centre	
Organizations and Clubs	If an academic club, can broaden your knowledge or experience in an area of study; can help you balance school with other enriching activities		Can help you develop skills, build knowledge, and make new contacts that may serve you in your working life	Depending on the club focus, can be an outlet for stress, a source of personal inspiration, a source of important friendships, an opportunity to help others
Fitness Centre(s)		Usually free or low cost to enrolled students		Provides opportunity to build fitness and reduce stress; may have weight room, track, aerobic or dance classes, martial arts, team sports, exercise machines, etc.

Table 1–1   How Resources Can Help You   (continued)

Resource	Academic Assistance	Financial Assistance	Job/Career Assistance	Personal Assistance
Bulletin Boards	List academic events, class information, changes and additions to schedules, office hours, academic club meetings	List financial aid seminars, job opportunities, scholarship opportunities	List career forums, job sign-ups, and employment opportunities; offer a place for you to post a message if you are marketing a service	List support group meetings
Housing and Transportation Office		Can help find the most financially beneficial travel or housing plan		Can help commuters with parking, bus or train service, and permits; can help with finding on- or off-campus housing
Career Planning and Placement Office		Can help add to your income through job opportunities	Job listings, help with résumés and interviews, possible interview appointments, factual information about the workplace (job trends, salaries, etc.)	
Tutors	One-on-one help with academic subjects; assistance with specific assignments		If you decide to become a tutor, a chance to find out if teaching and working with people is for you	
Student Health Office		May provide low-cost or no-cost health care to enrolled students; may offer reduced-cost prescription plan		Wellness care (regular examinations), illness care, hospital and specialist referrals, and prescriptions
Adult Education Centre	Academic help tailored to the returning adult student	May have specific financial-aid advice	May have job listings or other help with coordinating work and classes	May offer child-care assistance and opportunities to get to know other returning adults
Support Groups and Hotlines	If school-related, they offer a chance to hear how others have both stumbled and succeeded in school —and a chance to share your story			Personal help with whatever the hotline or support group specializes in; a chance to talk to someone whose job is to listen
School Publications/ Campus Radio and Television	Academic news and course changes	News about financial aid opportunities or work/study programs	Job listings, information about the workplace and the job market	Articles and announcements about topics that may help you

for each department. The calendar is an important resource in planning your academic career. When you have a question, consult the calendar first before you spend time and energy looking elsewhere.

Your *student handbook* looks beyond specific courses to the big picture, helping you to navigate student life. In it you will find some or all of the following, and maybe more: information on available housing (for on-campus residents) and on parking and driving (for commuters); overviews of the support offices for students, such as academic advising, counselling, career planning and placement, student health, disabled student services, child care, financial aid, and individual centres for academic subject areas such as writing or math; descriptions of special-interest clubs; and details about library and computer services. It may also list hours, locations, and phone numbers and addresses for all offices, clubs, and organizations.

Your student handbook will also describe important information such as how to add or drop a class, how the grading system works, campus rules, drug and alcohol policies, what kinds of records your school keeps, safety tips, and more. Keep your student handbook where you can find it easily, in your study area at home or someplace safe at school. The information it gives you can save you a lot of trouble when you need to find out information about a resource or service. If you call for locations and hours before you visit a particular office, you'll avoid the frustration of dropping by when the office is closed.

Making the most of your resources is one way to strive for success. The next section offers other strategies for you to consider.

How Can You Strive for Success?

Success is a process in motion, not a fixed goal. A successful person is one who is constantly learning, growing, and working toward personal and career goals. When people perceive success as an end point to a process instead of the process itself, they often wonder why they feel so unsatisfied when they get there. If you don't continue to change and grow and add new goals along the way, you may feel dissatisfied, empty, aimless, or stuck.

Striving for success is no easy task. It requires motivation, commitment, initiative, responsibility, positive thinking, and a willingness to face your fears. In combination, these six keys will keep you in motion toward new knowledge and opportunities.

Get Motivated

motivation

A force that moves a person to action, often inspired by an idea, a fact, an event, a goal.

Motivation is the energy that fuels your drive to achieve, and a motivator is anything that motivates you. There are at least as many motivators as there are people, and what motivates any given person can change from situation to situation or even from day to day. For example, some potential motivators for attending school could be supporting a family, learning a marketable skill, gaining earning potential, impressing others, or improving yourself.

It's nearly impossible to remain motivated continually. Motivation can slip away when you least expect to lose it. Everyone has energy highs and lows, and sometimes you don't feel like accomplishing anything. How can you renew lost motivation?

- ☺ **Spend time reflecting on why your goal is meaningful to you.** Remind yourself of what you wanted.

- ☺ **Make a decision to take one step toward your goal.** Sometimes feeling overwhelmed by a goal immobilizes you. Don't worry about tomorrow. Focus on the step you can take today.

- ☺ **After you take the first step, reward yourself for a job well done.** Rewards can be material (a new CD) or they can be more internal (a walk outside, time spent with a friend).

- ☺ **Examine and deal with your obstacles.** What's getting in your way? Maybe your health or finances have been troubling you. Whatever it is, make a commitment to deal with your problems as soon as they arise. They'll be more manageable that way.

- ☺ **Begin, or begin again.** If you can just get yourself started, you'll feel better as you continue working toward your goals. A law of physics, Newton's first law of motion, says that things in motion tend to stay in motion, and that things at rest tend to stay at rest. Be a thing in motion.

For example, to pass an early-morning writing class that you've already failed once, you decide to implement two strategies. First, you promise yourself that you will go to every class and turn in your work on time. Second, you make a commitment to write daily in a journal. Your motivation: Passing this course is necessary to continue your education, and the writing skills you learn will help you get a good job when you graduate. Plus, you promise yourself a reward: If you get at least a B- in the course, you will buy yourself that cordless phone you've been wanting.

To reach your goal, you remove obstacles to success. Instead of staying up late and being too tired to go to class, you start going to bed earlier. As a first step to getting up early, you put your alarm clock across the room so that you have to get up to shut it off. If you keep it up, your motivation should pay off. Even so, follow-through may be difficult for you. If you discover this is the case, you may want to shift to another strategy, such as trying to schedule afternoon classes in order to compensate for your sleep habits.

Make a Commitment

How do you focus the energy of motivation? Make a commitment. Commitment means that you do what you say you will do. It requires honesty and trustworthiness. When you honour a commitment, you prove to others as well as to yourself that your words and intentions can be trusted. A committed person follows through on a promise.

Commitment doesn't just refer to a personal relationship. You can apply the tasks of commitment—and the rewards—to academic goals, professional relationships, your working life, career goals, and self-improvement. Commitment often stretches over a period of time. You may commit to finishing school in three years, to working on your marriage, or to recycling

commitment
1) A pledge or promise to do something, or
2) dedication to a long-term course of action.

more often. Not only have you made a promise, but you hold yourself to that promise for as long as the commitment demands.

Commitment requires you to focus your energy on something specific. A general and daunting task such as ending world hunger or homelessness will probably intimidate you into staying motionless on the couch. In order to remain successfully committed, you need to break goals into manageable pieces, setting your specific goal and naming the steps of the process you will use to achieve it.

How do you go about making and keeping a commitment?

- **State your commitment concretely.** It's hard to commit to something like "I'm going to pass this course," because you haven't set yourself clear tasks. Commit to something specific.

- **Get started and note your progress.** The long road of a commitment can tire you out. Looking for improvements on the way, no matter how small, can keep you going.

- **Renew your commitment regularly.** How many times have you committed to making a change in your life, only to find that your resolve fades away in a few weeks—or even a few days? People have bursts of inspiration when they feel they could commit forever, but then everyday fatigue sets in and clouds the good intentions. You're not a failure if you lose momentum— it's normal. Recharge by reflecting on the positive effects of your commitment.

- **Keep track of your commitment.** Find ways to make sure you don't forget the commitments you have made. Make a list of commitments to keep in your date book. If commitments involve events or projects that take place on specific dates, be sure to note them on the calendar. Post notes to yourself on your refrigerator, your wall, or your mirror. Talk about your commitments with friends and family. Sometimes, just having someone supporting you and your goals helps you remain more accountable.

For example, you might make this specific commitment: "I will write in my journal every night before going to sleep." You make journal entries for two weeks, then evaluate what positive effects this daily practice has had on your writing ability. If you were to skip your journal entries for a week, you could renew your commitment by reminding yourself how keeping a journal exercised your writing ability and relieved stress. You might keep track of your commitment by telling a partner or housemate to check on you.

Making and keeping your commitments helps you keep a steady focus on your most important goals. It gives you a sense of accomplishment as you experience gradual growth and progress.

Take Initiative

initiative
The power to begin or to follow through energetically with a plan or task; determination.

When you take initiative, you push yourself to take that first difficult step. Initiative helps to get the pursuit of your goals off the ground. It jump-starts your journey and helps to renew motivation along the way. It enables you to respond continually to changes that occur.

Source: John Marshall, Binghamton Press and Sun Bulletin.

When you use initiative, you take the first step on your own instead of waiting for someone else to fix the problem or having to be dragged into it by people, rules, or requirements. You take initiative when you go to a counsellor for help with a personal problem, talk to a friend about something he or she said that upset you, raise your hand to speak in a classroom, come up with a better way to do a job at work, take a political stand by voting, or start doing fifty abdominal crunches every morning.

Initiative requires you to keep on top of your goals and to listen to your instincts. You may discover that you want to do more than what is expected, which can be positive both at school and in the workplace. Initiative is a spark plug. It ignites the fuel of your motivation and powers your passions and commitment.

Be Responsible

Being responsible is all about living up to your obligations, both those that are imposed on you and those that you impose on yourself. It means that you can address situations and challenges that arise in your daily life. Through action, you prove that you are responsible, or "response-able," able to respond. When something needs to be done, a responsible person does the work—as efficiently as possible, on time, and to the best of his or her ability.

Responsibility can take enormous effort. Throughout your life you will have moments when you just don't want to respond. In those moments, you need to weigh the positive and negative effects and decide if not responding is worth your while. However, being responsible has definite benefits. For one, you make a crucial impression on others. You earn the trust of your instructors, supervisors, relatives, and friends. When others trust you, they may give you increasing responsibility and opportunities for growth. Trust builds relationships, which in turn feed progress and success.

responsibility
The quality of being reliable, trustworthy, and accountable for one's actions.

When you are trusted you are also respected, and respect brings its own rewards. Supervisors promote employees they respect; instructors give respected students special duties or assignments; friends look to one another for advice and help when they respect each other. Even more important is the self-respect that emerges when you prove that you can live up to your promises. Responsible people are given power and opportunity because they have shown they are capable of making the best of both.

For example, when you complete class assignments on time, you demonstrate responsibility. When you correct errors and work on problem areas, you demonstrate a commitment to doing well. An instructor who sees these patterns of behaviour is likely to trust your judgment and may even allow you to do independent work for the course. You don't have to take on the world to show how responsible you can be. Responsibility shows in basic everyday actions: attending class, fulfilling requirements, turning in work on time, being a good friend or parent, and being true to your word.

Think Positively

Attitude is important to success. Many people believe that what happens in your life can be linked to how you feel about yourself and your place in the world. Ask yourself whether you see a glass as half empty or half full. You may not create instant success by seeing it as half full, but you can create a mindset that helps you seize opportunity and make the most of it.

Your attitudes influence your choices and affect how you perceive and relate to others. A positive attitude can open your mind to learning experiences and inspire you to take action. On the other hand, a negative attitude can hinder learning and stifle initiative. For example, say you are enrolled in a required course unrelated to your program or major. If you adopt the attitude that the course is a waste of time, chances are you won't learn much. If, however, you keep an open mind, the course might teach you something valuable or introduce you to a new area of interest.

positive self-talk
Supportive and positive-thinking thoughts and ideas that a person communicates to him- or herself.

One of the ways you can create a positive attitude is with positive self-talk. When you hear negative thoughts (I'm not very smart/I can't do it/I'm not good enough) in your mind, replace them with positive ones (I have a lot to offer/It won't be easy, but I'm smart enough to figure it out/I am talented). Talk to yourself as if you were talking to another person, someone you care a lot about. You would probably never talk to a friend as harshly as you talk to yourself at times. Take that to heart and be kind to yourself. The following hints will help you put positive self-talk into action.

Stop negative talk in its tracks and change it to positive talk. If you catch yourself thinking, "I can never write a decent paper," stop and say to yourself, "I can do better than that and next time I will." Then think over how you plan to do it.

Take a moment to pay yourself a general compliment: "I am a terrific, valuable, and powerful person." Or be specific. "I have really improved my spelling and proofreading." Some people use word calendars with daily affirmations. These are great reminders of positive self-talk.

Replace words of *obligation*, which take power from you, with words of personal *intent*.

I should	*becomes*	I choose to
I have to	*becomes*	I want to
I'll try	*becomes*	I will
I mean to	*becomes*	I promise to

Words of intent give you power and control because they imply a personal decision to act. When you say, "I *have* to be in class by 9," you're saying that someone else has power over you and has handed you a required obligation. When you say, "I *want* to be in class by 9 because I don't want to miss anything I need to learn about," you're saying that the choice is yours.

Note your successes. Even when you don't think you are at your best, don't let that diminish your victories. Congratulate yourself when you take any positive steps. Whether you do well on a paper, write in your journal for a week straight, get to class on time all week, or have fewer mistakes on this week's paper than last week's, each success helps you believe in yourself. Every step is a step in the right direction, no matter how small. Try keeping a list of your successes in a notebook.

It can be very difficult to think positively. If you have a deep-rooted feeling of unworthiness, you may want to see a counsellor. Many people have benefited from skilled professional advice.

Face Your Fears

Everyone experiences fear. Even when you are excited about a change, new experiences often feel frightening. The changes involved in pursuing an education can inspire fear. You wonder if you can handle the work and if you have chosen the right school or program. You may worry that family and friends may expect too much or may stand in your way. You may also have fears about the future. You ask yourself whether you'll be able to apply what you are learning in school to a job and whether you can earn a living.

Connected with the fear of change is the fear of independence. Surviving and learning to thrive in the world is tough—it's hard to earn and manage money, pay for shelter and food and bills, perhaps care for children or an aging relative, and still find time for rest and relaxation. You have chosen to get an education and move yourself along the road to independence. You should congratulate yourself on your actions: Some people back away from fears because they feel safer with the familiar—even if they don't like it.

The successful pursuit of an education demands a willingness to push your limits and face your fears. Only when you identify and confront your fears can you start to work through challenges. These five steps will help you face your fears with courage. Through the course of your life you will find yourself taking these steps again and again.

1. Acknowledge your specific fears. Just the act of naming your fear will begin to diminish it. Be as specific as you can. Knowing you fear a particular course may not inspire you to do anything

"They are able because they think they are able."

Virgil

"He has not yet learned the lesson of life who does not every day surmount a fear."

Ralph Waldo Emerson

Real World Perspective

How do I make the most of my post-secondary education?

Matt Millard, Undeclared Major

I decided to attend school so I could have a job doing what I really like instead of just doing it for the money. Even though I haven't decided what I want to do when I graduate, I know that I want to continue learning for a long time. I'd even like to continue on to get a Masters and maybe even a Ph.D. someday. So far, I'm mainly interested in the theatre and English, but I'm not quite sure where to go with it.

I try to take steps to better myself. Even though I'd like it to be more often, I work out at racquetball a couple of times a week. I also think it's important to help other people, so I make time to help my friends with their homework and stuff like that. My grades are average so I'd like them to get better. I'd also like to get a little more focused on what I want to declare as a major. Even though I think I'm doing fine handling university, I'd appreciate any suggestions you could give me. What steps do you think I need to take in order to get the most out of my learning?

Tamara Mandeville, Communications and Advertising

I am a graduate of the Communications Program at Brock University. Now I attend Mohawk College and I have noticed that there are many similarities as well as many differences. University is theory-based while college offers a more hands-on, practical experience.

My best college experience has been working for a full-service, student-run advertising agency where I am co-Public Relations/Event Coordinator. This is a real working agency doing advertising for non-profit organizations, and it has opened doors to the many fields of advertising, including public relations and promotions.

I felt that college was the next logical step after university to get some practical experience before I went to work, and college has definitely provided me with the experience and motivation I need to be successful in advertising. Having a job that I feel good about and can't wait to go to every day is very important to me.

Time management has become an essential aspect of my life. In university, I made a huge wall calendar that listed everything, day by day, that I had to do. This allowed me to see what assignments or tests were upcoming. In college, I have learned to make the most of my time by using a day planner, which I take with me everywhere. These methods have helped me get the most out of university and college, and they have also helped me maintain my good grades.

You're right about keeping your friends close. Friends are my sounding board. A few close friends that are willing to listen to me complain or lend me a shoulder to cry on when my computer crashes, are priceless. It's hard not to make and keep friends in university and college when everyone in your program is in the same boat.

Finally, "me time" is also an important concept that I have learned throughout university and college. Whether it's five minutes or an hour, getting away from all the stress and homework is necessary in order to keep my sanity and keep me motivated.

about it. Focusing in on a fear of an instructor, a particular skill requirement, or an assignment gives you something to work on.

2. **Decide which fears are real and which conceal something deeper.** Sometimes one fear is a mask for another larger one. If you fear a test, determine whether you fear the test itself or the fact that if you pass it, you will have to take a tougher class next semester. If you fear the test, you can take steps to prepare adequately for it. If you fear the next class, you might talk with your instructor about it.

3. **Decide on a plan of attack.** Evaluate what will help you overcome the fear you have identified. For example, if you are uneasy about your writing style, develop a realistic picture of your abilities by consulting your instructor, talking to friends in the class, or reading a variety of work by other writers.

4. **Move ahead with your plans.** Courage is the key to moving ahead. You may find that the drive to overcome fear forces you to work harder, resulting in even greater success than you imagined; or you may discover your fear is so great that you must change your plans. Take the steps that will help you most.

5. **Talk about your fears with people you trust.** Everyone has fears. Often the ideas other people have about gaining control can help you with your own fears. When you share strategies, everybody benefits.

If you acknowledge and evaluate them, fears can provide valuable clues to what blocks your success. They can guide you, showing you where you need a push or extra work, and they also can signal a need to make changes or open yourself up to new knowledge. You can apply this wisdom to your exploration of people who are different from you.

What Is Your Role in a Diverse World?

Diversity isn't just what happens in an international students club, in a business that tries to hire men and women from different backgrounds, or in a neighbourhood that is home to various cultural groups. Diversity is the mosaic of differences that envelops your life, your communities, your nation, and the world. Canada is officially multicultural, but diversity in our country also occurs in desires, traditions, religions, family backgrounds, genders, abilities, economic levels, ages, habits, lifestyle choices, careers, artistic expressions, modes of dress, foods, health conditions, perspectives, opinions, and experiences. Diversity touches each Canadian in a very personal way.

Diversity Is Real Life: Multiculturalism in Canada

You encounter diversity every day, even if you don't realize it. You're constantly bombarded with images and information in newspapers and magazines, on television, and on the radio that tell you about how different people think and live. We tend to focus on the kind of diversity we can see, but people who look similar to you may actually be different in many important ways. Think about the people you know. Your fellow student may have a different religion or a hidden disability, your cousin may oppose your political beliefs, or your co-worker may have a different sexual orientation. Canadian society is made up of people who transcend labels and have limitless worth.

Multiculturalism also means social reality in Canada. Look around you. Many ethnic and racial backgrounds are represented in your class. Many famous Canadians have come from other countries. For example, Canada's first prime minister, Sir John A. MacDonald, was born in Scotland, as was Alexander Graham Bell, who invented the telephone. Canadian filmmaker Ivan Reitman, who directed *Ghostbusters* and *Twins*, was born in the former Czechoslovakia. Cellist Ofra Harnoy is from Israel. Actor Keanu Reeves was born in Lebanon. Ernie Coombs, known as Mr. Dressup to generations of Canadian children, was born in the United States. The list of famous "immigrant Canadians" from diverse backgrounds is endless.

Acceptance of diversity has also become more important, because the world is becoming more interdependent. As people become more aware of other ways of living, they may tune in more to differences between "us" and "them." The knowledge of differences can be a benefit. Unfortunately, it can also be used to spread negative stereotypes about others. The problem is not in the differences but in the way in which people view and treat these differences.

Ethnocentrism

ethnocentrism
The condition of thinking that one's particular ethnic group is superior to others.

When groups of people believe that their way of thinking is the only way, or a better way than anyone else's, they are being ethnocentric. Ethnocentrism is the belief that one's particular group is better than anyone else's. It's important to be proud of your identity, but it's one thing to think your group is terrific and another thing to think that your group is superior to all other groups.

A group can be organized around any sort of uniqueness—the same skin colour, accent, country of origin, ideas, interests, religion, traditions, and much more. The problem arises when celebrating your own uniqueness leads to putting down someone else's. One example is thinking that when someone speaks with an accent, he or she doesn't know as much as you do. Another example is thinking that it is disrespectful for someone not to look you in the eye during a conversation. In some cultures, it is considered rude to look people in the eye, especially if the person happens to be an authority figure.

Ethnocentrism has many negative effects. It can get in the way of effective communication, as you will see in more detail when you read Chapter 8. It can prevent you from getting to know people from different backgrounds. It can result in people being shut out and denied opportunities that all people deserve. It limits you and your potential because it denies you exposure to new ideas that could help you grow and learn. Finally, it can hinder your ability to work with others, which can cause problems for you both at school and on the job.

Diversity and Teamwork

Much of what people accomplish they owe to teamwork. Think of the path of your accomplishments, and you will find that other people had roles in your success. When you earn a degree, complete a project, or raise a family, you don't do it alone. You are part of many hard-working teams. As the African proverb goes, it takes an entire village to raise a child.

Your success at school and at work depends on your ability to cooperate in a team setting. At school you will work with study groups, complete group projects, interact with instructors and administrators, and perhaps live with a roommate. At work you will regularly team up with co-workers to achieve goals. At home you work with family or housemates to manage the tasks and responsibilities of daily life. Your achievements depend on how you communicate, share tasks, and develop a common vision.

Any team will gain strength from the diversity of its members. In fact, diversity is an asset in a team. Consider a hockey team, composed of a centre, a left winger, a right winger, two defence, and a goalie. Each person has a different role and a different style of play, but only by combining their abilities can they achieve success. The more diverse the team members, the greater the chance that new ideas and solutions will find their way to the table, increasing the chances of solving any problem. As a member of any team, use these three strategies to maximize team success.

1. Open your mind and accept that different team members have valuable roles.

2. Consider the new information and ideas that others offer.

3. Evaluate contributions based on how they help solve the problem or achieve the goal rather than based on the identity of the person who had the idea. Successful teams use what works.

Living Your Role

It's not always easy to open your mind to differences. However, doing so can benefit both you and others around you. You may consider actions like these as you define your role in the diverse world:

- **Accept diversity as a fact of life.** Canada and the world will only continue to diversify. The more you adapt to and appreciate this diversity, the more enriched your life will be. Diversity is an asset, not a deficiency. Open your mind and learn about what is unfamiliar around you.

- **Celebrate your own uniqueness as well as that of others.** It's natural to think that your own way is the best way. Expand your horizons by considering your way as one good way and seeking out different ways to do things.

- ◌ **Consider new perspectives.** The wide variety of ideas and perspectives brought by people from all different groups and situations creates a wealth of thought from which the world can find solutions to tough and complex problems.

- ◌ **Continue to learn.** Education is one of the most productive ways to combat discrimination and become more open-minded. Classes such as sociology and ethics can increase your awareness of the lives, choices, and values of other people. Even though your personal beliefs may be challenged, facing how you feel about others is a positive step toward harmony among people.

Throughout this book you will find references to a diverse mixture of people in different life circumstances. Chapter 8 will go into more detail about communicating across lines of difference and addressing the problems that arise when people have trouble accepting each other's differences. Diversity is not a subject that you study at one point in the semester and then leave behind. It is a theme that touches every chapter in this book and every part of your life. Note especially the "Real World Perspective" feature in every chapter, which highlights people from different backgrounds who are struggling to learn about themselves and their world.

In Chinese writing, this character has two meanings: One is "chaos," the other is "opportunity." The character communicates the belief that every challenging, chaotic, demanding situation in life also presents an opportunity. By responding to challenges in a positive and active way, you can discover the opportunity that lies within the chaos.

Let this concept reassure you as you begin college or university. You may feel that you are going through a time of chaos and change. Remember that no matter how difficult the obstacles, you have the ability to persevere. You can create opportunities for yourself to learn, grow, and improve.

Chapter 1: Applications

Name _____   Date _____

 ## Key into Your Life:
Opportunities to Apply What You Learn

Exercise 1: Identify Yourself

Where do you fit in today's student population? Describe your particular circumstances, opinions, and needs in a short paragraph. Here are some questions to inspire thought:

- How do you describe yourself—your culture, ethnicity, gender, age, lifestyle?
- How long are you planning to spend in college/university?
- What do you expect out of your post-secondary experience?
- What resources do you plan to use?
- What is your work situation, if you work?
- What are your financial needs for college and living expenses?
- What are your career goals?
- How would you describe your family?
- What qualities make you special?

_____

_____

_____

_____

_____

_____

_____

Exercise 2: Brainstorm Your Ideal Life

Take some quiet time to think about your life. Spend a half-hour or so brainstorming everything that you wish you could be, do, have, or experience. List your wishes on a blank piece of paper, draw them, or depict them using cutouts from magazines—whatever you like best.

Here are some wish categories for you to consider, each with an example:

CATEGORY	EXAMPLES
Career choices (job, perks, schedule, opportunities)	I want to teach elementary school. I want a job that's within twenty minutes' driving time of where I live. I want health benefits.
Lifestyle issues (what type of house, cars you want to own, hobbies and interests)	I want to own instead of rent. I want to finish paying off my car. I want to spend more time exercising.
Finances	I want to pay off my credit card debt. I want to provide at least part of my tuition.
Family and relationships	I want to keep in touch with my parents. I want to spend more time with my child.
Serving and helping others	I want to see what I can do at the senior citizens' centre.
Creativity	I want to get my camera out and take pictures more often.
Experiences	I want to see Nova Scotia. I want to spend some time driving across Canada.
Other important wishes	I want to work harder to keep myself organized.

Now take a look at your list. You probably have a wide variety of details. To discover how your wishes relate to one another, group them in order of priority. Take four pieces of paper and label them *Priority 1*, *Priority 2*, *Priority 3*, and *Future Dreams*. Write each wish on the piece of paper where it fits, with *Priority 1* being the most important wishes, *Priority 2* the second most important, *Priority 3* the third most important, and *Future Dreams* the wishes that you would like to accomplish someday.

Look at your priority lists. What do your lists tell you about what is most important to you? What wishes are you ready to work toward right now? Choose three high-priority wishes that you want to work on this semester. List them here.

_____

_____

_____

Exercise 3: Experience the Success Strategies

Take one of the wishes you just listed and turn it into a goal for this semester. Make your goal as specific as possible first, for example, "I want to find a job that allows me to work at night and still have time to study for my day classes."

Your goal: _____

_____

1. Get Motivated. Explore your motivation by considering the following: Why is this goal important? What positive effects will achieving it bring you? What makes you want it? Describe your motivating factors here.

_____

_____

_____

2. Make a Commitment. Get specific about just how you will go about achieving your goal. Describe your commitment here. What steps will you take? How will you stay committed when the going gets tough?

_____

_____

_____

3. Take Initiative. Make that first step count. How can you set out to accomplish this goal on your own? What will show that you mean business? Describe how you will take the initiative.

_____

_____

_____

4. Be Responsible. How can you prove to yourself and others that you will meet your commitment? Explain how you will be responsible for moving toward your goal.

_____

_____

_____

5. Think Positively. If you have negative thoughts about your abilities, turn them around with positive self-talk. Write both the negative thoughts and the positive self-talk you will use to combat them.

_____

_____

_____

Exercise 4: Facing Your Fears

One valuable solution to any fear is to let go of the need to be perfect, which often prevents people from doing anything at all, and do something. The easiest way to do this is to break the task into manageable units and complete one step at a time. First, think of an activity you have been postponing because of fear (fear of success, of failure, of the task, or of perfectionism). Describe it here.

_____

_____

Now list five small activities that would get you closer to working through that fear. If you don't want to start a major project, for example, you could read a book on the subject, brainstorm what you already know about it, or just write one page about it.

1. _____

2. _____

3. _____

4. _____

5. _____

Commit yourself to one small step you will do within the next two days. State it here.

_____

List the time you will begin the activity and how much time you will spend doing it.

_____

What reward will you give yourself for having taken that step?

_____

After taking the step, describe how it felt.

_____

Affirm that you have taken that first step and are on the way to success by signing your name here and writing the date.

Signature _____   Date _____

Key to Cooperative Learning:
Building Teamwork Skills

Who Can Help You? Every school is unique and offers its own particular range of opportunities. Investigate your school. Use the resource table as a guide, and explore your student handbook. Make a check mark by the resources that you think will be most helpful to you.

Advisers and counsellors	_____	Support groups/hotlines	_____
Library/media centre	_____	Career/job placement office	_____
Instructors	_____	Administration	_____
Clubs/organizations	_____	Academic centres	_____
Bulletin boards	_____	School publications/TV and	
Student health centre	_____	radio stations	_____
Housing and transportation	_____	Tutoring	_____
Wellness/fitness centres	_____	Financial aid office	_____
Adult education centre	_____		

Gather in small groups; or, if you have a small class, work as one large group together. Each member of each group should choose one or more different resources (make sure no two people within a group explore the same resource). All resources on the following grid should be accounted for. Then, each group member will investigate his or her resources and fill in the information on the grid, answering the questions listed across the top of the grid. The two blank spaces at the bottom are for you to use if you find resources not listed here.

After each person has completed his or her investigation, meet again to exchange information and fill in the information on the grid. You now have a resource guide to which you can refer at any time. Write here how you will use the three resources that you feel will benefit you the most.

1. _____

_____

2. _____

_____

3. _____

_____

RESOURCE	WHO PROVIDES IT?	WHERE CAN YOU FIND IT?	WHEN IS IT AVAILABLE?	HOW CAN IT HELP YOU?	HOW DO YOU ASK FOR IT?	PHONE # OR OTHER KEY DETAILS
Administrative help						
Instructor advice						
Academic advising						
Personal counselling						
Financial aid						
Academic centres						
Organizations and clubs						
Bulletin boards						
Housing and transportation						
Career planning and placement						

RESOURCE	WHO PROVIDES IT?	WHERE CAN YOU FIND IT?	WHEN IS IT AVAILABLE?	HOW CAN IT HELP YOU?	HOW DO YOU ASK FOR IT?	PHONE # OR OTHER KEY DETAILS
Tutoring						
Student health						
Adult education centres						
Fitness						
Support groups/hotlines						
Disabled student services						
English as a Second Language						

Key to Self-Expression:
Discovery Through Journal Writing

To record your thoughts, use a separate journal or the lined page at the end of the chapter.

Your Diverse World: The Reality of Multiculturalism in Canada Describe one particular person with whom you interact, a person who is different from you in some way. What have you learned from your relationship with this person? What is positive about spending time with him or her? What is negative? What is positive and negative about spending time with people who seem very similar to you?

Key to Your Personal Portfolio:
Your Paper Trail to Success

Educational Contract This is the first item in your personal portfolio. Find a sturdy folder or notebook in which to keep each portfolio item you add as you read the chapters of this book. By the end of this course, you will have collected concrete evidence of your abilities and qualifications for success in the real world. Your portfolio will come in handy during your tenure as a student. You can also look back at it when you apply for jobs, because much of what you generate will give you practical help with the application, interview, and hiring processes in the workplace. In addition, your portfolio will help remind you of how much progress you've made and how far you've come.

Start your portfolio by drawing up a "contract" for your education. Think of it as a plan that spells out what you need to put into your educational process and what you expect to receive from your instructors, administrators, and other school personnel in exchange for your efforts. Create two lists, one for each of the following subjects:

⚙ What you expect from people and services at your school

⚙ What your school should expect from you

When you finish your contract, pair up with a fellow student. Go over your contracts together. Discuss with one another any additional insights you have, or any thoughts on whether these expectations and goals seem reasonable. Together you can clarify and revise your contract so that you have a better idea of what to expect.

Keep this contract until the end of the semester. When you finish this course, take it out and look at it again. See how your expectations of your school or yourself have changed as you have changed. Revise your contract so that you can renew your commitment to yourself as well as your drive to make sure your school does everything for you that it can.

Name _____ Date _____

Journal Entry

_____
_____
_____
_____
_____
_____
_____
_____
_____
_____
_____
_____
_____
_____
_____
_____
_____
_____
_____
_____
_____

2 Self-Awareness:
Knowing Who You Are and How You Learn

In this chapter, you will explore answers to the following questions:

⊙ Is there one best way to learn?

⊙ How can you discover your learning styles?

⊙ What are the benefits of knowing your learning styles?

⊙ How do you explore who you are?

⊙ How can you start thinking about choosing a major?

Learning is not something you do just in college or university. In its Employability Skills Profile, the Conference Board of Canada recognizes the need for employees to become lifelong learners. Throughout your life, learning can help you keep up with the rapid pace at which technology is changing the world. The Internet allows people to send documents and photographs over phone lines in the blink of an eye. Cameras, cars, stereos, and all kinds of other items have computer chips inside them that control their operation. Medical science has discovered how to isolate the genes that cause certain genetic diseases and characteristics.

Technology is changing so fast that you cannot learn today about everything that will be commonplace five years from now. However, you can learn how to be an effective learner in school and in the workplace so that you can keep pace with changes as they occur. In this chapter you will become aware of your learning style by completing three different learning style assessments. Each assessment will add a different dimension to the picture you are forming of yourself. You will then explore other important elements of self: your self-perception, your preferences, your habits, your abilities, and your attitudes.

Thinking It Through

Check those statements that apply to you right now:

☐ I'm not sure what "learning style" means.

☐ I feel out of touch in some of my classes.

☐ I have never evaluated my study habits.

☐ I don't know how my learning style and personality would be linked to the career I choose.

☐ I know I have some habits that I'd like to change.

☐ I don't know what I want to major in yet.

Is There One Best Way to Learn?

Your mind is the most powerful tool you will ever possess. You are accomplished at many skills and can process all kinds of information. However, when you have trouble accomplishing a particular task, you may become convinced that you can't learn how to do anything new. You may feel that those who can do what you can't have the "right" kind of ability. Not only is this perception incorrect, it can also damage your belief in yourself.

Every individual is highly developed in some abilities and underdeveloped in others. Many famously successful people were brilliant in one area but functioned poorly in other areas. Winston Churchill failed the sixth grade. Canadian actor Donald Sutherland failed engineering while at university. Louis Pasteur was a poor student in chemistry. Walt Disney was fired from a job and told he had no good ideas. What some might interpret as a deficiency or disability may be simply a different method of learning.

There is no one "best" way to learn. Instead, there are many different learning styles, and different styles are suited to different situations. Your individual learning profile is made up of a combination of learning styles. Each person's profile is unique. Just like personality traits, learning styles are part of your personal characteristics. Knowing how you learn is one of the first steps in discovering who you are.

learning style
A particular way in which the mind receives and processes information.

How Can You Discover Your Learning Styles?

Your brain is so complex that one inventory cannot give you all the information you need to maximize your learning skills. You will learn about and complete three assessments: the Learning-Styles Inventory, the Pathways to Learning inventory based on the Multiple Intelligences Theory, and the Personality Spectrum. Each of these assessments evaluates your mind's abilities in a different way, although they often have related ideas. Your results will combine to form your learning-styles profile, consisting of the styles and types that best fit the ways that you learn and interact with others. After you complete the various learning-styles inventories, you will read about strategies that can help you make the most of particular styles and types, both in school and beyond. Your learning-styles profile will help you to improve your understanding of yourself, how you learn, and how you may function as a learner in the Canadian workplace.

"To be what we are, and to become what we are capable of becoming, is the only end of life."

Robert Louis Stevenson

Learning-Styles Inventory

One of the first instruments to measure psychological types, the Myers-Briggs Type Indicator (MBTI), was designed by Katharine Briggs and her daughter, Isabel Briggs Myers. Later David Keirsey and Marilyn Bates combined the sixteen Myers-Briggs types into four temperaments. Barbara Soloman, Associate Director of the University Undesignated Student Program at North Carolina State University, has developed the following learning-styles inventory based on these theories and on her work with thousands of students.[1]

"Students learn in many ways," says Professor Soloman. "Mismatches often exist between common learning styles and standard teaching styles. Therefore, students often do poorly and get discouraged. Some students doubt themselves and doubt their ability to succeed in the curriculum of their choice. Some settle for low grades and even leave school. If students understand how they learn most effectively, they can tailor their studying to their own needs."

"Learning effectively" and "tailoring studying to your own needs" means choosing study techniques that help you learn. For example, if a student responds more to visual images than to words, he or she may want to construct notes in a more visual way. Or, if a student learns better when talking to people than when studying alone, he or she may want to study primarily in pairs or groups.

Learning-Styles Inventory

This inventory has four "dimensions," within each of which are two opposing styles. At the end of the inventory, you will have two scores in each of the four dimensions. The difference between your two scores in any dimension tells you which of the two styles in that dimension is dominant for you. A few people will score right in between the two styles, indicating that they have fairly equal parts of both styles. Following are brief descriptions of the four dimensions. You will learn more about them after you complete all three assessments, in the section on study strategies.

Active/Reflective. *Active* learners learn best by experiencing knowledge through their own actions. *Reflective* learners understand information best when they have had time to reflect on it on their own.

Factual/Theoretical. *Factual* learners learn best through specific facts, data, and detailed experimentation. *Theoretical* learners are more comfortable with big-picture ideas, symbols, and new concepts.

Visual/Verbal. *Visual* learners remember best what they see: diagrams, flow charts, time lines, films, and demonstrations. *Verbal* learners gain the most learning from reading, hearing spoken words, participating in discussion, and explaining things to others.

Linear/Holistic. *Linear* learners find it easiest to learn material presented step by step in a logical, ordered progression. Holistic learners progress in fits and starts, perhaps feeling lost for a while, but eventually seeing the big picture in a clear and creative way.

holistic
Relating to the wholes of complete systems rather than the analysis of parts.

Please complete this inventory by circling **a** or **b** to indicate your answer to each question. Answer every question and choose only one answer for each question. If both answers seem to apply to you, choose the answer that applies more often.

1. I study best
   a. in a study group.
   b. alone or with a partner.

2. I would rather be considered
   a. realistic.
   b. imaginative.

3. When I recall what I did yesterday, I am most likely to think in terms of
   a. pictures/images.
   b. words/verbal descriptions.

4. I usually think new material is
   a. easier at the beginning and then harder as it becomes more complicated.
   b. often confusing at the beginning but easier as I start to understand what the whole subject is about.

5. When given a new activity to learn, I would rather first
   a. try it out.
   b. think about how I'm going to do it.

6. If I were an instructor, I would rather teach a course
   a. that deals with real-life situations and what to do about them.
   b. that deals with ideas and encourages students to think about them.

7. I prefer to receive new information in the form of
   a. pictures, diagrams, graphs, or maps.
   b. written directions or verbal information.

8. I learn
   a. at a fairly regular pace. If I study hard I'll "get it" and then move on.
   b. in fits and starts. I might be totally confused and then suddenly it all "clicks."

9. I understand something better after
   a. I attempt to do it myself.
   b. I give myself time to think about how it works.

10. I find it easier
    a. to learn facts.
    b. to learn ideas/concepts.

11. In a book with lots of pictures and charts, I am likely to
    a. look over the pictures and charts carefully.
    b. focus on the written text.

12. It's easier for me to memorize facts from
    a. a list.
    b. a whole story/essay with the facts embedded in it.

13. I will more easily remember
    a. something I have done myself.
    b. something I have thought or read about.

14. I am usually
    a. aware of my surroundings. I remember people and places and usually recall where I put things.
    b. unaware of my surroundings. I forget people and places. I frequently misplace things.

15. I like instructors
    a. who put a lot of diagrams on the board.
    b. who spend a lot of time explaining.

16. Once I understand
    a. all the parts, I understand the whole thing.
    b. the whole thing, I see how the parts fit.

17. When I am learning something new, I would rather
    a. talk about it.
    b. think about it.

18. I am good at
    a. being careful about the details of my work.
    b. having creative ideas about how to do my work.

19. I remember best
    a. what I see.
    b. what I hear.

20. When I solve problems that involve some math, I usually
    a. work my way to the solutions one step at a time.
    b. see the solutions but then have to struggle to figure out the steps to get to them.

21. In a lecture class, I would prefer occasional in-class
    a. discussions or group problem-solving sessions.
    b. pauses that give opportunities to think or write about ideas presented in the lecture.

22. On a multiple-choice test, I am more likely to
    a. run out of time.
    b. lose points because of not reading carefully or making careless errors.

23. When I get directions to a new place, I prefer
    a. a map.
    b. written instructions.

24. When I'm thinking about something I've read,
    a. I remember the incidents and try to put them together to figure out the themes.
    b. I just know what the themes are when I finish reading and then I have to back up and find the incidents that demonstrate them.

25. When I get a new computer or VCR, I tend to
    a. plug it in and start punching buttons.
    b. read the manual and follow instructions.

26. In reading for pleasure, I prefer
    a. something that teaches me new facts or tells me how to do something.
    b. something that gives me new ideas to think about.

27. When I see a diagram or sketch in class, I am most likely to remember
    a. the picture.
    b. what the instructor said about it.

28. It is more important to me that an instructor
    a. lay out the material in clear, sequential steps.
    b. give me an overall picture and relate the material to other subjects.

SCORING SHEET: Use Table 2–1 to enter your scores.

1. Put 1's in the appropriate boxes in the table (e.g., if you answered **a** to Question 3, put a 1 in the column headed **a** next to the number 3).

2. Total the 1's in the columns and write the totals in the indicated spaces at the base of the columns.

Table 2-1 Learning-Styles Inventory Scores

	Actv/Refl			Fact/Theo			Visl/Vrbl			Linr/Hols	
Q #	a	b	Q#	a	b	Q#	a	b	Q#	a	b
1			2			3			4		
5			6			7			8		
9			10			11			12		
13			14			15			16		
17			18			19			20		
21			22			23			24		
25			26			27			28		

Write totals for each column in the spaces below.

3. For each of the four dimensions, circle your two scores on the bar scale and then fill in the bar between the scores. For example, if under "ACTV/REFL" you had 2 **a** and 5 **b** responses, you would fill in the bar between those two scores, as this sample shows:

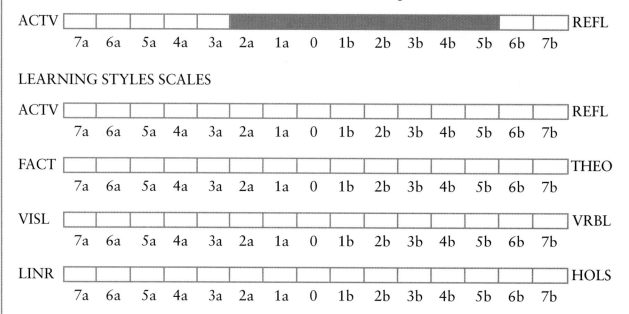

If your filled-in bar has the 0 close to its centre, you are well balanced on the two dimensions of that scale. If your bar is drawn mainly to one side, you have a strong preference for that one dimension and may have difficulty learning in the other dimension.

Continue on to the next assessment. After you complete all three, the next section of the chapter will help you understand and make use of your results from each assessment.

Multiple Intelligences Theory

Howard Gardner, a Harvard University professor, has developed a theory called Multiple Intelligences. He believes there are at least eight distinct intelligences possessed by all people, and that every person has developed some intelligences more fully than others. Most people have experienced a time when they learned something very quickly and comfortably. Most have also had the opposite experience when, no matter how hard they tried, something they wanted to learn just would not sink in. According to the Multiple Intelligences Theory, when you find a task or subject easy, you are probably using a more fully developed intelligence; when you have more trouble, you may be using a less developed intelligence.[2]

Following are brief descriptions of the focus of each of the intelligences. Study skills that reinforce each intelligence will be described later in the chapter.

intelligence
As defined by H. Gardner, an ability to solve problems or fashion products that are useful in a particular cultural setting or community.

kinesthetic
Coming from physical sensation caused by body movements and tensions.

- ⊙ **Verbal-Linguistic Intelligence**—ability to communicate through language (listening, reading, writing, speaking)
- ⊙ **Logical-Mathematical Intelligence**—ability to understand logical reasoning and problem solving (math, science, patterns, sequences)
- ⊙ **Bodily-Kinesthetic Intelligence**—ability to use the physical body skillfully and to take in knowledge through bodily sensation (coordination, working with hands)

- Visual-Spatial Intelligence—ability to understand spatial relationships and to perceive and create images (visual art, graphic design, charts and maps)

- Interpersonal Intelligence—ability to relate to others, noticing their moods, motivations, and feelings (social activity, cooperative learning, teamwork)

- Intrapersonal Intelligence—ability to understand one's own behaviour and feelings (independence, time spent alone)

- Musical Intelligence—ability to comprehend and create meaningful sound (music, sensitivity to sound)

- Naturalistic Intelligence—ability to understand features of the environment (interest in nature, environmental balance, ecosystem, stress relief brought by natural environments)

Please complete the following assessment of your multiple intelligences, called Pathways to Learning, developed by Joyce Bishop. It will help you determine which of your intelligences are most fully developed. Don't be concerned if some of your scores are low. That is true of most people, even your instructors and the authors of this book.

Pathways to Learning[3]

Developed by Joyce Bishop, Ph.D., and based upon Howard Gardner, *Frames of Mind: The Theory of Multiple Intelligences*.

Directions: Rate each statement as follows: Write the number of your response (1–4) on the line next to the statement and total each set of six questions.

rarely	sometimes	usually	always
1	2	3	4

1. _____ I enjoy physical activities.
2. _____ I am uncomfortable sitting still.
3. _____ I prefer to learn through doing.
4. _____ When sitting I move my legs or hands.
5. _____ I enjoy working with my hands.
6. _____ I like to pace when I'm thinking or studying.

_____ **TOTAL for Bodily-Kinesthetic**

13. _____ I enjoy telling stories.
14. _____ I like to write.
15. _____ I like to read.
16. _____ I express myself clearly.
17. _____ I am good at negotiating.
18. _____ I like to discuss topics that interest me.

_____ **TOTAL for Verbal-Linguistic**

7. _____ I use maps easily.
8. _____ I draw pictures/diagrams when explaining ideas.
9. _____ I can assemble items easily from diagrams.
10. _____ I enjoy drawing or photography.
11. _____ I do not like to read long paragraphs.
12. _____ I prefer a drawn map over written directions.

_____ **TOTAL for Visual-Spatial**

19. _____ I like math in school.
20. _____ I like science.
21. _____ I problem-solve well.
22. _____ I question how things work.
23. _____ I enjoy planning or designing something new.
24. _____ I am able to fix things.

_____ **TOTAL for Logical-Mathematical**

Pathways to Learning *(continued)*

Directions: Rate each statement as follows:
Write the number of your response (1–4) on the line
next to the statement and total each set of six questions.

rarely	sometimes	usually	always
1	2	3	4

25. _____ I listen to music.
26. _____ I move my fingers or feet when I hear music.
27. _____ I have good rhythm.
28. _____ I like to sing along with music.
29. _____ People have said I have musical talent.
30. _____ I like to express my ideas through music.

_____ **TOTAL for Musical**

31. _____ I like doing a project with other people
32. _____ People come to me to help settle conflicts.
33. _____ I like to spend time with friends.
34. _____ I am good at understanding people.
35. _____ I am good at making people feel comfortable.
36. _____ I enjoy helping others.

_____ **TOTAL for Interpersonal**

37. _____ I need quiet time to think.
38. _____ I think about issues before I want to talk.
39. _____ I am interested in self-improvement.
40. _____ I understand my thoughts and feelings.
41. _____ I know what I want out of life.
42. _____ I prefer to work on projects alone.

_____ **TOTAL for Intrapersonal**

43. _____ I enjoy nature whenever possible.
44. _____ I think about having a career involving nature.
45. _____ I enjoy studying plants, animals, or oceans.
46. _____ I avoid being indoors except when I sleep.
47. _____ As a child I played with bugs and leaves.
48. _____ When I feel stressed I want to be out in nature.

_____ **TOTAL for Naturalistic**

Write each of your eight intelligences in the column where it fits below. For each, choose the column that corresponds with your total in that intelligence.

SCORES OF 20–24 HIGHLY DEVELOPED		SCORES OF 14–19 MODERATELY DEVELOPED		SCORES BELOW 14 UNDERDEVELOPED	
Scores	Intelligences	Scores	Intelligences	Scores	Intelligences

Learning styles and multiple intelligences are gauges to help you understand yourself. Instead of labelling yourself narrowly using one category or another, learn as much as you can about your preferences and how you can maximize your learning. Most people are a blend of styles and preferences, with one or two being dominant. In addition, you may change preferences depending on the situation. For example, a student might find it easy to take notes in outline style when the instructor lectures in an organized way. However, if another instructor jumps from topic to topic, the student might choose to use the Cornell system or a think link (Chapter 6 goes into detail about note-taking styles).

The final assessment, through its evaluation of personality types, focuses on how you relate to others.

Personality Spectrum

A system that simplifies learning styles into four personality types has been developed by Joyce Bishop (1997). Her work is based on the Myers-Briggs and Keirsey theories discussed earlier in the chapter. The Personality Spectrum will give you a personality perspective on your learning styles. Please complete the following assessment.

Personality Spectrum

Joyce Bishop, Ph.D. (1997)

STEP 1. Rank in order all four responses to each question from <u>**most** like you (4)</u>, to <u>**least** like you (1)</u>. Place a 1, 2, 3, or 4 in each pink box next to the responses.

1. I like instructors who
   - a. tell me exactly what is expected of me.
   - b. make learning active and exciting.
   - c. maintain a safe and supportive classroom.
   - d. challenge me to think at higher levels.

2. I learn best when the material is
   - a. well organized.
   - b. something I can do hands-on.
   - c. about understanding and improving the human condition.
   - d. intellectually challenging.

3. A high priority in my life is to
   - a. keep my commitments.
   - b. experience as much of life as possible.
   - c. make a difference in the lives of others.
   - d. understand how things work.

4. Other people think of me as
   - a. dependable and loyal.
   - b. dynamic and creative.
   - c. caring and honest.
   - d. intelligent and inventive.

5. When I experience stress I would most likely
   - a. do something to help me feel more in control of my life.
   - b. do something physical and daring.
   - c. talk with a friend.
   - d. go off by myself and think about my situation.

(continued)

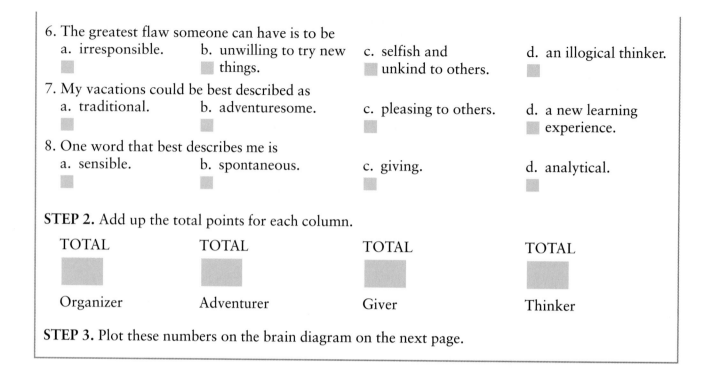

6. The greatest flaw someone can have is to be
   a. irresponsible. ▨
   b. unwilling to try new things. ▨
   c. selfish and unkind to others. ▨
   d. an illogical thinker. ▨

7. My vacations could be best described as
   a. traditional. ▨
   b. adventuresome. ▨
   c. pleasing to others. ▨
   d. a new learning experience. ▨

8. One word that best describes me is
   a. sensible. ▨
   b. spontaneous. ▨
   c. giving. ▨
   d. analytical. ▨

STEP 2. Add up the total points for each column.

TOTAL ▨   TOTAL ▨   TOTAL ▨   TOTAL ▨

Organizer   Adventurer   Giver   Thinker

STEP 3. Plot these numbers on the brain diagram on the next page.

Plotting your scores on Figure 2–1 will create a visual representation of your spectrum.

Your Personality Spectrum assessment can help you maximize your functioning at school and at work. Each personality type has its own abilities that improve work and school performance, suitable learning techniques, and ways of relating in interpersonal relationships. Table 2–2 explains what suits each type.

Table 2–2 Personality Spectrum at School and Work

Personality	Strengths at School and Work	Interpersonal Relationships
Organizer	• Can efficiently manage heavy workloads • Good organizational skills • Natural leadership qualities	• Loyal • Dependable • Traditional
Adventurer	• Adaptable to most changes • Creative and skillful • Dynamic and fast-paced	• Free • Exciting • Intense
Giver	• Always willing to help others • Honest and sincere • Good people skills	• Giving • Romantic • Warm
Thinker	• Good analytical skills • Can develop complex designs • Is thorough and exact	• Quiet • Good problem solver • Inventive

Figure 2-1

Personality Spectrum —Thinking Preferences & Learning Styles

Place a dot on the appropriate number line for each of your four scores and connect the dots. A new shape will be formed inside each square. Colour each shape differently.

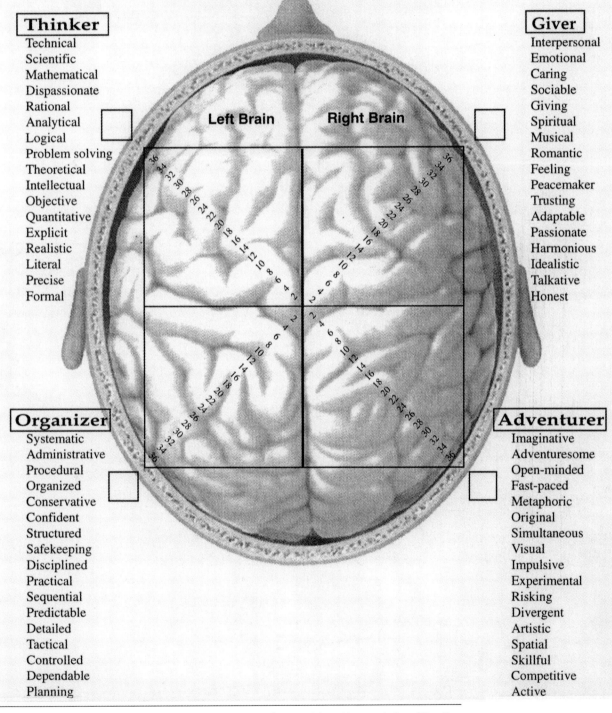

Thinker
Technical
Scientific
Mathematical
Dispassionate
Rational
Analytical
Logical
Problem solving
Theoretical
Intellectual
Objective
Quantitative
Explicit
Realistic
Literal
Precise
Formal

Giver
Interpersonal
Emotional
Caring
Sociable
Giving
Spiritual
Musical
Romantic
Feeling
Peacemaker
Trusting
Adaptable
Passionate
Harmonious
Idealistic
Talkative
Honest

Organizer
Systematic
Administrative
Procedural
Organized
Conservative
Confident
Structured
Safekeeping
Disciplined
Practical
Sequential
Predictable
Detailed
Tactical
Controlled
Dependable
Planning

Adventurer
Imaginative
Adventuresome
Open-minded
Fast-paced
Metaphoric
Original
Simultaneous
Visual
Impulsive
Experimental
Risking
Divergent
Artistic
Spatial
Skillful
Competitive
Active

Left Brain   Right Brain

Source: *Understanding Psychology*, 3rd ed., Charles G. Morris. © 1996. Adapted by permission of Prentice-Hall, Inc., Upper Saddle River, NJ.

What Are the Benefits of Knowing Your Learning Styles?

Determining your learning-styles profile takes work and self-exploration. For it to be worth your while, you need to understand what knowing your profile can do for you. The following sections will discuss benefits specific to study skills as well as more general benefits.

Study Benefits

Most students aim to maximize learning while minimizing frustration and time spent studying. If you know your particular learning style, you can use techniques that complement it. Such techniques take advantage of your highly developed areas while helping you through your less-developed ones. For example, say you perform better in smaller, discussion-based classes. When you have the opportunity, you might choose a course section that is smaller or that is taught by an instructor who prefers group discussion. You might also apply specific strategies to improve your retention in a lecture situation.

This section describes the techniques that tend to complement the strengths and shortcomings of each style. Students in Professor Soloman's program made many of these suggestions according to what worked for their own learning styles. Concepts from different assessments that benefit from similar strategies are grouped together. In Figure 2–2, you can see which styles tend to be dominant among students.

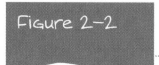

Figure 2–2   Percentages of Students with Particular Learning Styles

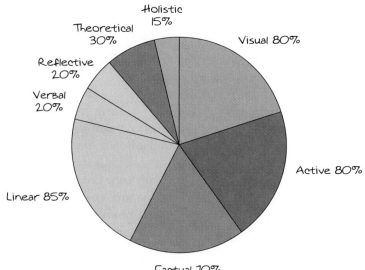

Source: Barbara Soloman, North Carolina State University.

Remember that you may have characteristics from many different styles, even though some are dominant. Therefore, you may see suggestions for styles other than your dominant ones that may apply to you. What's important is that you use what works. Note the boxes next to the names of each style or type. In order to spot your best suggestions quickly, mark your most dominant styles or types by making check marks in the appropriate boxes.

Are You Active or Reflective?

Active learners ☐ include Bodily-Kinesthetic ☐ and Interpersonal ☐ learners as well as Adventurers ☐ . They like to apply the information to the real world, experience it in their own actions, or discuss or explain to others what they have learned.

Student-suggested strategies for active learners:

- Study in a group in which members take turns explaining topics to each other and then discussing them.
- Think of practical uses of the course material.
- Pace and recite while you learn.
- Act out material or design games.
- Use flash cards with other people.
- Teach the material to someone else.

Reflective learners ☐ include Intrapersonal ☐ and Logical/Mathematical ☐ learners as well as Thinkers ☐ . They retain and understand information better after they have taken time to think about it.

Student-suggested strategies for reflective learners:

- Study in a quiet setting.
- When you are reading, stop periodically to think about what you have read.
- Don't just memorize material; think about why it is important and to what it relates, considering the causes and effects involved.
- Write short summaries of what the material means to you.

Are You Factual or Theoretical?

Factual learners ☐ and Organizers ☐ prefer concrete and specific facts, data, and detailed experimentation. They like to solve problems with standard methods and are patient with details. They don't respond well to surprises and unique complications that upset normal procedure. They are good at memorizing facts.

Student-suggested strategies for factual learners:

- Ask the instructor how ideas and concepts apply in practice.
- Ask for specific examples of the ideas and concepts.
- Brainstorm specific examples with classmates or by yourself.
- Think about how theories make specific connections with the real world.

<u>Theoretical learners</u> ☐ are often also <u>Logical/Mathematical</u> ☐ and prefer innovation and theories. They are good at grasping new concepts and big-picture ideas. They dislike repetition and fact-based learning. They are comfortable with symbols and abstractions, often connecting them with prior knowledge and experience. Most classes are aimed at theoretical learners.

Student-suggested strategies for theoretical learners:

- If a class deals primarily with factual information, try to think of concepts, interpretations, or theories that link the facts together.
- Because you become impatient with details, you may be prone to careless mistakes on tests. Read directions and entire questions before answering, and be sure to check your work.
- Look for systems and patterns that arrange facts in a way that makes sense to you.
- Spend time analyzing the material.

Are You Visual/Spatial or Verbal/Linguistic?

<u>Visual/Spatial learners</u> ☐ remember best what they see: diagrams, flow charts, time lines, films, and demonstrations. They tend to forget spoken words and ideas. Classes generally don't include much visual information. Note that although words written on paper or shown with an overhead projector are something you see, visual learners learn most easily from visual cues that don't involve words.

Student-suggested strategies for visual/spatial learners:

- Add diagrams to your notes whenever possible. Dates can be drawn on a time line; math functions can be graphed; percentages can be drawn in a pie chart.
- Organize your notes so that you can clearly see main points and supporting facts and how things are connected. (You will learn more about different styles of note taking in Chapter 6.)
- Connect related facts in your notes by drawing arrows.
- Colour-code your notes using different coloured highlighters so that everything relating to a particular topic is the same colour.

<u>Verbal/Linguistic learners</u> ☐ (often also <u>Interpersonal</u> ☐) remember much of what they hear and more of what they hear and then say. They benefit from discussion, prefer verbal explanation to visual demonstration, and learn effectively by explaining things to others. Because written words are processed as verbal information, verbal learners learn well through reading. The majority of classes, since they present material through the written word, lecture, or discussion, are geared to verbal learners.

Student-suggested strategies for verbal learners:

- Talk about what you learn. Work in study groups so that you have an opportunity to explain and discuss what you are learning.
- Read the textbook and highlight no more than 10 per cent.

- ☺ Rewrite your notes.
- ☺ Outline chapters.
- ☺ Recite information or write scripts and debates.

Are You Linear or Holistic?

<u>Linear learners</u> ☐ **find it easiest to learn material presented in a logical, ordered progression.** They solve problems in a step-by-step manner. They can work with sections of material without yet fully understanding the whole picture. They tend to be stronger when looking at the parts of a whole rather than understanding the whole and then dividing it up into parts. They learn best when taking in material in a progression from easiest to more complex to most difficult. Many courses are taught in a linear fashion.

Student-suggested strategies for linear learners:

- ☺ If you have an instructor who jumps around from topic to topic, spend time outside of class with the instructor or a classmate who can help you fill the gaps in your notes.
- ☺ If class notes are random, rewrite the material according to whatever logic helps you understand it best.
- ☺ Outline the material.

<u>Holistic learners</u> ☐ **learn in fits and starts.** They may feel lost for days or weeks, unable to solve even the simplest problems or show the most basic understanding, until they suddenly "get it." They may feel discouraged when struggling with material that many other students seem to learn easily. Once they understand, though, they tend to see the big picture to an extent that others may not often achieve. They are often highly creative.

Student-suggested strategies for the holistic learner:

- ☺ Recognize that you are not slow or stupid. Don't lose faith in yourself. You will get it!
- ☺ Before reading a chapter, preview it by reading all the subheadings, summaries, and any margin glossary terms. The chapter may also start with an outline and overview of the entire chapter.
- ☺ Instead of spending a short time on every subject every night, try setting aside evenings for specific subjects and immerse yourself in just one subject at a time.
- ☺ Try taking difficult subjects in summer school when you are handling fewer courses.
- ☺ Try to relate subjects to other things you already know. Keep asking yourself how you could apply the material.

Study Techniques for Additional Multiple Intelligences

People who score high in <u>Musical/Rhythmic</u> ☐ intelligence have strong memories for rhymes and can be energized by music. They often have a song running through their minds and find themselves tapping a foot or their fingers when they hear music.

Student-suggested strategies for musical/rhythmic people:

- Create rhymes out of vocabulary words.
- Beat out rhythms when studying.
- Play instrumental music while studying if it does not distract you, but first determine what type of music improves your concentration the most.
- Take study breaks and listen to music.
- Write a song about your topic.

<u>Naturalistic learners</u> ☐ feel energized when they are connected to nature. Their career choices and hobbies reflect their love of nature.

Student-suggested strategies for naturalistic people:

- Study outside whenever practical but only if it is not distracting.
- Explore subject areas that reflect your love for nature. Learning is much easier when you have a passion for it.
- Relate abstract information to something concrete in nature.
- Take breaks with something you love from nature—a walk, watching your fish, or a nature video. Use nature as a reward for getting other work done.

Study Techniques for Different Personality Types

The different personality types of the Personality Spectrum combine the learning styles and multiple intelligences you have explored. Table 2–3 shows learning techniques that benefit each type.

General Benefits

Although schools have traditionally favoured verbal-linguistic students, there is no general advantage to one style over another. The only advantage is in discovering your profile through accurate and honest analysis. Following are three general benefits of knowing your learning styles.

1. You will have a better chance of avoiding problematic situations. If you don't explore what works best for you, you risk forcing yourself into career or personal situations that stifle your creativity, development, and happiness. Knowing how you learn and how you relate to the world can help you make smarter choices.

2. You will be more successful on the job. Your learning style is essentially your working style. If you know how you learn, you will be able to look for an environment that suits you best and you'll be able to work effectively on work teams. This will prepare you for successful employment in the twenty-first century.

3. You will be better able to target areas that need improvement. The more you know about your learning styles, the more you will be able to pinpoint the areas that are more difficult for you. That has two advantages. First, you can begin to work on difficult

Table 2-3 Types and Learning Techniques

Personality Type	Related Learning Styles	Learning Techniques to Use
Organizer	Factual, Linear	• Organize material before studying. • Whenever possible, select instructors who have well-planned courses. • Keep a daily planner and to-do list.
Adventurer	Active, Bodily-Kinesthetic	• Keep study sessions moving quickly. • Make learning fun and exciting. • Study with other Adventurers but also with Organizers.
Giver	Interpersonal	• Form study groups. • Help someone else learn. • Pick classes that relate to your interest in people.
Thinker	Reflective, Intrapersonal, Logical-Mathematical, Theoretical	• Study alone. • Allow time to think about material. • Choose intellectually challenging classes and instructors.

areas, step by step. Second, when a task comes up that requires a skill that is tough for you, you can either take special care with it or suggest someone else whose style may be better suited to it.

Your learning-styles profile is one important part of self-knowledge. Next you will explore other important factors that help to define you.

How Do You Explore Who You Are?

You are an absolutely unique individual. Although you may share individual characteristics with others, your combination of traits is one of a kind. It could take a lifetime to learn everything there is to know about yourself, because you are constantly changing. However, you can start by exploring these facets of yourself: self-perception, interests, habits, abilities, and limitations.

Self-Perception

It is difficult to have an accurate image of yourself. Unfortunately, many people err on the side of negativity. Feeling inadequate from time to time is normal, but a constantly negative self-perception can have destructive effects. Look at

self-perception
How one views oneself; one's opinion of oneself.

Real World Perspective

How can I adjust my learning style to my instructors' teaching styles?

Patti Reed-Zweiger, Part-Time Student

This last year I took a class in math that left me extremely stressed and exhausted. The way the teacher presented the material just didn't work for me. He threw out way too much information in a short period of time with little or no tools for completing the tasks. I really think he was unprepared. When he'd get to class, he'd fumble through his book for a while until he latched onto something to share. Sometimes, he'd spend the whole class answering a ques-

tion or two about the homework and then, at the very last minute, give us a new assignment for the next class. We'd leave without any understanding of what we were to accomplish. It seems to me this teacher did very little teaching.

I'm a police officer, so I'm used to handling enormous pressure, but in this case, nothing seemed to work. I'd leave in tears, class after class. This is frustrating for me. I'm 40 years old and very confident and yet in this class I felt like I was back in grade school again. I felt inadequate, foolish, and out of control. So much so that I would become sick to my stomach—nauseous. I wouldn't wish this experience on my worst enemy. What can I do to succeed in math and still maintain my self-esteem? At this point, I'm ready to drop it altogether.

Jacque Hall, Business Major

You're not alone. Math is frightening to most people. When I began taking math classes, I felt like a total failure. In fact, I dropped out of my Math 102 class. I just couldn't handle it. That's the first thing I'd recommend to you. Get out of the class if the teacher is not what you need. But make sure you talk with the teacher first and see if there's something the two of you can do to make the class successful for you. If you feel that it just won't work, let it go and try to find a

better situation for yourself. Math is hard enough without subjecting yourself to inadequate teaching. I found that networking with other students on what classes and instructors to take really helped. The younger students always seem to know who the best teachers are.

If you can afford the additional time, I recommend you audit a class. If that isn't an option, hire a math tutor or take advantage of the math lab on a regular basis. Most importantly, remember that you are not a failure. And you're also not alone. I have felt a great deal of despair over math myself. I have seen people cry in class and others leave in total frustration. At some time or other, every student is going to run into a teacher or a classroom situation that leaves them feeling dissatisfied. Do your part by communicating with the teacher. If that doesn't work, move on. I'm glad I did.

people you know who think that they are less intelligent, capable, or attractive than they really are. Observe how that shuts down their confidence and motivation. You do the same to yourself when you perceive yourself negatively.

Negative self-perception has a series of effects that lead to a self-fulfilling prophecy—something that comes true because you have convinced yourself it will: First you believe that you are incapable of being or doing something, then you neglect to try, and finally, you most likely don't do or become what you had already decided was impossible.

For example, say you think you can't pass a certain course. Since you feel you don't have a chance, you don't put as much effort into the work for that course. Sure enough, at the end of the semester, you don't pass. The worst part is that you may see your failure as proof of your incapability, instead of realizing that you didn't allow yourself to try. This chain of events can occur in many situations. When it happens in the workplace, people lose jobs. When it happens in personal life, people lose relationships.

Negative self-images may come from one or more different sources. Here are some possibilities:

- **Critical parents or guardians.** All children hear some criticism. But if you hear repeated negative comments and receive little positive reinforcement, you may believe what you hear.

- **Instructors or other authority figures.** As with parents, critical authority figures who focus on the negative may influence your self-perception.

- **Magazines, television, and other media.** The media set a standard by what they convey to be the right way to look, behave, and work. If you and your life don't seem to match this standard, you may take that as a negative reflection on yourself.

- **Unrealistic expectations.** Many people expect too much of themselves. When they don't live up to these expectations, they are often their own worst critics, labelling the effort a "failure" and playing a constant inner tape of negative self-talk.

Refine your self-image so that it reflects more of your true self. These strategies might help.

- **Believe in yourself.** If you don't believe in yourself, others may have a harder time believing in you. Work to eliminate negative self-talk. Have faith in your abilities. When you set your goals, stick to them. Know that your mind and will are very powerful.

- **Talk to other people whom you trust.** People who know you well often have a more realistic perception of you than you do of yourself.

- **Take personal time.** Stress makes having perspective on your life more difficult. Take time out to clear your mind and think realistically about who you are and who you want to be.

- **Look at all of the evidence.** Mistakes can loom large in your mind. Consider what you do well and what you have accomplished as carefully as you consider your stumbles.

"The greatest discovery of any generation is that human beings can alter their lives by altering their attitudes of mind."

Albert Schweitzer

Building a positive self-perception is a lifelong challenge. If you maintain a bright but realistic vision of yourself, it will take you far along the road toward achieving your goals.

Interests

Taking some time now to explore your interests will help you later when you select a major and a career. You may be aware of many of your general interests already. For example, you can ask yourself:

- What areas of study do I like?
- What activities make me happy?
- What careers seem interesting to me?
- What kind of daily schedule do I like to keep (early riser, night owl)?
- What type of home and work environment do I prefer?

Interests play an important role in the workplace. Many people, however, do not take their interests seriously when choosing a career. Some make salary or stability their first priority. Some feel they have to take the first job that comes along. Some may not realize they can do better. Not considering what you are interested in may lead to an area of study or a job that leaves you unhappy, uninterested, or unfulfilled.

Choosing to consider your interests and happiness takes courage but brings benefits. Think about your life. You spend hours of time both attending classes and studying outside of class. You will spend at least eight hours a day, five or more days a week, up to fifty or more weeks a year as a working contributor to the world. Although your studies and work won't always make you deliriously happy, it is possible to spend your school and work time in a manner that suits you.

Here are three positive effects of focusing on your interests.

1. You will have more energy. Think about how you feel when you are looking forward to seeing a special person, participating in a favourite sports activity, or enjoying some entertainment. When you're doing something you like, time seems to pass very quickly. Contrast this with how you feel about disagreeable activities. The difference in your energy level is immense. You will be able to get much more done in a subject or career area that you enjoy.

2. You will perform better. When you were in high school, you probably got your best grades in your favourite classes and excelled in your favourite activities. That doesn't change as you get older. You will usually find the most success in work that you like to do. The more you like something, the harder you work at it—and the harder you work, the more you will improve.

3. You will have a positive attitude. A positive attitude creates a positive environment and might even make up for areas in which you lack ability or experience. On the other hand, even if you perform well, a negative attitude can sour the atmosphere for

attitude

A state of mind or feeling toward something.

your co-workers and may ultimately cost you your job. This is especially important when working in a team with others. Because businesses currently emphasize teamwork to such a great extent, your ability to maintain a positive attitude might mean the difference between success and failure.

Habits

A preference for a particular action that you do a certain way, and often on a regular basis or at certain times, is a habit. You might have a habit of showering in the morning, eating raisins, channel surfing with the television remote control, hitting the snooze button on your clock, talking for hours on the phone, or studying late at night. Your habits reveal a lot about you. Some habits you consider to be good habits, and some may be bad habits.

Bad habits earn that title because they can prevent you from reaching important goals. Some bad habits, such as chronic lateness, cause obvious problems. Other habits, such as renting movies three times a week, may not seem bad until you realize that you needed to spend those hours studying. People maintain bad habits because they offer immediate, enjoyable rewards, even if later effects are negative. For example, eating out frequently may drain your budget, but at first it seems easier than shopping for food, cooking, and washing dishes.

Good habits are those that have positive effects on your life. You often have to wait longer and work harder to see a reward for good habits, which makes them harder to maintain. If you cut out fattening foods, you won't lose weight in two days. If you reduce your nights out to gain study time, your grades won't improve in a week. When you strive to maintain good habits, trust that the rewards are somewhere down the road. Changing a habit can be a long process.

Take time to evaluate your habits. Look at the positive and negative effects of each, and decide which are helpful and which harmful to you. Here are steps you can take to change a habit that has more negative effects than positive ones.

1. Be honest about your habits. Admitting negative or destructive habits can be hard to do. You can't change a habit until you admit that it is a habit.

2. Recognize the habit as troublesome. Sometimes the trouble may not seem to come directly from the habit. For example, spending every weekend working on the house may seem important, but you may be overdoing it and ignoring friends and family members.

3. Decide to change. You might realize what your bad habits are but not yet care about their effects on your life. Until you are convinced that you will receive something positive and useful from changing, your efforts will not get you far.

4. Start today. Don't put it off until after this week, after the family reunion, or after the semester. Each day lost is a day you haven't had the chance to benefit from a new lifestyle.

"Habit is Heaven's own redress: it takes the place of happiness."
Alexander Pushkin

5. **Change one habit at a time.** Changing and breaking habits is difficult. Attempting to be perfect overnight will only frustrate you. Trying to spend more time with your family, reduce time spent watching television, increase studying, and save more money all at once can bring on a fit of deprivation, sending you scurrying back to all your old habits. Easy does it.

6. **Reward yourself appropriately for positive steps taken.** If you earn a good grade, avoid slacking off on your studies the following week. If you've lost weight, avoid celebrating in a doughnut shop. Choose a reward that will not encourage you to stray from your target.

7. **Keep it up.** To have the best chance at changing a habit, be consistent for at least three weeks. Your brain needs time to become accustomed to the new habit. If you go back to the old habit during that time, you may feel like you're starting all over again.

8. **Don't get too discouraged.** Rarely does someone make the decision to change and do so without a setback or two. Being too hard on yourself might cause frustration that tempts you to give up and go back to the habit.

Abilities

Everyone's abilities include both strengths and limitations. Both are part of you. Examining both strengths and limitations is part of establishing the kind of clear vision of yourself that will help you maximize your potential.

Strengths

As you think about your preferences, your particular strengths will come to mind, because you often like best the things you can do well. Some strengths seem to be natural—things you learned to do without ever having to work too hard. Others you struggled to develop and continue to work hard to maintain. Asking yourself these questions may help you define more clearly what your abilities are:

- ⚙ What have I always been able to do well?
- ⚙ What have others often praised about me?
- ⚙ What do I like most about myself, and why?
- ⚙ What is my learning-styles profile?
- ⚙ What are my accomplishments—at home, at school, at work?

As with your preferences, knowing your abilities will help you find a job that makes the most of them. When your job requires you to do work you like, you are more likely to perform to the best of your ability. Keep that in mind as you explore career areas. Assessments and inventories that will help you further assess your abilities may be available at your school's career centre or library. Once you know yourself, you will be better able to set appropriate goals.

Limitations

Nobody is perfect, and no one is good at everything. Everyone has limitations. That doesn't mean they are any easier to take, however. Limitations can make you feel frustrated, stressed, or angry. You may feel as though no one else has the limitations you have, or that no one else has as many.

There are three ways to deal with your limitations. The first two—ignoring them or dwelling on them—are the most common. Both are natural, but neither is wise. The third way is to face them and to work to improve them while keeping the strongest focus on your abilities.

Ignoring your limitations can cause you to be unable to accomplish your goals. For example, say you are an active, global learner with a well-developed interpersonal intelligence. You have limitations in logical-mathematical intelligence and in linear thought. Ignoring that fact, you decide that you can make good money in computer programming, and you sign up for math and programming courses. You certainly won't fail automatically. However, if you ignore your limited ability in those courses and don't seek extra help, you may have more than a few stumbles.

Dwelling on your limitations can make you forget you have any strengths at all. This results in negative self-talk and a poor self-perception. Continuing the example, if you were to dwell on your limitations in math, you might stop trying altogether.

Facing limitations and working to improve them is the best response. A healthy understanding of your limitations can help you avoid troublesome situations. In the above example, you could face your limitations in math and explore other career areas that use your more well-developed abilities and intelligences. If you decided to stick with computer technology, you could study an area of the field that focuses on management and interpersonal relationships. Or you could continue to aim for a career as a programmer, taking care to seek special help in areas that give you trouble.

How Can You Start Thinking About Choosing a Major?

While many students come to university or college knowing what they want to study, many do not. That's completely normal. University or college is a perfect time to begin exploring your different interests. In the process, you may discover talents and strengths you never realized you had. For example, taking an environmental class may teach you that you have a passion for finding solutions to pollution problems. You may discover a talent for public speaking and decide to explore on-camera journalism.

While some of your explorations may take you down paths that don't resonate with your personality and interests, each experience will help to clarify who you really are and what you want to do with your life. Thinking about choosing a major involves exploring potential majors, being open to changing majors, and linking majors to career areas.

major
A subject of academic knowledge chosen as a field of specialization, requiring a specific course of study.

Exploring Potential Majors

Here are some steps to help you explore majors that may interest you.

Take a variety of classes. Although you will generally have core requirements to fulfill, use your electives to branch out. Try to take at least one class in each area that sparks your interest.

Don't rule out subject areas that aren't classified as "safe." Friends or parents may have warned you against pursuing certain careers, encouraging you to stay with "safe" careers that pay well. Even though financial stability is important, following your heart's dreams and desires is equally important. Choosing between the "safe" path and the path of the heart can be challenging. Only you can decide which is the best for you.

Spend time getting to know yourself, your interests, and your abilities. The more you know about yourself, the more ability you will have to focus on areas that make the most of who you are and what you can do. Pay close attention to those areas that inspire you to greater heights and those areas that seem to deaden your initiative.

Work closely with your adviser. Begin discussing your major early on with your adviser, even if you don't intend to declare a major right away. For any given major, your adviser may be able to tell you about both the corresponding department at your school and the possibilities in related career areas. You may also discuss with your adviser the possibility of a double major (completing the requirements for two different majors) or designing your own major, if your school offers an opportunity to do so.

Take advantage of other resources. Seek opinions from instructors, friends, and family members. Talk to students who have declared majors that interest you. Explore the course materials your college or university gives you in order to see what majors your school offers.

Develop your critical-thinking skills. Working toward any major will help you develop your most important skill—knowing how to use your mind. Critical thinking is the most crucial ingredient in any recipe for school and career success. More than anything, your future career and employer will depend on your ability to think clearly, effectively, creatively, and wisely, and to contribute to the workplace by truly making a difference.

Changing Majors

Some people may change their minds several times before honing in on a major that fits. Although this may add to the time you spend in university or college, being happy with your decision is important. For example, an education major may begin student teaching only to discover that she really doesn't feel comfortable in front of students. Or, like Donald Sutherland, a student may declare engineering as a major only to realize that his or her passion is in acting.

If this happens to you, don't be discouraged. You're certainly not alone. Changing a major is much like changing a job. Skills and experiences from one job will assist you in your next position, and some of the courses from your first major may apply—or even transfer as credits—to your next major. Talk with your academic adviser about any desire to change majors. Sometimes an adviser can speak to department heads in order to get the maximum number of credits transferred to your new major.

Whatever you decide, realize that you do have the right to change your mind. Continual self-discovery is part of the journey. No matter how many detours you make, each interesting class you take along the way helps to point you toward a major that feels like home.

Linking Majors to Career Areas

The point of declaring and pursuing a major is to help you reach a significant level of knowledge in one subject, often in preparation for a particular career area. Before you discard a major as not practical enough, consider where it might be able to take you. Thinking through the possibilities may open doors that you never knew existed. Besides finding an exciting path, you may discover something highly marketable and beneficial to humankind as well.

For each major there are many career options that aren't obvious right away. For example, a student working toward a teaching certification doesn't have to teach public school. This student could develop curricula, act as a consultant for businesses, develop an online education service, teach overseas, or create a cable television program. The sky's the limit.

Explore the educational requirements of any career area that interests you. Your choice of major may be more or less crucial depending on the career area. For example, pursuing a career in medicine almost always requires a major in some area of the biological sciences, while aspiring lawyers may have majored in anything from political science to philosophy. Many employers are more interested in your ability to think than in your specific knowledge, and therefore may not pay as much attention to your major as they do to your critical-thinking skills. Ask advisers or people in your areas of interest what educational background is necessary or helpful to someone pursuing a career in that area.

The Personality Page
www.personalitypage.com/

This Web site helps students link their personality with careers that suit those personality types. It's an excellent place to start exploring your academic and career possibilities.

Ontario Institute for Studies in Education
www.oise.utoronto.ca/ ~mpress/eduweb.html

OISE is a centre for education research in Canada, and the Web site contains a very comprehensive list of colleges and universities in Canada. Should you discover that your current educational path isn't the right one, you can shop around using this site.

Sabiduría

In Spanish, the term *sabiduría* represents the two sides of learning—both knowledge and wisdom. Knowledge—building what you know about how the world works—is the first part. Wisdom—deriving meaning and significance from knowledge, and deciding how to use that knowledge—is the second. As you continually learn and experience new things, the sabiduría you build will help you make knowledgeable and wise choices about how to lead your life.

Think of this concept as you discover more about how you learn and receive knowledge in all aspects of your life—in school, work, and personal situations. As you learn how your unique mind works and how to use it, you can more confidently assert yourself. As you expand your ability to use your mind in different ways, you can create lifelong advantages for yourself.

Chapter 2: Applications

Name _____ Date _____

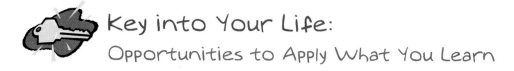 Key into Your Life:
Opportunities to Apply What You Learn

Exercise 1: How Do You Learn Best?

Start by writing your scores next to each term.

LEARNING-STYLES INVENTORY	PATHWAYS TO LEARNING	PERSONALITY SPECTRUM
_____ Active	_____ Bodily-Kinesthetic	_____ Organizer
_____ Reflective	_____ Visual-Spatial	_____ Adventurer
_____ Factual	_____ Verbal-Linguistic	_____ Giver
_____ Theoretical	_____ Logical-Mathematical	_____ Thinker
_____ Visual	_____ Musical	
_____ Verbal	_____ Interpersonal	
_____ Linear	_____ Intrapersonal	
_____ Holistic	_____ Naturalist	

Circle your highest preferences (highest scores) for each assessment. What positive experiences have you had at work and school that you can link to the strengths you circled? _____

_____

_____

_____

What negative experiences have you had that may be related to your least-developed learning styles or intelligences? _____

_____

_____

_____

Exercise 2: Making School More Enjoyable

List two required classes that you are not necessarily looking forward to taking. Discuss what parts of your learning-styles profile may relate to your lack of enthusiasm. Name learning-styles-related study techniques that may help you get the most out of the class and enjoy it more.

CLASS	REASON FOR LACK OF ENTHUSIASM	LEARNING OR STUDY TECHNIQUES
1.		
2.		

Exercise 3: Your Habits

You have the power to change your habits. List three habits that you want to change. Discuss the effects of each and how those effects keep you from reaching your goals.

HABIT	EFFECTS THAT PREVENT YOU FROM REACHING GOALS
1.	
2.	
3.	

Out of these three, put a star by the habit you want to change first. Write down a step you can take today toward overcoming that habit.

_____

_____

_____

What helpful habit do you want to develop in its place? For example, if your problem habit were a failure to express yourself when you are angry, a replacement habit might be to talk calmly about situations that upset you as soon as they arise. If you have a habit of cramming for tests at the last minute, you could replace it with a regular study schedule that allows you to cover your material bit by bit over a longer period of time.

_____

_____

One way to help yourself abandon your old habit is to think about how your new habit will improve your life. List two benefits of your new habit.

1. _____

2. _____

Give yourself one month to complete your habit shift. Set a specific deadline. Keep track of your progress by indicating on a chart or calendar how well you did each day. If you avoided the old habit, write an X below the day. If you used the new one, write an N. Therefore, a day when you only avoided the old habit will have an X; a day when you did both will have both letters; a day when you did neither will be left blank. You can use the chart below or mark your own calendar. Try pairing up with another student and arranging to check up on each other's progress.

1	2	3	4	5	6	7	8	9	10	11	12	13	14	15	16
17	18	19	20	21	22	23	24	25	26	27	28	29	30	31	

Don't forget to reward yourself for your hard work. Write here what your reward will be when you feel you are on the road to a new and beneficial habit.

_____

_____

_____

Exercise 4: Interests, Majors, and Careers

Start by listing activities and subjects you like.

1. _____

2. _____

3. _____

4. _____

5. _____

6. _____

Name three majors that might relate to your interests and help you achieve your career goals.

1. _____

2. _____

3. _____

For each major, name a corresponding career area you may want to explore.

1. _____

2. _____

3. _____

Keep these majors and career areas in mind as you gradually narrow your course choices in the time before you declare a major.

 Key to Cooperative Learning:
Building Teamwork Skills

Personality Spectrum Gather in small groups with people of the same Personality Spectrum (all Organizers or Adventurers or Givers or Thinkers). With your group complete the chart on page 67 on notebook paper or on a large flip chart.

You may want to present this information to the entire class to enable everyone to have a better understanding and acceptance of each other's unique personalities. You might also brainstorm strategies for dealing with your spectrum's struggles and stressors, and present those ideas to the class as well.

YOUR PERSONALITY SPECTRUM	
Strengths	Struggles
1.	1.
2.	2.
3.	3.
4.	4.
5.	5.
Stressors	Careers
1.	1.
2.	2.
3.	3.
4.	4.
5.	5.

EXAMPLE FOR AN ADVENTURER	
Strengths	Struggles
1. Flexibility	1. Meeting deadlines
2. Creativity	2. Focusing on details
Stressors	Careers
1. Anything boring	1. Business owner
2. Traditional structure	2. Designer

Key to Self-Expression:
Discovery Through Journal Writing

To record your thoughts, use a separate journal or the lined page at the end of the chapter.

Your Learning-Styles Profile Discuss the insights you have gained, through exploring your learning-styles profile, about your strengths and struggles at school and work. What new strengths have come to your attention? What struggles have you become aware of that you couldn't explain before? Talk about how your insights may have changed the way you see yourself.

Key to Your Personal Portfolio:
Your Paper Trail to Success

Self-Portrait Use this exercise to synthesize everything you have been exploring about yourself into one comprehensive "self-portrait." You will design your portrait in "think link" style, using words and visual shapes to describe your self-perception, learning-styles profile, attitudes, habits, preferences, and abilities.

A think link is a visual construction of related ideas, similar to a map or web, that represents your thought process. Ideas are written inside geometric shapes, often boxes or circles, and related ideas and facts are attached to those ideas by lines drawn connecting the shapes. You will learn more about think links in the note-taking section in Chapter 6.

Use the style shown in the example in Figure 2–3, or create your own. For example, in this exercise you may want to create a "wheel" of ideas coming off your central shape, entitled "Myself." Then, spreading out from each of those ideas (abilities, learning style, etc.) you would draw lines connecting all of the thoughts that go along with that idea. Connected to "Abilities," for example, might be "singing," "good memory," "get along with people," "math skills." You don't have to use the wheel image. You might want to design a tree-like think link, or a line of boxes with connecting thoughts written below the boxes, or anything else you like. Let your design reflect who you are, just as the think link itself does.

Figure 2–3   Sample Self-Portrait Think Link

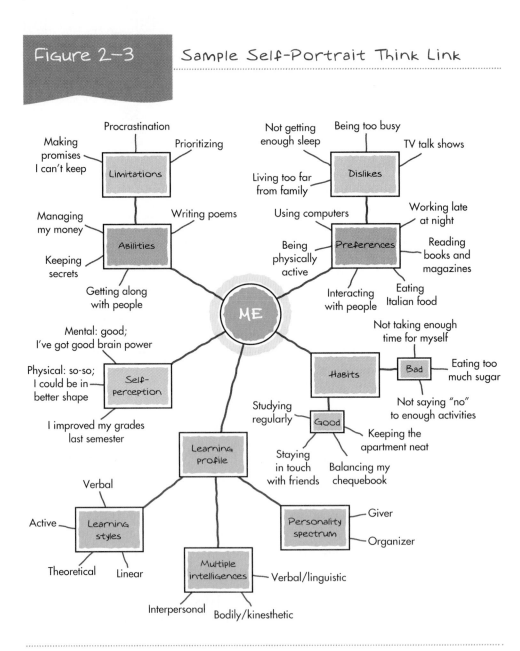

Name _____ Date _____

Journal Entry

3 Goal Setting and Time Management:

Mapping Your Course

In this chapter, you will explore answers to the following questions:

☉ What defines your values?

☉ How do you set and achieve goals?

☉ What are your priorities?

☉ How can you manage your time?

☉ Why is procrastination a problem?

People dream of what they want out of life, but not everyone knows how to turn dreams into reality. Often dreams and goals seem far off in time, too difficult, or even completely unreachable. It may seem that there is a vast desert between where you are now and where you aspire to be. You can build paths through the desert by identifying the steps you need to take, one by one, to arrive at your destination. The steps are goals. When you set goals, prioritize, and manage your time effectively, you increase your ability to take those steps to achieve your long-term goals.

The pursuit of personal and professional goals gives your life meaning. This chapter explains how taking specific steps toward goals can help you turn your dreams into reality. You will explore how your values relate to your goals. You will see how to create a framework for your life's goals—a personal mission statement—and how to set long-term and short-term goals. You will discover how setting priorities can help you work toward your goals more efficiently. The Conference Board of Canada identifies the ability to set goals and to manage time as two critical personal management skills for Canadian workers. The section on time management will discuss how to translate those goals into daily, weekly, monthly, and yearly steps to give shape and purpose to their achievement. Finally, you will explore the topic of procrastination, how it affects your life, and what you can do to minimize the problems it may cause.

Thinking It Through

Check those statements that apply to you right now:

- ❏ I haven't thought much about the sources of my values.

- ❏ I set goals but don't always feel that I achieve them.

- ❏ I feel that my priorities have changed since entering college or university.

- ❏ I have a date book but I don't use it all that much.

- ❏ I know it doesn't help me, but I procrastinate.

- ❏ I don't think about the future; I just let things happen to me.

What Defines Your Values?

values
Principles or qualities that one considers important, right, or good.

Your personal values are the beliefs that guide your choices. Examples of Canadian values include family togetherness, getting a good education, caring for others, and having worthwhile employment. The sum total of all your values is your *value system*. You demonstrate your particular value system in the priorities you set, how you communicate with others, your family life, your educational and career choices, and even the material things with which you surround yourself.

Looking at sources is a good first step in the exploration of your values.

Sources of Values

Values are choices. You are in control of choosing what you value. It may not always seem that way, however, because people often choose their values based on what others value or what society or the media seem to value. A value system is constructed over time, using information from many different sources.

Sources of values include the following:

- Parents, guardians, or relatives
- Friends and peers
- Religious belief and study
- Instructors, supervisors, mentors, and other authority figures
- Books, magazines, television, or other media
- Workplace and school

A particular value may come from one or more sources. For example, a student may value education (primary source: parents), music (primary sources: media and friends), and spiritual life (primary sources: religious leaders and grandparents). Another student may have abandoned all of the values that he or she grew up with and instead adopted the values of a trusted mentor. Still another may find that adopting certain values became important in order to succeed in a particular career area. Being influenced by the values of others is natural, although you should take care to follow what feels right to you.

Choosing and Evaluating Values

Examining the sources of your values can help you define those values, trace their origin, and question the reasons why you have adopted them. Value sources, however, aren't as important as the process of considering each value carefully to see if it makes sense to you. Some of your current values may have come from television or other media but still ring true. Some may come from what others have taught you. Some you may have constructed from your own personal experience and opinion. You must make the final decision about what to value, regardless of the source.

Each individual value system is unique, even if many values come from other sources. Your value system is yours alone. Your responsibility is to make sure that your values are your own choice, and not the choices of others. Make value choices for yourself based on what feels right for you, for your life, and for those who are touched by your life.

You can be more sure of making choices that are right for you if you try to always question and evaluate your values. Before you adopt a value, ask yourself: Does it feel right? What effects might it have on my life? Am I choosing it to please someone else, or is it truly my choice? Values are a design for life, and you are the one who has to live the life you design.

Because changes in your life and new experiences may bring a change in values, you should continue to evaluate values as time goes by. Periodically evaluate the effects that having each value has on your life, and see if a shift in values might suit your changing circumstances. The difficulty of a divorce may have a positive result: a new value of independence and individuality. After growing up in a homogeneous community, a student who meets other students from unfamiliar backgrounds may learn a new value of living in a multicultural country like Canada. Your values will grow and develop as you do if you continue to think them through.

How Values Relate to Goals

Understanding your values will help you set career and personal goals, because the most ideal goals help you achieve what you value. If you value spending time with your family, related goals may include living near your parents or writing to your grandmother every week. A value of financial independence may generate goals, such as working while going to school and keeping credit-card debt low, that reflect the value. If you value helping others, try to make time for volunteer work.

Goals enable you to put values into practice. When you set and pursue goals that are based on values, you demonstrate and reinforce values through taking action. The strength of those values, in turn, reinforces your goals. You will experience a much stronger drive to achieve if you build goals around what is most important to you.

How Do You Set and Achieve Goals?

A goal can be something as concrete as buying a Canada Savings Bond or as abstract as working to control your temper. When you set goals and work to achieve them, you engage your intelligence, abilities, time, and energy in order to move ahead. From major life decisions to the tiniest day-to-day activities, setting goals will help you define how you want to live and what you want to achieve.

Paul Timm, a best-selling author and teacher who is an expert in self-management, feels that focus is a key ingredient in setting and achieving goals. "Focus adds power to our actions. If somebody threw a bucket of water on you, you'd get wet, and probably get mad. But if water was shot at you

"Obstacles are what people see when they take their eyes off the goal."
Subway Bulletin Board

goal
An end toward which effort is directed; an aim or intention.

through a high-pressure nozzle, you might get injured. The only difference is focus."[1] Each part of this section will explain ways to focus your energy through goal setting. You can set and achieve goals by defining a personal mission statement, placing your goals in long-term and short-term time frames, evaluating goals in terms of your values, and linking your goals to five life areas.

Identifying Your "Personal Mission Statement"

Some people go through their lives without ever really thinking about what they can do or what they want to achieve. When duties and demands fill your days, it's easy to lose your drive. If you choose not to set goals or explore what you want out of life, you may look back on your past with a sense of emptiness. You may not know what you've done or why you did it. However, you can avoid that emptiness by periodically taking a few steps back and thinking about where you've been and where you want to be.

One helpful way to determine your general direction is to write a *personal mission statement*. Dr. Stephen Covey, author of the bestseller *The Seven Habits of Highly Effective People*, defines a mission statement as a philosophy that outlines what you want to be (character), what you want to do (contributions and achievements), and the principles by which you live. "A personal mission statement based on correct principles becomes the same kind of standard for an individual," he says. "It becomes a personal constitution, the basis for making major, life-directing decisions, the basis for making daily decisions in the midst of the circumstances and emotions that affect our lives. It empowers individuals with the same timeless strength in the midst of change."[2]

Your personal mission isn't written in stone. It should change as you move from one phase of life to the next—from single person to spouse, from parent to single parent to caregiver of an older parent. Stay flexible and re-evaluate your personal mission from time to time.

Here is author Carol Carter's personal mission statement:

> My mission is to use my talents and abilities to help people of all ages, stages, backgrounds, and economic levels achieve their human potential through fully developing their minds and their talents. I also aim to balance work with people in my life, understanding that my family and friends are a priority above all else.

A company, like a person, needs to establish standards and principles that guide its many activities. Companies often have mission statements so that each member of the organization, from the custodian to the president, clearly understands what he or she needs to achieve. If a company fails to identify its mission, a million well-intentioned employees might focus their energies in just as many different directions, creating chaos and low productivity.

Here is a mission statement from Canadian Tire. Notice how it reinforces the company's goals of leadership and excellence.

> To be the first choice for Canadians in Automotive, Sports and Leisure, and Home products, providing total customer value through customer-driven, focused assortments and competitive operations.

You will have an opportunity to write your own personal mission statement at the end of this chapter. Writing a mission statement is much more than an in-school exercise. It is truly for you. Thinking through your personal mission can help you begin to take charge of your life. It helps to put you in control instead of allowing circumstances and events to control you. If you frame your mission statement carefully so that it truly reflects your goals, it can be your guide in everything you do.

Placing Goals in Time

Everyone has the same twenty-four hours in a day, but it often doesn't feel like enough. Have you ever had a busy day flash by so quickly that it seems you accomplished nothing? Have you ever felt that way about a longer period of time, like a month or even a year? Your commitments can overwhelm you unless you decide how to use time to plan your steps toward goal achievement.

If developing a personal mission statement establishes the big picture, placing your goals within particular time frames allows you to bring individual areas of that picture into the foreground. It's a rare goal that is reached overnight. Lay out the plan by breaking a long-term goal into stages of what you will accomplish in one day, one week, one month, six months, one year, five years, ten years, even twenty years. Planning your progress step by step will help you maintain your efforts over the extended time period often needed to accomplish a goal. Goals fall into two categories: long-term and short-term.

Setting Long-Term Goals

Establish first the goals that have the largest scope, the *long-term goals* that you aim to attain over a lengthy period of time, up to a few years or more. As a student, you know what long-term goals are all about. You have set yourself a goal to attend school and earn a degree, diploma, or certificate. Completing your education is an admirable goal that takes a good number of years to reach.

Some long-term goals are lifelong, such as a goal to continually learn more about yourself and the world around you. Others have a more definite end, such as a goal to complete a course successfully. To determine your long-term goals, think about what you want out of your professional, educational, and personal life. Here is Carol Carter's long-term goal statement:

<u>Carol's Goals:</u>   To accomplish my mission through writing books, giving seminars, and developing programs that create opportunities for students to learn and develop. To create a personal, professional, and family environment that allows me to manifest my abilities and duly tend to each of my responsibilities.

For example, you may establish long-term goals such as these:

- I will graduate from school and know that I have learned all that I could, whether my grade point average shows it or not.
- I will use my current and future job experience to develop practical skills that will help me later in life.
- I will build my leadership and teamwork skills by forming positive, productive relationships with classmates, instructors, and co-workers.

Long-term goals don't have to be lifelong goals. Think about your long-term goals for the coming year. Considering what you want to accomplish in a year's time will give you clarity, focus, and a sense of what needs to take place right away. When Carol thought about her long-term goals for the coming year, she came up with the following list:

1. Develop programs to provide internships, scholarships, and other quality initiatives for students.
2. Write a book for students emphasizing an interactive, highly visual approach to learning.
3. Allow time in my personal life to eat well, run five days a week, and spend quality time with family and friends. Allow time daily for quiet reflection and spiritual devotion.

In the same way that Carol's goals are tailored to her personality and interests, your goals should reflect who you are. Personal missions and goals are as unique as each individual. Continuing the example above, you might adopt these goals for the coming year:

- I will earn passing grades in all my classes.
- I will look for a part-time job with a local newspaper or newsroom.
- I will join two clubs and make an effort to take leadership roles in each.

Setting Short-Term Goals

When you divide your long-term goals into smaller, manageable goals that you hope to accomplish within a relatively short time, you are setting *short-term goals*. Short-term goals narrow your focus, helping you to maintain your progress toward your long-term goals. They are the steps that take you where you want to go. Say you have set the above three long-term goals. To stay on track toward those goals, you may want to accomplish these short-term goals in the next six months:

"When men are arrived at the Goal, they should not turn Back"

Plutarch

- I will pass Business Writing I so that I can move on to Business Writing II.
- I will make an effort to ask my co-workers for advice on how to get into the news business.
- I will attend four monthly meetings of the Journalism Club.

These same goals can be broken down into even smaller parts, such as one month.

- I will complete five of the ten essays for Business Writing.
- I will have lunch with my office mate at work so that I can talk with her about her work experience.
- I will write an article for next month's Journalism Club newsletter.

In addition to monthly goals, you may have short-term goals that extend for a week, a day, or even a couple of hours in a given day. Take as an example the article you have planned to write for the next month's Journalism Club newsletter. Such short-term goals may include the following:

- Three weeks from now: Have a final draft ready. Submit it to the editor of the newsletter.
- Two weeks from now: Have a second draft ready, and give it to one more person to review.
- One week from now: Have a first draft ready. Ask my writing instructor to review it.
- Today by the end of the day: "Freewrite" about the subject of the article, and narrow it down to a specific topic.
- By 3 P.M. today: Brainstorm ideas and subjects for the article (more on brainstorming and freewriting in Chapter 6).

As you consider your long-term and short-term goals, notice how all of your goals are linked to one another. As Figure 3–1 shows, your long-term goals establish a context for the short-term goals. In turn, your short-term goals make the long-term goals seem clearer and more reachable. The whole system works to keep you on track.

Linking Goals with Values

If you are not sure how to start formulating your mission, look to your values to guide you. Define your mission and goals based on what is important to you.

If you value physical fitness, your mission statement might emphasize your commitment to staying in shape throughout your life. Your long-term goal might be to run a marathon, while your short-term goals might involve your weekly exercise and eating plan. Similarly, if you value a close family, your personal mission might emphasize how you want to maintain family ties and stability. In this case, your long-term goals might involve finding a job that allows for family time or living in a town close to your parents. Your short-term goals may focus on helping your son learn a musical instrument or having dinner with your family at least twice a week.

D. Richard Compton
home.golden.net/~drc/

This Canadian motivational speaker has tips and advice on goal setting and time management. The site includes links to motivational and goal-setting specialists, and offers trial versions of goal-setting software.

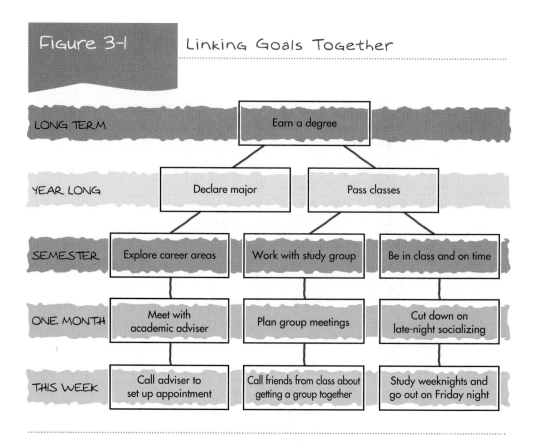

Figure 3-1   Linking Goals Together

Current and Personal Values Mean Appropriate Goals

When you use your values as a compass for your goals, make sure the compass is pointed in the direction of your real feelings. Watch out for the following two pitfalls that can occur:

Setting goals according to other peoples' values. Friends or family may encourage you to strive for what they think you should value, rather than what is right for you. If you follow their advice without believing in it, you may have a harder time sticking to your path. For example, someone who attends school primarily because a parent or spouse thought it was the right thing to do may have less motivation and initiative than someone who made an independent decision to become a student. Look hard at what you really want, and why. Staying in tune with your own values will help you make decisions that are right for you.

Setting goals that reflect values you held in the past. What you felt yesterday may no longer apply, because life changes can alter your values. The best goals reflect what you believe today. For example, a person who has been through a near-fatal car accident may experience a dramatic increase in how he or she values time with friends and family, and a drop in how he or she values material possessions. Someone who survives a serious illness may value healthy living above all else. Keep in touch with changes in your life so that your goals can reflect who you are.

Goals in Five Life Areas

All goals are not the same, because they involve different parts of your life and different values. Approach goal setting by establishing your long-term and short-term goals within five different areas: personal, family, school/career, financial, and lifestyle. As you set your goals in each area, remember that all your goals are interconnected. A financial goal, for example, will affect a career goal and a lifestyle goal.

Personal. This category includes your character, personality, physical appearance, and conduct. Do you want to gain confidence and knowledge? Develop a lean, athletic physique? Stop hanging out with people who bring you down? You can set your personal goals by taking a hard look at the difference between who you are and who you want to be.

Family. Do you want to stay single or marry? Do you want to have one or more children? If you have already started to build a family, do you want it to grow? Do you want to address problems with parents, improve your relationship with your spouse, or change the way you relate to your family? Do you want to live near relatives or far away from them? The goals you set can help you build a solid, satisfying family life.

School/career. What kinds of subjects or career field do you prefer? In school, consider the classes, instructors, class schedule, and available diplomas, degrees, or certificates. Think about your commitment to academic excellence and whether honours and awards are important goals. Then, think about the job you want after you graduate. Consider the requirements (diplomas, degrees, certificates, or tests), job duties, hours, co-workers, salary, transportation, and company size and style that might be associated with your ideal job. Do you want to become a manager, a supervisor, an independent contractor, or a business owner? How much responsibility do you want? Identify goals that can point you toward your ideal education and career.

Financial. How much money do you need to pay your bills, maintain your chosen lifestyle, and save for the future? Do you need to borrow money for school or a major purchase such as a car? Do you already have heavy monthly bills that you want to reduce? Compare your current financial picture to how comfortable you eventually want to be, and set goals that will help you bridge the gap. These goals will also affect the career you choose.

Lifestyle. Where do you want to live (city, suburbs, country), and in what kind of space (apartment, condominium, townhouse, single- or multi-family house)? What kinds of values do you want to live by and encourage in others? How do you equip yourself with the skills necessary for dealing with diverse people? With whom do you want to live (extended/immediate family, roommates, friends, no one)? What do you want to give back to your community through service or volunteer work? What do you like to do in your leisure time? Consider goals that allow you to live the way you want to live.

Setting and working toward goals can be frightening and difficult at times. Like learning a new physical task, it takes a lot of practice and repeated efforts. As long as you do all that you can to achieve a goal, you haven't failed, even if you don't achieve it completely or in the time frame you had planned. Even one step in the right direction is an achievement. For example, if you wanted to raise your course grade to a B from a D, and you ended up with a C, you have still accomplished something important.

Identifying Educational Goals

Education is a major part of your life right now. In order to define a context for your school goals, explore why you have decided to pursue an education. People have many reasons for attending college or university. You may identify with one or more of the following possible reasons.

- I want to earn a higher salary.
- I want to build marketable skills.
- My supervisor at work says that a degree will help me move ahead in my career.
- Most of my friends are going.
- I want to be a student and learn all that I can.
- It seems like the only option for me right now.
- I am recently divorced and need to find a way to earn money.
- Everybody in my family goes to college or university; it's expected.
- I don't feel ready to jump into the working world yet.
- I received a scholarship.
- My friend loves her job and encouraged me to take courses in the field.
- My parent (or a spouse or partner) pushed me to go to school.
- I am pregnant and need to increase my skills so I can provide for my baby.
- I am studying for a specific career.
- I don't really know.

All of these answers are legitimate, even the last one. Being honest with yourself is crucial if you want to discover who you are and what life paths make sense for you. Whatever your reasons are for being in school, you are at the gateway to a journey of discovery.

It isn't easy to enroll in college or university, pay tuition, decide what to study, sign up for classes, gather the necessary materials, and actually get yourself to the school and into the classroom. Many people drop out at different places along the way, but somehow your reasons have been compelling enough for you to have arrived at this point.

Don't worry if you go through periods of low motivation. Remember, asking important questions gives you power to make responsible decisions that are yours and yours alone. Recharge by asking yourself: What do I want out of my life? What would I like people to say about me? What is important to me? Now and again you may let a day get past you without making any progress, but don't let a whole life go by.

Achieving goals becomes easier when you are realistic about what is possible. Setting priorities will help you make that distinction.

What Are Your Priorities?

When you set a priority, you identify what's important at any given moment. *Prioritizing* helps you focus on your most important goals, even when they are difficult to achieve. If you were to pursue your goals in no particular order, you might tackle the easy ones first and leave the tough ones for later. The risk is that you might never reach for goals that are important to your success. Setting priorities helps you focus your plans on accomplishing your most important goals.

To explore your priorities, think about your personal mission and look at your goals in the five life areas: personal, family, school/career, financial, and lifestyle. These five areas may not all be equally important to you right now. At this stage in your life, which two or three are most critical? Is one particular category more important than others? How would you prioritize your goals from most important to least important?

You are a unique individual, and your priorities are yours alone. What may be top priority to someone else may not mean that much to you, and vice versa. You can see this in Figure 3–2, which compares the priorities of two very different students. Each student's priorities are listed in order, with the first priority at the top and the lowest priority at the bottom.

priority
An action or intention that takes precedence in time, attention, or position.

Figure 3–2   Two Students Compare Priorities

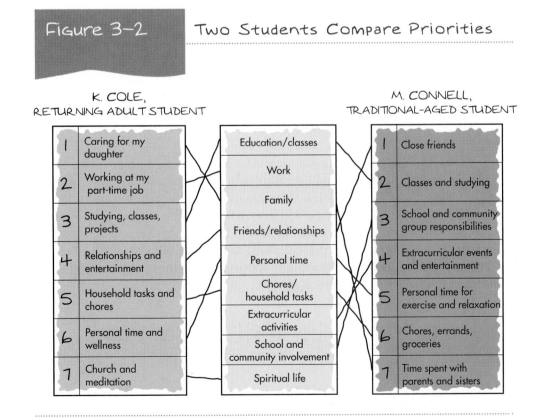

K. COLE,
RETURNING ADULT STUDENT

1	Caring for my daughter
2	Working at my part-time job
3	Studying, classes, projects
4	Relationships and entertainment
5	Household tasks and chores
6	Personal time and wellness
7	Church and meditation

Education/classes
Work
Family
Friends/relationships
Personal time
Chores/household tasks
Extracurricular activities
School and community involvement
Spiritual life

M. CONNELL,
TRADITIONAL-AGED STUDENT

1	Close friends
2	Classes and studying
3	School and community group responsibilities
4	Extracurricular events and entertainment
5	Personal time for exercise and relaxation
6	Chores, errands, groceries
7	Time spent with parents and sisters

First and foremost, your priorities should reflect your personal goals. In addition, they should reflect your relationships with others. For example, if you are a parent, your children's needs will probably be high on the priority list. You may decide to go back to school so you can get a better job, earn more money, and give them a better life. If you are in a committed relationship, you may consider the needs of your partner. You may schedule your classes so that you and your partner are home together as often as possible. Even as you consider the needs of others, however, you should never lose sight of your personal goals. Be true to your goals and priorities so that you can make the most of who you are.

Setting priorities moves you closer to accomplishing specific goals. It also helps you begin planning to achieve your goals within specific time frames. Being able to achieve your goals is directly linked to effective time management.

How Can You Manage Your Time?

Time is one of your most valuable and precious resources. Unlike money, or opportunity, or connections, time doesn't discriminate—everyone has the same twenty-four hours in a day, every day. Your responsibility—and your potential for success—lies in how you use yours. You cannot manipulate or change how time passes, but you can spend it taking steps to achieve your goals. Efficient time management helps you achieve your goals in a steady, step-by-step process.

People have a variety of different approaches to time management. Your learning style (this is explained in more detail in Chapter 2) can help you identify the particular way you currently use your time. For example, factual and linear learners tend to organize activities within a framework of time. Because they stay aware of how long it takes them to do something or travel somewhere, they are usually prompt. Theoretical and holistic learners tend to miss the passing of time while they are busy thinking of something else. Because they focus on the big picture, they may neglect details such as structuring their activities within available time. They frequently lose track of time and may often be late without meaning to be.

Time management, like physical fitness, is a lifelong pursuit. No one can plan a perfect schedule or build a terrific physique and then be "done." You'll work at time management throughout your life, and it can be tiring. Your ability to manage your time will vary with your mood, your stress level, how busy you are, and other factors. You're human, so don't expect perfection. Just do your best. Time management involves taking responsibility for how you spend your time, building a schedule, and making your schedule work through lists and other strategies.

Pace Productivity
www.GetMoreDone.com/
tips.html

This Canadian consulting firm offers free advice on the fine art of time management. These tips might help you gain a few hours of study time each week.

Taking Responsibility for How You Spend Your Time

Being in control of how you manage your time is a key factor in taking responsibility for yourself and your choices. When you plan your activities with an eye to achieving your most important goals, you are taking personal responsibility for how you live. Life changes and the judgments of others are among the factors that can affect your control.

Life Changes

Life's sudden changes and circumstances often make you feel out of control. One minute you seem to be on track, and the next minute chaos hits: Your car breaks down; your relationship falls apart; you fail a class; you or your child develops a medical problem; you get laid off at work. Coping with all of these changes can cause stress. As your stress level rises, your sense of control dwindles.

Although you cannot always choose your circumstances, you might be able to choose how to handle them. Dr. Covey says that language is important in trying to take action. Using language like "I have to" and "They made me" robs you of personal power. For example, saying that you "have to" go to school or move out of your parents' house can make you feel that others control your life. However, language like "I have decided to" and "I prefer" helps energize your power to choose. Then you can turn "I have to go to school" into "I prefer to go to school rather than work in a dead-end job."

Judgments of Others

The judgments of others can also intimidate you into not taking responsibility for your time. A student who feels that no one will hire him because of his weight may not search for jobs. A student who feels her instructor is prejudiced against her might not study for that instructor's course. Try not to let these barriers rob you of your control of your time. Early in his life, Malcolm X was told that he had no business aspiring to be a lawyer in spite of his excellent record as a student. He was constantly demeaned because of his race. However, he did not let the ignorance of others stand in his way.

Instead of giving in to others' judgments, try to choose actions that improve your circumstances. If you lose a job, spending an hour a day investigating other job opportunities is a better use of your time than watching television. If you have trouble with an instructor, you can address the problem with that instructor directly and try to make the most of your time in the course. If that doesn't work, you can drop the course, spend that time in other important pursuits, and retake the course in summer school while working part time. Try to find an option that will allow you to be in control of your time.

Time can be your ally if you make smart choices about how to use it. Building a schedule can help you decide when to accomplish the activities you choose.

judgments
Considered opinions, assessments, or evaluations.

"The right time is any time that one is still so lucky as to have.... Live!"

Henry James

Building a Schedule

Just as a road map helps you travel from place to place, a *schedule* is a time-and-activity map that helps you get from the beginning of the day (or week, or month) to the end as smoothly as possible. A written schedule helps you gain control of your life. Schedules have two major advantages: They allocate segments of time for the fulfillment of your daily, weekly, monthly, and longer-term goals, and they serve as a concrete reminder of tasks, events, due dates, responsibilities, and deadlines. Few moments are more stressful than suddenly realizing you have forgotten to pick up a prescription, take a test, or be on duty at work. Scheduling can help you avoid events like these.

Keep a Date Book

Gather the tools of the trade: a pen or pencil and a *date book* (sometimes called a planner). Some of you already have date books and may have used them for years. Others may have had no luck with them or have never tried. Even if you feel you are not the type of person who would use one, give it a try. A date book is indispensable for keeping track of your time. Paul Timm says, "Most time management experts agree that rule number one in a thoughtful planning process is: Use some form of a planner where you can write things down."

There are two major types of date books. The *day-at-a-glance* version devotes a page to each day. While it gives you ample space to write the day's activities, this version makes it difficult to see what's ahead. The *week-at-a-glance* book gives you a view of the week's plans, but has less room to write per day. If you write out your daily plans in detail, you might like the day-at-a-glance version. If you prefer to remind yourself of plans ahead of time, try the book that shows a week's schedule all at once. Some date books contain additional sections that allow you to note plans and goals for the year as a whole and for each month. You can also create your own sheets for yearly and monthly notations in a notepad section, if your book has one, or on plain paper that you can then insert into the book.

Another option to consider is an *electronic planner*. These are compact mini-computers that can hold a large amount of information. You can use them to schedule your days and weeks, make to-do lists, and create and store an address book. Electronic planners are powerful, convenient, and often fun. On the other hand, they certainly cost more than the paper version, and you can lose a lot of important data if something goes wrong with the computer inside. Evaluate your options and decide what you like best.

Set Weekly and Daily Goals

The most ideal time management starts with the smallest tasks and builds to bigger ones. Setting short-term goals that tie in to your long-term goals gives you the following benefits:

- Increased meaning for your daily activities
- Shaping your path toward the achievement of your long-term goals
- A sense of order and progress

For college and university students as well as working people, the week is often the easiest unit of time to consider at one glance. Weekly goal-setting and planning allows you to keep track of day-to-day activities while giving you the larger perspective of what is coming up during the week. Take some time before each week starts to remind yourself of your long-term goals. Keeping long-term goals in mind will help you determine related short-term goals you can accomplish during the week to come.

Figure 3–3 shows parts of a daily schedule and a weekly schedule.

Link Daily and Weekly Goals with Long-Term Goals

After you evaluate what you need to accomplish in the coming year, semester, month, week, and day in order to reach your long-term goals, use your sched-

Figure 3–3 Daily and Weekly Schedules

2001		
MONDAY, MARCH 26		**PRIORITY**

TIME	TASKS	
7:00 AM		
8:00	Up at 8am – finish homework	☆
9:00		
10:00	Business Administration	☆
11:00	Renew driver's licence	
12:00 PM		
1:00	Lunch	
2:00	Writing Seminar (peer editing today)	☆
3:00		
4:00	check on Ms. Schwartz's office hrs.	
5:00	5:30 work out	
6:00	↳6:30	
7:00	Dinner	
8:00	Read two chapters for Business Admin.	
9:00		
10:00		
11:00		

Monday, March 26

8			
9	BIO 212	CALL: Maggie Blair	
10		Financial Aid Office	1
11	CHEM 203	EMS 262 ☆Paramedic role-play ☆	2
12			3
Evening	6pm yoga class		4

Tuesday, March 27

8	Finish reading assignment!		5
9		Work @ library	
10	ENG 112		1
11		(study for quiz)	2
12			3
Evening			4

Wednesday, March 28

8		↓ until 7pm	5
9	BIO 212	Meet w/adviser	
10			1
11	CHEM 203☆ QUIZ☆	EMS 262	2
12			3
Evening	6pm Aerobics	☆ Pick up photos	4
			5

ule to record those steps. Write down the short-term goals that will enable you to stay on track. Here is how a student might map out two different goals over a year's time.

This year:	Complete enough courses to graduate. Improve my physical fitness.
This semester:	Complete my accounting class with a B average or higher. Lose 10 pounds and exercise regularly.
This month:	Set up study-group schedule to coincide with quizzes. Begin walking and weight lifting.
This week:	Meet with study group; go over material for Friday's quiz. Go for a fitness walk three times; go to weight room twice.
Today:	Go over Chapter 3 in accounting text. Walk for 40 minutes.

Prioritize Goals

Prioritizing enables you to use your date book with maximum efficiency. On any given day, your goals will have varying degrees of importance. Record your goals first, and then label them according to level of importance, using these categories: Priority 1, Priority 2, and Priority 3. Identify these categories using any code that makes sense to you. Some people use numbers, as above. Some use letters (A, B, C). Some write activities in different colours according to priority level. Some use symbols (*, +, -).

Priority 1 activities are the most important things in your life. They may include attending class, picking up a child from daycare, putting gas in the car, and paying bills.

Priority 2 activities are part of your routine. Examples include grocery shopping, working out, participating in a school organization, or cleaning. Priority 2 tasks are important but more flexible than Priority 1's.

Priority 3 activities are those you would like to do but can reschedule without much sacrifice. Examples might be a trip to the mall, a visit with a friend, a social phone call, a sports event, a movie, or a hair appointment. As much as you would like to accomplish them, you don't consider them urgent. Many people don't enter Priority 3 tasks in their date books until they are sure they have time to get them done.

Prioritizing your activities is essential for two reasons. First, some activities are more important than others, and effective time management requires that you focus most of your energy on Priority 1 items. Second, looking at all your priorities helps you plan when you can get things done. Often, it's not possible to get all your Priority 1 activities done early in the day, especially if these activities involve scheduled classes or meetings. Prioritizing helps you set Priority 1 items and then schedule Priority 2 and 3 items around them as they fit.

Keep Track of Events

Your date book also enables you to schedule *events*. Rather than thinking of events as separate from goals, tie them to your long-term goals just as you would your other tasks. For example, attending a wedding in a few months contributes to your commitment to spending time with your family. Being aware of quiz dates, due dates for assignments, and meeting dates will aid your goals to achieve in school and become involved.

Note events in your date book so that you can stay aware of them ahead of time. Write them in daily, weekly, monthly, or even yearly sections, where a quick look will remind you that they are approaching. Writing them down will also help you see where they fit in the context of your other activities. For example, if you have three big tests and a presentation all in one week, you'll want to take time in the weeks before to prepare for them all.

Following are some kinds of events worth noting in your date book:

- Due dates for papers, projects, presentations, and tests
- Important meetings, medical appointments, or due dates for bill payments
- Birthdays, anniversaries, social events, holidays, and other special occasions
- Benchmarks for steps toward a goal, such as due dates for sections of a project or a deadline for losing five pounds on your way to losing twenty

List Low-Priority Goals Separately

Priority 3 tasks can be hard to accomplish. As the least important tasks, they often get put off from one day to the next. You may spend valuable time rewriting these items day after day in your date book instead of getting them done. One solution is to keep a list of Priority 3 tasks in a separate place in your date book. That way, when you have an unexpected pocket of free time, you can consult your list and see what you have time to accomplish—making a trip to the post office, writing a card, returning a borrowed tape, giving some clothes to charity, going to the hardware store. Keep this list current by crossing off items as you accomplish them and writing in new items as soon as you think of them. Rewrite the list when it gets too messy.

Time Management Strategies

Managing time takes thought and energy. Here are some additional strategies to try.

1. Plan your schedule each week. Before each week begins, note events, goals, and priorities. Look at the map of your week to decide where to fit activities like studying and Priority 3 items. For example, if you have a test on Thursday, you can plan study sessions on the days up until then. If you have more free time on Tuesday and Friday than on other days, you can plan workouts or Priority 3 activities at those times. Looking at the whole week

Real World Perspective

Karin Lounsbury, Returning Mature Student

I decided to return to school when I had just turned 40. I didn't like feeling dependent on my husband for my financial security so I thought that I'd do something about it. I also did it for my two children. My marriage had been shaky for quite a few years and I was scared to death that I wouldn't be able to provide for them on my own. Even though I'd worked in the business world for a long time, the salary was never very good. I was over-  experienced and underpaid. I thought that by completing my education, I could find a great job that would allow me to support my family. Although I knew that university would be challenging, I wasn't concerned with the workload—I'm used to carrying a lot of responsibilities, probably more than most people, in fact. Besides my two young children, I'm married to a man who lost both his legs. He's in a wheelchair, which means a lot of extra work falls on my shoulders.

These last few months everything seems to be falling apart. My husband and I decided to get a divorce; my son has been struggling at school; my mother was just diagnosed with cancer; and I feel like I can hardly keep my head above water. All of this is taking a toll on my grades. I'm usually so emotionally and physically exhausted by the end of the day, I just don't have the energy to put into my work. When I'm at school, I'm distracted thinking about the future. I don't want to drop out of school but I also don't want my kids to suffer when they need me so badly. How can I get through this difficult time and still accomplish my educational goals?

Kath Myers, Mature Student, Social Service Worker Program

Like many Canadians, I decided to return to school later in life. I was out of school for twenty-two years when I returned full time in my late 30s. I returned for personal reasons: My kids were getting older and I wanted new challenges out of life. I was tired of working dead-end jobs, plus I wanted a job where I would be able to help people. I took a six-month outreach course here at Mohawk College and decided to go back to school full time.

Attending classes with students half your age is different. Call it the generation gap or whatever; there is a difference between coming to college out of high school and being a mature student. Students often look up to me for guidance and support.

There are many challenges. I am a single mother with three kids and I want to be there for them when they need me. Sometimes I don't get to my homework until after they are in bed. Be warned: There will be times when there will be a strain between your role as a mom and your role as a student. At first, my kids had some difficulty adjusting to mom not being there 24/7, but we were able to work out our problems.

From a financial standpoint, I was lucky enough to receive a scholarship. Be sure you find out about and make use of what your college has to offer regarding scholarships and awards.

One final note: No one told me about the stress and time management associated with coming back to school. I got frazzled, was tired, and felt worn out. I went to a friend who gave me some advice on how to handle school. Find a way to manage your time and resources. It takes a lot to be successful at college. You need to be dedicated and determined to get what you want. Time management will help you achieve your goals.

will help you avoid being surprised by something you have forgotten was coming up.

2. **Make and use to-do lists.** Use a *to-do list* to record the things you want to accomplish. If you generate a daily or weekly to-do list on a separate piece of paper, you can look at all tasks and goals at once. This will help you consider time frames and priorities. You might want to prioritize your tasks and transfer them to appropriate places in your date book. Some people create daily to-do lists right on their date book pages. You can tailor a to-do list to an important event such as exam week or an especially busy day when you have a family gathering or a presentation to make. This kind of specific to-do list can help you prioritize and accomplish an unusually large task load.

3. **Make thinking about time a priority.** Mr. Timm recommends that you devote a minimum of ten to fifteen minutes a day to planning your schedule. Although making a schedule takes time, it can mean hours of saved time later. Say you have two errands to run, both on the other side of town. Not planning ahead could result in your driving across town twice in one day. The extra driving time is far more than it would have taken to plan the day in advance.

4. **Refer to your schedule.** Many people make detailed schedules, only to forget to look at them. Carry your date book wherever you go and check it throughout the day. Find a date book size you like—there are books that fit into your briefcase, bag, or even your pocket.

5. **Post monthly and yearly calendars at home.** Keeping a calendar on the wall will help you stay aware of important events. You can purchase one or draw it yourself, month by month, on plain paper. Use a yearly or a monthly version (Figure 3–4 shows part of a monthly calendar) and keep it where you can refer to it often. If you live with family or friends, make the calendar a group project so that you stay aware of each other's plans. Knowing each other's schedules can also help you avoid scheduling problems such as two people needing the car at the same time or one partner scheduling a get-together when the other has to work.

6. **Schedule downtime.** When you're wiped out from too much activity, you don't have the energy to accomplish much with your time. A little downtime will refresh you and improve your attitude. Even half an hour a day will help. Fill the time with whatever relaxes you—having a snack, reading, watching TV, playing a game or sport, walking, writing, or just doing nothing. Make downtime a priority.

7. **Be flexible.** Since priorities determine the map of your day, week, month, or year, any priority shift can jumble your schedule. Be ready to reschedule your tasks as your priorities change. On Monday, a homework assignment due in a week might be Priority 2. By Saturday, it has become Priority 1. On some days a

University of Waterloo
www.adm.uwaterloo.ca/
infocs/Study/time.html

This Canadian Web page is dedicated to helping post-secondary students with the task of time management. It asks you to keep track of your time for one week, and then offers advice on how to cultivate any wasted hours.

downtime
Quiet time set aside for relaxation and low-key activity.

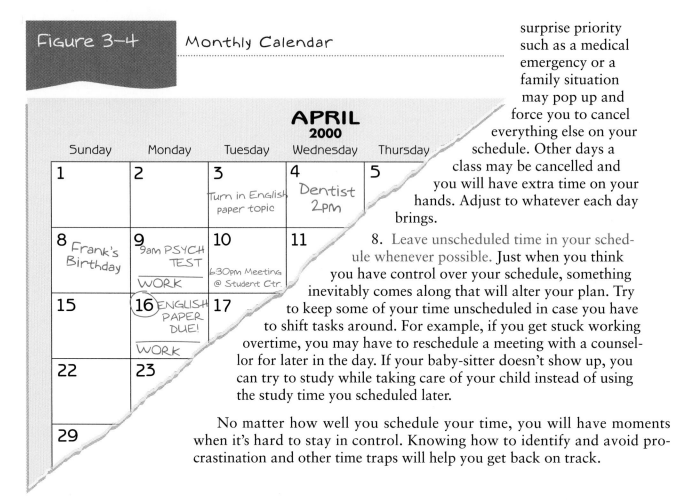

Figure 3-4   Monthly Calendar

APRIL 2000

Sunday	Monday	Tuesday	Wednesday	Thursday
1	2	3 _Turn in English paper topic_	4 _Dentist 2pm_	5
8 _Frank's Birthday_	9 _9am PSYCH TEST_ _WORK_	10 _6:30pm Meeting @ Student Ctr._	11	
15	16 _ENGLISH PAPER DUE!_ _WORK_	17		
22	23			
29				

surprise priority such as a medical emergency or a family situation may pop up and force you to cancel everything else on your schedule. Other days a class may be cancelled and you will have extra time on your hands. Adjust to whatever each day brings.

8. Leave unscheduled time in your schedule whenever possible. Just when you think you have control over your schedule, something inevitably comes along that will alter your plan. Try to keep some of your time unscheduled in case you have to shift tasks around. For example, if you get stuck working overtime, you may have to reschedule a meeting with a counsellor for later in the day. If your baby-sitter doesn't show up, you can try to study while taking care of your child instead of using the study time you scheduled later.

No matter how well you schedule your time, you will have moments when it's hard to stay in control. Knowing how to identify and avoid procrastination and other time traps will help you get back on track.

Why Is Procrastination a Problem?

procrastination
The act of putting off something that needs to be done.

Procrastination occurs when you postpone unpleasant or burdensome tasks. People procrastinate for different reasons. Having trouble with goal setting is one reason. People may project goals too far into the future, set unrealistic goals that are too frustrating to reach, or have no goals at all. People also procrastinate because they don't believe in their ability to complete a task or don't believe in themselves in general. As natural as these tendencies are, they can also be extremely harmful. If continued over a period of time, procrastination can develop into a habit that will dominate a person's behaviour. Following are some ways to face your tendencies to procrastinate and *just do it!*

Strategies to Fight Procrastination

Weigh the benefits (to you and others) of completing the task versus the effects of procrastinating. What rewards lie ahead if you get it done? A burden off your shoulders? Some free time? Career advancement? What will be the effects if you continue to put it off? Which situation has better effects? Chances are you will benefit more in the long term from facing the task head-on.

Set reasonable goals. Plan your goals carefully, allowing enough time to complete them. Unreasonable goals can be so intimidating that you do nothing at all. "Pay off the credit-card bill next month" could throw you. However, "Pay off the credit-card bill in six months" might inspire you to take action.

Get started. Going from doing nothing to doing something is often the hardest part of avoiding procrastination. You might want to use the motivation techniques from Chapter 1 to help you take the first step. Once you start, you may find it easier to continue.

Break the task into smaller parts. If a task seems overwhelming, look at it in terms of its parts. How can you approach it step by step? If you can concentrate on achieving one small goal at a time, the task may become less of a burden.

Ask for help with tasks and projects at school, work, and home. You don't always have to go it alone. Instructors, supervisors, and family members can lend support, helping you to complete a dreaded task. For example, if you have put off an intimidating assignment, ask your instructor for guidance. If you avoid a project because you dislike the employee with whom you have to work, talk to your supervisor about adjusting the assignment of tasks or personnel. If you need accommodations because of a disability, don't assume that others know about it. Once you identify what's holding you up, see who can help you face the task.

Don't expect perfection. No one is perfect. Being able to do something flawlessly is not a requirement for trying. Most people learn by starting at the beginning and wading through plenty of mistakes and confusion. It's better to try your best than to do nothing at all.

Consider how you would operate if you were looking forward to something you really wanted to do. You might not be late if you were headed to the airport for a flight to the Bahamas! See if you can transfer that behaviour to a task that isn't quite as much fun.

Procrastination is natural, but it can cause you problems if you let it get the best of you. When that does happen, take some time to think about the causes. What is it about this situation that frightens you or puts you off? Answering that question can help you address what causes lie underneath the procrastination. These causes might indicate a deeper problem that needs to be solved.

Other "Time Traps" to Avoid

Procrastination isn't the only way to spend your time in less-than-productive ways. Keep an eye out for these situations too:

Saying "yes" when you really don't have the time. Many people, in their desire to please others, agree to help with tasks they can't easily fit into their schedule. Being reliable is great, but not when it is at your own expense. Learn to say "no" when you need to. First, resist the temptation to respond right away. Then ask yourself what effects a new responsibility will have on your schedule. Be honest with yourself about whether you have the time to

Essay Motivation
www.iss.stthomas.edu/
studyguides/attmot3.htm
www.utexas.edu/student/
lsc/makinggrade/
procrastination.html

Looking for motivation to help you write that essay? These Web pages help you understand the consequences of procrastination. Don't do it later; do it now!

make a new commitment. If it will cause you more trouble than it seems to be worth, say "no" graciously.

Studying at a bad time of day. At what point in the day do you have the most energy? Is that when you study? If not, you may be wasting time. When you are tired, you may need extra time to fully understand your material. If you study when you are most alert, you will be able to take in more information in less time.

Studying in a distracting location. Find an environment that helps you maximize study time. If you need to be alone to concentrate, for example, studying near family members or roommates might interfere with your focus. Conversely, people who require a busier environment to stay alert might need to choose a more active setting.

Not thinking ahead. Forgetting important things is a big time drain. One book left at home can cost you extra time going back and forth. One forgotten phone call can mean you have to do what you wanted to ask someone else to do. Five minutes of scheduling in the morning or during the night before can save you hours.

Not curbing your social time. Time passes quickly when you're having fun. You plan to make a quick telephone call and the next thing you know you've been talking for an hour, losing time you could have used for studying or sleeping. Don't cut out all socializing, but wear a watch and stay aware of the time. If friends invite you for dinner and you know you can't spend a whole evening out, consider joining them after dinner for coffee and dessert. Your friends will most likely respect your priorities and you will respect yourself when you see the rewards.

Not delegating. No one can take a test, read a chapter, or eat a meal for you, but you can delegate some tasks to other people. A relative might be able to shovel your walk or cut your grass. A friend going to the post office could pick up some stamps for you. Another day-care parent might be able to pick up your child on a day when your time runs short. Check into those possibilities, and don't forget to return the favour.

Pushing yourself too far. You've probably experienced one of those study sessions during which, at a certain point, you realize that you haven't absorbed anything for the last hour. Sometimes you just need a break. Stay aware of your energy level, and when you just can't seem to concentrate anymore, take a refresher—stretch, get a drink or a snack, go for a walk, take a nap. You're much better off using some of your time to revive yourself, rather than trying in vain to focus on your work.

In Hebrew, the word *chai* means "life," representing all aspects of life—spiritual, emotional, family, educational, and career. Individual Hebrew characters have number values. Because the characters in the word *chai* add up to eighteen, the number eighteen has come to be associated with good luck. The word *chai* is often worn as a good-luck charm. As you plan your goals, think about your view of luck. Many people feel that a person can create his or her own luck by pursuing goals persistently and staying open to possibilities and opportunities. Canadian novelist Robertson Davies once said, "What we call luck is the inner man externalized. We make things happen to us."

Consider that your vision of life may largely determine how you live. You can prepare the way for luck by establishing a personal mission and forging ahead toward your goals. If you believe that the life you want awaits you, you will be able to recognize and make the most of luck when it comes around. *L'Chaim*—to life, and good luck.

Chapter 3: Applications

Name _____ Date _____

Key into Your Life:
Opportunities to Apply What You Learn

Exercise 1: Your Values

Begin to explore your values by rating the following values on a scale from 1 to 4, 1 being least important to you, and 4 being most important. If you have values that you don't see in the chart, list them in the blank spaces and rate them.

VALUE	RATING	VALUE	RATING
Knowing yourself		Mental health	
Physical health		Fitness and exercise	
Spending time with your family		Close friendships	
Helping others		Education	
Being well paid		Being employed	
Being liked by others		Free time/vacations	
Enjoying entertainment		Time to yourself	
Spiritual/religious life		Reading	
Keeping up with the news		Staying organized	
Being financially stable		Having an intimate relationship	
Creative/artistic pursuits		Self-improvement	
Lifelong learning		Facing your fears	

Considering your priorities, write your top five values here:

1. _____

2. _____

3. _____

4. _____

5. _____

Exercise 2: Your Personal Mission Statement

Using the personal mission statement examples in the chapter as a guide, consider what you want out of your life and create your own personal mission statement. You can write it in paragraph form, in a list of long-term goals, or in the form of a think link. Take as much time as you need in order to be as complete as possible. Write a draft on a separate sheet of paper and take time to revise it before you write the final version here. If you have created a think link rather than a verbal statement, attach it separately.

_____

_____

_____

_____

_____

_____

_____

_____

_____

Exercise 3: Establishing and Tracking Long-Term Goals

The chapter described the importance of goal setting in five different life areas. For each area, name an important long-term goal for your own life. Then imagine that you will begin working toward each goal. Indicate the steps you will take to achieve your goals on a short-term and long-term basis. Write what you hope to accomplish in the next year, the next six months, the next month, the next week, and the next day.

Your Goal	One Year	Six Months	One Month	One Week	One day
Example: I want to develop a better relationship with my father.	Instead of moving, I will complete my course of study at a school near my parents' home.	I will work to understand our relationship by talking with a counsellor at school.	I will see my counsellor every two weeks and make sure that I see my father at least once.	I will see if my father needs help with anything around the house this weekend.	I will call my dad after the hockey game because I know he'll be watching it.
Personal					
Family					
School/career					
Financial					
Lifestyle					

Exercise 4: Why Are You Here?

Why did you decide to enroll in school? Do any of the reasons listed in the chapter fit you? Do you have other reasons all your own? Many people have more than one answer. Write up to five here.

_____

_____

_____

_____

Take a moment to think about the reasons you outlined above. Which reasons are most important to you? Why? Prioritize your reasons by writing 1 next to the most important, 2 next to the second most important, etc.

How do you feel about your reasons? You may be proud of some. On the other hand, you may not feel comfortable with others. Which do you like or dislike and why?

_____

_____

_____

_____

Exercise 5: Short-Term Scheduling

Take a close look at your schedule for the coming month, including events, important dates, and steps toward goals. On the calendar layout that follows, fill in the name of the month and appropriate numbers for the days. Then record everything you need to be aware of, including the following:

- ⊛ Due dates for papers, projects, and presentations
- ⊛ Test dates
- ⊛ Important meetings, medical appointments, and due dates for bill payments
- ⊛ Birthdays, anniversaries, and other special occasions
- ⊛ Steps toward long-term goals

This kind of chart will help you see the big picture of your month. To stay on target from day to day, check these dates against the entries in your date book and make sure that they are indicated there as well.

Month Chart

Exercise 6: Discover How You Spend Your Time

In the chart below, estimate the total time you think you spend per week on each listed activity. Then add the hours together. If your number is over 168 (the number of hours in a week), rethink your original estimates and recalculate the total so that it equals or is less than 168.

ACTIVITY	ESTIMATED TIME SPENT
Class	
Work	
Studying	
Sleeping	
Eating	
Family time/child care	
Commuting/travelling	
Chores and personal business	
Friends and important relationships	
Telephone time	
Leisure/entertainment	
Spiritual life	
Total	

When your estimate equals or is less than 168, subtract that number (the total number of hours you estimate you spend on these activities) from 168. Whatever is left over is your estimate of hours that you spend in unscheduled activities.

168

Minus total _____

Unscheduled time _____

Now spend a week recording exactly how you spend your time. The following chart has blocks showing half-hour increments. As you go through the week, write in what you do each hour, indicating when you started and when you stopped. Don't forget things that don't feel like "activities," such as sleeping, relaxing, and watching TV. Also, beware of recording how you want to spend your time or how you think you *should have* spent your time; be perfectly honest about your schedule. There are no wrong answers.

| MONDAY | | TUESDAY | | WEDNESDAY | | THURSDAY | |
TIME	ACTIVITY	TIME	ACTIVITY	TIME	ACTIVITY	TIME	ACTIVITY
5:00 am		5:00 am		5:00 am		5:00 am	
5:30 am		5:30 am		5:30 am		5:30 am	
6:00 am		6:00 am		6:00 am		6:00 am	
6:30 am		6:30 am		6:30 am		6:30 am	
7:00 am		7:00 am		7:00 am		7:00 am	
7:30 am		7:30 am		7:30 am		7:30 am	
8:00 am		8:00 am		8:00 am		8:00 am	
8:30 am		8:30 am		8:30 am		8:30 am	
9:00 am		9:00 am		9:00 am		9:00 am	
9:30 am		9:30 am		9:30 am		9:30 am	
10:00 am		10:00 am		10:00 am		10:00 am	
10:30 am		10:30 am		10:30 am		10:30 am	
11:00 am		11:00 am		11:00 am		11:00 am	
11:30 am		11:30 am		11:30 am		11:30 am	
12:00 pm		12:00 pm		12:00 pm		12:00 pm	
12:30 pm		12:30 pm		12:30 pm		12:30 pm	
1:00 pm		1:00 pm		1:00 pm		1:00 pm	
1:30 pm		1:30 pm		1:30 pm		1:30 pm	
2:00 pm		2:00 pm		2:00 pm		2:00 pm	
2:30 pm		2:30 pm		2:30 pm		2:30 pm	
3:00 pm		3:00 pm		3:00 pm		3:00 pm	
3:30 pm		3:30 pm		3:30 pm		3:30 pm	
4:00 pm		4:00 pm		4:00 pm		4:00 pm	
4:30 pm		4:30 pm		4:30 pm		4:30 pm	
5:00 pm		5:00 pm		5:00 pm		5:00 pm	
5:30 pm		5:30 pm		5:30 pm		5:30 pm	
6:00 pm		6:00 pm		6:00 pm		6:00 pm	
6:30 pm		6:30 pm		6:30 pm		6:30 pm	
7:00 pm		7:00 pm		7:00 pm		7:00 pm	
7:30 pm		7:30 pm		7:30 pm		7:30 pm	
8:00 pm		8:00 pm		8:00 pm		8:00 pm	
8:30 pm		8:30 pm		8:30 pm		8:30 pm	
9:00 pm		9:00 pm		9:00 pm		9:00 pm	
9:30 pm		9:30 pm		9:30 pm		9:30 pm	
10:00 pm		10:00 pm		10:00 pm		10:00 pm	
10:30 pm		10:30 pm		10:30 pm		10:30 pm	
11:00 pm		11:00 pm		11:00 pm		11:00 pm	
11:30 pm		11:30 pm		11:30 pm		11:30 pm	

FRIDAY		SATURDAY		SUNDAY	
TIME	ACTIVITY	TIME	ACTIVITY	TIME	ACTIVITY
5:00 am		5:00 am		5:00 am	
5:30 am		5:30 am		5:30 am	
6:00 am		6:00 am		6:00 am	
6:30 am		6:30 am		6:30 am	
7:00 am		7:00 am		7:00 am	
7:30 am		7:30 am		7:30 am	
8:00 am		8:00 am		8:00 am	
8:30 am		8:30 am		8:30 am	
9:00 am		9:00 am		9:00 am	
9:30 am		9:30 am		9:30 am	
10:00 am		10:00 am		10:00 am	
10:30 am		10:30 am		10:30 am	
11:00 am		11:00 am		11:00 am	
11:30 am		11:30 am		11:30 am	
12:00 pm		12:00 pm		12:00 pm	
12:30 pm		12:30 pm		12:30 pm	
1:00 pm		1:00 pm		1:00 pm	
1:30 pm		1:30 pm		1:30 pm	
2:00 pm		2:00 pm		2:00 pm	
2:30 pm		2:30 pm		2:30 pm	
3:00 pm		3:00 pm		3:00 pm	
3:30 pm		3:30 pm		3:30 pm	
4:00 pm		4:00 pm		4:00 pm	
4:30 pm		4:30 pm		4:30 pm	
5:00 pm		5:00 pm		5:00 pm	
5:30 pm		5:30 pm		5:30 pm	
6:00 pm		6:00 pm		6:00 pm	
6:30 pm		6:30 pm		6:30 pm	
7:00 pm		7:00 pm		7:00 pm	
7:30 pm		7:30 pm		7:30 pm	
8:00 pm		8:00 pm		8:00 pm	
8:30 pm		8:30 pm		8:30 pm	
9:00 pm		9:00 pm		9:00 pm	
9:30 pm		9:30 pm		9:30 pm	
10:00 pm		10:00 pm		10:00 pm	
10:30 pm		10:30 pm		10:30 pm	
11:00 pm		11:00 pm		11:00 pm	
11:30 pm		11:30 pm		11:30 pm	

Now go through this chart and look at how many hours you actually spent on the activities for which you estimated your hours before. Tally the hours in the boxes in the following table using straight tally marks; round off to half hours and use a short tally mark for a half-hour spent. At the far right of the table, total the hours for each activity.

ACTIVITY	TIME TALLIED OVER ONE-WEEK PERIOD	TOTAL TIME IN HOURS
Example: Class	‖‖ ‖‖‖ ‖‖ ‖‖ ‖	16.5
Class		
Work		
Studying		
Sleeping		
Eating		
Family time/child care		
Commuting/travelling		
Chores and personal business		
Friends and important relationships		
Telephone time		
Leisure/entertainment		
Spiritual life		

Add the totals on the right to find your GRAND TOTAL: _____

Compare your grand total to your estimated grand total; compare your actual activity hour totals to your estimated activity hour totals. What matches and what doesn't? Describe the similarities and differences.

_____

_____

_____

_____

_____

What is the one biggest surprise about how you spend your time?

_____

_____

_____

_____

Name one change you would like to make in how you spend your time.

_____

_____

_____

_____

Think about what kinds of changes you could make that will help you improve your ability to set and achieve goals. Ask yourself important questions about what you do daily, weekly, and monthly. On what activities do you think you should spend more or less time? For this last chart, write the hours for each activity that represent your ideal week.

ACTIVITY	IDEAL TIME IN HOURS
Class	
Work	
Studying	
Sleeping	
Eating	
Family time/child care	
Commuting/travelling	
Chores and personal business	
Friends and important relationships	
Telephone time	
Leisure/entertainment	
Spiritual life	

Exercise 7: To-Do Lists

Make a to-do list for what you have to do tomorrow. Include all tasks
—Priority 1, 2, and 3—and events.

TOMORROW'S DATE: _____

1. _____

2. _____

3. _____

4. _____

5. _____

6. _____

7. _____

8. _____

9. _____

10. _____

11. _____

12. _____

Use the coding system of your choice to indicate priority level of both tasks
and events. Place a check mark by the items that are important enough to note
in your date book. Use this list to make your schedule for tomorrow in the date
book, making a separate list for Priority 3 items. At the end of the day, evaluate this system. Did the to-do list help you? How did it make a difference? If
you liked this exercise, use it as a guide for making regular to-do lists.

_____

_____

_____

_____

Exercise 8: Your Procrastination Habits

Name up to three habitual excuses that you use in order to avoid something
you don't want to do.

1. _____

2. _____

3. _____

What are the effects of your procrastination? Discuss how procrastination may affect the quality of your work, motivation, productivity, ability to be on time, grades, or self-perception.

_____

_____

_____

_____

_____

Think about a specific time when you procrastinated. Describe what happened.

_____

_____

_____

_____

_____

Choose one of your procrastination habits you want to change. You may want to use the habit-breaking techniques you explored in Chapter 2. What do you plan to work on, and how?

_____

_____

_____

Once you've had a chance to work on this habit, describe what happened. Did you make progress? How did it help you to fight your procrastination?

_____

_____

_____

_____

Key to Cooperative Learning:
Building Teamwork Skills

Individual Priorities In a group of three or four people, brainstorm a list of long-term goals and have one member of the group write them down. From that list, pick ten goals to which everyone can relate. Each group member should then take five minutes alone to evaluate the relative importance of the ten goals and rank them in the order that he or she prefers. Use a 1 to 10 scale, with 1 being the highest priority and 10 the lowest.

Display the rankings of each group member side by side. How many different orders are there? Discuss why each person has a different set of priorities, and be open to different views. What factors in different people's lives have caused them to select particular rankings? If you have time, discuss how priorities have changed for each group member over the course of a year, perhaps by having each person re-rank the goals according to his or her needs of a year ago.

Key to Self-Expression:
Discovery Through Journal Writing

To record your thoughts, use a separate journal or the lined page at the end of the chapter.

Downtime Think about the last two weeks. When did you last have some downtime for yourself? What did you do? How did you feel? Make an effort to schedule downtime into your plans at some point in the next couple of days. Describe in a few sentences your idea of a perfect day spent alone—what you would do, where you would go, how you hope it would help you.

Key to Your Personal Portfolio:
Your Paper Trail to Success

Your Mission, Goals, and Priorities Looking again at the five life areas in which you set goals—personal, family, school/career, fnancial, and lifestyle—select and write down your most important long-term goals, up to five for each category. Use a separate sheet of paper for each set of goals. Look at your lists, then rewrite them on the bottom half of each sheet, ranking them in order of priority, with the most important first.

On another sheet of paper, rewrite all twenty-five goals on one list. Then use your chosen coding system to assign them Priority 1, Priority 2, or Priority 3 status.

Both kinds of goal sheets illustrate what is important to you. One shows you what is most important within particular categories, and the other shows you what takes priority when all goals are considered together.

Recopy your mission statement onto another separate sheet of paper, allowing yourself to make any changes that occur to you.

Keep your goal/priority sheets and your mission statement in your portfolio. A couple of times during the semester, take them out to make any necessary changes. Your instructor may assign mission-statement revisions from time to time. By the end of this course, your mission statement may change as a result of what you have learned about yourself.

In the future, you may have to prove to a prospective employer that you know how to set, pursue, and achieve your goals, no matter how hard they may be. Learning to do this on a personal level is one of the best ways to show someone that you can have the same success professionally.

Journal Entry

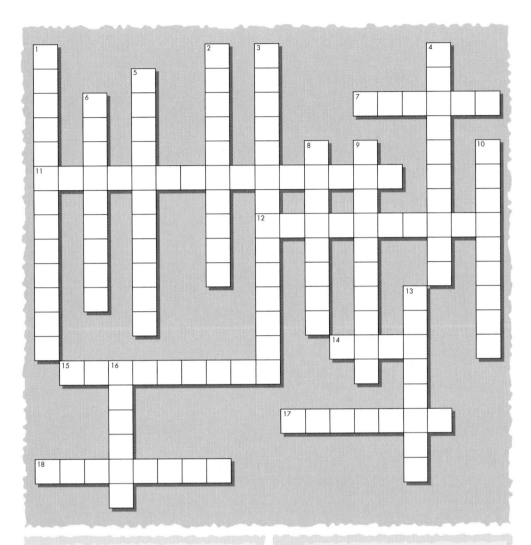

ACROSS

7. preferences for actions done in a certain way, often on a regular basis or at particular times
11. the act of putting off the doing of something that should be done
12. determination; the power to begin or to follow through with a plan or task
14. the end toward which effort is directed
15. the variety that occurs in every aspect of of humanity
17. a learning style that focuses on facts, data, and detailed experimentation
18. a time-and-activity map that allocates time for tasks and serves as a reminder

DOWN

1. a type of intelligence that focuses on an ability to relate to others and their feelings
2. a promise or pledge to do something in the future
3. the quality or state of being reliable or trustworthy
4. to list or rate in order of importance
5. a learning style that focuses on big-picture ideas, symbols, and new concepts
6. people, organizations, or services that supply help and support
8. state of mind or feeling toward something
9. a force that moves a person to action, often inspired by an idea, event, or goal
10. adherence to a code of moral values; honesty
13. to authorize or entrust another person with a task that you don't necessarily have to do yourself
16. principles, standards, or qualities considered important, right, or good

PART 2

Developing Your Learning Skills

4 Critical and Creative Thinking:

Tapping the Power of Your Mind

In this chapter, you will explore answers to the following questions:

- What is critical thinking?

- How does your mind work?

- How does critical thinking help you solve problems and make decisions?

- How do you construct an effective argument?

- How do you establish truth?

- Why shift your perspective?

- Why plan strategically?

- How can you develop your creativity?

Your mind's powers show in everything you do, from the smallest chores (comparing prices on cereals at the grocery store) to the most complex situations (figuring out how to earn money after being laid off). Your mind is able to process, store, and create with the facts and ideas it encounters. Critical and creative thinking are what enable those skills to come alive.

Understanding how your mind works, both its simple actions and its more involved thinking processes, is the first step toward critical thinking. When you have that understanding, you can perform the essential critical thinking task: asking important questions about ideas and information. This chapter will show you both the mind's basic actions and the thinking processes that use those actions. You will explore what it means to be an open-minded, critical, and creative thinker, able to ask and understand questions that promote your success in college or university, career, and life.

Thinking It Through

Check those statements that apply to you right now:

☐ I'm not quite sure what "critical thinking" means.

☐ I am usually happy with how I've solved a problem.

☐ When I have to make a decision, I often have a hard time making up my mind.

☐ Plan for next year? I can hardly get past next week.

☐ I'm not sure I often take the time to question the validity of my opinions.

☐ I find it hard to convince anyone that my argument makes sense.

☐ I think my perspective is generally on target.

☐ I consider myself to be a creative person.

History of Critical
Thinking
www.criticalthinking.org/
university/univlibrary/
cthistory.nclk

From Socrates to John Dewey, the
history and principles of critical
thinking are explained and examined in detail.

What Is Critical Thinking?

Critical thinking is thinking that goes beyond the basic recall of information. If the word *critical* sounds negative to you, consider that the dictionary defines its meaning as "indispensable" and "important." Critical thinking is important thinking that involves asking questions. Using critical thinking, you question established ideas, create new ideas, turn information into tools to solve problems and make decisions, and take the long-term view as well as the day-to-day view.

A critical thinker asks as many kinds of questions as possible. The following are examples of possible questions about a given piece of information: *Where did it come from? What could explain it? In what ways is it true or false, and what examples could prove or disprove it? How do I feel about it, and why? How is this information similar to or different from what I already know? Is it good or bad? What causes led to it, and what effects does it have?* Critical thinkers also try to transform information into something they can use. They ask themselves whether the information can help them solve a problem, make a decision, create something new, or anticipate the future. Such questions help the critical thinker learn, grow, and create.

Not thinking critically means not asking questions about information or ideas. A person who does not think critically tends to accept or reject information or ideas without examining them. Table 4–1 compares how a critical thinker and a non-critical thinker might respond to particular situations.

Asking questions (the focus of the table), considering without judgment as many responses as you can, and choosing responses that are as complete and accurate as possible are the ingredients that make up the skill of critical thinking.

Critical Thinking Is a Skill

Critical thinking has only recently begun to be taught as such in schools. It used to be assumed that students possessed various levels of thinking ability that would either stay the same or develop naturally in the course of studying particular subjects. Education used to focus primarily on teaching information rather than on how to question and process that information. Now, educators have begun to see critical thinking as a skill that can be taught to students at all different levels of thinking ability. Anyone can develop the ability to think critically.

Learning information is still an important part of education, and is in fact a crucial component of critical thinking. For instance, part of the skill of critical thinking is comparing new information with what you already know. Your prior knowledge provides a framework within which to ask questions about and evaluate a new piece of information. Without a solid base of knowledge, critical thinking is harder to achieve. For example, thinking critically about the statement "Shakespeare's character King Richard III is like an early version of Adolf Hitler" is impossible without basic knowledge of World War II and Shakespeare's play *Richard III*.

Table 4-1 Not Thinking Critically vs. Thinking Critically

Your Role	Situation	Non-Questioning Response	Questioning Response
Student	Instructor is lecturing on the prime minister's alleged role during the 1999 pepper-spray incident.	You assume that everything your instructor tells you is true.	You consider what the instructor says, write down questions about issues you want to clarify, and initiate discussion with the instructor or other classmates.
Parent	Instructor discovers your child lying about something at school.	You're mad at your child and believe the instructor, or you think the instructor is lying.	You ask both instructor and child about what happened, and you compare their answers, evaluating who you think is telling the truth. You discuss the concepts of lying/honesty with your child.
Spouse/Partner	Your partner feels that he or she no longer has quality time with you.	You think he or she is wrong and defend yourself.	You ask how long he/she has felt this way, ask your partner and yourself why this is happening, and explore how you can improve the situation.
Employee	Your supervisor is angry at you.	You ignore or avoid your supervisor, or you deny responsibility for what the supervisor is angry about.	You are willing to discuss the situation; you ask what you could have done better; you ask what changes you can make in the future.
Neighbour	People who are different from you move in next door.	You ignore or avoid them; you think their way of living is strange.	You introduce yourself; you offer to help if they need it; you respectfully explore what's different about them.
Citizen	You encounter a homeless person.	You avoid the person—and the issue of homelessness.	You examine whether the community has a responsibility to the homeless and, if you find that it does, you explore how to fulfill that responsibility.
Consumer	You want to buy a car.	You decide on a brand-new car and don't think through how you will handle the payments.	You consider the different effects of buying a new car vs. buying a used car; you look at your financial situation to see what kind of payment you can handle each month.

The skill of critical thinking focuses on generating questions about statements and information. To examine potential critical-thinking responses in more depth, explore the different questions that a critical thinker may have about one particular statement.

A Critical-Thinking Response to a Statement

Consider the following statement of opinion: *"My obstacles are keeping me from succeeding in school. Other people make it through school because they don't have to deal with the obstacles that I have."*

Non-questioning thinkers may accept an opinion such as this as an absolute truth, believing that their obstacles will hinder their success. As a result, on the road to achieving their goals, they may lose the motivation to overcome those obstacles. In contrast, critical thinkers would take the opportunity to examine the opinion through a series of questions. Here are some examples of questions one student might ask (the type of each question is indicated in parentheses):

Confused by Critical Thinking?
www.criticalthinking.org/
university/univlibrary/
Gloss/intro.nclk

This site offers a glossary of all the terms you will need to understand to apply critical thinking to your academic studies.

"What exactly are my obstacles? I define my obstacles as a heavy work schedule, single parenting, being in debt, and returning to school after ten years out."* **(recall)**

"Are there other cases different from mine? I do have one friend who is going through problems worse than mine, and she's getting by. I also know another guy who doesn't have too much to deal with that I can see, and yet he's struggling just like I am."* **(difference)**

"What is an example of someone who has had success despite having to overcome obstacles? Country singer Shania Twain's parents were killed in a car crash when she was just 22 years old. After their death, Shania became the head of the household, and continued to sing and write songs while taking care of her four younger sisters and brothers. She didn't give up her goals in spite of the obstacles she faced. She used her singing and songwriting abilities not only as a way to put food on the table, but as a way to cope. Her dream of becoming a successful singer did not die because of this tragedy."* **(idea to example)**

"What conclusion can I draw from my questions? From thinking about my friend and about Shania Twain, I would say that people can successfully overcome their obstacles by working hard and not giving up, focusing on their abilities, and concentrating on their goals."* **(example to idea)**

"Who has problems similar to mine? Well, if I consider my obstacles specifically, I might say that single parents and returning adult students will all have trouble in school. But that is not necessarily true. People in all kinds of situations may still become successful."* **(similarity)**

"Why do I think this? Perhaps I am scared of returning to school and adjusting to a new environment. Maybe I am afraid to challenge myself, which I haven't done in a long time. Whatever the cause, the effect is that I feel bad about myself and don't work to the best of my abilities, and that can hurt both me and my family, who depend on me."* **(cause and effect)**

"How do I evaluate the effects of this statement? I think it's harmful. When we say that obstacles equal difficulty, we can damage our desire to try to overcome those obstacles. When we say that successful people don't have obstacles, we might overlook that some very successful people have to deal with hidden disadvantages such as learning disabilities or abusive families."* **(evaluation)**

Remember these types of questions. When you explore the seven mind actions later in the chapter, refer to these questions to see how they illustrate the different actions your mind performs.

The Value of Critical Thinking

Critical thinking has many important advantages. Following are some ways you may benefit from putting energy into critical thinking.

You will increase your ability to perform thinking processes that help you reach any kind of school, career, or life goal. Critical thinking is a learned skill, just like shooting a puck or making roses with frosting or using a word-processing program on the computer. As with any other skill, the more you use it, the better you become. The more you ask questions, the better you think. The better you think, the more effective you will be when completing schoolwork, managing your personal life, and performing on the job. You will learn more about different critical-thinking processes later in this chapter.

You can produce knowledge, rather than just reproduce it. When you think critically and ask questions, the interaction of new information with what you already know creates new knowledge. When you think critically about lectures or reading materials, rather than just learn them for a test, you will retain knowledge that will serve you after you leave school. The usefulness of knowledge comes in when you apply it to new and different situations. It won't mean much for an early-childhood-education student to quote the stages of child development on an exam unless he or she can make judgments about children's needs when on the job.

You can be a valuable employee. You probably won't be a failure in the workplace if you follow directions. However, you will be even more valuable if you think critically and ask strategic questions about how to make improvements, large or small. Questions could range from "Is there a better way to deliver phone messages?" to "How can we increase business to keep from going under?" An employee who shows the initiative to think critically will be more likely to earn responsibility and promotions. According to the Conference Board of Canada, the ability to "think critically and act logically to evaluate situations, solve problems, and make decisions" is a key employability skill.[1]

You can increase your creativity. You cannot be a successful critical thinker without being able to come up with new and different questions to ask, possibilities to explore, and ideas to try. Creativity is essential to producing what is new. Being creative generally improves your outlook, your sense of humour, and your perspective as you cope with problems. Later in this chapter, you will look at ways to awaken and increase your natural creativity.

In the next section, you will read about the seven basic actions your mind performs when asking important questions. These actions are the basic blocks you will use to build the critical-thinking processes you will explore later in the chapter.

The Value of Critical Thinking
www.criticalthinking.org/ university/univlibrary/ intraits.nclk

The Conference Board of Canada lists the ability to "think critically and logically" as an important employability skill. This link offers reasons why critical thinking makes you a better person.

"We do not live to think But, on the contrary, we think in order that we may succeed in surviving."
José Ortega y Gasset

How Does Your Mind Work?

Critical thinking depends on a thorough understanding of the workings of the mind. Your mind has some basic moves, or actions, some combination of which it uses each time you think. Sometimes it uses one action by itself, but most often it uses two or more.

Mind Actions: The Thinktrix

You can identify your mind's actions using a system called the Thinktrix, developed by educators Frank Lyman, Arlene Mindus, and Charlene Lopez.[2] They studied how students think and named seven mind actions that are the basic building blocks of thought. These actions are not new to you, although some of their names may be. They represent the ways in which you think all the time.

Through exploring these actions, you can go beyond just thinking and learn *how* you think. This will help you take charge of your own thinking. The more you know about how your mind works, the more control you will have over thinking processes such as problem solving, decision making, creating, and strategic planning.

Following are explanations of each of the mind actions. Each explanation has the name of the action, words that define it, and examples that explain it. As you read, write your own examples in the blank spaces provided. Each action is also represented by a picture or *icon* that helps you visualize and remember it.

Recall: *Facts, sequence, and description.* This is the simplest action. When you recall you describe facts, objects, or events, or put them into sequence. *Examples:*

- Naming the prime ministers of Canada, in order
- Remembering your best friends' phone numbers

Your example: Recall some important events this month. _____

_____

_____

The icon: A string tied around a finger is a familiar image of recall or remembering.

Similarity: *Analogy, likeness.* This action examines what is **similar** about one or more things. You might compare situations, ideas, people, stories, events, or objects. *Examples:*

- Comparing notes with another student to see what facts and ideas you have both considered important
- Analyzing the arguments you've had with your partner this month and seeing how they all seem to be about the same problem

Your example: State what is similar about two of your best friends. _____

_____

_____

The icon: Two alike objects, in this case triangles, indicate similarity.

Difference: *Distinction, contrast.* This action examines what is **different** about one or more situations, ideas, people, stories, events, or objects, by contrasting them with one another. *Examples:*

- Seeing how two instructors differ in style—one divides the class into small groups and encourages discussion; the other keeps desks in straight lines and lectures for most of the class

- Contrasting a weekday during which you work half the day and go to school half the day with a weekday during which you attend class and then have the rest of the day to study

Your example: Explain how your response to a course you like differs from your response to a course you don't like as much. _____

_____

_____

The icon: Two differing objects, in this case a triangle and a square, indicate difference.

Cause and effect: *Reasons, consequences, prediction.* Using this action, you look at what has **caused** a fact, situation, or event, and/or what **effects**, or consequences, come from it. In other words, you examine both what led up to something and what will follow because of it. *Examples:*

- Staying up late at night causes you to oversleep, which has the effect of your being late to class. This causes you to miss some of the material, which has the further effect of your having problems on the test.

- By paying your phone and utility bills on time, you create effects such as a better credit rating, uninterrupted service, and a better relationship with your service providers.

Your example: Name what causes you to like your favourite class, and the effects that liking the class has on you. _____

_____

_____

The icon: The pin pricking a balloon indicates cause and a predicted effect.

Example to idea: *Generalization, classification, conceptualization.* From one or more **examples** (facts or events), you develop a general **idea** or ideas.

Grouping facts or events into patterns may allow you to make a general statement about several of them at once. Classifying a fact or event helps you build knowledge. This mind action moves from the specific to the general. *Examples:*

- You have had trouble finding a baby-sitter who can match your schedule. A classmate even brought her child to class once. Your brother has had to drop off his daughter at your mom's and doesn't like being unable to see her all day. From these examples, you derive the idea that your school needs an on-campus daycare program.

- You see a movie and you decide it is mostly about pride.

Your example: Name examples of activities you enjoy, and from them, come up with an idea of your choice of vacation. _____

_____

_____

The icon: The arrow and "EX" pointing to a light bulb on their right indicate how an example or examples lead to the idea (the light bulb, lit up).

Idea to example: *Categorization, substantiation, proof.* In a reversal of the previous action, you take an **idea** or ideas and think of **examples** (events or facts) that support or prove that idea. This mind action moves from the general to the specific. *Examples:*

- When you write a paper, you start with a thesis statement, which communicates the central idea: "Men are favoured over women in the modern workplace." Then you gather examples to back up that idea: Men make more money on average than women in the same jobs; there are more men in upper management positions than there are women; and women can be denied advancement when they make their families a priority.

- You talk to your instructor about changing your major, giving examples that support your idea: You have worked in the field to which you want to change; you have fulfilled some of the requirements for that major already; and you are unhappy with your current course of study.

Your example: Name an admirable person. Give three examples of why that person is admirable. _____

_____

_____

The icon: In a reversal of the previous icon, this one starts with the light bulb and has an arrow pointing to "EX." This indicates that you start with the idea, the lit bulb, and then branch into the example or examples that support the idea.

Evaluation: *Value, judgment, rating.* Here you **judge** whether something is useful or not useful, important or unimportant, good or bad, or right or wrong by identifying and weighing its positive and negative effects (pros and cons). Be sure to consider the specific situation at hand (a cold drink might be good on the beach in August, not so good in the snowdrifts in January). With the facts you have gathered, you determine the value of something in terms of both predicted effects and your own needs. Cause-and-effect analysis always accompanies evaluation. *Examples:*

- You decide to try taking later classes for a semester. You schedule classes in the afternoons and spend your nights on the job. You find that instead of getting up early to use the morning time, you tend to sleep in and then get up not too long before you have to be at school. From those harmful effects, you evaluate that it doesn't work for you. You decide to schedule earlier classes next time.

- Someone offers you a chance to cheat on a test. You evaluate the potential effects if you are caught. You also evaluate the long-term effects on you of not actually learning the material. You decide that it isn't worth your while to participate in the plan to cheat.

Your example: Evaluate your mode of transportation to school. _____

_____

_____

The icon: A set of scales out of balance indicates how you weigh positive and negative effects to arrive at an evaluation.

You may want to use a *mnemonic device*—a memory tool, explained in more detail in Chapter 7—to remember the seven mind actions. Try recalling them using the word DECRIES—each letter is the first letter of a mind action. You can also make a sentence of words that each start with a mind action's first letter. Here's an example: "Really Smart Dogs Cook Eggs In Enchiladas" (the first letter of each word stands for one of the mind actions).

How Mind Actions Build Thinking Processes

The seven mind actions are the fundamental building blocks that your mind uses every day. Note that you will rarely use them one at a time in a step-by-step process, as they are presented here. You will usually combine them, overlap them, and repeat them more than once, using different actions for different situations. For example, when you want to say something nice at the end of a date, you might consider past comments that had an effect *similar* to what you want now. When a test question asks you to explain what prejudice is, you might name similar *examples* that show your *idea* of what prejudice means.

When you combine mind actions in working toward a specific goal, you are performing a thinking process. The next few sections will explore six of the most important critical-thinking processes: solving problems, making decisions, constructing effective arguments, establishing truth, shifting your perspective, and planning strategically. Each thinking process helps you succeed by directing your critical thinking toward the achievement of your goals. Figure 4–3, which appears later in the chapter, shows all of the mind actions and thinking processes together and reminds you that the mind actions form the core of the thinking processes.

How Does Critical Thinking Help You Solve Problems and Make Decisions?

"It is a Bad plan that admits of no modification."

Publilius Syrus

Problem solving and decision making are probably the two most crucial and common thinking processes. Each one requires various mind actions. They overlap somewhat, because every problem that needs solving requires you to make a decision. However, not every decision requires that you solve a problem (for example, not many people would say that deciding what to order in a restaurant is a problem). Each process will be considered separately here. You will notice similarities in the steps involved in each.

Although both of these processes have multiple steps, you will not always have to work your way through each step. As you become more comfortable with solving problems and making decisions, your mind will automatically click through the steps you need whenever you encounter a problem or decision. Also, you will become more adept at evaluating which problems and decisions need serious consideration and which can be taken care of more quickly and simply.

Problem Solving

Life constantly presents problems to be solved, ranging from average daily problems (how to manage study time or learn not to misplace your keys) to life-altering situations (how to care for a sick elderly relative or design a custody plan during a divorce). Choosing a solution without thinking critically may have negative effects. For example, if you decide to move a sick elderly relative into your home without considering the effects of your work schedule, the relative may be alone in the evenings with no one to help should a medical emergency arise. However, if you use the steps of the following problem-solving process to think critically, you have the best chance of coming up with a favourable solution.

You can apply this problem-solving plan to any situation or issue that you want to resolve. Using the following steps will maximize the number of possible solutions you generate and will allow you to explore each one as fully as possible.

1. State the problem clearly. What are the facts? *Recall* the details of the situation. Be sure to name the problem specifically, without focusing on causes or effects. For example, a student might state this as a problem: "I'm not understanding the class material."

However, that may be a *cause* of the actual problem at hand: "I'm failing my economics quizzes."

2. Analyze the problem. What is happening that, in your opinion, needs to change? In other words, what *effects* does the situation have that cause a problem for you? What *causes* these effects? Look at the *causes and effects* that surround the problem. Continuing the example of the economics student, if some effects of failing quizzes include poor grades in the course and disinterest, some causes may include poor study habits, poor test-taking skills, lack of sleep, or not understanding the material.

3. Brainstorm possible solutions. Brainstorming will help you think of examples of similar problems and how you solved them. Consider what is different about this problem, and see if the thoughts you generate might lead you to new possible solutions. You will find more about brainstorming on pages 139 and 140 of this chapter. *It's very important to base your possible solutions upon* **causes***, rather than* **effects***.* Getting to the heart of a problem requires addressing the cause, not simply putting a bandage on the effect. If the economics student were to aim for better assignment grades to offset the low quiz grades, that might raise his average but wouldn't address the cause of not understanding the material. Looking at this cause, on the other hand, might lead him to work on study habits or seek help from his instructor, a study group, or a tutor.

> **brainstorming**
> The spontaneous, rapid generation of ideas or solutions, undertaken by a group or an individual, often as part of a problem-solving process.

4. Explore each solution. Why might your solution work? Why not? Might a solution work partially, or in a particular situation? *Evaluate* the pros and cons, or the positive and negative effects, of each idea. Create a chain of causes and effects in your head, as far into the future as you can, to see where you think this solution would lead. The economics student might consider the effects of improved study habits, more sleep, tutoring, or dropping the class.

5. Choose and execute the solution you decide is best. Decide how you will put your solution to work. Then, execute your solution. The economics student could decide on a combination of improved study habits and tutoring.

6. Evaluate the solution that you acted upon, looking at its *effects*. What are the positive and negative effects of what you did? In terms of your needs, was it a useful solution or not? Could the solution use any adjustments or changes in order to be more useful? Would you do the same again or not? Evaluating his choice, the economics student may decide that the effects are good but that his fatigue still causes a problem.

7. Continue to refine the solution. Problem solving is always a process. You may have opportunities to apply the same solution over and over again. Re-evaluate regularly, making changes that you think will make the solution better. The economics student may decide to continue to study more regularly but, after a few weeks of tutoring, could opt to trade in the tutoring time for

some extra sleep. He may decide to take what he has learned from the tutor so far and apply it to his increased study efforts.

Using this process will enable you to solve personal, educational, and workplace problems in a thoughtful and comprehensive way. Figure 4–1 is a think link that demonstrates a way to visualize the flow of problem solving. Figure 4–2 contains a sample of how one person used this plan to solve a problem. Figure 4–2 represents the same type of plan as 4–1 but gives room to write, so that it can be used in the problem-solving process.

Decision Making

Although every problem-solving process involves making a decision (by which you decide which solution to try), not all decisions involve solving problems. Decisions are choices. Making a choice, or decision, requires

Figure 4–1   Problem-Solving Plan

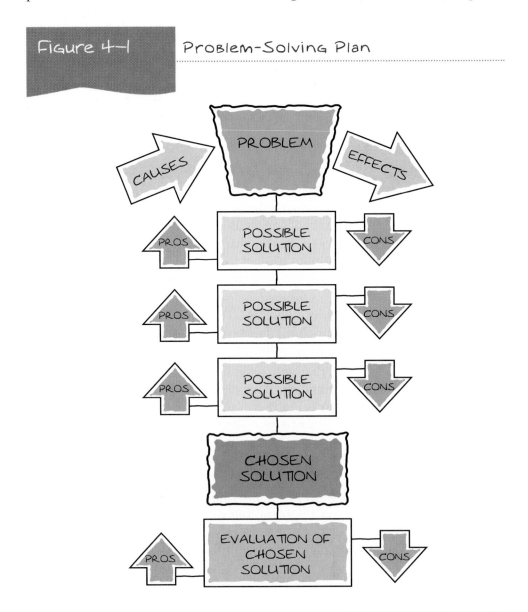

Figure 4-2   How One Student Worked Through a Problem

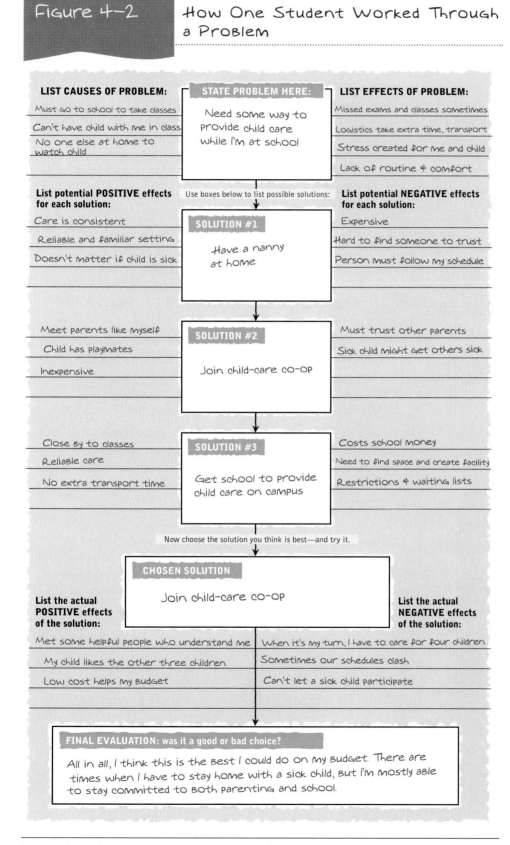

LIST CAUSES OF PROBLEM:

Must go to school to take classes

Can't have child with me in class

No one else at home to watch child

STATE PROBLEM HERE:

Need some way to provide child care while I'm at school

LIST EFFECTS OF PROBLEM:

Missed exams and classes sometimes

Logistics take extra time, transport

Stress created for me and child

Lack of routine & comfort

List potential POSITIVE effects for each solution:

Care is consistent

Reliable and familiar setting

Doesn't matter if child is sick

Use boxes below to list possible solutions:

SOLUTION #1

Have a nanny at home

List potential NEGATIVE effects for each solution:

Expensive

Hard to find someone to trust

Person must follow my schedule

Meet parents like myself

Child has playmates

Inexpensive

SOLUTION #2

Join child-care co-op

Must trust other parents

Sick child might get others sick

Close by to classes

Reliable care

No extra transport time

SOLUTION #3

Get school to provide child care on campus

Costs school money

Need to find space and create facility

Restrictions & waiting lists

Now choose the solution you think is best—and try it.

CHOSEN SOLUTION

Join child-care co-op

List the actual POSITIVE effects of the solution:

Met some helpful people who understand me

My child likes the other three children

Low cost helps my budget

List the actual NEGATIVE effects of the solution:

When it's my turn, I have to care for four children

Sometimes our schedules clash

Can't let a sick child participate

FINAL EVALUATION: was it a good or bad choice?

All in all, I think this is the best I could do on my budget. There are times when I have to stay home with a sick child, but I'm mostly able to stay committed to both parenting and school.

Source: Adapted from a learning aid developed by Frank T. Lyman, Jr., Ph.D., University of Maryland, 1983.

thinking critically through all of the possible choices and evaluating which will work best for you and for the situation. Decisions large and small come up daily, hourly, even every few minutes. Do you call your landlord when the heat isn't coming on? Do you drop a course? Should you stay in a relationship? Can you work part time without your job interfering with school?

Before you begin the decision-making process, evaluate the level of the decision you are making. Do you have to decide what to have for lunch (usually a minor issue), or whether to quit a good job (often a major life change)? Some decisions are little, day-to-day considerations that you can take care of quickly on your own. Others require thoughtful evaluation, time, and perhaps the input of others you trust. The following is a list of steps to take in order to think critically through a decision.

1. Decide on a goal. Why is this decision necessary? In other words, what result do you want from this decision? Considering the *effects* you want can help you formulate your goal. For example, say a student currently attends university. Her goal is to become a physical therapist. The school has a good program, but her financial situation has changed and has made this school too expensive for her.

2. Establish needs. *Recall* the needs of everyone (or everything) involved in the decision. The student needs a school with a full physical therapy program; she and her parents need to cut costs (her father changed jobs and her family cannot continue to afford the current school); she needs to be able to transfer credits.

3. Name, investigate, and evaluate available options. Brainstorm possible choices, and then look at the facts surrounding each. *Evaluate* the good and bad effects of each possibility. Weigh these effects and judge which is the best course of action. Here are some possibilities that the student in the example might consider:

   ○ *Continue at university.* **Positive effects:** I wouldn't have to adjust to a new place or to new people. I could continue my course work as planned. **Negative effects:** I would have to find a way to finance most of my tuition and costs on my own, whether through loans, grants, or work. I'm not sure I could find time to work as much as I would need to, and I don't think I would qualify for as much aid as I now need.

   ○ *Transfer to the community college.* **Positive effects:** They have many of the courses I need to continue with the physical therapy curriculum. The school is twenty minutes from my parents' house, so I could live at home and avoid paying housing costs. Some credits may be transferable. The tuition is extremely reasonable. **Negative effects:** I don't know anyone there. I would be less independent. Community colleges don't offer a bachelor's degree.

4. **Decide on a plan of action and pursue it.** Make a choice based on your evaluation, and act on your choice. In this case the student might decide to go to the community college for two years and then transfer back to university to earn a bachelor's degree in physical therapy. Although she might lose some independence and contact with friends, the positive effects are money saved, opportunity to spend time on studies rather than working to earn tuition money, and the availability of classes that match the physical therapy program requirements.

5. **Evaluate the result.** Was it useful? Not useful? Some of both? Weigh the positive and negative effects. The student may find that it can be hard living at home, although her parents are adjusting to her independence and she is trying to respect their concerns as parents. Fewer social distractions result in her getting more work done. The financial situation is much more favourable. All things considered, her evaluation is that this decision was a good one.

Making important decisions can take time. Think through your decision thoroughly, considering your own ideas as well as those of others you trust, but don't hesitate to act once you have your plan. You cannot benefit from your decision until you act upon it and follow through.

How Do You Construct an Effective Argument?

In this case, "argument" does not refer to a fight you would have with someone; it is a persuasive case that you make to prove or disprove a point. In every aspect of your life you will encounter situations in which your success depends on your being able to persuade someone to agree with you on some idea. You may need to convince an instructor that you deserve a second chance on an assignment; you may need to persuade a parent that you're making the right choice in a relationship; you may need to persuade a prospective employer that you are the one for the job.

> **persuade**
> To convince someone through argument or reasoning to adopt a belief, position, or course of action.

When you come to crossroads in your life, much is at stake—a grade, a relationship, a job, and more. If you want your persuasive argument to help you achieve what's at stake, you require the use of your critical thinking. Put the mind actions to work asking questions about the situation, using the following steps:

Establish the goal—what's at stake. No argument is an absolute guarantee of achieving a goal, but a persuasive argument will give you your best shot. Ask yourself what you want. As an example, imagine that you want a raise and promotion to a new position at work.

Gather examples that support your idea. What can you say that will support your request? In this case, your examples may be that you have worked at this company part time for a year and full time for half of a year; you are almost always on time; you have received good reviews from your supervisor; and you have ideas for the position to which you want to be promoted.

Anticipate questions. What will the other person or people ask you to explain? In the promotion example, they could ask you about your prior track record, what you have achieved in your current position, what you know about the position you want to take, whether you know the people you would be working with, and what new and creative ideas you have.

Anticipate points against you. What might someone bring up that argues against your position? Whatever you think of, decide what you will say to oppose it. If your supervisor says that you can't handle the longer hours the new position would require, you may respond that you have looked into adjusting your school schedule. If the supervisor says that you don't have the necessary experience, you may respond that you have studied the job or talked with people who do that type of work.

Be flexible. You never know what will happen as you present your argument. You might not even need to push; on the other hand, it may turn out to be much tougher than you thought. By rehearsing your response to questions beforehand, you will be as prepared as possible to handle any twists and turns the conversation may take.

How Do You Establish Truth?

Investigating the truth and accuracy of information is an important critical-thinking process. In order to seek truth through critical thinking, you must question the validity of statements or information. Critical-thinking experts Sylvan Barnet and Hugo Bedau state that when you test for the truth of a statement, you "determine whether what it asserts corresponds with reality; if it does, then it is true, and if it doesn't, then it is false."[3] In order to determine to what degree a statement "corresponds with reality," ask questions based on the mind actions. The search for truth takes two primary forms: distinguishing fact from opinion, and challenging assumptions.

Distinguishing Fact from Opinion

Fact, according to the dictionary, is information presented as objectively real. *Opinion* is defined as a belief, conclusion, or judgment. Being able to evaluate what in a piece of reading material is fact and what is opinion is crucial to your understanding of the material. Fact and opinion generate different reactions in a reader. If you decide that a statement is opinion, you may focus on deciding whether you agree with that opinion, based on how it is explained and supported. If you decide that a statement is fact, you have agreed to accept it as true, and your focus moves to evaluating how that fact is used to support other ideas or opinions.

Fact and opinion may overlap. Opinions can be proved to be partially or completely factual after investigation. Statements that seem factual may emerge as opinions if any part of them is proven wrong through questioning. Qualifiers, such as *all, none, never, often, sometimes,* and *many,* will often mean the difference between fact and opinion. Absolute qualifiers such as *all* and *none* indicate an opinion more often than a fact, while indefinite qualifiers such as *some* and *many* may make a fact out of what seems to be an opinion. For example, "All college students need to take math" is an opinion, whereas "Some college students need to take math" is a fact.

Both facts and opinions require investigation through questioning. Even though opinions would seem to require more examination than facts, some opinions masquerade as facts and are revealed only through examination. For example, an article may state, "Twenty to thirty minutes of vigorous exercise three to five times a week is essential for good health." That may sound like a fact. When you examine it through questioning, however, you may reveal it as the opinion of the author. To be safe, consider all statements opinions until proven otherwise. Questions you may ask include the following:

- What facts or examples provide evidence of truth?
- How does the maker of the statement know this to be true?
- Is there another fact that disproves this statement or information, or shows it to be an opinion?
- How reliable are the sources of information?
- What about this statement is similar to or different from other information I consider to be fact?
- How could I test the validity of this statement or information?

Even though you may find a truth in and agree with the statement after examining how the author supports it, the statement remains an opinion. The observation that some healthy people do not exercise in this way proves that the statement is not completely factual.

Take a different statement as another example. It has been stated as a fact that the economically poor take unfair advantage of the welfare system. A critical thinker who questions this statement may find that the statement is actually an opinion with some degree of truth. Some citizens may try to cheat the welfare system, while others may have an honest claim to their welfare cheques and may try hard to find work. See Table 4–2 for some more examples of factual statements vs. statements of opinion.

Another crucial step in determining the truth is to question the assumptions that you and others hold, which are the underlying force in shaping opinions.

Challenging Assumptions

"If it's more expensive, it's better." "It's best to start your day before 8 A.M." "Famous people have easy lives." These statements reveal assumptions—often evaluations, or generalizations, based on observing cause and effect—that can sometimes hide within seemingly truthful assertions. Important life choices can come from your assumptions—you may assume that you should get married and have children, own a car, or eat three meals a day. Many people

assumption
An idea or statement accepted as true without examination or proof.

Table 4–2 Examples of Facts and Opinions		
Subject	Factual Statement	Statement of Opinion
Animal speed	The cheetah has been clocked at speeds that prove it to be the world's fastest animal.	No animal can ever escape the speed of the cheetah.
Weather	It's raining outside.	This is the worst rainstorm in recent history.
Fats in foods	Two slices of stuffed-crust pizza have more fat than a Big Mac.™	Diners will have more luck avoiding fat at a burger joint than at a pizza place.

live without questioning what their assumptions are or whether they make sense, nor do they challenge the assumptions of others.

Assumptions come from sources such as parents or relatives, television and other media, friends, and your personal experiences. As much as you think such assumptions work for you, it's just as possible that they don't. Assumptions can close your mind to opportunities and even harm people. For example, the old false assumption that people who speak with a regional or foreign accent are somehow less intelligent or less qualified has caused a great deal of harm through the years.

Think critically to uncover and investigate assumptions. Ask these questions:

1. Is the truth of this statement supported by fact, or does the statement hide an assumption?
2. In what cases is this assumption true or not true? What examples prove or disprove it?
3. Has making this assumption benefited me or others? Has it hurt me or others? In what ways?
4. If someone taught me this assumption, why? Did that person think it over or just accept it?
5. What harm could be done by always taking this assumption as fact?

For example, here's how you might use these questions to investigate the following statement: "The most productive schedule involves getting started early in the day."

1. This statement hides an assumption that the morning is the time when all people feel most energetic and are able to get a lot of things done.
2. The assumption may be generally true for people who enjoy early morning hours and have good energy during that part of the day. But the assumption may be not true for people who work best in the afternoon or evening hours.

3. Society's basic standard of daytime classes and 8 A.M. to 5 P.M. working hours supports this assumption. Therefore, the assumption may work for people who have early jobs and classes or children who get up early. It may not work, however, for people who work late or overnight shifts or who take classes in the evening.

4. Maybe people who believe this assumption to be true were raised in a household where people started their days early. Or, perhaps they just say this because it goes along with what seems to be society's standard. Still, there are plenty of people who operate on a different schedule and yet enjoy successful, productive lives.

5. Taking this assumption as fact could hurt people who don't operate at their peak in the earlier hours. For example, if a "night owl" tries to conform to an early schedule of classes, he or she might experience concentration problems that would not necessarily occur during later classes. In situations that favour their particular characteristics—later classes; jobs that start in the late morning, afternoon, or evening; or career areas that don't require early morning work—such people have just as much potential to succeed as anyone else.

Be careful to look for and question all assumptions, not just the ones that seem problematic right from the start. It's a rare assumption that is *completely* "good" or "bad." Because assumptions may work differently in different situations, a generally good assumption may even cause problems under particular circumstances. Every new situation is worth a critical look. Here are two examples of assumptions that may have both good and bad sides:

"We should keep finding new uses for computers." Computers have improved industry and communication. However, many people have lost their jobs because what they used to do by hand is now being performed by a computer. Some people may become addicted to computers and neglect other important activities. You also may miss talking to a real person when you get a computer answering system on the phone—"Press '7' if you want…"

"Never argue in front of a child." It can be extremely damaging for children to witness angry or even violent arguments in the home. However, it can be helpful for them to see parents or guardians work through problems reasonably and try to find solutions. In this way the child sees that people can work through conflict in a positive way and bring about a useful result.

Why Shift Your Perspective?

Seeing the world only from your perspective, or point of view, is inflexible, limiting, and frustrating to both you and others. You probably know how hard it can be to relate to someone who cannot understand your situation—a co-worker who's annoyed that you leave early on Thursdays for physical therapy, a parent who doesn't see why you can't take a study break to visit, a

perspective
A mental point of view or outlook, based on a cluster of related assumptions, incorporating values, interests, and knowledge.

Real World Perspective

How can I find a satisfactory solution to my problem?

Chelsea Phillips, Environmental Science Major

This year I'm involved in a field study program called Earth Lands. I live and work in a sustainable community and study ecological issues. There are nine of us that live together. All of us are environmental activists and we agree to live by certain principles. The lodge we live in is run by solar power. We use kerosene and flashlights, too. Our food is entirely vegan, which means that we not only don't eat meat, we also don't eat other foods that come from animals, like milk and butter.

Five of the participants in the program, including myself, are here as paying students. The other members are brought in to live with us and support us as we learn about the environment and community living. When we got involved, we believed the program was an entirely collaborative effort—at least that's what the brochure said. We're starting to find out, however, that there is a subtle power structure that exists between the five of us and the group called the "Centring Team." We don't have as much input as we'd like into the schedule or decisions that need to be made. Because we're learning how to build community and resolve problems, I'd like to find a way to resolve this feeling of separation between the two groups. I'd like to see much more dialogue and collaboration so that we're all equal participants. What process could I initiate that would address this problem and allow for more equality within our community?

Raymond Reyes, Community and Organizational Consultant

There seems to be a "tale of two cities" here, where there are two distinct groups of people. I would recommend that you revisit and "reclaim" the core principles that you have said were agreed upon by everyone in the community. There is an obvious gap between what has been said and reality. As a community, you need to journey into the gap, or what Plato called "the fertile void." You may want to  give serious consideration to identifying and inviting an individual who can guide you through a process to establish a greater level of trust and authenticity and to do some team building.

Communities and other "learning organizations" need to address what I often refer to as the "other three R's" of education: relationship, relevance, and respect. First, address the need for honest and healthy relationships by specifically identifying and working through the trust and power issues. Secondly, make the core principles upon which your community is based more relevant so that the members truly "own" them, whether they are paying students or part of the "Centring Team." Lastly, your community needs to establish a social culture that has "wake up" calls that remind everyone to practise respect. Just as you are practising respect for our Earth Mother, your community needs to have the daily fellowship behaviours that are likewise respectful.

friend who can't understand why you would date someone of a different race. Seeing beyond one's own perspective can be difficult, especially when life problems and fatigue take their toll.

On the other hand, when you shift your own perspective to consider someone else's, you open the lines of communication. Trying to understand what other people feel, need, and want makes you more responsive to them. They then may feel respected by you and respond to you in turn. For example, if you want to add or drop a course and your adviser immediately says it's impossible, the last thing you may feel like doing is pouring your heart out. On the other hand, if your adviser asks to hear your point of view, you may sense that your needs are respected. Because the adviser wants to hear from you, you feel valued; that may encourage you to respond, or even to change your mind.

Every time you shift your perspective, you can also learn something new. There are worlds of knowledge and possibilities outside your individual existence. You may learn that what you eat daily may be against someone else's religious beliefs. You may discover people who don't fit a stereotype. You may find different and equally valid ways of getting an education, living as a family, relating to one another, having a spiritual life, or spending free time. Above all else, you may see that each person is entitled to his or her own perspective, no matter how foreign it may be to you.

Asking questions like these will help you maintain flexibility and openness in your perspective.

- What is similar and different about this person/belief/method and me/my beliefs/my methods?

- What positive and negative effects come from this different way of being/acting/believing? Even if this perspective seems to have negative effects for me, how might it have positive effects for others, and therefore have value?

- What can I learn from this different perspective? Is there anything I could adopt for my own life—something that would help me improve who I am or what I do? Is there anything I wouldn't do myself but that I can still respect and learn from?

Shifting your perspective is at the heart of all successful communication. Each person is unique. Even within a group of people similar to yourself, there will be a great variety of perspectives. Whether you decide that each world community has different customs or you understand that a friend can't go out on weekends because he spends that time with his mother, you have increased your wealth of knowledge and shown respect to others. Being able to shift perspective and communicate more effectively may mean the difference between success and failure in today's diverse working world.

Why Plan Strategically?

If you've ever played a game of chess or checkers, participated in a wrestling or martial arts match, or had a drawn-out argument, you have had experience with strategy. In those situations and many others, you continually have

strategy
A plan of action designed to accomplish a specific goal.

to think through and anticipate the moves the other person is about to make. Often you have to think about several possible options that person could put into play, and consider what you would counter with should any of those options occur. In competitive situations, you try to outguess the other person with your choices. The extent of your strategic skills can determine whether you will win or lose.

Strategy is the plan of action, the method, the "how" behind any goal you want to achieve. Specifically, strategic planning means having a plan for the future, whether you are looking at the next week, month, year, ten years, or fifty years. It means exploring the future positive and negative effects of the choices you make and actions you take today. You are planning strategically right now just by being in school. You made a decision that the sacrifices involved in attending a post-secondary institution are a legitimate price to pay for the skills, contacts, and opportunities that will help you in the future.

You don't have to compete against someone else in order to be strategic. You can be strategic on your own or even in a cooperative situation. For example, as a student, you are challenging yourself to achieve. You are learning to set goals for the future, analyze what you want in the long term, and prepare for the job market to increase your career options. Being strategic with yourself means challenging yourself as you would challenge a competitor, urging you to demand that you work to achieve your goals with conviction and determination.

What are the benefits, or positive effects, of strategic planning?

Strategy is an essential skill in the workplace. A food company that wants to develop a successful health-food product needs to examine the anticipated trends in health consciousness. A lawyer needs to think through every aspect of the client's case, anticipating how to respond to any allegation the opposing side will bring up in court. Strategic planning creates a vision into the future that allows the planner to anticipate all kinds of possibilities and, most importantly, to be prepared for them.

Strategic planning powers your short-term and long-term goal setting. Once you have set goals, you need to plan the steps that will help you achieve those goals over time. For example, a strategic thinker who wants to own a home in five years' time might drive a used car and cut out luxuries, put a small amount of money every month into a mutual fund, and keep an eye on current mortgage rates. In class, a strategic planner will think critically about the material presented, knowing that information is most useful later on if it is clearly understood.

Strategic planning helps you keep up with technology. As technology develops more and more quickly, jobs become obsolete. It's possible to spend years in school training for a career area that will be drying up when you are ready to enter the work force. When you plan strategically, you can take a broader range of courses or choose a major and career that are expanding. This will make it more likely that your skills will be in demand when you graduate.

Effective critical thinking is essential to strategic planning. If you aim for a certain goal, what steps will move you toward that goal? What positive effects do you anticipate these steps will have? How do you evaluate your past

Figure 4-3   The Wheel of Thinking

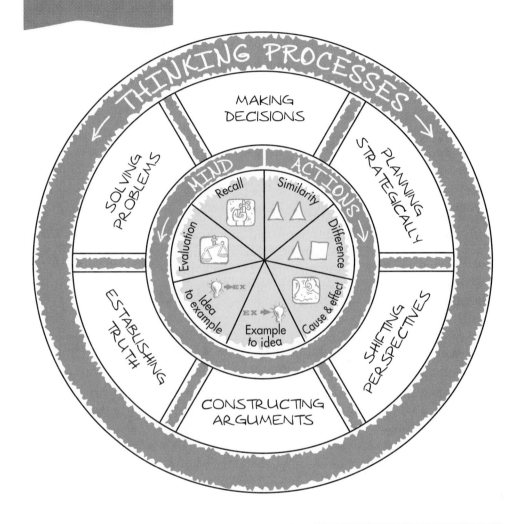

experiences with planning and goal setting? What can you learn from similar or different previous experiences in order to take different steps today? Critical thinking runs like a thread through all of your strategic planning.

Here are some tips for becoming a strategic planner:

Develop an appropriate plan. What approach will best achieve your goal? What steps toward your goal will you need to take one year, five years, ten years, or twenty years from now?

Anticipate all possible outcomes of your actions. What are the positive and negative effects that may occur?

Ask the question "how?" How do you achieve your goals? How do you learn effectively and remember what you learn? How do you develop a productive idea on the job? How do you distinguish yourself at school and at work?

Use human resources. Talk to people who are where you want to be, whether professionally or personally. What helped them to get there? Ask them what they believe are the important steps to take, degrees to earn, training to have, knowledge to gain.

In each thinking process, you use your creativity to come up with ideas, examples, causes, effects, and solutions. You have a capacity to be creative, whether you are aware of it or not. Open up your mind and awaken your creativity. It will enhance your critical thinking and make life more enjoyable.

How Can You Develop Your Creativity?

creativity

The ability to produce something new through imaginative skill.

Everyone is creative. Although the word "creative" may seem to refer primarily to artists, writers, musicians, and others who work in fields in which creative aspects are in the forefront, creativity comes in many other forms. It is the power to create anything, whether it is a solution, idea, approach, tangible product, work of art, system, program—anything at all. To help you expand your concept of creativity, here are some examples of day-to-day creative thinking:

- Figuring out an alternative plan when your baby-sitter unexpectedly cancels on you
- Planning how to coordinate your work and class schedules
- Talking through a problem with an instructor, and finding a way to understand each other
- Working to improve a relationship with a partner, child, parent, or friend
- Planning a budget so that you can pay your bills on time each month

Creative innovations introduced by all kinds of people continually expand and change the world. Here are some that have had an impact:

- Agnes Macphail, Cairine Wilson, Nellie McClung, and other women fought for and won the right for women to be active members of the Canadian political process.
- Art Fry and Spencer Silver invented the Post-It™ note in 1980, enabling people to save paper and protect documents by using removable notes.
- Henry Ford introduced the assembly-line method of automobile construction, making cars cheap enough to be available to the average citizen.
- Rosa Parks refused to give up her seat on the bus to a white person, thus setting off a chain of events that gave rise to the American civil rights movement.

◦ Tim Collings, an Engineering teacher at Simon Fraser University, was concerned about the effects of television violence on children. He developed the "violence chip," or V-Chip. Once installed in a television, it allows parents to determine which programs are acceptable for their children to watch and which are not.

Even though these particular innovations had wide-ranging effects, the characteristics of these influential innovators can be found in all people who exercise their creative capabilities.

Characteristics of Creative People

Creative people think in fresh new ways that improve the world and increase productivity, consistently responding to change with new ideas. Roger von Oech, an expert on creativity, highlights this kind of flexibility: "I've found that the hallmark of creative people is their mental flexibility," he says. "Like race-car drivers who shift in and out of different gears depending on where they are on the course, creative people are able to shift in and out of different types of thinking depending on the needs of the situation at hand….They're doggedly persistent in striving to reach their goals."[4]

T. Z. Tardif and F. J. Sternberg[5] say that creative people are perceived as having particular characteristics. See Table 4–3 for these characteristics and examples.

Creative people combine ideas and information in ways that form completely new solutions, ideas, processes, uses, or products. Children often can tap into this creative freedom more easily than adults. Whether they make up a new game, wear a bowl as a hat, or create forts from chairs and blankets, they create naturally without worrying that their ideas might not be "right." See if you can retrieve some of that creative freedom from your childhood, using the suggestions you are about to read.

Enhancing Your Creativity

You are naturally creative. One way to spur your creative ability is to allow yourself to explore new territory and adjust to change. Although it may feel risky and uncomfortable to try out new ideas or behaviour, it can open you to new and exciting possibilities. Your creative spirit may thrive in a state of change. When you feel yourself resisting change, remember that exploring new ideas doesn't mean that what you were doing before was wrong. You are just responding to change with flexibility and creativity.

Table 4–3 Characteristics of Creative People

Characteristic	Example
Willingness to take risks	Taking a difficult, high-level course
Tendency to break away from customary limitations	Entering a marathon race, particularly when physically disabled
Tendency to seek challenges and new experiences	Taking on an internship in an unfamiliar and high-pressure workplace
Broad range of interests in which he or she becomes absorbed	Inventing new moves on the basketball court and playing guitar at an open-mike night
Ability to make unique things out of available materials and objects	Making curtains out of bedsheets or writing a poem
Tendency to question social norms and assumptions	Adopting a child of a different ethnic background than the family's
Willingness to deviate from popular opinion	Working for a small, relatively unknown political party
Curiosity and inquisitiveness	Wanting to know how a computer program works; asking about the secret to a cooking trick

Source: Adapted from "What do we know about creativity?" in R. J. Sternberg (ed.), *The Nature of Creativity*, London, Cambridge University Press, 1988.

Following are some ways to enhance your creativity, adapted from material by J. R. Hayes.[6]

Take the broadest possible perspective. At first, a problem may look like "My child won't stay quiet when I study." If you take a wider look, you may discover hidden causes or effects of the problem, such as "I haven't chosen the best time of day to study," or "We haven't had time together, so he feels lonely," or "I need to plan activities for him in advance."

Choose the best atmosphere. T. M. Amabile says that people are more creative and imaginative when they spend time around other creative folk.[7] Spend time around innovative people whose thinking inspires you.

Give yourself time. Rushing can stifle your creative ability. When you allow time for thought to percolate, or you focus on a problem and then return to it after taking a break, you may increase your creative output. In addition, when you derive ideas and choose solutions, avoid evaluating them right away. If you criticize your creative ideas too soon, you tend to derail them.

Gather varied input. The more information and ideas you gather as you think, the more material you have to build a creative idea or solution. Every new piece of input offers a new perspective that may enlighten you.

Here are a few additional creativity tips from Roger von Oech.[8]

Don't get hooked on finding the one right answer. There can be many "right answers" to any question, depending on your point of view. Shift your perspective and come up with a few. The more you generate, the better your chance of finding the best one.

Don't always be logical. Following strict logic may cause you to miss analogies or ignore your hunches.

Break the rules sometimes. All kinds of creative breakthroughs have occurred because someone bypassed the rules. Women and minorities can vote and hold jobs because someone broke a rule—a law—many years ago. When necessary, challenge rules with creative ideas.

Be impractical. Ask yourself, "What if?" Use your imagination to consider what would happen if you didn't follow the accepted pattern. Too great an emphasis on practicality can narrow the scope of your ideas.

Let yourself play. People often hit upon their most creative ideas when they aren't trying to think about anything at all—when they are exercising, socializing, playing around, or just relaxing. Often when your mind switches into play mode, it can more freely generate new thoughts.

> "The world of reality has its limits. The world of imagination is boundless."
>
> Jean Jacques Rousseau

Let yourself go a little crazy. It's easy to conform to peer pressure and to do what everyone else does. Although you may feel weird doing something completely different, that independence could lead to some unique ideas. The idea for Velcro™ came from examining how a burr sticks to clothing. What seems like a crazy idea might turn into a brilliant discovery.

Don't fear failure. Even Michael Jordan got cut from the basketball team as a high school sophomore in Wilmington, N.C., and John F. Kennedy, Jr. needed a couple of tries to pass the exam to be licenced to practise law. If you insist on getting it right all the time, you may miss out on the creative path—often paved with failures—that leads to the best possible solution. Failure can open your mind to new possibilities and reveal to you the value of critical thinking.

Always consider yourself creative. Use your positive self-talk. Telling yourself you are a creative person can help you act like one.

Brainstorming is a creative process that may combine many of these creativity strategies. You can use brainstorming for problem solving, decision making, and preparing to write an essay or paper. Anytime you need to free your mind to consider new possibilities, you can brainstorm.

Brainstorming Toward a Creative Answer

You are brainstorming when you approach a problem by letting your mind free-associate and come up with as many possible ideas, examples, or solutions as you can, without immediately evaluating them as good or bad.

Brainstorming is also referred to as divergent thinking—you start with the issue or problem and then let your mind diverge, or go in as many different directions as it wants, in search of ideas or solutions. Here are some rules for successful brainstorming:[9]

Don't evaluate or criticize an idea right away. Write down your ideas so that you remember them. Evaluate later, after you have had a chance to think about them. Try to avoid criticizing other people's ideas as well. Students often become stifled when their ideas are evaluated during brainstorming.

Focus on quantity; don't worry about quality until later. Try to generate as many ideas or examples as you can. The more thoughts you generate, the better the chance that one may be useful. Brainstorming works well in groups. Group members can become inspired by, and make creative use of, one another's ideas.

Let yourself consider wild and wacky ideas. Trust yourself to fall off the edge of tradition when you explore your creativity. Sometimes the craziest ideas end up being the most productive, positive, workable solutions around.

Remember, creativity can be developed if you have the desire and patience. Be gentle with yourself in the process. Most people are harsher with themselves and their ideas than is necessary. Your creative expression will become freer with practice.

Creativity and Critical Thinking

Critical thinking and creativity work hand in hand. Critical thinking is inherently creative, because it requires you to take the information you are given and come up with original ideas or solutions to problems. For example, you can brainstorm to generate possible causes of a certain effect. If the effect you were examining was fatigue in afternoon classes, you might come up with possible causes such as lack of sleep, too much morning caffeine, a diet heavy in carbohydrates, a natural tendency toward low energy at that time, or an instructor who doesn't inspire you. Through your consideration of causes and solutions, you have been thinking both creatively and critically.

Creative thinkers and critical thinkers have similar characteristics—both consider new perspectives, ask questions, don't hesitate to question accepted assumptions and traditions, and persist in the search for answers. Only through thinking critically and creatively can you freely question, brainstorm, and evaluate in order to come up with the most fitting ideas, solutions, decisions, arguments, and plans.

You use critical-thinking mind actions throughout everything you do in school and in your daily life. In this chapter and in some of the other study skills chapters, you will notice mind-action icons placed where they can help you to label your thinking.

Κρινειν

The word "critical" is derived from the Greek word *krinein*, which means to separate in order to choose or select. To be a mindful and aware critical thinker, you need to be able to separate, evaluate, and select ideas, facts, and thoughts.

Think of this concept as you apply critical thinking to your reading, writing, and interaction with others. Be aware of the information you take in and of your thoughts, and be selective as you process them. Critical thinking gives you the power to make sense of life by deliberately selecting how to respond to the information, people, and events that you encounter.

Chapter 4: Applications

Name _____   Date _____

Key into Your Life:
Opportunities to Apply What You Learn

Exercise 1: The Seven Mind Actions

One way to explore the seven mind actions is to apply them to a vocabulary word. Choose a vocabulary word from a course you are taking now.
    Write your word here: _____

Recall. Write the definition here. Include two sentences—from the dictionary or from your class materials—that contain the word.

_____

_____

_____

Similarity. What synonyms—words with similar meanings—can you name?

_____

_____

Difference. What antonyms—words with opposite meanings—can you name?

_____

_____

Cause and effect. What effect is caused by using this word—what tone or connotation does it have? _____

_____

_____

Example to idea. From looking at the synonyms and sentences, create a definition in your own words. _____

_____

Idea to example. From the idea or the definition, show an example of the use of the word by placing it in a sentence that you create.

_____

_____

Evaluation. How well does the word fit in the sentence you have written? Explain. _____

_____

_____

Using the mnemonic devices suggested in Chapter 7, on pages 237 and 238, will also help you remember mind actions. Try inventing your own mnemonic device for the actions. Write it here or, if it is a mental picture, describe it.

_____

_____

_____

_____

Exercise 2: Making a Decision

In this series of exercises you will make a personal decision using the seven mind actions and the decision-making steps described in this chapter. Before you proceed through each of the steps, write here an important personal decision you have to make. Choose a decision that you want to act on and will be able to address soon.

_____

_____

Step 1   Name Your Goal
Be specific: What goal, or desired effects, do you seek from this decision? For example, if your decision is a choice between two jobs, the effects you want might be financial security, convenience, experience, or anything else that is a priority to you. It could also be a combination of these effects. Write down the desired effects that together make up your goal. Note priorities by numbering the effects in order of importance.

_____

_____

Step 2   Establish Needs
Who and what will be affected by your decision? If you are deciding how to finance your education and you have a family to support, you must take into consideration their financial needs as well as your own when exploring options.

List here the people/things/situations that may be affected by your decision and indicate how your decision will affect them.

_____

_____

_____

_____

_____

_____

EX →

Step 3   Check Out Your Options

Look at all the options you can imagine. Consider options even if they seem impossible or unlikely—you can evaluate them later. Some decisions only have two options (to move to a new apartment or not, to get a new roommate or not); others have a wider selection of choices. For example, if you are a full-time student and the parent of a child, you must coordinate your class schedule with the child's needs. Options could be the following: (1) put the child in day care; (2) ask a relative to care for the child; (3) hire a full-time nanny; or (4) arrange your class schedule so that you can balance the duties with another parent.

First, list the possible options for your own personal decision. Then evaluate the positive and negative effects of each.

Option 1 _____

Positive effects _____

Negative effects _____

Option 2 _____

Positive effects _____

Negative effects _____

Option 3 _____

Positive effects _____

Negative effects _____

Option 4 _____

Positive effects _____

Negative effects _____

Have you or someone else ever made a decision similar to the one you are about to make? What can you learn from that decision that may help you?

_____

_____

Step 4   Make Your Decision and Pursue It to the Goal
Taking your entire analysis into account, decide what to do. Write your decision here.

_____

_____

_____

Next is perhaps the most important step: <u>Act on your decision</u>.

Step 5   Evaluate the Result
After you have acted on your decision, evaluate how everything turned out. Did you achieve what you wanted to? What were the effects on you? On others? On the situation? To what extent were they positive, negative, or some of both?

List four effects here. Name each effect, circle *Positive* or *Negative*, and explain that evaluation.

Effect _____

    Positive   *Negative*

Why? _____

Effect _____

    Positive   *Negative*

Why? _____

Effect _____

    Positive   *Negative*

Why? _____

Effect _____

    Positive   *Negative*

Why? _____

Final evaluation: Write one statement in reaction to the decision you made. Indicate whether you feel the decision was useful or not useful, and why. Indicate any adjustments that could have made the effects of your decision more positive.

_____

_____

_____

_____

Exercise 3: Brainstorming on the Idea Wheel

Your creative mind can solve problems when you least expect it. Many people report having sudden ideas while exercising, driving, showering, upon waking, or even when dreaming. When the pressure is off, the mind is often freer to roam through uncharted territory and bring back treasures.

To make the most of this "mind-float," grab ideas right when they surface. If you don't, they can roll back into your subconscious as if on a wheel. Since you never know how big the wheel is, you can't be sure when that particular idea will roll to the top again. That's one of the reasons writers carry notebooks—they need to grab thoughts when they come to the top of the wheel.

Name a problem, large or small, to which you haven't yet found a satisfactory solution. Do a brainstorm without the time limit. Be on the lookout for ideas, causes, effects, solutions, or similar problems coming to the top of your wheel. The minute it happens, grab this book and write your idea next to the problem. Take a look at your ideas later and see how your creative mind may have pointed you toward some original and workable solutions. You may want to keep a book by your bed to catch ideas that pop up before, during, or after sleep.

Problem: _____

Ideas: _____

_____

_____

_____

_____

_____

_____

Exercise 4: Constructing an Argument About Assumptions and Perspectives

Name an assumption that you know is common, or that you have made yourself. It can be about anything—people, lifestyles, education, differences, money, relationships, etc. Write it here:

_____

_____

Now you will construct two arguments: one that supports the assumption, and one that disputes it. Use your mind actions to ask important questions as you construct your arguments—think of cases or examples that fit and don't fit the assumption, positive and negative effects of believing the assumption, similar and different assumptions, and what experiences might cause the assumption.

Argument supporting _____

_____

_____

_____

Argument disputing _____

_____

_____

_____

Analyze each argument. Which perspective seems more open-minded? Which works better for situations in your life? Which perspective is closer to your own? Can you learn anything from the perspective that is different from your own?

_____

_____

_____

_____

Key to Cooperative Learning:
Building Teamwork Skills

Group Problem Solving As a class, brainstorm a list of problems in your lives. Write the problems on the board or on a large piece of paper attached to an easel. Include any problems you feel comfortable discussing with others. Such problems may be in the categories of schoolwork, relationships, job stress, discrimination, parenting, housing, procrastination, and others. Divide into groups of two to four, with each group choosing or being assigned one problem on which to work. Use the empty problem-solving flow chart on the next page to fill in your work.

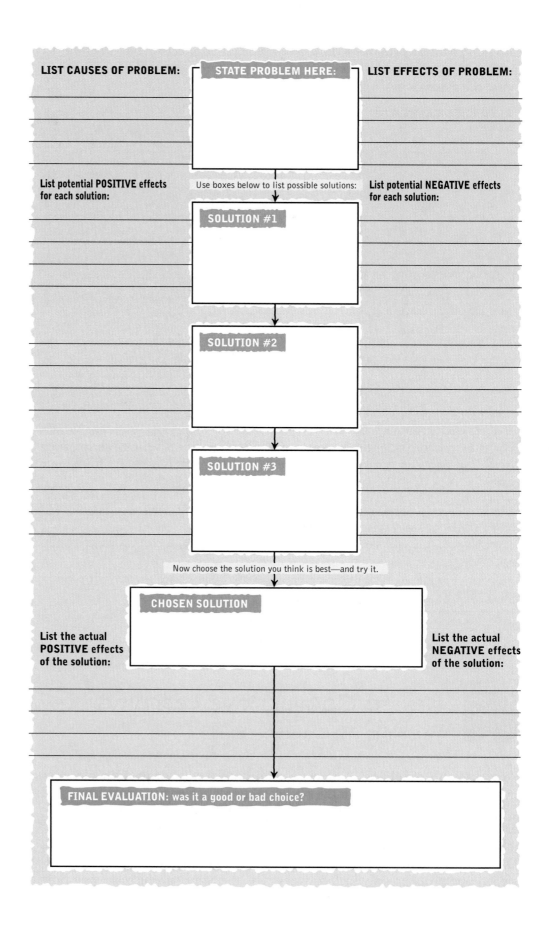

1. **Identify the problem.** As a group, state your problem specifically, without causes ("I'm not attending all of my classes" is better than "lack of motivation"). Then, look at the causes and effects that surround it. Record the effects that the problem has on your lives. List what causes the problem. Remember to look for "hidden" causes (you may perceive that traffic makes you late for school, but the hidden cause might be that you don't get up early enough to have adequate commuting time in the morning).

2. **Brainstorm possible solutions.** Determine the most likely causes of the problem; from those causes, derive possible solutions. Record all the ideas that group members offer. After ten minutes or so, each group member should choose one possible solution to explore independently.

3. **Explore each solution.** In thinking independently through the assigned solution, each group member should (a) weigh the positive and negative effects, (b) consider similar problems, (c) determine whether the problem requires a different strategy from other problems like it, and (d) describe how the solution affects the causes of the problem. Evaluate your assigned solution. Is it a good one? Will it work?

4. **Choose your top solution(s).** Come together again as a group. Take turns sharing your observations and recommendations, then take a vote: Which solution is the best? You may have a tie or may combine two different solutions. Either way is fine. Different solutions suit different people and situations. Although it's not always possible to reach agreement, try to find the solution that works for most of the group.

5. **Evaluate the solution you decide is best.** When you decide on your top solution or solutions, discuss what would happen if you went through with it. What do you predict would be the positive and negative effects of this solution? Would it turn out to be a truly good solution for everyone?

Key to Self-Expression:
Discovery Through Journal Writing

To record your thoughts, use a separate journal or the lined page at the end of the chapter.

Strategic Planning Discuss your abilities and limitations in how you set and plan your short-term and long-term goals. Do you tend to plan ahead of time? Why or why not? What do you like and dislike about strategically planning ahead? Do you have a hard time seeing beyond the present, or do you like to predict what will happen in the future? Discuss a long-term goal in terms of what you want in one year, five years, ten years, and twenty years. How do you plan to accomplish this goal? What steps will you take? What do you want to achieve?

Key to Your Personal Portfolio:
Your Paper Trail to Success

A Critical Evaluation of Your Habits You studied habits and how to change them in Chapter 2. Evaluate your habits now using your critical- and creative-thinking skills; decide what changes you want to make.

Your first step is to recall your habits. They can be work-related, school-related, family-related, personal—anything at all. Don't censor; make a list of good and bad habits alike.

Rewrite your list, dividing the habits into two columns: Helpful (good) and Harmful (bad).

Evaluate your habits: Rank each habit according to how strong a hold it has on you. In terms of their effects, which do you feel are the two most helpful and two most harmful habits? Circle them.

Start a new page for each of the four habits you circled. For each, answer these questions:

- What circumstances caused this habit?

- What effects, positive or negative, does this habit have? In other words, what rewards or negative consequences come about because of it?

- Do you want to keep or to change/stop this habit?

Use your problem-solving skills. For each habit you want to change, build a habit-altering solution to the problems that the habit causes. Create a problem-solving flow chart or think link. You may want to include a plan for developing a new habit in its place.

Record your habit-changing progress on the page you have devoted to that habit. You can list events as they occur or make a calendar in which you mark days that you avoided or changed habitual behaviour. Make a tangible record of the effects of your work on the habit. Refer to the section on habits in Chapter 2 for more detailed information.

Keep your habit lists and your four habit-evaluation pages in your portfolio. As you gradually make changes, update your lists. If you successfully change a harmful habit, cross it off, circle the habit that you now consider the worst, and set to work on it.

Habits take consistent effort to change. You may find that your will to change fades in and out, depending on the circumstances of your life. Don't criticize yourself if you slip. Just ask yourself questions about why it happened, and work to get back on track toward your goal. Given the chance, your mind has the power to bring strong and positive changes to your life.

Name _____ Date _____

Journal Entry

---

5 Reading and Studying:

Maximizing Written Resources

In this chapter, you will explore answers to the following questions:

- ❁ What are some challenges of reading?

- ❁ Why define your purpose for reading?

- ❁ How can PQ3R help you study?

- ❁ How can you read critically?

- ❁ What resources does your library offer?

The society you live in revolves around the written word. Although the growth of computer technology may seem to have made technical knowledge more important than reading, the focus on word processing and computer handling of documents has actually increased the need for employees who function at a high level of literacy. The Conference Board of Canada says that workers need to be able to "read, comprehend, and use written materials" in order to be effective workers in the Canadian workplace.[1]

Two crucial keys to your post-secondary success are reading and studying. If you read thoroughly and understand what you read, and if you achieve your study goals, you can improve your capacity to learn and understand. In this chapter you will learn how you can overcome barriers to successful reading and benefit from defining a purpose each time you read. You will explore the PQ3R study technique and see how critical reading can help you maximize your understanding of any text. Finally, the chapter will provide an overview of your library's resources.

Thinking It Through

Check those statements that apply to you right now:

☐ I frequently experience "circuit overload" because my instructors give me so much to read in so little time.

☐ I find myself struggling to get through many of my texts.

☐ When I read rapidly, I have trouble understanding or remembering what I read.

☐ When I learn a new vocabulary word, I often don't remember the definition for long.

☐ When I study, I often have to read the same material over and over again in order to get a grasp of it.

☐ I don't usually study with a group of classmates.

☐ I'm not that familiar with my school's library.

What are Some Challenges of Reading?

Whatever your skill level, you will encounter challenges that make reading more difficult, such as an excess of reading assignments, difficult texts, distractions, a lack of speed and comprehension, and insufficient vocabulary. Following are some ideas about how to meet these challenges. Note that if you have a reading disability, if English is not your primary language, or if you have limited reading skills, you may need additional support and guidance. Most colleges and universities provide services for students through a reading centre or tutoring program. Take the initiative to seek help if you need it. Many accomplished learners have benefited from help in specific areas.

Dealing with Reading Overload

Reading overload is part of almost every post-secondary experience. On a typical day, you may be faced with reading assignments that look like this:

- An entire textbook chapter on Louis Riel and the Métis uprising of 1870 (Canadian history)
- An original research study on the stages of sleep (psychology)
- Section I of Margaret Atwood's *The Handmaid's Tale* (Canadian literature)

Reading all this and more leaves little time for anything else unless you read selectively and skillfully. You can't control your reading load. You can, however, improve your reading skills. The material in this chapter will present techniques that can help you read and study as efficiently as you possibly can, while still having time left over for other things.

Working Through Difficult Texts

Textbook Terror
www.adm.uwaterloo.ca/
infocs/Study/reading.html

Your textbooks may be challenging. This University of Waterloo Web site offers clear and simple advice on how to read your textbooks more effectively.

While many textbooks are useful teaching tools, some can be poorly written and organized. Students using texts that aren't well written may blame themselves for the difficulty they're experiencing. Because texts are often written with the purpose of challenging the intellect, even well-written and organized texts may be difficult and dense to read. Generally, the further you advance in your education, the more complex your required reading is likely to be. For example, your sociology professor may assign a chapter on the dynamics of social groups, including those of dyads and triads. When is the last time you heard the terms *dyads* and *triads* in normal conversation? You may feel at times as though you are reading a foreign language as you encounter new concepts, words, and terms.

Assignments can also be difficult when the required reading is from primary sources rather than from texts. *Primary sources* are original documents rather than another writer's interpretation of these documents. They include:

- historical documents
- works of literature (novels, poems, and plays)

- scientific studies, including laboratory reports and accounts of experiments
- journal articles

The academic writing found in journal articles and scientific studies is different from other kinds of writing. Some academic writers assume that readers understand sophisticated concepts. They may not define basic terms, provide background information, or supply a wealth of examples to support their ideas. As a result, concepts may be difficult to understand.

Making your way through poorly written or difficult reading material is hard work that can be accomplished through focus, motivation, commitment, and skill. The following strategies may help.

Approach your reading assignments head-on. Be careful not to prejudge them as impossible or boring before you even start to read.

Accept the fact that some texts may require some extra work and concentration. Set a goal to make your way through the material and learn, whatever it takes.

When a primary source discusses difficult concepts that it does not explain, put in some extra work to define such concepts on your own. Ask your instructor or other students for help. Consult reference materials in that particular subject area, other class materials, dictionaries, and encyclopedias. You may want to make this process more convenient by creating your own mini-library at home. Collect reference materials that you use often, such as a dictionary, a thesaurus, a Canadian writer's style handbook, and perhaps an atlas or computer manual. You may also benefit from owning reference materials in your particular areas of study. "If you find yourself going to the library to look up the same reference again and again, consider purchasing that book for your personal or office library," advises library expert Sherwood Harris.[2]

Look for order and meaning in seemingly chaotic reading materials. The information you will find in this chapter on the PQ3R reading technique and on critical reading will help you discover patterns and achieve a greater depth of understanding. Finding order within chaos is an important skill, not just in the mastery of reading, but in life as well. This skill can give you power by helping you "read" (think through) work dilemmas, personal problems, and educational situations.

"No Barrier of the senses shuts me out from the sweet, gracious discourse of my book friends. They talk to me without embarrassment or awkwardness."

Helen Keller

Managing Distractions

With so much happening around you, it's often hard to keep your mind on what you are reading. Distractions take many forms. Some are external: the sound of a telephone, a friend who sits next to you at lunch and wants to talk, a young child who asks for help with homework. Other distractions come from within. As you try to study, you may be thinking about your parent's health, an argument you had with a friend or partner, a paper due in art history, or a site on the Internet that you want to visit.

Real World Perspective

How can I cope with a learning disability?

Clacy Albert, Communications Major

All my life I've felt different. I just couldn't seem to learn the way other kids did. I felt stupid and afraid that other people would think I couldn't do anything right. I wouldn't raise my hand in class because I was afraid of being laughed at. I wouldn't volunteer for games because I was afraid I'd let my team down. Study groups were impossible for me. I didn't want anyone to know that I was different. Because of this, my self-esteem really suffered. I became very quiet.

It wasn't until I was in grade 10 that a teacher recognized that something was wrong with the way I learned. It was my math teacher who saw that I couldn't recognize certain patterns. I would see things in reverse or not be able to recognize a pattern at all. He sat down with my parents and helped them understand that something was wrong. Unfortunately, the school I attended didn't have any testing for learning disabilities, so I let it go until I was in university. When I enrolled they told us about the learning disability resource centre. My mom suggested I finally get the testing I needed. I'm glad I did, because now I know that I have dyslexia and need special assistance to handle my studies. I wish there was mandatory testing for this disability in grade school. If there had been I wouldn't have suffered so deeply all these years. What suggestions do you have for helping me cope with this disability?

Edith Hall, Senior Sales Representative—Prentice Hall

I have a different disability but one that causes similar problems. I have Attention Deficit Hyperactivity Disorder (ADHD) and the fact that it was undiagnosed and untreated for many years has caused many problems in my life. It wasn't until I was six years out of university that I was diagnosed with ADHD. And the great thing about it is I don't feel crazy anymore.  Now I know why I can't sit still for long periods and why I can't complete large and/or long projects like non-ADHD people can.

I think acknowledging that I had a disorder and then accepting it were the biggest steps to coping and living with this disorder. The other thing I have done is to get educated. I have read almost anything I can get my hands on. I am also involved in a support group. Having other people I can talk with about how my brain affects my behaviour and my life truly is one of the best coping strategies I know.

Having a disability or disorder is not a bad thing. Ennis Cosby, slain son of comedian Bill Cosby, said of his dyslexia, "The day I found out I had dyslexia was the best day of my life." Finding out he had dyslexia relieved him of the belief that he was dumb or stupid or slow. For me, like Ennis Cosby, finding out I had ADHD was a great day in my life because I now had tools and help to be different...and I no longer felt alone.

Identify the Distraction and Choose a Suitable Action

Pinpoint what's distracting you before you decide what kind of action to take. If the distraction is *external* and *out of your control*, such as construction outside your building or a noisy group in the library, try to move away from it. If the distraction is *external* but *within your control*, such as the television, telephone, or children, take action. For example, if the television or phone is a problem, turn off the TV or unplug the phone for an hour. Figure 5–1 explores some ways that parents or other people caring for children may be able to maximize their study efforts.

Figure 5–1

Managing Children While Studying

Explain what your education entails. Tell them how it will improve both your life and theirs. This applies, of course, to older children who can understand the situation and compare it to their own schooling.

Keep them up to date on your schedule. Let them know when you have a big test or project due and when you are under less pressure, and what they can expect of you in each case.

Keep them active while you study. Give them games, books, or toys to occupy them. If there are special activities that you like to limit, such as watching videos on TV, save them for your study time.

Find help. Ask a relative or friend to watch your children or arrange for a child to visit a friend's house. Consider trading baby-sitting hours with another parent, hiring a sitter to come to your home, or using a daycare centre that is private or school-sponsored.

Offset study time with family time and rewards. Children may let you get your work done if they have something to look forward to, such as a movie night, a trip for ice cream, or something else they like.

Study on the phone. You might be able to have a study session with a fellow student over the phone while your child is sleeping or playing quietly.

Special Notes for Infants

Study at night if your baby goes to sleep early, or in the morning if your baby sleeps late.

Study during nap times if you aren't too tired yourself.

Lay your notes out and recite information to the baby. The baby will appreciate the attention, and you will get work done.

Put baby in a safe and fun place while you study, such as a playpen, motorized swing, or jumping seat.

If the distraction is *internal*, there are a few strategies to try that may help you clear your mind. You may want to take a break from your studying and tend to one of the issues that you are worrying about. Physical exercise may relax you and bring back your ability to focus. For some people, studying while listening to music helps to quiet a busy mind. For others, silence may do the trick. If you need silence to read or study and cannot find a truly quiet environment, consider purchasing sound-muffling headphones or even earplugs.

Find the Best Place and Time to Read

Any reader needs focus and discipline in order to concentrate on the material. Finding a place and time that minimize outside distractions will help you achieve that focus. Here are some suggestions:

Read alone unless you are working with other readers. Family members, friends, or others who are not in study mode may interrupt your concentration. If you prefer to read alone, establish a relatively interruption-proof place and time, such as an out-of-the-way spot at the library or an after-class hour in an empty classroom. If you study at home and live with other people, you may want to place a "Quiet" sign on the door. Some students benefit from reading with other students. If this helps you, plan to schedule a group reading meeting in which you read sections of the assigned material and then break to discuss them.

Find a comfortable location. Many students study in the library on a hard-backed chair. Others prefer a library easy chair, a chair in their room, or even the floor. The spot you choose should be comfortable enough for hours of reading, but not so comfortable that you fall asleep. Also, make sure that you have adequate lighting and aren't too hot or too cold.

Choose a regular reading place and time. Choose a spot you like and return to it often. Also, choose a time when your mind is alert and focused. Some students prefer to read just before or after the class for which the reading is assigned. Eventually, you will associate preferred places and times with focused reading.

If it helps you concentrate, listen to soothing background music. The right music can drown out background noises and relax you. However, the wrong music can make it impossible to concentrate; for some people, silence is better. Experiment to learn what you prefer: If music helps, stick with the type that works best. A personal headset makes listening possible no matter where you are.

Turn off the television. For most people, reading and TV don't mix.

Building Comprehension and Speed

Most students lead busy lives, carrying heavy academic loads while perhaps holding down a job or even caring for a family. It's difficult to make time to study at all, let alone handle the enormous reading assignments for your different classes. Increasing your reading comprehension and speed will save you valuable time and effort.

Rapid reading won't do you any good if you can't remember the material or answer questions about it. However, reading too slowly can be equally inefficient because it often eats up valuable study time and gives your mind space to wander. Your goal is to read for maximum speed *and* comprehension. Focus on comprehension first, because greater comprehension is the primary goal and also promotes greater speed.

Methods for Increasing Reading Comprehension

Following are some specific strategies for increasing your understanding of what you read:

Continually build your knowledge through reading and studying. More than any other factor, what you already know before you read a passage will determine your ability to understand and remember important ideas. Previous knowledge, including vocabulary, facts, and ideas, gives you a context for what you read.

Establish your purpose for reading. When you establish what you want to get out of your reading, you will be able to determine what level of understanding you need to reach and, therefore, on what you need to focus.

Remove the barriers of negative self-talk. Instead of telling yourself that you cannot understand, think positively. Tell yourself: *I can learn this material. I am a good reader.*

Think critically. Ask yourself questions. Do you understand the sentence, paragraph, or chapter you just read? Are ideas and supporting examples clear to you? Could you clearly explain what you just read to someone else?

context
Written or spoken knowledge that can help to illuminate the meaning of a word or passage.

Methods for Increasing Reading Speed

The following suggestions will help increase your reading speed.

- Try to read groups of words rather than single words.
- Avoid pointing your finger to guide your reading, since this will slow your pace.
- Try swinging your eyes from side to side as you read a passage, instead of stopping at various points to read individual words.

⊙ When reading narrow columns, focus your eyes in the middle of the column and read down the page. With practice, you'll be able to read the entire column width.

⊙ Avoid vocalization when reading.

⊙ Avoid thinking each word to yourself as you read it, a practice known as *subvocalization*. Subvocalization is one of the primary causes of slow reading speed.

vocalization

The practice of speaking the words and/or moving your lips while reading.

Expanding Your Vocabulary

Lifelong learners consider their vocabulary a work in progress, because they never finish learning new words. A strong vocabulary increases reading speed and comprehension—when you understand the words in your reading material, you don't have to stop as often to think about what they mean. No matter how strong or weak your vocabulary is, you can improve it by using a dictionary, reading and writing words in context, and learning common prefixes and suffixes.

Use a Dictionary

When reading a textbook, the first "dictionary" to search is the text glossary. Textbooks often include an end-of-book glossary that explains technical words and concepts. The definitions there are usually limited to the meaning of the term as it is used in the text.

Standard dictionaries provide a broader treatment. They give you all kinds of information about each word, including its origin, pronunciation, part of speech, synonyms (words that are similar), antonyms (words with opposite meanings), and multiple meanings. By using a dictionary whenever you read, you will increase your general comprehension. Buy a standard dictionary and keep it nearby. Don't hesitate to make notations in it when you need to. Consult your dictionary when you need help understanding a passage that contains unfamiliar key words.

You may not always have time for the following suggestions, but when you can use them, they will make your dictionary use as productive as possible.

Read every meaning of a word, not just the first. Think critically about which meaning suits the context of the word in question and choose the one that makes the most sense to you.

Substitute a word or phrase from the definition for the word. Use the definition you have chosen. Imagine, for example, that you encounter the following sentence and do not know what the word *indoctrinated* means:

The cult indoctrinated its members to reject society's values.

When you search the dictionary, you find several alternate definitions, including *brainwashed, instructed,* and *trained exhaustively.* You decide that the definition closest to the correct meaning is *brainwashed.* Substituting this term, the sentence reads:

The cult brainwashed its members to reject society's values.

Keep a journal of every new word you learn, including definitions. Review the journal on a regular basis and watch your vocabulary grow.

Read and Write Words in Context

Most people learn words best when they read and use them in written or spoken language. Although reading a definition tells you what a word means, you may have difficulty remembering that definition because you have no former knowledge, or context, to which you can connect or compare it. Using a word in context after defining it will help to anchor the information so that you can continue to build upon it.

Here are some strategies for using context to solidify your learning of new vocabulary words.

Use new words in a sentence or two right away. Do this immediately after reading their definitions, while everything is still fresh in your mind.

Reread the sentence where you originally saw the word. Go over it a few times to make sure that you understand how the word is used.

Use the word over the next few days whenever it may apply. Try it while talking with friends, writing letters or notes, or in your own thoughts.

Consider where you may have seen or heard the word before. When you learn a word, going back to sentences you previously didn't understand may help you to broaden your understanding of its meaning. For example, when most children learn to sing "O Canada," they memorize the words by rote without understanding exactly what "patriot" means. Later, when they learn the definition of "patriot," the anthem provides a context for the word that helps them understand it more fully.

Seek knowledgeable advice. If after looking up a word you still have trouble with its meaning, ask your instructor or a friend if he or she can help you figure it out.

If you keep a vocabulary journal, include sentences that place the word in context. Write sentences near the word's definition.

Learn Prefixes and Suffixes

Often, if you understand part of a word, you will be able to figure out what the entire word means. Particularly helpful is a working knowledge of common prefixes and suffixes. *Prefixes* are word parts that are added to the beginning of a root, while *suffixes* are added to the end of the root. Table 5–1 contains prefixes and suffixes you may encounter.

Facing the challenges of reading is only the first step. The next important step is to examine why you are reading any given piece of material.

Why Define Your Purpose for Reading?

As with all other aspects of your education, asking important questions will enable you to make the most of your efforts. When you define your purpose,

Online Dictionaries
www.onelook.com/

If you can't find your handy dictionary, the Internet offers a variety of online dictionaries. This site offers you access to almost 600 dictionaries. It also generates all possible meanings for the words.

root
The central part or basis of a word, around which prefixes and/or suffixes can be added to produce different words.

Table 5-1   Common Prefixes and Suffixes

Prefix	Primary Meaning	Example
a-, ab-	from, away	abstain, avert
ad-, af-, at-	to	adhere, affix, attain
con-, cor-, com-	with, together	convene, correlate, compare
di-	apart	divert, divorce
il-	not	illegal, illegible
ir-	not	irresponsible
post-	after	postpone, postpartum
sub-, sup-	under	subordinate, suppose

Suffix	Primary Meaning	Example
-able	able	recyclable
-arium	place for	aquarium, solarium
-cule	very small	molecule
-ist	one who	pianist
-meter	measure	thermometer
-ness	state of	carelessness
-sis	condition of	hypnosis
-y	inclined to	sleepy

you ask yourself *why* you are reading a particular piece of material. One way to do this is by completing this sentence: "In reading this material, I intend to define/learn/answer/achieve..." With a clear purpose in mind, you can decide how much time and what kind of effort to expend on various reading assignments. Nearly 375 years ago, Francis Bacon, the English philosopher and essayist, recognized that

> Some books are to be tasted, others to be swallowed, and some few to be chewed and digested; that is, some books are to be read only in parts, others to be read but not curiously; and some few to be read wholly, and with diligence and attention.

Achieving your reading purpose requires adapting to different types of reading materials. Being a flexible reader—adjusting your reading strategies and pace—will help you to adapt successfully.

Purpose Determines Reading Strategy

With purpose comes direction; with direction comes a strategy for reading. Following are four reading purposes, examined briefly. You may have one or more for each piece of reading material you approach.

Purpose 1: Read to Evaluate Critically. Critical evaluation involves approaching the material with an open mind, examining causes and effects, evaluating ideas, and asking questions that test the strength of the writer's argument and that try to identify assumptions. Critical reading is essential for you to demonstrate an understanding of material that goes beyond basic recall of information. You will read more about critical reading later in the chapter.

Purpose 2: Read for Comprehension. Much of the studying you do involves reading for the purpose of comprehending the material. The two main components of comprehension are *general ideas* and *specific facts/examples*. These components depend on one another. Facts and examples help to explain or support ideas, and ideas provide a framework that helps the reader to remember facts and examples.

> *General Ideas.* General-idea reading is rapid reading that seeks an overview of the material. You may skip entire sections as you focus on headings, subheadings, and summary statements in search of general ideas.

> *Specific Facts/Examples.* At times, readers may focus on locating specific pieces of information—for example, the stages of intellectual development in young children. Often, a reader may search for examples that support or explain more general ideas—for example, the causes of economic recession. Because you know exactly what you are looking for, you can skim the material at a rapid rate. Reading your texts for specific information may help before taking a test.

Purpose 3: Read for Practical Application. A third purpose for reading is to gather usable information that you can apply toward a specific goal. When you read a computer software manual, an instruction sheet for assembling a gas grill, or a cookbook recipe, your goal is to learn how to do something. Reading and action usually go hand in hand.

Purpose 4: Read for Pleasure. Some materials you read for entertainment, such as *The Hockey News* magazine or the latest John Grisham courtroom thriller. Entertaining reading may also go beyond materials that seem obviously designed to entertain. Whereas some people may read a Jane Austen novel for comprehension, as in a class assignment, others may read her books for pleasure.

> "All that mankind has done, thought, gained, or been: it is lying as in magic preservation in the pages of books."
>
> Thomas Carlyle

Purpose Determines Pace

George M. Usova, senior education specialist and graduate professor at The Johns Hopkins University in Baltimore, Maryland, explains: "Good readers are flexible readers. They read at a variety of rates and adapt them to the reading *purpose* at hand, the *difficulty* of the material, and their *familiarity* with the subject area."[3] As Table 5–2 shows, good readers link the pace of reading to their reading purpose.

Table 5-2   Linking Purpose to Pace

Type Of Material	Reading Purpose	Pace
Academic readings • textbooks • original sources • articles from scholarly journals • online publications for academic readers • laboratory reports • required fiction	• Critical analysis • Overall mastery • Preparation for tests	• Slow, especially if the material is new and unfamiliar
Manuals • instructions • recipes	• Practical application	• Slow to medium
Journalism and nonfiction for the general reader • nonfiction books • newspapers • magazines • online publications for the general public	• Understanding of general ideas, key concepts, and specific facts for personal understanding and/or practical application	• Medium to fast
Nonrequired fiction	• Understanding of general ideas, key concepts, and specific facts for enjoyment	• Variable, but tending toward the faster speeds

Source: Adapted from Nicholas Reid Schaffzin, *The Princeton Review Reading Smart*, New York, Random House, 1996, p. 15.

So far, this chapter has focused on reading. Recognizing obstacles to effective reading and defining the various purposes for reading lay the groundwork for effective *studying*—the process of mastering the concepts and skills contained in your texts.

How Can PQ3R Help You Study Reading Materials?

When you study, you take ownership of the material you read. You learn it well enough to apply it to what you do. For example, by the time students studying to be computer-hardware technicians complete their coursework, they should be able to assemble various machines and analyze hardware problems that lead to malfunctions.

Studying also gives you mastery over *concepts*. For example, a dental hygiene student learns the causes of gum disease, a biology student learns what happens during photosynthesis, and a business student learns about marketing research.

This section will focus on a technique that will help you learn and study more effectively as you read your textbooks.

Preview-Question-Read-Recite-Review (PQ3R)

PQ3R is a technique that will help you grasp ideas quickly, remember more, and review effectively and efficiently for tests. The symbols P-Q-3-R stand for *preview, question, read, recite,* and *review*—all steps in the studying process. Developed more than fifty-five years ago by Francis Robinson, the technique is still being used today because it works.[4] It is particularly helpful for studying texts. When reading literature, read the work once from beginning to end to appreciate the story and language. Then, reread it using PQ3R to master the material.

Moving through the stages of PQ3R requires that you know how to skim and scan. Skimming involves rapid reading of various chapter elements, including introductions, conclusions, and summaries; the first and last lines of paragraphs; boldfaced or italicized terms; pictures, charts, and diagrams. In contrast, scanning involves the careful search for specific facts and examples. You will probably use scanning during the *review* phase of PQ3R when you need to locate and remind yourself of particular information. In a chemistry text, for example, you may scan for examples of how to apply a particular formula.

Preview

The best way to ruin a "whodunit" novel is to flip through the pages to find out how everything turned out. However, when reading textbooks, previewing can help you learn, and is encouraged. *Previewing* refers to the process of surveying, or pre-reading, a book before you actually study it. Most textbooks include devices that give students an overview of the text as a whole as well as of the contents of individual chapters. As you look at Figure 5–2 on the following page, think about how many of these devices you already use.

skimming
Rapid, superficial reading of material that involves glancing through to determine central ideas and main elements.

scanning
Reading material in an investigative way, searching for specific information.

PQ3R Online
www.angelo.edu/
~jmiazga/1201/PQ3R/

This online PowerPoint presentation explains how the PQ3R process can make you a better reader.

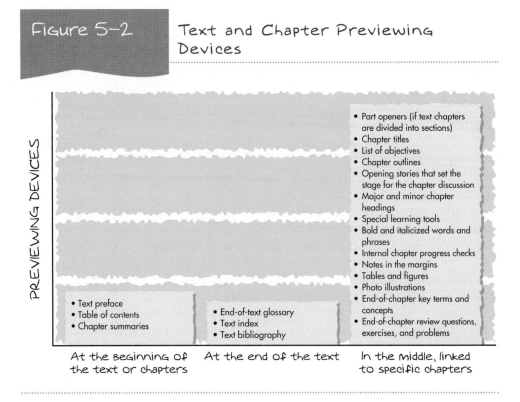

FIGURE 5-2   Text and Chapter Previewing Devices

PREVIEWING DEVICES

- Part openers (if text chapters are divided into sections)
- Chapter titles
- List of objectives
- Chapter outlines
- Opening stories that set the stage for the chapter discussion
- Major and minor chapter headings
- Special learning tools
- Bold and italicized words and phrases
- Internal chapter progress checks
- Notes in the margins
- Tables and figures
- Photo illustrations
- End-of-chapter key terms and concepts
- End-of-chapter review questions, exercises, and problems

- Text preface
- Table of contents
- Chapter summaries

- End-of-text glossary
- Text index
- Text bibliography

At the beginning of the text or chapters   At the end of the text   In the middle, linked to specific chapters

Question

Your next step is to examine the chapter headings and then write questions linked to those headings. These questions will focus your attention and increase your interest, helping you relate new ideas to what you already know and building your comprehension. You can take questions from the textbook or from your lecture notes, or come up with them on your own when you preview, based on the ideas you think are most important.

I. THE CONSUMER BUYING PROCESS	I. WHAT IS THE CONSUMER BUYING PROCESS?
A. Problem/Need Recognition	A. Why must consumers first recognize a problem or need before they buy a product?
B. Information Seeking	B. What is information seeking and who answers consumers' questions?
C. Evaluation of Alternatives	C. How do consumers evaluate different products to narrow their choices?
D. Purchase Decisions	D. Are purchasing decisions simple or complex?
E. Post-Purchase Evaluations	E. What happens after the sale?

Here is how this technique works. The column on the left contains primary- and secondary-level headings from a section of *Business*, an introductory text by Ricky W. Griffin and Ronald J. Ebert. The column on the right rephrases these headings in question form.

There is no "correct" set of questions. Given the same headings, you would create your own particular set of questions. The more useful kinds of questions are ones that engage the critical-thinking mind actions and processes found in Chapter 4.

Read

Your questions give you a starting point for *reading*, the first *R* of PQ3R. Read the material with the purpose of answering each question you raised. Pay special attention to the first and last lines of every paragraph, which should tell you what the paragraph is about. As you read, record key words, phrases, and concepts in your notebook. Some students divide the notebook into two columns, writing questions on the left and answers on the right. This method, known as the Cornell note-taking system, is described in more detail in Chapter 6.

If you own the textbook, marking it up—in whatever ways you prefer—is a must. The notations that you make will help you to interact with the material and make sense of it. You may want to write notes in the margins, circle key ideas, or highlight key sections. Some people prefer to underline, although underlining adds more ink to the lines of text and may overwhelm your eye. Although writing in a textbook makes it difficult to sell the book back to the bookstore, the increased depth of understanding you can gain is worth the investment.

Highlighting may help you pinpoint material to review before an exam. Here are some additional tips on highlighting.

Get in the habit of marking the text *after* you read the material. If you do it while you are reading, you may wind up marking less important passages.

Highlight key terms and concepts. Mark the examples that explain and support important ideas. You might try highlighting ideas in one colour, and examples in another.

Highlight figures and tables. They are especially important if they summarize text concepts.

Avoid overmarking. A phrase or two is enough in most paragraphs. Set off long passages with brackets rather than marking every line.

Write notes in the margins with a pen or pencil. Comments like "main point" and "important definition" will help you find key sections later on.

Be careful not to mistake highlighting for learning. You will not necessarily learn what you highlight unless you review it carefully. You may benefit from writing the important information you have highlighted into your lecture notes.

One final step in the reading phase is to divide your reading into digestible segments. Many students read from one topic heading to the next, then stop. Pace your reading so that you understand as you go. If you find you are losing the thread of the ideas you are reading, you may want to try smaller segments, or you may need to take a break and come back to it later.

Recite

Once you finish reading a topic, stop and answer the questions you raised about it in the Q stage of PQ3R. You may decide to recite each answer aloud, silently speak the answers to yourself, tell the answers to another person as though you were teaching him or her, or write your ideas and answers in brief notes. Writing is often the most effective way to solidify what you have read. Use whatever techniques best suit your learning-styles profile (see Chapter 2).

After you finish one section, move on to the next. Then repeat the question-read-recite cycle until you complete the entire chapter. If during this process you find yourself fumbling for thoughts, it means that you do not yet "own" the ideas. Reread the section that's giving you trouble until you master its contents. Understanding each section as you go is crucial because the material in one section often forms a foundation for the next.

Review

Review soon after you finish a chapter. Here are some techniques for reviewing.

- Skim and reread your notes. Then try summarizing them from memory.
- Answer the text's end-of-chapter review, discussion, and application questions.
- Quiz yourself, using the questions you raised in the Q stage. If you can't answer one of your own or one of the text's questions, go back and scan the material for answers.
- Review and summarize in writing the sections and phrases you have highlighted.
- Create a chapter outline in standard outline form or think-link form.
- Reread the preface, headings, tables, and summary.
- Recite important concepts to yourself, or record important information on a cassette tape and play it on your car's tape deck or your Walkman.
- Make flash cards that have an idea or word on one side and examples, a definition, or other related information on the other. Test yourself.
- Think critically: Break ideas down into examples, consider similar or different concepts, recall important terms, evaluate ideas, and explore causes and effects.
- Make think links that show how important concepts relate to one another.

Remember that you can ask your instructor if you need help clarifying your reading material. Your instructor is an important resource. Pinpoint the material you want to discuss, schedule a meeting with him or her during office hours, and come prepared with a list of questions. You may also want to ask what materials to focus on when you study for tests.

If possible, you should review both alone and with study groups. Reviewing in as many different ways as possible increases the likelihood of retention. Figure 5–3 shows some techniques that will help a study group maximize its time and efforts.

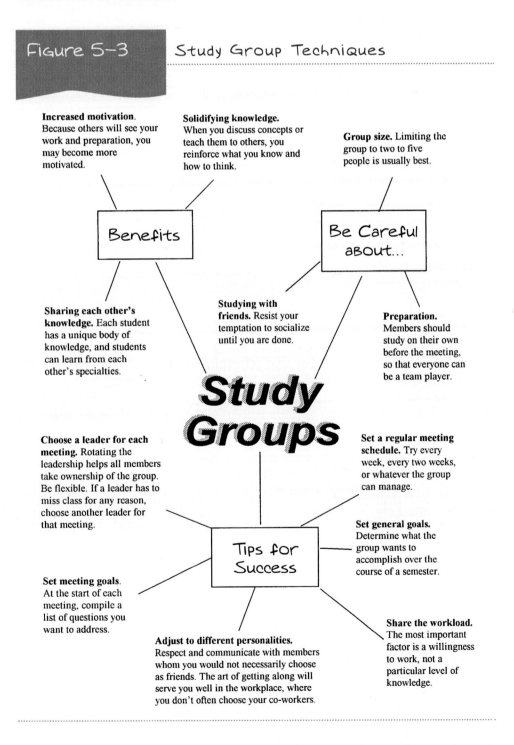

Figure 5–3   Study Group Techniques

Increased motivation. Because others will see your work and preparation, you may become more motivated.

Solidifying knowledge. When you discuss concepts or teach them to others, you reinforce what you know and how to think.

Group size. Limiting the group to two to five people is usually best.

Benefits

Be Careful about...

Sharing each other's knowledge. Each student has a unique body of knowledge, and students can learn from each other's specialties.

Studying with friends. Resist your temptation to socialize until you are done.

Preparation. Members should study on their own before the meeting, so that everyone can be a team player.

Study Groups

Choose a leader for each meeting. Rotating the leadership helps all members take ownership of the group. Be flexible. If a leader has to miss class for any reason, choose another leader for that meeting.

Set a regular meeting schedule. Try every week, every two weeks, or whatever the group can manage.

Tips for Success

Set general goals. Determine what the group wants to accomplish over the course of a semester.

Set meeting goals. At the start of each meeting, compile a list of questions you want to address.

Adjust to different personalities. Respect and communicate with members whom you would not necessarily choose as friends. The art of getting along will serve you well in the workplace, where you don't often choose your co-workers.

Share the workload. The most important factor is a willingness to work, not a particular level of knowledge.

Table 5-3 Use PQ3R to Become an Active Reader

Active readers tend to . . .

Divide material into manageable sections

Write questions

Answer questions through focused note taking

Recite, verbally and in writing, the answers to questions

Highlight key concepts

Focus on main ideas found in paragraphs, sections, and chapters

Recognize summary and support devices

Answer end-of-chapter questions and applications

Create chapter outlines

Create think links that map concepts in a logical way

Make flash cards and study them

Recite what they learned into a tape recorder and play the tape back

Rewrite and summarize notes and highlighted materials from memory

Explain what they read to a family member or friend

Analyze tables, figures, and photos

Form a study group

Repeating the review process renews and solidifies your knowledge. That is why it is important to set up regular review sessions—for example, once a week. As you review, remember that refreshing your knowledge is easier and faster than learning it the first time.

As you can see in Table 5–3, using PQ3R is part of being an active reader. Active reading involves the specific activities that help you retain what you learn.

Putting PQ3R to Work

The following is an excerpt from *Principles of Microeconomics, First Canadian Edition*.[5] Apply the PQ3R technique as you read it. Think through the major points of the passage and use the margins and/or the space below to make any notes, comments, or questions.

_____

_____

_____

_____

_____

FIRMS AND HOUSEHOLDS:
THE BASIC DECISION-MAKING UNITS

Throughout this book, we discuss and analyze the behaviour of two fundamental decision-making units: *firms*—the primary producing units in an economy—and *households*—the consuming units in an economy. Both are made up of people performing different functions and playing different roles. In essence, then, what we are developing is a theory of human behaviour.

firm *An organization that transforms resources (inputs) into products (outputs). Firms are the primary producing units in a market economy.*

A **firm** exists when a person or a group of people decides to produce a product or products by transforming *inputs* (that is, resources in the broadest sense) into *outputs* (the products that are sold in the market). Some firms produce goods; others produce services. Some are large, some are small, and some are in between. But all firms exist to transform resources into things that people want. The Toronto Symphony Orchestra takes labour, land, a building, musically talented people, electricity, and other inputs and combines them to produce concerts. The production process can be extremely complicated. The first flutist in the orchestra, for example, uses training, talent, previous performing experience, a score, an instrument, the conductor's interpretation, and her own feelings about the music to produce just one contribution to an overall performance.

Most firms exist to make a profit for their owners, but some do not. Your university, for example, fits the description of a firm: It takes inputs in the form of labour, land, skills, books, and buildings and produces a service that we call education. Although it sells that service for a price, it does not exist to make a profit, but rather to provide education of the highest quality possible.

Still, most firms exist to make a profit. They engage in production because they can sell their product for more than it costs to produce it. The analysis of firm behaviour that follows rests on the assumption that *firms make decisions in order to maximize profits.*

entrepreneur *A person who organizes, manages, and assumes the risks of a firm, taking a new idea or a new product and turning it into a successful business.*

An **entrepreneur** is one who organizes, manages, and assumes the risks of a firm. It is the entrepreneur who takes a new idea or a new product and turns it into a successful business. All firms have implicit in them some element of entrepreneurship. When a new firm is created—whether a proprietorship, a partnership, or a corporation—someone must organize the new firm, arrange financing, hire employees, and take risks. That person is an entrepreneur. Sometimes existing companies introduce new products, and sometimes new firms develop or improve an old idea, but at the root of it all is entrepreneurship, which some see as the core of the free enterprise system.

At the root of the debate about the potential of free enterprise in formerly socialist Eastern Europe is the question of entrepreneurship. Does an entrepreneurial spirit exist in that part of the world? If not, can it be developed? Without it the free enterprise system breaks down.

households *The consuming units in an economy.*

The consuming units in an economy are **households.** A household may consist of any number of people: a single person living alone, a married couple with four children, or 15 unrelated people sharing a house. Household decisions are presumably based on the individual tastes and preferences of the consuming unit. The household buys what it wants and can afford. In a large, heterogeneous, and open society such as Canada, wildly different tastes find expression in the marketplace. A six-block walk in any direction on any street in Montreal or a drive from Yonge and Bloor streets north into rural Ontario should be enough to convince anyone that it is difficult to generalize about what people like and do not like.

Even though households have wide-ranging preferences, they also have some things in common. All—even the very rich—have ultimately limited incomes, and all must pay in some way for the things they consume. While households may have some control over their incomes—they can work more or less—they are also constrained by the availability of jobs, current wages, their own abilities, and their accumulated and inherited wealth (or lack thereof).

Source: Principles of Microeconomics, First Canadian Edition, by Karl E. Case, Ray C. Fair, J. Frank Strain, and Michael R. Veall, © 1998. Reprinted by permission of Prentice Hall Canada Inc., Scarborough, Ontario.

After reading the excerpt using PQ3R, answer the following questions. Try not to look back at the material. Instead, examine whether the PQ3R system helped you remember the key points of the passage.

1. What are the two decision-making units called?

   _____

   _____

2. Most firms exist to make a profit. True or false? _____

3. Someone who organizes, manages, and assumes risks is called a(n):

   _____

4. A household:
   a. is the consuming unit in an economy.
   b. may consist of any number of people.
   c. has ultimately limited incomes.
   d. is constrained by the availability of jobs.
   e. all of the above.

How Can You Read Critically?

Your textbooks will often contain features that highlight important ideas and help you determine questions to ask while reading. As you advance in your education, however, many reading assignments will not be so clearly marked, especially if they are primary sources. You will need critical-reading skills in order to select the important ideas, identify examples that support them, and ask questions about the text without the aid of any special features or tools.

Critical reading enables you to consider reading material carefully, developing a thorough understanding of it through evaluation and analysis. A critical reader is able to discern what in a piece of reading material is true or useful, such as when using material as a source for an essay. A critical reader can also compare one piece of material to another and evaluate which makes more sense, which proves its thesis more successfully, or which is more useful for the reader's purpose.

Critical reading is reading that transcends taking in and regurgitating material. You can read critically by using PQ3R to get a basic idea of the material, asking questions based on the critical-thinking mind actions, and engaging your critical-thinking processes.

Use PQ3R to "Taste" Reading Material

Sylvan Barnet and Hugo Bedau, authors of *Critical Thinking, Reading, and Writing: A Brief Guide to Argument,* suggest that the active reading of PQ3R will help you form an initial idea of what a piece of reading material is all about. Through previewing, skimming for ideas and examples, highlighting and writing comments and questions in the margins, and reviewing, you can develop a basic understanding of its central ideas and contents.[6]

Summarizing, part of the review process in PQ3R, is one of the best ways to develop an understanding of a piece of reading material. To construct a summary, focus on the central ideas of the piece and the main examples that support those ideas. A summary does *not* contain any of your own ideas or your evaluation of the material. It simply condenses the material, making it easier for you to focus on the structure of the piece and its central ideas when you go back to read more critically. At that point, you can begin to evaluate the piece and introduce your own ideas. Using the mind actions will help you.

summary

A concise restatement of the material, in your own words, that covers the main points.

Ask Questions Based on the Mind Actions

The essence of critical reading, as with critical thinking, is asking questions. Instead of simply accepting what you read, seek a more thorough understanding by questioning the material as you go along. Using the mind actions of the Thinktrix to formulate your questions will help you understand the material.

What parts of the material you focus on will depend on your purpose for reading. For example, if you are writing a paper on Canada's role in World War II, you might spend your time focusing on how certain events fit your thesis. If you are comparing two pieces of writing that contain opposing arguments, you may focus on picking out their central ideas and evaluating how well the writers use examples to support these ideas.

You can question any of the following components of reading material:

- The central idea of the entire piece
- A particular idea or statement
- The examples that support an idea or statement
- The proof of a fact
- The definition of a concept

Following are some ways to critically question your reading material, based on the mind actions. Apply them to any component you want to question by substituting the component for the words "it" and "this."

<u>Similarity:</u>	What does this remind me of, or how is it similar to something else I know?
<u>Difference:</u>	What different conclusions are possible?
	How is this different from my experience?
<u>Cause and effect:</u>	Why did this happen, or what caused this?
	What are the effects or consequences of this?
	What effect does the author want to have, or what is the purpose of this material?
	What effects support a stated cause?

<u>Example to idea:</u>	How would I classify this, or, what is the best idea to fit this example(s)?
	How would I summarize this, or what are the key ideas?
	What is the thesis or central idea?
<u>Idea to example:</u>	What evidence supports this, or what examples fit this idea?
<u>Evaluation:</u>	How would I evaluate this? Is it valid or pertinent?
	Does this example support my thesis or central idea?

Engage Critical-Thinking Processes

Certain thinking processes from Chapter 4 can help to deepen your analysis and evaluation of what you read. These processes are establishing truth, constructing an argument, and shifting perspective. Within these processes you will ask questions that use the mind actions.

Establishing Truth

With what you know about how to seek truth, you can evaluate any statement in your reading material, identifying it as fact, opinion, or assumption and challenging how it is supported. Evaluate statements, central ideas, or entire pieces of reading material using questions such as the following:

- Is this true? How does the writer know?
- How could I test the validity of this?
- What assumptions underlie this?
- What else do I know that is similar to or different from this?
- What information that I already know supports or disproves this?
- What examples disprove this as fact or do not fit this assumption?

For example, imagine that a piece of writing states, "The dissolving of the family unit is the main cause of society's ills." You may question the truth of this statement by looking at what facts and examples support it. You may question the writer's sources of information. You may investigate its truth by reading other materials. You could discern that some hidden assumptions underlie this statement, such as an assumed definition of what a family is or of what constitutes "society's ills." You could also find examples that do not fit this assumption, such as successful families that don't fit the definition of "family" used by the writer.

Constructing an Argument

When your reading material contains one or more arguments, you can use what you know about arguments to evaluate whether the writer has constructed his or her argument effectively. Ask questions like the following:

- What is the purpose of the writer's argument?
- Do I believe this? How is the writer trying to persuade me?
- If the author uses cause-and-effect reasoning, does it seem logical?
- Do the examples adequately support the central idea of the argument?
- What different and perhaps opposing arguments seem just as valid?
- If I'm not sure whether I believe this, how could I construct an opposing argument?

Don't rule out the possibility that you may agree wholeheartedly with an argument. However, use critical thinking to make an informed decision, rather than accepting the argument outright.

Shifting Perspective

Your understanding of perspective will help you see that many reading materials are written from a particular perspective. Perspective often has a strong effect on how the material is presented. For example, if a recording artist and a music censorship advocate were to each write a piece about a controversial song created by that artist, their different perspectives would result in two very different pieces of writing.

To analyze perspective, ask questions like the following:

What perspective is guiding this? What are the underlying ideas that influence this material?

Who wrote this, and what may be the author's perspective? For example, a piece on a new drug written by an employee of the drug manufacturer may differ from a doctor's evaluation of the drug.

What does the title of the material tell me about its perspective? For example, a piece entitled "New Therapies for Diabetes" may be informational, and "What's Wrong With Insulin Injections" may intend to be persuasive.

How does the material's source affect its perspective? For example, an article on Quebec separatism published in *Le Devoir* may be more favourable and one-sided than one published in *The Globe and Mail*.

Seek Understanding

Reading critically allows you to investigate what you read so that you can reach the highest possible level of understanding. Think of your reading process as an archaeological dig. The first step is to excavate a site and uncover the artifacts. In reading, that corresponds to your initial preview and reading of the material. As important as the excavation is, the process would be incomplete if you stopped there and just took home a bunch of items covered in dirt. The second half of the process is to investigate each item, evaluate what all of those items mean, and derive new knowledge and ideas from what you discover. Critical reading allows you to complete that crucial second half of the process.

As you work through all of the different requirements of critical reading, remember that critical reading takes *time* and *focus*. Finding a time, place, and purpose for reading, something which is covered earlier in the chapter, is crucial to successful critical reading. Give yourself a chance to gain as much as possible from what you read.

No matter where or how you prefer to study, your school's library (or libraries) can provide many useful services to help you make the most of classes, reading, studying, and assignments.

What Does Your Library Offer?

"With one day's reading a man may have the key in his hands."

Ezra Pound

Your library can help you search for all kinds of information. First, learn about your library, its resources, and its layout. While some schools have only one library, other schools have a library network that includes one or more central libraries and smaller, specialized libraries that focus on specific academic areas. Take advantage of library tours, training sessions, and descriptive pamphlets. Spend time walking around the library on your own. If you still have questions, ask a librarian. A simple question can save hours of searching. The following sections will help you understand how your library operates.

General Reference Works

General reference works give you an overview and lead you to more specific information. These works cover topics in a broad, nondetailed way. General reference guides are found in the front of most libraries and are often available on CD-ROM, a compact disc that contains millions of words and images. You access this information by inserting the disc into a specially designed computer. Among the works that fall into this category are:

- encyclopedias—for example, the multivolume *The Canadian Encyclopedia Plus* (on CD-ROM)
- almanacs—*The Canadian Global Almanac*
- dictionaries—*Gage Canadian Dictionary*
- biographical reference works—*Merriam-Webster's Biographical Dictionary*

Specialized Reference Works

Look at *specialized reference works* to find more specific facts. Specialized reference works include encyclopedias and dictionaries that focus on a narrow field. The short summaries you will find there focus on critical ideas. Bibliographies that accompany the articles point you to the names and works of recognized experts. Examples of specialized references include *Canada's Law on Child Sexual Abuse: A Handbook,* and the *Canadian Education Index*.

Library Book Catalogue

Found near the front of the library, the *book catalogue* lists every book the library owns. The listings usually appear in three separate categories: authors' names, book titles, and subjects. Not too long ago, most libraries stored their book catalogue on index-sized cards in hundreds of small drawers. Today, many libraries have replaced these cards with computers. Using a terminal that has access to the library's computer records, you can search by author, title, and subject.

The computerized catalogue in your school's library is probably connected to the holdings of other college and university libraries. This gives you an online search capacity, which means that if you don't find the book you want in your local library, you can track it down in another library and request it through an interlibrary loan. *Interlibrary loan* is a system used by many colleges and universities to allow students to borrow materials from a library other than the one at their school. Students request materials through their own library, to which the materials are eventually delivered by the outside library. If you are in a rush, keep in mind that interlibrary loan may take a substantial amount of time.

Periodical Indexes

Periodicals are magazines, journals, and newspapers that are published on a regular basis throughout the year. Examples include *The Financial Post, The Globe and Mail*, and *Maclean's*. Many libraries display periodicals that are up to a year or two old and convert older copies to microfilm or microfiche (photocopies of materials reduced greatly in size and printed on film readable in a special reading machine—*microfilm* is a strip of film, and *microfiche* refers to individual leaves of film). Finding articles in Canadian publications involves a search of periodical indexes. A widely used index is the *Canadian Periodical Index*. It indexes articles in more than 400 general-interest magazines and journals.

Electronic Research

You will also find complete source material through a variety of electronic sources, including the Internet, online services, and CD-ROM. Here is a sampling of the kind of information you will find:

- Complete articles from thousands of journals and magazines
- Complete articles from newspapers around the world
- Government data on topics as varied as agriculture, transportation, and labour
- Business documents, including corporate annual reports

Your library is probably connected to the *Internet*, a worldwide computer network that links government, university, research, and business computers.

Tapping into the *World Wide Web*—a tool for searching the huge libraries of information stored on the Internet—gives you access to billions of written words and graphic images. If your college or university has its own Internet home page, start by spending some time browsing through it.

Although most libraries do not charge a fee to access the Internet, they may charge when you connect to commercial online services. Ask your librarian about all fees and restrictions. Libraries also have electronic databases on CD-ROM. A database is a collection of data—or, in the case of most libraries, a list of related resources that all focus on one specific subject area—arranged so that you can search through it and retrieve specific items easily. For example, the DIALOG Information System includes hundreds of small databases in specialized areas. CD-ROM databases are generally smaller than online databases and are updated less frequently. However, there is never a user's fee.

читать

This word may look completely unfamiliar to you, but anyone who can read the Russian language and alphabet will know that it means "read." People who read languages that use different kinds of characters, such as Russian, Japanese, or Greek, learn to process those characters as easily as you process the letters of your native alphabet. Your mind learns to process individually each letter or character you see. This ability enables you to move to the next level of understanding—making sense of those letters or characters when they are grouped to form words, phrases, and sentences.

Think of this concept when you read. Remember that your mind is an incredible tool, processing unmeasurable amounts of information so that you can understand the concepts on the page. Give it the best opportunity to succeed by reading as often as you can and by focusing on all of the elements that help you read to the best of your ability.

Chapter 5: Applications

Name _____   Date _____

 Key into Your Life:
Opportunities to Apply What You Learn

Exercise 1: Studying a Text Page

The following page is from the Groups and Organizations chapter in the third Canadian edition of *Sociology*, a Prentice Hall Canada text.[7] Using what you learned in this chapter about study techniques, complete the questions on the next page.

works: people who live in small communities have more kin in their networks than people who live in large settlements (Marsden, 1987; Markovsky et al., 1993; Kadushin, 1995; O'Brien, Hassinger, and Dersham, 1996).

In a study of "intimate networks" in East York (a Toronto borough), Wellman (1979) found that almost everyone could name one to six intimates outside the home, only half of whom were kin. While most of their intimate contacts lived within Metropolitan Toronto, only 13 percent lived in the neighbourhood. In other words, Wellman's respondents felt close to people who were widely dispersed. Neither weak-tie networks nor the intimate variety are geographically bound.

Finally, new information technology has generated a global network of unprecedented size in the form of the Internet. The "Cyber-Society" box takes a closer look at the impacts of this twenty-first century form of communication. Global Map 7–1 shows access to the Internet around the world.

FORMAL ORGANIZATIONS

Throughout human history, most people lived in small groups of family members and neighbours; this pattern was still widespread in Canada a century ago. Today, families and neighbourhoods persist, of course, but our lives revolve far more around **formal organizations**, *large, secondary groups that are organized to achieve their goals efficiently.*

Formal organizations, such as corporations or government agencies, differ from families and neighbourhoods: their greater size renders social relationships less personal and fosters a planned, formal atmosphere. In other words, formal organizations operate to accomplish complex jobs rather than to meet personal needs.

When you think about it, organizing a society with thirty million members is a remarkable feat. Countless tasks are involved, from collecting taxes to delivering the mail. To meet most of these responsibilities, we rely on large, formal organizations. The Canadian government, our largest formal organization, employs about one million people in provincial, federal, and municipal government and the armed forces. Such vast organizations develop lives and cultures of their own, so that as members come and go,

the statuses they fill and the roles they perform remain unchanged over the years.

TYPES OF FORMAL ORGANIZATIONS

Amitai Etzioni (1975) has identified three types of formal organizations, distinguished by why people participate—utilitarian organizations, normative organizations, and coercive organizations.

Utilitarian Organizations

Just about everyone who works for income is a member of a *utilitarian organization*, which pays its members for their efforts. Large business enterprises, for example, generate profits for their owners and income in the form of salaries and wages for their employees. Joining utilitarian organizations is usually a matter of individual choice, although most people must join one or another utilitarian organization to make a living.

Normative Organizations

People join normative organizations not for income but to pursue goals they consider morally worthwhile. Sometimes called *voluntary associations*, these include community service groups (such as the Lions Club or Kiwanis), political parties, churches, and other organizations concerned with specific social issues. Historically, women played a greater role than men in voluntary and charitable organizations, in part because of their more limited involvement in the paid labour force.

Americans have long been characterized as "joiners" and still are involved, disproportionately, as members of voluntary associations (Curtis, Grabb, and Baer, 1992). Figure 7–3 provides a comparative glance at membership in cultural or educational organizations for selected countries, and reveals that Canadians are not too far behind their American neighbours.

Coercive Organizations

In Etzioni's typology, *coercive organizations* are distinguished by involuntary membership. That is, people are forced to join the organization as a form of punishment (prisons) or treatment (psychiatric hospitals). Coercive organizations have extraordinary physical features, such as locked doors and barred windows, and

Source: *Sociology*, 3rd Canadian Edition, John J. Macionis and Linda M. Gerber, © 1999. Reprinted by permission of Prentice Hall Canada Inc., Toronto, Ontario.

1. Identify the headings on the page and the relationship among them. Which headings are primary-level headings; which are secondary; which are tertiary? Which heading serves as an umbrella for the rest?

    _____

    _____

    _____

2. What do the headings tell you about the content of the page? _____

    _____

    _____

3. Identify the boldfaced and italicized terms. How do they differ?

    _____

    _____

4. After reading the chapter headings, write three study questions. List the questions below:

    _____

    _____

    _____

    _____

    _____

5. Highlight key phrases and sentences. Write short marginal notes to help you review the material at a later point.

6. After reading this page, list four key concepts that you will need to study:

    a. _____

    b. _____

    c. _____

    d. _____

Exercise 2: Building Your Vocabulary

Look again at the textbook page you just worked with. Are there any words that are new to you? If so, write them below and look them up in the dictionary. Write the definition next to the word and then include the word in your own sentence. If there are no unfamiliar words in this page, choose three words from any reading assignment you have this week.

1. _____

_____

2. _____

_____

3. _____

_____

Exercise 3: Focusing on Your Purpose for Reading

Read the following paragraphs on kinetic and potential energy and the first law of thermodynamics taken from *Life On Earth* by Teresa Audesirk and Gerald Audesirk.[8] When you have finished, answer the questions below.

Among the fundamental characteristics of all living organisms is the ability to guide chemical reactions within their bodies along certain pathways. The chemical reactions serve many functions, depending on the nature of the organism: to synthesize the molecules that make up the organism's body, to reproduce, to move, even to think. Chemical reactions either require or release **energy**, which can be defined simply as *the capacity to do work*, including synthesizing molecules, moving things around, and generating heat and light. In this chapter we discuss the physical laws that govern energy flow in the universe, how energy flow in turn governs chemical reactions, and how the chemical reactions within living cells are controlled by the molecules of the cell itself. Chapters 7 and 8 focus on photosynthesis, the chief "port of entry" for energy into the biosphere, and glycolysis and cellular respiration, the most important sequences of chemical reactions that release energy.

Energy and the Ability to Do Work

As you learned in Chapter 2, there are two types of energy: **kinetic energy** and **potential energy**. Both types of energy may exist in many different forms. Kinetic energy, or *energy of movement*, includes light (movement of photons), heat (movement of molecules), electricity (movement of electrically charged particles), and movement of large objects. Potential energy, or *stored energy*, includes chemical energy stored in the bonds that hold atoms together in molecules, electrical energy stored in a battery, and positional energy stored in a diver poised to spring (Fig. 4-1). Under the right conditions, kinetic energy can be transformed into potential energy, and vice versa. For example, the diver converted kinetic energy of movement into potential energy of position when she climbed the ladder up to the platform; when she jumps off, the potential energy will be converted back into kinetic energy.

To understand how energy flow governs interactions among pieces of matter, we need to know two things: (1) the quantity of available energy and (2) the usefulness of the energy. These are the subjects of the laws of thermodynamics, which we will now examine.

The Laws of Thermodynamics Describe the Basic Properties of Energy

All interactions among pieces of matter are governed by the two **laws of thermodynamics**, physical principles that define the basic properties and behavior of energy. The laws of thermodynamics deal with "isolated systems," which are any parts of the universe that cannot exchange either matter or energy with any other parts. Probably no part of the universe is completely isolated from all possible exchange with every other part, but the concept of an isolated system is useful in thinking about energy flow.

The First Law of Thermodynamics States That Energy Can Neither Be Created nor Destroyed

The **first law of thermodynamics** states that within any isolated system, energy can neither be created nor destroyed, although it can be changed in form (for example, from chemical energy to heat energy). In other words, within an isolated system *the total quantity of energy remains constant*. The first law is therefore often called the law of conservation of energy. To use a familiar example, let's see how the first law applies to driving your car (Fig. 4-2). We can consider that your car (with a full tank of gas), the road, and the surrounding air roughly constitute an isolated system. When you drive your car, you convert the potential chemical energy of gasoline into kinetic energy of movement and heat energy. The total amount of energy that was in the gasoline before it was burned is the same as the total amount of this kinetic energy and heat.

An important rule of energy conversions is this: Energy always flows "downhill," from places with a high concentration of energy to places with a low concentration of energy. This is the principle behind engines. As we described in Chapter 2, temperature is a measure of how fast molecules move. The burning gasoline in your car's engine consists of molecules moving at extremely high speeds: a high concentration of energy. The cooler air outside the engine consists of molecules moving at much lower speeds: a low concentration of energy. The molecules in the engine hit the piston harder than the air molecules outside the engine do, so the piston moves upward, driving the gears that move the car.

Work is done. When the engine is turned off, it cools down as heat is transferred from the warm engine to its cooler surroundings. The molecules on both sides of the piston move at the same speed, so the piston stays still. No work is done.

Source: *Life on Earth* by Teresa Audesirk and Gerald Audesirk, © 1997. Reprinted by permission of Prentice-Hall, Inc., Upper Saddle River, NJ.

a. *Reading for critical evaluation.* Evaluate the material by answering these questions:

Were the ideas clearly supported by examples? If you feel one or more were not supported, give an example.

_____

_____

_____

_____

Did the author make any assumptions that weren't examined? If so, name one or more.

_____

_____

Do you disagree with any part of the material? If so, which part, and why?

_____

_____

_____

Do you have any suggestions for how the material could have been presented more effectively?

_____

_____

_____

_____

b. *Reading for practical application.* Imagine you have to give a presentation on this material the next time the class meets. On a separate sheet of paper, create an outline or think link that maps out the key elements you would discuss.

c. *Reading for comprehension.* Answer the following questions to determine the level of your comprehension.

Name the two types of energy.

Which one "stores" energy?

Can kinetic energy be turned into potential energy?

What is the term that describes the basic properties and behaviours of energy?

Mark the following statements as true (T) or false (F).

_____ Within any isolated system, energy can be neither created nor destroyed.

_____ Energy always flows downhill, from high concentration levels to low.

_____ All interactions among pieces of matter are governed by two laws of thermodynamics.

_____ Some parts of the universe are isolated from other parts.

 # Key to Cooperative Learning:
Building Teamwork Skills

Reading and Group Discussion Divide into small groups, ideally groups of four. Take five minutes to independently read the excerpt from "The New Rung on the Corporate Ladder" on page 184. Each person should select one of the following questions to focus on while reading. If your group is smaller than four, eliminate unselected questions. If your group is larger than four, some questions may have to be shared between two group members.

1. What role do internships play in today's corporate hiring process?
2. If you were a manager for a company, why would you want to hire someone who has had practical experience during college or university?
3. What did Dan Kosta gain from taking a semester off from school for his internship?
4. How would an intern learn about business from the bottom up?

Use your critical-reading skills to explore your selected question. Focus on finding ideas that help to answer the question and examples that support those ideas. Consider other information you know, relevant to your question, that may be similar to or different from the material in the passage. If your questions look for causes or effects, scan for them in the passage. Be sure to make notes as you write.

When you have finished reading critically, gather as a group. Each person (or pair) should take a turn presenting the question, the response and/or answer to the question that was derived through critical reading, and any other ideas that came up while reading. The group then has an opportunity to present any other ideas they want to add to the discussion of that question. Continue until each person has had a chance to present what they worked on.

From "The New Rung on the Corporate Ladder," by Emma J. Taylor.

Gone are the days of the entry-level jobs; the internship has replaced it as the low rung on the corporate ladder. Summer internships have long been the de facto third semester of school, adding ballast and diversity to otherwise short résumés, but these days even three summer stints aren't always enough to secure you the right position. Recent grads are now turning to year-long postcollege internships, and undergrads are taking time off from school to fill low-paying or unpaid positions, all in the effort to prove they're ready to face the responsibility of full-time jobs. And employers are taking note.

"Work experience has a higher value than most educational experiences," says Patrick Scheetz, author of a nationwide hiring survey. "It is the employer's expectation," he explains. "If you went into heart surgery, you would ask if the surgeon had ever operated on a heart before. Why wouldn't an employer ask the same question of you?" Of last year's new hires, according to the survey, nearly 50 percent had completed career-related internships. "Work plays a big part in your development as a prospective employee," Scheetz says.

In other words, employers like to see you pay your dues.

Dan Kosta paid his when he took a semester off to intern with Paul Shaffer on *The Late Show with David Letterman*. He dealt with a lot of downtime and pulled some gofer details, but in the entertainment industry, as in many others, the mudsucking internship is virtually a prerequisite.

"It's backroom to backstage," Kosta says of his experience at *The Late Show*. "It's really about being there. I learned more about the entertainment industry in the first two weeks I was there than I could have taking any kind of class or reading any kind of book. It's just hands-on knowledge. You see how everything works, from the top to the bottom. And you're the bottom."

Source: Emma Taylor, "The New Rung on the Corporate Ladder," *Tools for Life*, 1.2 (Spring 1997): 17–18.

Key to Self-Expression:
Discovery Through Journal Writing

To record your thoughts, use a separate journal or the lined page at the end of the chapter.

Reading Challenges What is your most difficult challenge when reading assigned materials? A challenge might be a particular kind of reading material, a reading situation, or the achievement of a certain goal when reading. Considering the tools that this chapter presents, make a plan that addresses this challenge. What techniques might be able to help you most? How and when will you try them out? What positive effects do you anticipate they may have on you?

Key to Your Personal Portfolio:
Your Paper Trail to Success

Evaluate Your Reading and Study Skills On a separate sheet of paper, evaluate your current reading and studying skills. Analyze the current status of each of the following skill areas, what you are doing to improve your performance in each area, and your long-term and short-term goals for skill improvement. Define your short-term goal in terms of what you hope to accomplish after one month and your long-term goal in terms of what you hope to accomplish in one year.

Skill Areas

- Ability to define your reading purpose
- Progress in increasing your reading speed
- Progress in increasing your reading comprehension
- Vocabulary building
- Use of PQ3R
- Identification and use of text-previewing devices
- Participation in a study group
- Ability to understand and use visual aids

Use your item-by-item analysis as an action plan that will help you improve your skills. For example, if you currently spend no time building your vocabulary, your short-term goal may be to add five new words a week to your vocabulary, with your end-of-year goal the "ownership" of more than 200 new words. To accomplish this, you could do more reading and upgrade the quality of your reading material. One way to do this is to start reading a national paper like *The Globe and Mail*, which is available online and at your library. You may also want to keep a list of the unfamiliar words you encounter as you read, look them up in a dictionary, and use them in a sentence.

As part of your plan, prioritize the items on the list. For example, you may decide that your number-one priority is perfecting the use of PQ3R, while the item of least importance is forming a study group, since you study best alone.

As the year progresses, monitor your accomplishments in each area. You may decide to modify your action plan based on how the elements of the plan affect your school performance. If you work as well as attend class, consider the reading that you have to do on the job—newspapers, journals, or any other information—along with your school reading when you activate your plan and monitor your progress.

Name _____ Date _____

Journal Entry

6 Note Taking and Writing:

Harnessing the Power of Words and Ideas

In this chapter, you will explore answers to the following questions:

⊙   How can note taking help you?

⊙   Which note-taking system should you use?

⊙   How can you write faster when you take notes?

⊙   How can you become a good writer?

⊙   What are the elements of effective writing?

⊙   What is the writing process?

Words, joined to form ideas, are tools that have enormous power. Whether you write an essay, a memo to a supervisor, or a love letter over e-mail, words allow you to take your ideas out of the realm of thought and give them a form that other people can read and consider. You can harness their power and make it your own. Set a goal for yourself: Strive continually to improve your knowledge of how to use words to construct understandable ideas.

This chapter will teach you the note-taking skills you need to record information successfully. It will show you how to express your written ideas completely and how good writing is linked to clear thinking. In class or at work, taking notes and writing well will help you stand out from the crowd. Being able to "write effectively in the language business is conducted" is an essential skill, according to the Conference Board of Canada.[1]

Thinking It Through

Check those statements that apply to you right now:

- ☐ I would like to take good notes in class, but I can't seem to accurately record the instructor's ideas on paper.

- ☐ I use one note-taking system for every purpose.

- ☐ No matter how fast I go, I can't write down everything the instructor says.

- ☐ I don't know why I have to write well for my career choice.

- ☐ When I begin to write, I rarely think about the people who will read my work.

- ☐ The best writers can write a perfect paper the first time around.

- ☐ When I revise and edit a paper, I focus on getting my words right, and I leave everything else alone.

How Does Taking Notes Help You?

Notes help you learn when you are in class, doing research, or studying. Since it is virtually impossible to take notes on everything you hear or read, the act of note taking encourages you to decide what is worth remembering. Looking at the positive effects of note taking will help you see why good note taking is a useful habit (see Table 6–1).

Recording Information in Class

Your notes have two purposes: First, they should reflect what you heard in class; and second, they should be a resource for studying, writing, or comparing with your text material.

Preparing to Take Class Notes

Taking good class notes depends on good preparation, including the following:

- If your instructor assigns reading on a lecture topic, you may choose to complete the reading before class so that the lecture becomes more of a review than an introduction.

- Use separate pieces of letter-size paper for each class. If you use a three-ring binder, punch holes in papers your instructor hands out and insert them immediately following your notes for that day.

- Choose a comfortable seat where you can easily see and hear, and be ready to write as soon as the instructor begins speaking.

- Choose a note-taking system that helps you handle the instructor's speaking style. While one instructor may deliver organized lectures at a normal speaking rate, another may jump from topic to topic or speak very quickly.

- Set up a support system with a student in each class. That way, when you are absent, you can get the notes you missed.

Table 6–1   The Value of Notes
✓   Your notes provide material that helps you study information and prepare for tests.
✓   When you take notes, you become an active, involved listener and learner.
✓   Notes help you think critically and organize ideas.
✓   The information you learn in class may not appear in any text; you will have no way to study it without writing it down.
✓   If it is difficult for you to process information while in class; having notes to read and make sense of later can help you learn.
✓   Note taking is a skill for life that you will use on the job and in your personal life.

What to Do During Class

Because no one has the time to write down everything he or she hears, the following strategies will help you choose and record what you feel is important, in a format that you can read and understand later.

Lecture Notes: The 5 R's
www.iss.stthomas.edu/
studyguides/lcturnote.htm

This site offers tips on using a five-step process for taking lecture notes. The 5 R's are record, reduce, recite, reflect, and review.

- ☺ Date each page. When you take several pages of notes during a lecture, add an identifying letter or number to the date on each page: 11/27 A, 11/27 B,...or 11/27—1 of 3, 11/27—2 of 3.

- ☺ Add the specific topic of the lecture at the top of the page. For example:

  11/27 A—<u>Marshall McLuhan: The Medium is the Message</u>

- ☺ If your instructor jumps from topic to topic during a single class, try starting a new page for each topic.

- ☺ Ask yourself critical-thinking questions as you listen: Do I need this information? Is the information important or is it just a digression? Is the information fact or opinion? If it is opinion, is it worth remembering? (Chapter 4 offers ideas about how to distinguish between fact and opinion.)

- ☺ Record whatever an instructor emphasizes (see Figure 6–1 for details).

- ☺ Continue to take notes during class discussions and question-and-answer periods. What your fellow students ask the instructor about may help you as well.

- ☺ Leave one or more blank spaces between points. This white space will help you review your notes, because information will appear in self-contained sections.

- ☺ Draw pictures and diagrams that help illustrate ideas.

- ☺ Indicate material that is especially important with a star, with underlining, using a highlighter pen, or by writing words in capital letters.

- ☺ If you cannot understand what the instructor is saying, leave a space and place a question mark in the margin. Then ask the instructor to explain the idea again after class, or discuss it with a classmate. Fill in the blank when the idea is clear.

- ☺ Take notes until the instructor stops speaking. Students who stop writing a few minutes before the class is over may miss critical information.

- ☺ Make your notes as legible, organized, and complete as possible. Your notes are only useful if you can read and understand them.

Make Notes a Valuable After-Class Reference

Class notes are a valuable study tool when you review them regularly. Try to begin your review within a day of the lecture. Read over the notes to learn the information, clarify abbreviations, fill in missing information, and underline or highlight key points. Try to review each week's notes at the end

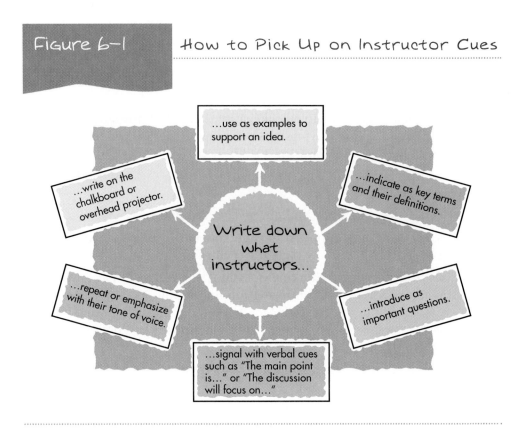

Figure 6-1   How to Pick Up on Instructor Cues

Write down what instructors...

...use as examples to support an idea.

...write on the chalkboard or overhead projector.

...indicate as key terms and their definitions.

...repeat or emphasize with their tone of voice.

...introduce as important questions.

...signal with verbal cues such as "The main point is..." or "The discussion will focus on..."

of that week. Think critically about the material, in writing, study group discussions, or quiet reflective thought, using the following questions.

- What do these ideas mean? What examples support or negate them?
- How do I evaluate these ideas? Why are they important?
- How do these ideas, facts, and statements fit together? Is there any missing information?

Summarizing your notes is another important review technique. Summarizing involves critically evaluating which ideas and examples are most important and writing them in a condensed form. You may prefer to summarize as you review your notes, although you might also try summarizing your notes from memory after you review them.

You can take notes in many ways. Different note-taking systems suit different people and situations. Explore each system and choose what works for you.

What Note-Taking System Should You Use?

You will benefit most from the system that feels most comfortable to you. As you consider each system, remember the learning-styles profile you compiled

"Omit needless words... This requires not that the writer make all his sentences short, or that he avoid all detail and treat his subjects only in outline, But that every word tell."

William Strunk, Jr.[2]

in Chapter 2. The most common note-taking systems include outlines, the Cornell system, and think links.

Taking Notes in Outline Form

When a reading assignment or lecture seems well organized, you may choose to take notes in outline form. *Outlining* shows the relationships among ideas and their supporting examples through the use of line-by-line phrases set off by varying indentations.

Formal outlines indicate ideas and examples using Roman numerals, capital and lower-case letters, and numbers. When you are pressed for time, such as during class, you can use an informal system of consistent indenting and dashes instead. Formal outlines also require at least two headings on the same level—that is, if you have a II A you must also have a II B. Figure 6–2 on the following page shows an outline on early Canadian history.

Taking Notes
www.yorku.ca/admin/cdc/
lsp/note/note6.htm

The Counselling and Development Centre at York University offers this primer on how to take notes in class and from your textbook.

Cornell Explained
www.eiu.edu/~lrnasst/
notes.html

This thorough Web site not only explains the Cornell note-taking system, but also discusses other strategies to help you take better notes before, during, and after class.

Guided Notes

From time to time, an instructor may give you a guide, usually in the form of an outline, to help you take notes in class. This outline may be on a page that you receive at the beginning of the class, on the board, or on an overhead projector.

Although *guided notes* help you follow the lecture and organize your thoughts during class, they do not replace your own notes. Because they are more of a basic outline of topics than a comprehensive coverage of information, they require that you fill in what they do not cover in detail. If you "tune out" in class because you think that the guided notes are all you need, you will most likely miss important information.

When you receive guided notes on paper, write directly on the paper if there is room. If not, use a separate sheet and write on it the outline categories that the guided notes suggest. If the guided notes are on the board or an overhead, copy them down, leaving plenty of space in between for your own notes.

Using the Cornell Note-Taking System

The *Cornell note-taking system*, also known as the T-note system, was developed more than forty-five years ago by Walter Pauk at Cornell University.[3] The system is successful because it is simple—and because it works. It consists of three sections on ordinary note paper:

- ◎ *Section 1*, the largest section, is on the right. Record your notes here in informal outline form.

- ✳ *Section 2*, to the left of your notes, is the *cue column*. Leave it blank while you read or listen, then fill it in later

Figure 6-2   Sample Formal Outline

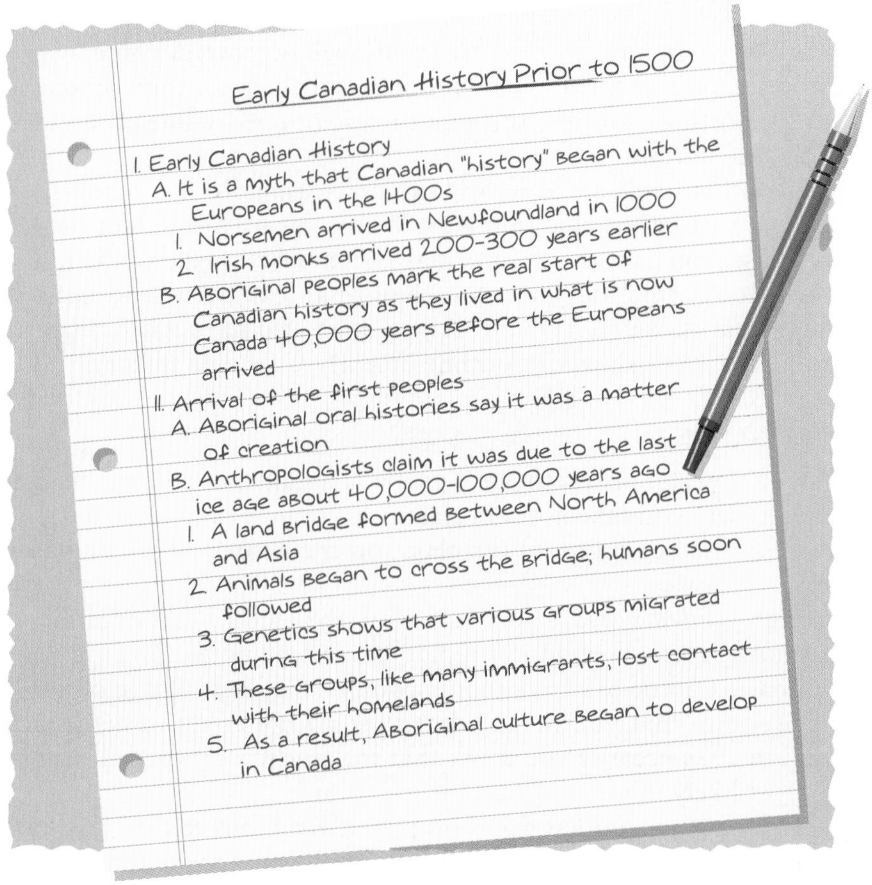

Early Canadian History Prior to 1500

I. Early Canadian History
   A. It is a myth that Canadian "history" began with the Europeans in the 1400s
      1. Norsemen arrived in Newfoundland in 1000
      2. Irish monks arrived 200-300 years earlier
   B. Aboriginal peoples mark the real start of Canadian history as they lived in what is now Canada 40,000 years before the Europeans arrived
II. Arrival of the first peoples
   A. Aboriginal oral histories say it was a matter of creation
   B. Anthropologists claim it was due to the last ice age about 40,000-100,000 years ago
      1. A land bridge formed between North America and Asia
      2. Animals began to cross the bridge; humans soon followed
      3. Genetics shows that various groups migrated during this time
      4. These groups, like many immigrants, lost contact with their homelands
      5. As a result, Aboriginal culture began to develop in Canada

as you review. You might fill it with comments that highlight main ideas, clarify meaning, suggest examples, or link ideas and examples. You can even draw diagrams.

⊙ *Section 3*, at the bottom of the page, is the *summary area*, where you summarize the notes on the page. When you review, use this section to reinforce concepts and provide an overview.

When you use the Cornell system, create the note-taking structure before class begins. Picture an upside-down letter T and use Figure 6–3 as your guide. Make the cue column about 7 centimetres wide and the summary area 5 centimetres tall. Figure 6–3 shows how a student used the Cornell system to take notes in an introduction-to-business course.

Creating a Think Link

A *think link*, also known as a mind map, is a visual form of note taking. When you draw a think link, you diagram ideas using shapes and lines that link ideas

Figure 6-3 Notes Taken Using the Cornell System

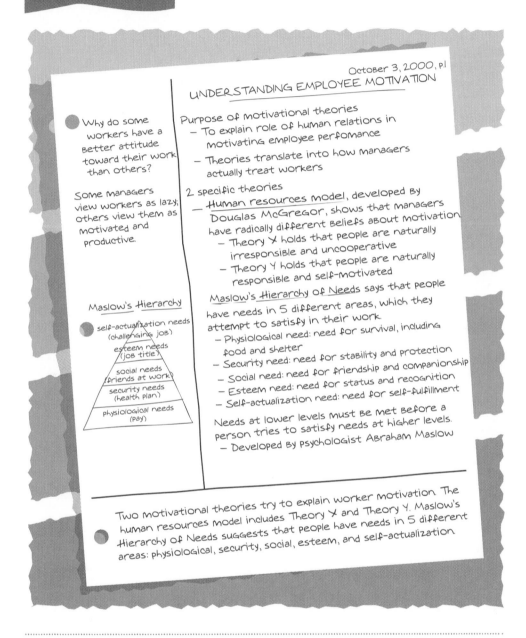

and supporting details and examples. The visual design makes the connections easy to see, and the use of shapes and pictures extends the material beyond mere words. Many learners respond well to the power of visualization. You can use think links to brainstorm ideas for paper topics as well.

One way to create a think link is to start by circling your topic in the middle of a sheet of unlined paper. Next, draw a line from the circled topic and write the name of the first major idea at the end of that line. Circle the idea as well. Then jot down specific facts related to the idea, linking them to the

visualization

The interpretation of verbal ideas through the use of mental visual images.

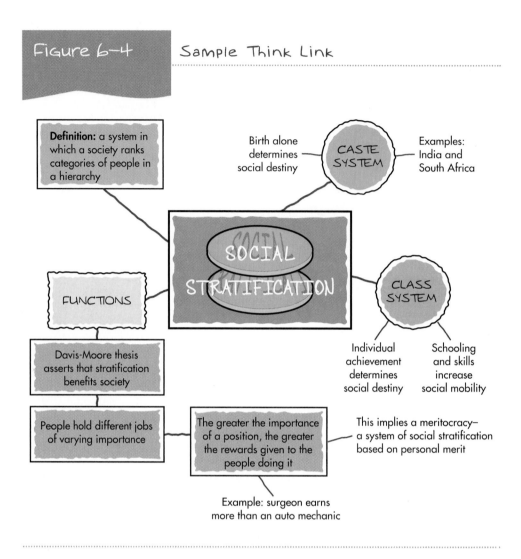

Figure 6-4   Sample Think Link

idea with lines. Continue the process, connecting thoughts to one another using circles, lines, and words.

A think link may be difficult to construct in class, especially if your instructor speaks quickly. In this case, use another note-taking system during class. Then make a think link as you review. Figure 6–4 shows a think link on a sociology concept called *social stratification*.

Once you choose a note-taking system, your success will depend on how well you use it. Personal shorthand will help you make the most of whatever system you choose.

How Can You Write Faster When Taking Notes?

When taking notes, many students feel they can't keep up with the instructor. Using some personal shorthand (not standard secretarial shorthand) can help to push the pen faster. *Shorthand* is writing that shortens words or replaces them with symbols. Because you are the only intended reader, you can misspell and abbreviate words in ways that only you understand.

The only danger with shorthand is that you might forget what your writing means. To avoid this problem, review your shorthand notes while your abbreviations and symbols are fresh in your mind. If there is any confusion, spell out words as you review.

Here are some suggestions that will help you master this important skill:

1. Use the following standard abbreviations in place of complete words:

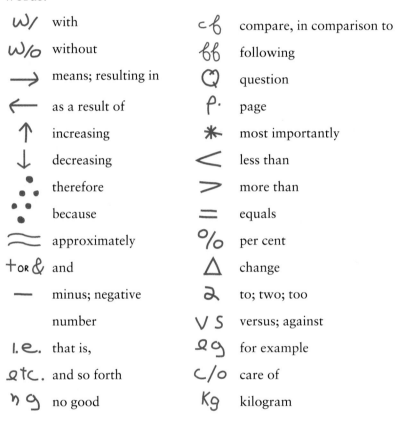

w/	with	c̸	compare, in comparison to
w/o	without	ƒƒ	following
→	means; resulting in	☺	question
←	as a result of	p.	page
↑	increasing	*	most importantly
↓	decreasing	<	less than
∴	therefore	>	more than
∵	because	=	equals
≈	approximately	%	per cent
+ or &	and	△	change
—	minus; negative number	2	to; two; too
		VS	versus; against
i.e.	that is,	eg	for example
etc.	and so forth	c/o	care of
ng	no good	Kg	kilogram

2. Shorten words by removing vowels from the middle of words:

   prps   =   purpose
   Crvtte =   Corvette (as on a vanity licence plate for a car)

3. Substitute word beginnings for entire words:

   assoc   =   associate; association
   info   =   information

4. Form plurals by adding s:

   prblms =   problems
   prntrs =   printers

5. Make up your own symbols and use them consistently:

   b/4   =   before
   2thake =   toothache

6. Learn to rely on key phrases instead of complete sentences ("German—nouns capitalized" instead of "In the German language, all nouns are capitalized.")

While note taking focuses on taking in ideas, writing focuses on expressing them. Next you will explore the roles that writing can play in your life.

How Can You Become a Good Writer?

Essay Writing 101
www.iss.stthomas.edu/
studyguides/wrtstr.htm

This site is an excellent resource if you're new to writing essays and term papers at a post-secondary level. It gives advice on how to write various types of term papers, including literature, expository, and persuasive essays. It also includes a comprehensive bibliography of online resources.

Inkspot
www.inkspot.com

Like to write? Inkspot is a Canadian site for aspiring writers.

Good writing depends upon and reflects clear thinking. Therefore, a clear thought process is the best preparation for a well-written document, and a well-written document shows the reader a clear thought process. Good writing also depends on reading. The more you expose yourself to the work of other writers, the more you will develop your ability to express yourself well. Not only will you learn more words and ideas, but you will also learn about all the different ways a writer can put words together in order to express ideas. In addition, critical reading generates new ideas, ideas you can use in your writing.

In school, almost any course you take will require you to write essays or papers in order to communicate your knowledge and thought process. In order to express yourself successfully in those essays and papers, you need good writing skills. Knowing how to write and express yourself is essential outside of school as well, as the following example demonstrates. Imagine that you run a summer internship program at a major television network. You have two qualified student candidates who are vying for one internship position. Parts of both students' letters to you are shown in Figures 6–5 and 6–6.

Read both figures before continuing with the text on the next page.

| Figure 6–5 | First Student's Writing Sample |

I am a capable student who'se interests are many. I like the news business so much so that I want you to offer me the internship with your company.

My experience will impress you, as I'm sure you will agree I am a reporter for the college news station, and I can be a reporter for you as well. If you let me try. Instructors who know my work like my style. I prefer to think of myself as an individuel with a unique style that nothing can match.

Figure 6-6   Second Student's Writing Sample

From the time I was 8 years old, I was hooked on the news. Instead of watching cartoons on television, I watched Lloyd Robertson, Valerie Pringle, and Peter Mansbridge. I remember the day that CTV started a 24-hour all-news network, CTV News Net.

It seemed like a natural step to go into the news business. I started in high school as a reporter, and then I became editor-in-chief of the school paper. At university, I am majoring in broadcast journalism, and I am also working at the school radio station. Even though I'm starting at the bottom, I believe that there's a learning opportunity around every corner. By the time I take on my first reporting assignment next year, I feel that my knowledge and experience will have grown. I hope it will be enough to make me a competent journalist.

Which candidate would you choose? The second student's letter is well written, persuasive, logical, and error free. In contrast, the first student's letter is not thought through clearly and has technical errors. Good writing quality gives the edge to student number two.

Instructors, supervisors, and other people who see your writing judge your thinking ability based on what you write and how you write it. Over the next few years you may write papers, essays, answers to essay test questions, job application letters, résumés, business proposals and reports, memos to co-workers, and letters to customers and suppliers. Good writing skills will help you achieve the goals you set out to accomplish with each writing task.

What Are the Elements of Effective Writing?

Every writing situation is different, dependent upon three elements. Your goal is to understand each element before you begin to write:

- *Your purpose:* What do you want to accomplish with this particular piece of writing?
- *Your topic:* What is the subject about which you will write?
- *Your audience:* Who will read your writing?

Figure 6–7 shows how these elements are interdependent. Just as a triangle needs three points to be complete, a piece of writing needs these three elements.

Figure 6-7   The Three Elements of Writing

Writing Purpose

Writing without first establishing your purpose is like driving without deciding where you want to go. You'll get somewhere, but chances are it won't be the right place. Therefore, when you write, always define what you want to accomplish before you begin.

There are many different purposes for writing. However, the two purposes you will most commonly use in classwork and on the job are to inform and to persuade.

The purpose of *informative writing* is to present and explain ideas. A research paper on how hospitals use donated blood to save lives informs readers without trying to mold opinion. The writer presents facts in an unbiased way, without introducing a particular point of view. Most newspaper articles, with the exception of the opinion and editorial pages, are examples of informative writing.

Persuasive writing has the purpose of convincing readers that your point of view is correct. Often, persuasive writing seeks to change the mind of the reader. For example, as a member of the student health committee, you may write a newspaper column attempting to persuade readers to give blood. Examples of persuasive writing include newspaper editorials, business proposals, and books and magazine articles with a distinct point of view.

Additional possible writing purposes include *entertaining* the reader and *narrating* (describing an image or event to the reader). Although most of your writing in school will inform or persuade, you may occasionally need to entertain or narrate as well. Sometimes purposes will even overlap—you might write an informative essay that entertains at the same time.

Knowing Your Audience

In almost every case, a writer creates written material so that it can be read by others. The two partners in this process are the writer and the audience. Knowing who your audience is will help you communicate successfully.

Key Questions About Your Audience

In school, your primary audience is your instructor. For many assignments, instructors will want you to assume that they are "typical readers," rather

audience
The reader or readers of any piece of written material.

Real World Perspective

How can I improve my writing?

Erica Epstein, Education Major

I don't know if it was the school's fault or mine, but by the time I was in high school, I didn't read or do homework. I just stopped paying attention. The classes were too boring. Fifteen weeks of the same topic was redundant. I think education should be interesting. The material should  be tied in with something else so it has meaning. Instead, the teacher feeds you the information so you don't really have to put in much effort. But now, even though I do all right, I have to work really hard to write a good paper. I think if I'd had a better start I wouldn't have to spend so much time rewriting my papers.

My teachers say the main problem is with my grammar. I tend to go from the past tense to the present tense in the wrong places. I just don't make proper sentences. I also have trouble organizing my material. I jump in and start writing. But I end up starting somewhere in the middle when I should be somewhere else. This is really frustrating. I had to take the writing class twice because I didn't get a high enough score the first time. I passed it this semester. I go to the writing centre. They help me outline what I'm going to write. But I still end up rewriting my work before it's what I want. It's been really helpful but I know I still need to do more. What suggestions do you have?

Tom Smith, Criminology Major

First of all, just like you, I get help from the writing centre at my school. They know a lot about what different instructors expect of you, particularly the technical stuff like footnote and bibliography requirements. They also give great advice about phrasing and punctuation. I also ask  several of my friends to edit my papers. Usually, they'll focus in on the weaker points and then I can make the changes and strengthen my work. If your papers are sounding too chatty, this would probably be the best thing for you to do. Other people can often show you where you've gotten off the point. I'm never bothered by their comments. In fact, I'm grateful because it helps my papers be more professional. By the time three or four people have read my work, I'm usually pretty sure I've handled the problems. I usually edit my papers about three or four times before I turn them in, to make sure I got my point across. I also try and look at my paper from an opposing perspective or different viewpoint. That way I can be sure my arguments are clear. Finally, if you don't have a reference book for writers, I suggest you go to the bookstore and pick one up. And don't forget to use your spell-check and thesaurus. That way you'll be sure your spelling is correct and you can increase your vocabulary with every paper you write.

Writing Tips
www.brocku.ca/english/
jlye/index.
html#style

Professor John Lye's Course and
Source Page at Brock University
contains many links to help you
get started on writing that essay
you've been putting off.

than informed instructors. Writing for typical readers usually means that you should be as complete as possible in your explanations.

At times you may write papers in which you intend to address informed instructors or a specific reading audience other than your instructors. In such cases, you may ask yourself some or all of the following questions, depending on which are relevant to your topic.

- What are my readers' ages, cultural backgrounds, interests, and experiences?

- What are their roles? Are they instructors, students, employers, or customers?

- How much do they know about my topic? Are they experts in the field or beginners?

- Are they interested, or do I have to convince them to read what I write?

- Can I expect my audience to have an open or closed mind?

After you answer the questions about your audience, take what you have discovered into consideration as you write.

Your Commitment to Your Audience

Your goal is to organize your ideas so that readers can follow them. Suppose, for example, you are writing an informative research paper for a non-expert audience on using online services to find a job. One way to accomplish your goal is to first explain what these services are and the kinds of help they offer, then describe each service in detail. Conclude with how these services will change job hunting in the twenty-first century.

Effective and successful writing involves following the steps of the *writing process*.

What Is the Writing Process?

The writing process provides an opportunity for you to state and refine your thoughts until you have expressed yourself as clearly as possible. Critical thinking plays an important role every step of the way. The four main parts of the process are planning, drafting, revising, and editing.

Planning

Planning gives you a chance to think about what to write and how to write it. Planning involves brainstorming for ideas, defining and narrowing your topic by using prewriting strategies, conducting research if necessary, writing a thesis statement, and writing a working outline. Although the steps in preparing to write are listed in sequence, in reality the steps overlap one another as you plan your document.

Open Your Mind Through Brainstorming

Whether your instructor assigns a partially defined topic (Canadian author Sonia Sarfati) or a general category within which you make your own choice (Canadian children's authors), you should brainstorm to develop ideas about what you want to write. Brainstorming is a creative technique that involves generating ideas about a subject without making judgments. You may want to look at the section on creativity in Chapter 4 for more details.

First, let your mind wander! Write down anything on the assigned subject that comes to mind, in no particular order. Then, organize that list into an outline or think link that helps you see the possibilities more clearly. To make the outline or think link, separate list items into general ideas or categories and sub-ideas or examples. Then associate the sub-ideas or examples with the ideas they support or fit. Figure 6–8 shows a portion of an outline that a student, Sam Gordon, constructed from his brainstorming list. The assignment is a five-paragraph essay on a life-changing event. Here, only the subject that Sam eventually chose is shown broken down into different ideas.

Figure 6–8	Part of a Brainstorming Outline

A life-changing event...
- Family
- Childhood
→ Watching wrestling with my father
- High school sports
  → Football, hockey and amateur wrestling
    - Wrestling camp in Alberta
      ∘ A dream come true
      ∘ Hart Brothers
    - Physical conditioning
      ∘ Nightly training
      ∘ 3-5 hour sessions
      ∘ Painful exercises
Dream turned into a nightmare
      ∘ Drastic weight loss
      ∘ A matter of survival
      ∘ Still have respect for wrestling

Narrow Your Topic Through Prewriting Strategies

When your brainstorming has generated some possibilities, you can narrow your topic. Focus on the sub-ideas and examples from your initial brainstorming session. Because they are relatively specific, they will be more likely to point you toward possible topics.

Choose one or more sub-ideas or examples that you like and explore them using prewriting strategies such as brainstorming, freewriting, and asking journalists' questions.[4] Prewriting strategies will help you decide which of your possible topics you would most like to pursue.

prewriting strategies
Techniques for generating ideas about a topic and finding out how much you already know before you start your research and writing.

Brainstorming The same process you used to generate ideas will also help you narrow your topic further. Generate thoughts about the possibility you have chosen and write them down. Then, organize them into categories, noticing any patterns that appear. See if any of the sub-ideas or examples might make good topics.

Freewriting Another stream-of-consciousness technique that encourages you to put down ideas on paper as they occur to you is called *freewriting*. When you freewrite, you write whatever comes to mind without censoring your ideas or worrying about grammar, spelling, punctuation, or organization. Freewriting helps you think creatively and gives you an opportunity to begin weaving in information that you know. Freewrite on the sub-ideas or examples you have created to see if you want to pursue any of them. Here is a sample of freewriting:

> My chance to train at the Hart Brothers Wrestling Camp was an influence on my life. I used to watch wrestling with my Dad when I was a kid. I was told that to be successful in wrestling, you had to be in really good shape. I figured my years of high school football and amateur wrestling had me in shape. Boy, was I wrong! We trained on our own during the day. We met every night for several hours to jog, ride bikes and lift weights. Ed and Keith were in charge of training me. We had to practise doing knee bends: about 200 each night. We also had a chance to practise taking falls in a ring that they had set up at the gym. Being flexible was an important point for wrestlers at the camp. All these things made you tough. At the end of the first week of camp, I had lost a ton of weight and a lot of my enthusiasm for wrestling. Although I had been a fan of wrestling for a lot of years and had been planning to go to wrestling camp since I started high school, I had come to the conclusion that it wasn't for me. At least I can say that while I didn't finish the course, I did survive it.

Asking journalists' questions When journalists start working on a story, they ask themselves Who? What? Where? When? Why? and How? You can use these *journalists' questions* to focus your thinking. Ask these questions about any sub-idea or example to discover what you may want to discuss. For example:

Who?	Who was at wrestling camp? Who influenced me the most?
What?	What about wrestling changed my life? What did we do?
When?	When in my life did I go to wrestling camp, and for how long?
Where?	Where was camp located? Where did we spend our day-to-day time?
Why?	Why did I decide to go there? Why was it such an important experience?
How?	How did we train in the camp? How were we treated? How do I feel about not achieving my goal?

As you prewrite, don't forget to focus on the paper length, due date of your assignment, and any other requirements (such as topic area or purpose). These requirements influence your choice of a final topic. For example, if you had a month to write an informative, twenty-page paper on learning disabilities, you might choose to discuss the symptoms, diagnosis, effects, and treatment of Attention Deficit Disorder (ADD). If you were given a week to write a five-page persuasive essay, you might write about how elementary students with ADD need special training.

Prewriting will help you develop a topic broad enough to give you something with which to work but narrow enough to be manageable. Prewriting also helps you see what you already know and what you don't. If your assignment requires more than you know, you may need to do research.

Conduct Research

Much of the writing you do in college or university, such as a short composition essay, or an exam, will rely on what you already know about a subject. In these cases, prewriting strategies may generate all the ideas and information you need. In other writing situations, outside sources are necessary. Try doing your research in stages. In the first stage, look for a basic overview that can help you write a thesis statement. In the second stage, go into more depth in your research, tracking down information that will help you fill in the gaps and complete your thoughts.

Write a Thesis Statement

Your work up until this point has prepared you to write a *thesis statement*, the central message you want to communicate. The thesis statement states your subject and point of view, reflects your writing purpose and audience, and acts as the organizing principle of your paper. It tells your readers what they should expect to read. Here is an example from Sam's paper:

Topic	Hart Brothers Wrestling Camp
Purpose	To inform and narrate
Audience	Instructor with unknown knowledge about the topic

Thesis statement   It may look easy on television, but it's not. Although I was a high school football and hockey player and a fan of wrestling for many years, nothing I had experienced prepared me for the longest week of my life: my week at the Hart Brothers Wrestling Camp.

A thesis statement is just as important in a short document, such as a letter, as it is in a long paper. For example, when you write a job application letter, a clear thesis statement will help you tell the recruiter why you deserve the job.

Write a Working Outline

The final step in the preparation process involves writing a working outline. Use this outline as a loose guide instead of a finalized structure. As you draft your paper, your ideas and structure may change many times. Only through allowing changes and refinements to happen can you get closer and closer to what you really want to say. Some students prefer a more formal outline structure, while others like to use a think link. Choose whatever form suits you best.

Create a Checklist

Use the checklist in Table 6–2 to make sure your preparation is complete. Under "Date Due," create your own writing schedule, giving each task an intended completion date. Work backwards from the date the assignment is due and estimate how long it will take to complete each step. Refer to Chapter 3 for time-management skills that will help you schedule your writing process.

As you develop your schedule, keep in mind that you'll probably move back and forth between tasks. You might find yourself doing two and even three things on the same day. Stick to the schedule as best you can, while balancing the other demands of your busy life, and check off your accomplishments on the list as you complete them.

Table 6-2 Preparation Checklist

Date Due	Task	Is It Complete?
	Brainstorm	
	Define and narrow	
	Use prewriting strategies	
	Conduct research if necessary	
	Write thesis statement	
	Write working outline	
	Complete research	

Drafting

Some people aim for perfection when they write a first draft. They want to get everything right—from word choice to tone to sentence structure to paragraph organization to spelling, punctuation, and grammar. Try to resist this tendency, because it may lead you to shut the door on ideas before you even know they are there.

A *first draft* involves putting ideas down on paper for the first time—but not the last! You may write many different versions of the assignment until you like what you see. Each version moves you closer to communicating exactly what you want to say in the way you want to say it. The process is like starting with a muddy pond and gradually clearing the mud away until the pond is a clear body of water, showing the rocks and the fish underneath the surface. Think of your first draft as a way of establishing the pond before you start clearing it up.

The elements of writing a first draft are freewriting, crafting an introduction, organizing the ideas in the body of the paper, formulating a conclusion, and citing sources. When you think of drafting, it might help you to imagine that you are creating a kind of "writing sandwich." The bottom slice of bread is the introduction, the top slice is the conclusion, and the sandwich stuffing—the body of your paper—is made up of central ideas and supporting examples (see Figure 6–9).

Freewriting Your Draft

If the introduction, body, and conclusion are the three parts of the sandwich, freewriting is the process of searching the refrigerator for the ingredients and laying them all out on the table. Take everything that you have developed in

> "Clear a space for the writing voice...you cannot will this to happen. It is a matter of persistence and faith and hard work. So you might as well just go ahead and get started."
>
> Anne Lamott[5]

| Figure 6-9 | Create a "Writing Sandwich" in Your First Draft |

the planning stages and freewrite a very rough draft. Don't censor yourself. For now, don't consciously think about your introduction, conclusion, or structure within the body of the paper. Focus on getting your ideas out of the realm of thought and onto the paper, in whatever form they prefer to be at the moment.

When you have the beginnings of a paper in your hands, you can start to shape it into something with a more definite form. First, work on how you want to begin your paper.

Writing an Introduction

The introduction tells your readers what the rest of the paper will contain. Including the thesis statement is essential. Here, for example, is a draft of an introduction for Sam's paper about wrestling camp. The thesis statement is underlined at the end of the paragraph:

> As a boy, I watched some greats of the sport with my father—wrestlers like Whipper Billy Watson and Stu Hart would grace our television set Saturday afternoons. The kids in my class would often pretend to be wrestlers; we would act like our heroes during recess and after school. However, unlike most people, I had the chance to train at a professional wrestling school when I graduated from high school. <u>Though this had been a lifelong goal of mine, nothing I had done could have prepared me for what I experienced during my week at the Hart Brothers Wrestling Camp in Alberta.</u>

hooks
Elements—including facts, quotes, statistics, questions, stories, or statements—that catch the reader's attention and encourage him or her to continue to read.

When you write an introduction, you might try to draw the reader in with an anecdote—a story that is directly related to the thesis. You can try other hooks, including a relevant quotation, dramatic statistics, and questions that encourage critical thinking. Whatever strategy you choose, be sure it is linked to your thesis statement. In addition, try to state your purpose without referring to its identity as a purpose. For example, in your introductory paragraph, state "Computer technology is infiltrating every aspect of business," instead of, "In this paper, my purpose is to prove that computer technology is infiltrating every aspect of business."

After you have an introduction that seems to set up the purpose of your paper, work on making sure the body fulfills that purpose.

Creating the Body of a Paper

The body of the paper contains your central ideas and supporting evidence. *Evidence*—proof that informs or persuades—comprises the facts, statistics, examples, and expert opinions that you know or have gathered during research.

Look at the array of ideas and evidence within your draft in its current state. Think about how you might group certain items of evidence with the particular ideas they support. Then, when you see the groups that form, try to find a structure that helps you to organize them into a clear pattern. Here are some strategies to consider.

Arrange ideas by time. Describe events in order or in reverse order.

Arrange ideas according to importance. You can choose to start with the idea that carries the most weight and move to ideas with less value or influence. You can also move from the least important to the most important idea.

Arrange ideas by problem and solution. Start with a specific problem, then discuss one or more solutions.

Writing the Conclusion

Your conclusion is a statement or paragraph that provides closure for your paper. Aim to summarize the information in the body of your paper, as well as to critically evaluate what is important about that information. Try one of the following devices:

- ◉ A summary of main points (if material is longer than three pages)
- ◉ A story, a statistic, a quote, or a question that makes the reader think
- ◉ A "call to action"
- ◉ A look to the future

As you work on your conclusion, try not to introduce new facts or to restate what you feel you have proved ("I have successfully proven that violent cartoons are related to increased violence in children."). Let your ideas as they are presented in the body of the paper speak for themselves. Readers should feel that they have reached a natural point of completion.

Crediting Authors and Sources

When you write a paper using any materials other than your own thoughts and recollections, the ideas you gathered in your research become part of your own writing. This does not mean that you can claim these ideas as your own or fail to attribute them to someone. You need to credit authors for their ideas and words in order to avoid plagiarism.

Writers own their writings just as a computer programmer owns a program that he or she designed or a photographer owns an image that he or she created. A piece of writing and its ideas are the writer's products—her or his "intellectual property." Using an idea, phrase, or word-for-word paragraph without crediting its author is the same as using a computer program without buying it or printing a photograph without paying the photographer. It is just as serious as any other theft, and may have unfavourable consequences. Most colleges and universities have stiff penalties for plagiarism, as well as for any other cheating offence.

plagiarism
The act of using someone else's exact words, figures, unique approach, or specific reasoning without giving appropriate credit.

To avoid plagiarism, learn the difference between a quotation and a paraphrase. A *quotation* refers to a source's exact words, which are set off from the rest of the text by quotation marks. A *paraphrase* is a restatement of the quotation in your own words, using your own sentence structure. Restatement means to completely rewrite the idea, not just to remove or replace a few words. A paraphrase may not be acceptable if it is too close to the original. Figure 6–10 demonstrates these differences.

Plagiarism often begins by accident when you research. You may forget to include quotation marks around a word-for-word pickup from the source,

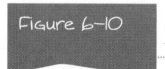

FiGure 6–10   Avoid Plagiarism by Learning How to Paraphrase[6]

QUOTATION

> "The most common assumption that is made by persons who are communicating with one another is...that the other perceives, judges, thinks, and reasons the way he does. Identical twins communicate with ease. Persons from the same culture but with a different education, age, background, and experience often find communication difficult. North American managers communicating with managers from other cultures experience greater difficulties in communication than with managers from their own culture."[7]

UNACCEPTABLE PARAPHRASE
(the underlined words are taken directly from the quoted source)

> When we communicate, we assume that the person to whom we are speaking <u>perceives, judges, thinks, and reasons the way</u> we do. This is not always the case. Although <u>identical twins communicate with ease, persons from the same culture but with a different education, age, background, and experience often</u> encounter communication problems. Communication problems are common among North American managers as they attempt to <u>communicate with managers from other cultures</u>. They experience greater communication problems than when they communicate <u>with managers from their own culture</u>.

ACCEPTABLE PARAPHRASE

> Many people fall into the trap of believing that everyone sees the world exactly as they do and that all people communicate based on the same assumptions. This belief is difficult to support even within our own culture as Blacks, Polish-Canadians, Asian-Canadians, and others often attempt unsuccessfully to find common ground. When intercultural differences are thrown into the mix, such as when North American managers working abroad attempt to communicate with managers from other cultures, clear communication becomes even harder.

or you may intend to cite or paraphrase but never find the time to do so. To avoid forgetting, try writing something like "Quotation from original; rewrite later" next to quoted material, and note at that time the specifics of the original document (title, author, source, page number, etc.), so you won't have to spend hours trying to locate it later.

Even an acceptable paraphrase requires a citation of the source of the ideas within it. Take care to credit any source that you quote, paraphrase, or use as evidence. To credit sources, write a footnote or endnote that describes the source. Use the format preferred by your instructor. Writing handbooks such as the *MLA Handbook*[8] contain acceptable formats. Your school calendar or student handbook probably has information about your school's plagiarism policy.

Continue Your Checklist

Create a checklist for your first draft (see Table 6–3). The elements of a first draft do not have to be written in order. In fact, many writers prefer to write the introduction after they complete the body of the paper, so the introduction will accurately reflect the paper's content and tone. Whatever order you choose, make sure your schedule allows adequate time to get everything done—with enough time left over for revisions.

Revising

When you *revise,* you critically evaluate the word choice, paragraph structure, and style of your first draft to see how it works. Any draft, no matter how good, can always be improved. Be thorough as you add, delete, replace, and reorganize words, sentences, and paragraphs. You may want to print out your draft and then spend time making notes and corrections on that hard copy before you make changes on a typewritten or computer-generated version.

In addition to revising on your own, some of your classes may include peer review (having students read each other's work and offer suggestions). A

Table 6-3 First Draft Checklist

Date Due	Task	Is It Complete?
	Freewrite a draft	
	Plan and write the introduction	
	Organize the body of the paper	
	Include research evidence in the body	
	Plan and write the conclusion	
	Check for plagiarism and rewrite passages to avoid it	
	Credit your sources	

peer reviewer can tell you what comes across well and what may be confusing. Having a different perspective on your writing is extremely valuable. Even if you don't have an organized peer-review system, you may want to ask a classmate to review your work as a favour to you.

The elements of revision include being a critical writer, evaluating paragraph structure, and checking for clarity and conciseness.

Being a Critical Writer

Critical thinking is as important in writing as it is in reading. Thinking critically when writing will help you move your papers beyond restating what you have researched and learned. Of course, your knowledge is an important part of your writing. What will make your writing even more important and unique, however, is how you use critical thinking to construct your own new ideas and knowledge from what you have learned.

The key to critical writing is asking the question, "So what?" For example, if you were writing a paper on nutrition, you might discuss a variety of good eating habits. Asking "So what?" could lead you into a discussion of *why* these habits are helpful, or what positive effects they have. If you were writing a paper on the theme of the family in the works of filmmaker Atom Egoyan, you might list all the examples you noticed. Then, asking "So what?" could lead you to evaluate why that theme is so strong and what idea you think those examples convey.

As you revise, ask yourself questions that can help you think through ideas and examples, come up with your own original insights about the material, and be as complete and clear as possible. Use the mind actions to guide you. Here are some examples of questions you may ask:

  Are these examples clearly connected to the idea?

 Are there any similar concepts or facts I know of that can add to how I support this?

 What else can I recall that can help to support this idea?

 In evaluating any event or situation, have I clearly indicated the causes and effects?

 What new idea comes to mind when I think about these examples or facts?

How do I evaluate any effect/fact/situation? Is it good or bad, useful or not?

What different arguments might a reader think of that I should address here?

Finally, critical thinking can help you evaluate the content and form of your paper. As you start your revision, ask yourself the following questions:

- Will my audience understand my thesis and how I've supported it?
- Does the introduction prepare the reader and capture attention?
- Is the body of the paper organized effectively?
- Is each idea fully developed, explained, and supported by examples?
- Are my ideas connected to one another through logical transitions?
- Do I have a clear, concise, simple writing style?
- Does the paper fulfill the requirements of the assignment?
- Does the conclusion provide a natural ending to the paper, and give a good summary?

Evaluating Paragraph Structure

Think of your individual paragraphs as mini-versions of your paper as a whole, each with an introduction, a body, and a conclusion. Make sure each paragraph has a *topic sentence* that states the paragraph's main idea (a topic sentence does for a paragraph what a thesis statement does for an entire paper). The rest of the paragraph should support that idea by presenting examples and other evidence. Topic sentences may occur just after the first sentence of a paragraph, at the end, or at the beginning. For example:

> When I arrived at camp, I had little idea of what to expect. <u>While I used to weight train, jog, and ride my bike for conditioning, nothing prepared me for the reality of the Hart camp.</u> From the first day, they meant business. Each session began with a mile and a half run through the Alberta foothills. Then the real fun began. The stretching and agility exercises were designed to improve stamina and improve balance while in the wrestling ring.

Examine how your paragraphs flow one into the other by evaluating your use of transitions. For example, words like *also, in addition*, and *next* indicate that another idea is coming. Similarly, *finally, as a result*, and *in conclusion* tell readers a summary is on its way.

transitions
Words and phrases that connect thoughts, helping readers move from one idea or paragraph to the next.

Checking for Clarity and Conciseness

Aim to say what you want to say in the clearest, most efficient way possible. A few well-chosen words will do your ideas more justice than a flurry of language. Try to eliminate extra words and phrases. Rewrite wordy phrases in a more concise, conversational way. For example, you can write "if" instead of

Editing Online
webster.commnet.
edu/hp/pages/darling/
grammar/composition/
editing.htm

Your paper isn't finished until
you've edited your rough draft.
This site offers you a list of what
to leave in and what to leave out
of your paper.

Spelling and Grammar
www.bartleby.com/141/
index.html

Don't forget to check your paper
for grammatical and spelling
errors. The classic writer's
resource, *Elements of Style*,
is available online.

Guide to Grammar and
Writing
cctc.commnet.edu/hp/
pages/darling/
grammar.htm

Here is a Web site with everything
you ever wanted to know about
run-on sentences but were afraid
to ask.

"in the event that," or "now" instead of "this point in time." "Capriciously, I sauntered forth to the entryway and pummelled the door that loomed so majestically before me," might become, "I skipped to the door and knocked loudly."

Editing

In contrast to the critical thinking of revising, *editing* involves correcting technical mistakes in spelling, grammar, and punctuation, as well as checking style consistency for elements such as abbreviations and capitalizations. Editing comes last, after you are satisfied with your ideas, organization, and style of writing. If you use a computer, you might want to use the grammar-check and spell-check functions to find mistakes. A spell-checker helps, but you still need to check your work on your own. While a spell-checker won't pick up the mistake in the following sentence, someone who is reading for sense will:

They are not hear on Tuesdays.

Look also for *sexist language*, which characterizes people based on their gender. Sexist language often involves the male pronoun *he* or *his*. For example, "An executive often spends hours each day going through his electronic mail" implies that executives are always men. A simple change will eliminate the sexist language: "Executives often spend hours each day going through their electronic mail," or, "An executive often spends hours each day going through his or her electronic mail." Try to be sensitive to words that leave out or slight women. *Mail carrier* is preferable to *mailman; police officer* to *policeman.*

Proofreading is the last stage of editing, occurring when you have a final version of your paper. Proofreading means reading every word and sentence in the final version to make sure it is accurate. Look for technical mistakes, run-on sentences, sentence fragments, incorrect word usage, and references that aren't clear.

Teamwork can be a big help as you edit and proofread, because another pair of eyes may see errors that you didn't notice on your own. If possible, have someone look over your work. Ask for feedback on what is clear and what is confusing. Then ask the reader to edit and proofread for errors.

There are many Canadian stylebooks available. *The Writer's Brief Handbook: Canadian Edition,*[10] by Alfred Rosa, Paul Eschholz, and John Roberts, includes information about Canadian spelling and grammar, sexism and bias in language, and up-to-date information about formatting your essays. If you're serious about writing, get a Canadian style guide for your reference shelf.

A Final Checklist

You are now ready to complete your revising and editing checklist. All the tasks listed in Table 6–4 should be complete when you submit your final paper.

Your final paper reflects all the hard work you put in during the writing process. Figure 6–11 shows the final version of Sam's paper.

"See revision as 'envisioning again.' If there are areas in your work where there is a blur or vagueness, you can simply see the picture again and add the details that will bring your work closer to your mind's picture."
Natalie Goldberg[9]

TaBLe 6-4 Revising and Editing Checklist

Date Due	Task	Is It Complete?
	Check the body of the paper for clear thinking and adequate support of ideas	
	Finalize introduction and conclusion	
	Check word spelling and usage	
	Check grammar	
	Check paragraph structure	
	Make sure language is familiar and concise	
	Check punctuation	
	Check capitalization	
	Check transitions	
	Eliminate sexist language	

FiGure 6-11

March 19, 1998

Sam Gordon

THE PAIN ISN'T FAKE

Bitten by the wrestling bug at an early age, I was determined to become a professional wrestler. As a child, I used to watch wrestling with my father Saturday afternoons. At school, my friends and I used to act out the role of "good guys" and "bad guys" during recess. As a teenager, I participated in a variety of contact sports. When I graduated from high school and the opportunity arose to attend a professional wrestling camp, I jumped at the chance. What I discovered was that while it might look easy on television, in reality, it's hard.

Located in the foothills of Alberta is the small town of Okotoks, home of the Hart Brothers Wrestling Camp. The Harts are recognized as some of the best trainers. They have built a strong reputation for running one of the most physically demanding schools in the world. Their philosophy comes from the patriarch of the family, Stu Hart. The wrestling world affectionately knows his training basement as the "dungeon." Many a spirit (and bone) have been broken here. His sons have continued his reputation for toughness, and, once a year, take in a new set of trainees. Any notion of wrestling camp as an acting school for "fakers" is quickly dismissed during the first training session. Let me explain.

When I arrived at camp, I, like most others, had little idea of what to expect. The camp itself is regimented in its methods. One of Stu Hart's sons, Keith, was in charge of my sessions, which were held five nights a week and lasted between three and five hours. Each session began with a mile-and-a-half run up and down the Alberta foothills. Once we returned to the camp, we had to do stretching exercises. Part of the workout was designed to improve your flexibility, and we would sit on the ground with the bottoms of our feet touching and our knees pointed out. Then, a 265-pound man would stand on our inner thighs, putting incredible pressure on the muscles and ligaments in our upper legs. As you can imagine, this stretching exercise brought tears to many eyes, mine included.

The session did not end there. From the stretching exercises, we began to learn how to take "bumps." The term "bump" refers to a wrestler falling down during a match. At the Hart camp, they teach many different ways of taking bumps. While it may sound simple to get into the ring and start falling down, there is a right way and a wrong way to take a bump without causing serious harm to yourself. When we first started taking bumps, many of my colleagues began to vomit. This is the body's natural reaction to the stress it takes when a person takes a bump. Adjusting to bumps, combined with the rigours of training, take their toll on the weight of the students. They told us that most students could expect to lose approximately 20 pounds during the first week of camp. I lost 35 pounds in my first four days alone.

Survival is a key word when describing the Hart wrestling camp. The Harts not only run a tough camp, they also run a professional and legitimate business. Most trainees, myself included, cannot get used to the punishment and decide to leave. The intensity of the training is physically taxing. The Harts were gracious enough to reimburse most of my money because I couldn't last a full week at their camp. I left Okotoks a little poorer, but a lot wiser. I had a new found respect for those who wrestled professionally. I still watch wrestling with my father Saturday afternoons, but with a more critical eye and admiration for its participants, especially any wrestler with the last name "Hart."

Suà

Suà is a Shoshone word, derived from the Uto-Aztecna language, meaning "think." While much of the Native American tradition in the Americas focuses on oral communication, written languages have allowed Native American perspectives and ideas to be understood by readers outside the Native American culture. The writings of Leslie Marmon Silko, J. Scott Momaday, and Sherman Alexis have expressed important insights that all readers can consider.

Think of *suà*, and of how thinking can be communicated to others through writing, every time you begin to write. The power of writing allows you to express your own insights so that others can read them and perhaps benefit from knowing them. Explore your thoughts, sharpen your ideas, and remember the incredible power of the written word.

Chapter 6: Applications

Name _____ Date _____

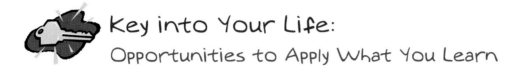 **Key into Your Life:**
Opportunities to Apply What You Learn

Exercise 1: Evaluate Your Notes

Choose one particular class period from the last two weeks. Have a classmate photocopy his or her notes from that period for you. Then evaluate your notes by comparing them with your classmate's.

- ☼ Do your notes make sense?
- ☼ How is your handwriting?
- ☼ Do the notes cover everything that was brought up in class?
- ☼ Are there examples to back up ideas?
- ☼ What note-taking system is used?
- ☼ Will these notes help you study?

Write your evaluation here _____

_____

_____

_____

_____

_____

What ideas or techniques from your classmate's notes do you plan to use in the future? _____

_____

_____

Exercise 2: Class vs. Reading

Pick a class for which you have a regular textbook. Choose a set of class notes on a subject that is also covered in that textbook. Read the textbook section that corresponds to the subject of your class notes, taking notes as you go. Compare your reading notes to the notes you took in class.

Did you use a different system with the textbook, or the same as in class? Why? _____

_____

_____

Which notes can you understand better? Why do you think that's true?

_____

_____

_____

_____

What did you learn from your reading notes that you want to bring to your class note-taking strategy? _____

_____

_____

Exercise 3: Audience Analysis

As a reporter for your student newspaper, you have been assigned the job of writing a story about some part of campus life. The choice is yours, and you submit the following suggestions to your editor-in-chief:

- The campus parking lot squeeze: too many cars and too few spaces
- Diversity: How students accept differences and live and work together
- Drinking on campus: Is the problem getting better or worse?

Your editor-in-chief asks you the following questions about reader response. Consider that your readers may include students, faculty and administrators, and community members.

1. Would readers care enough about each subject to read the entire article?

_____

_____

_____

_____

2. How would you adjust your writing according to whether readers know or don't know about the subject? _____

_____

_____

_____

_____

_____

_____

3. Which article idea is likely to have the greatest appeal to all the audiences? Why? _____

_____

_____

_____

4. For each topic, name the audience (or audiences) that you think would be most interested. If you think one audience would be equally interested in more than one topic, you can name that audience more than once.

   Campus parking lot _____

   Student diversity _____

   Drinking on campus _____

5. How can you make a specific article interesting to a general audience?

_____

_____

_____

_____

_____

Exercise 4: Prewriting

Choose a topic you are interested in and know something about—for example, sports, handling stress in a stressful world, our culture's emphasis on beauty and youth, or child rearing. Narrow your topic, then use the following prewriting strategies to discover what you already know about the topic and what you would need to learn if you had to write an essay about the subject for one of your classes. (If necessary, continue this prewriting exercise on a separate sheet of paper.)

   Brainstorm your ideas: _____

_____

_____

_____

_____

_____

_____

Freewrite: _____

_____

_____

_____

_____

_____

Ask journalists' questions: _____

_____

_____

_____

_____

_____

_____

Exercise 5: Writing a Thesis Statement

Write two thesis statements for each of the following topics. The first statement should try to inform the reader, while the second should try to persuade. In each case, writing a thesis statement will require that you narrow the topic:

◉ *The rising cost of a post-secondary education*

   Thesis with an informative purpose _____

_____

_____

Thesis with a persuasive purpose _____

_____

_____

⚙ *Taking care of your body and mind*

Thesis with an informative purpose _____

_____

_____

Thesis with a persuasive purpose _____

_____

_____

⚙ *Career choice*

Thesis with an informative purpose _____

_____

_____

Thesis with a persuasive purpose _____

_____

_____

 ## Key to Cooperative Learning: Using Teamwork Skills

Collaborative Writing In many jobs, you may be asked to work with other employees to produce written documents, including reports, proposals, procedure manuals, and even important letters and memos. Writing in groups, also known as *collaborative writing*, involves planning, drafting, revising, and editing.

To see what collaborative writing is like, join with three classmates and choose a general topic you are all interested in—for example, "What Universities and Colleges Can Do to Help Students Juggle School, Work, and Family" or "Teaching Safer Sex in an Age When Sex Isn't Safe." Now imagine that you and other group members have to write a persuasive paper on some aspect of this topic. Writing the paper involves the following steps:

- Each group member should spend an hour in the library to get an overview of the topic so that everyone is able to write about it in general terms.

- The group should come together to brainstorm the topic, narrow its focus, and come up with a thesis. Use your research and thesis to write a working outline that specifies what the paper will say and the approach it will take. Divide the writing assignment into parts and assign a part to each group member.

- Each group member should *draft* his or her portion of the paper. Each section should be about two to three paragraphs long.

- Photocopy each draft and give a copy to each group member. Working independently, each person should use the suggestions in this chapter to *evaluate and revise* each section. Afterwards, come together as a group to hammer out differences and prepare a final, unedited version.

- Photocopy this version and distribute it to group members. Have everyone *edit* the material, looking for mistakes in spelling, grammar, punctuation, and usage. Incorporate the group's changes into a final version you all agree on, and ask every group member to read it. The group's goal is to produce a finished paper that satisfies the thesis and also looks good.

- Working alone, each group member should answer the following questions. Finally, compare your responses with those of other group members:

1. What do you see as the advantages and disadvantages of collaborative writing? Is it difficult or easy to write as a team member?_____

_____

_____

_____

2. What part of the collaborative writing project worked best? Where did you encounter problems? _____

_____

_____

_____

3. What did you learn from this experience that will make you a more effective collaborative writer on the next project? _____

_____

_____

Key to Self-Expression:
Discovery Through Journal Writing

To record your thoughts, use a separate journal or the lined page at the end of the chapter.

Your Relationship with Words Some people love to work with words—writing them, reading them, speaking them—while others would rather do anything else. Do you enjoy writing in school, or does writing intimidate you? Do you write anything outside of school? Discuss how you feel about writing.

Key to Your Personal Portfolio:
Your Paper Trail to Success

Writing Sample: A Job Interview Letter To get a job interview, you may have to write a letter describing your background and value to the company. (Remember how the sample letters on pages 198 and 199 affected the internship choice.) Practise writing this letter, and make the result part of your portfolio. Write a one-page, three-paragraph cover letter to a prospective employer. (The letter will accompany your résumé.) Be creative—you may use fictitious names, but select a career and industry that interest you. Use the following business letter format:

Firstname Lastname
1234 Your Street
Your Province, Your Postal Code

January 1, 2001

Ms. Prospective Employer
Prospective Company
5432 Their Street
Their Province, Their Postal Code

Dear Ms. Employer:

First paragraph . . .

Second paragraph . . .

Third paragraph . . .

Sincerely,

sign your name here

Firstname Lastname

Enclosure(s) (*use this notation if you have included a résumé or other item with your letter*)

Introductory paragraph: Start with an attention getter—a statement that convinces the employer to read on. For example, name a person the employer knows who told you to write, or refer to something positive about the company that you read about in the paper. Identify the position for which you are applying and tell the employer that you are interested in working for the company.

Middle paragraph: Sell your value. Try to convince the employer that hiring you will help the company in some way. Centre your "sales effort" on your experience in school and the workplace. If possible, tie your qualifications to the needs of the company. Refer indirectly to your enclosed résumé.

Final paragraph: Close with a call to action. Ask the employer to call you, or tell the employer to expect your call to arrange an interview.

Exchange first drafts with a classmate. Read each other's letter and make notes in the margins. Discuss each letter, and make whatever corrections are necessary to produce a well-written, persuasive letter. Create a final draft for your portfolio.

Name _____ Date _____

Journal Entry

_____
_____
_____
_____
_____
_____
_____
_____
_____
_____
_____
_____
_____
_____
_____
_____
_____
_____
_____
_____

7 Listening, Memory, and Test Taking:
Taking in, Retaining, and Demonstrating Knowledge

In this chapter, you will explore answers to the following questions:

- Why is listening a skill?

- How can you improve your listening skills?

- How does memory work?

- How can you improve your memory?

- How can tape recorders help you listen, remember, and study?

- How can preparation help improve test scores?

- What strategies can help you succeed on tests?

- How can you learn from test mistakes?

College and university expose you to facts, opinions, and ideas. It is up to you to take in, retain, and demonstrate knowledge of what you learn, for use in or out of school. You can accomplish these goals through active listening, focused use of your memory skills, and thorough preparation for taking tests.

Listening is one of the primary ways of taking in information. You listen as instructors discuss concepts, as members of a study group share ideas, or as friends share their thoughts. Memory skills can help you retain what you've listened to so that you can recall it for a paper, a discussion, or a test. After you've listened and remembered, test taking is your key to demonstrating what you have learned to your instructor or others. Test taking demands preparation and strategy. In this chapter, you will learn strategies to improve your ability to take in, remember, and show knowledge of what you have learned. The Conference Board of Canada claims that being able to "listen to, understand, and learn" is an important skill Canadian employers look for in prospective employees.[1]

Thinking It Through

Check those statements that apply to you right now:

☐ Although I listen to my instructors, I often do not remember what they say.

☐ When I listen, I tend not to think about what the speaker is saying.

☐ I use memory games to help me remember important information.

☐ I spend a lot of time memorizing information for a test, but I forget almost everything after the test is over.

☐ I get very tense before and during an exam.

☐ I don't think that my test performance really reflects what I can do.

Why Is Listening a Skill?

The act of hearing isn't quite the same as the act of listening. While *hearing* refers to sensing spoken messages from their source, *listening* involves a complex process of communication. Successful listening results in the speaker's intended message reaching the listener. In school, and at home, poor listening results in communication breakdowns and mistakes, and skilled listening promotes progress and success.

Ralph G. Nichols, a pioneer in listening research, studied 200 students at the University of Minnesota over a nine-month period. His findings, summarized in Table 7–1, demonstrate that effective listening depends as much on a positive attitude as on specific skills.[2]

To overcome barriers, explore what the listening process is and the reasons it can be hard to listen well.

Table 7-1   What Helps and Hinders Listening

Listening is helped by . . .	Listening is hindered by . . .
. . . making a conscious decision to work at listening; viewing difficult material as a listening challenge.	. . . caring little about the listening process; tuning out difficult material.
. . . fighting distractions through intense concentration.	. . . refusing to listen at the first distraction.
. . . continuing to listen when a subject is difficult or dry, in the hope that one might learn something interesting.	. . . giving up as soon as one loses interest.
. . . withholding judgment until hearing everything.	. . . becoming preoccupied with a response as soon as a speaker makes a controversial statement.
. . . focusing on the speaker's theme by recognizing organizational patterns, transitional language, and summary statements.	. . . getting sidetracked by unimportant details.
. . . adapting note-taking style to the unique style and organization of the speaker.	. . . always taking notes in outline form, even when a speaker is poorly organized; this can lead to frustration.
. . . pushing past negative emotional responses and forcing oneself to continue to listen.	. . . letting an initial emotional response shut off continued listening.
. . . using excess thinking time to evaluate, summarize, and question what one just heard and anticipate what will come next.	. . . thinking about other things and, as a result, missing much of the message.

The Stages of Listening

Listening is made up of four stages that build on one another: sensing, interpreting, evaluating, and reacting. These stages take the message from the speaker to the listener and back to the speaker (see Figure 7–1).

During the *sensation stage* (also known as *hearing*), your ears pick up sound waves and transmit them to the brain. For example, you are sitting in class and hear your instructor say, "The only opportunity to make up last week's test is Tuesday at 5 P.M."

In the *interpretation stage*, listeners attach meaning to a message. This involves understanding what is being said and relating it to what you already know. For example, when you hear this message, you relate it to your knowledge of the test, whether you need to make it up, and what you are doing on Tuesday at 5 P.M.

In the *evaluation stage* of listening, you decide how you feel about the message—whether, for example, you like it or agree with it. This involves considering the message as it relates to your needs and values. In this example, if you do need to make up the test but have to work Tuesday at 5 P.M., you evaluate that you aren't thrilled with the message.

The final stage of listening involves a *reaction* to the message in the form of direct feedback. Your reaction, in this example, may be to raise your hand or stick around after class and ask the instructor if there is any alternative to that particular make-up test time.

Figure 7–1 Stages of Listening

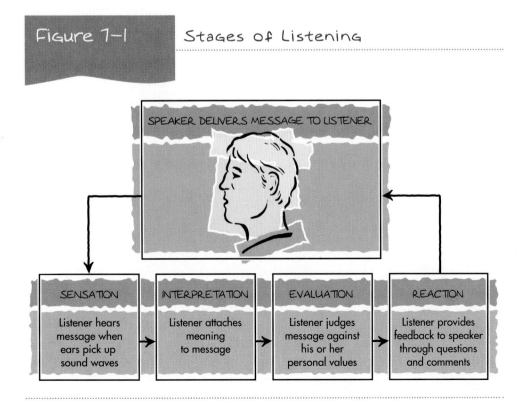

How Can You Improve Your Listening Skills?

Listening is a teachable—and learnable—skill. Improving your learning skills involves managing listening challenges and becoming an active listener. Although becoming a better listener will help in every class, it is especially important in subject areas that are difficult for you.

Manage Listening Challenges

Classic studies have shown that immediately after listening, students are likely to recall only half of what was said. This is partly due to particular listening challenges, including divided attention and distractions, the tendency to shut out the message, the inclination to rush to judgment, and partial hearing loss or learning disabilities.[3] To help create a positive listening environment, in both your mind and your surroundings, explore how to manage these challenges.

Divided Attention and Distractions

Imagine you are talking with a friend at a noisy party when, suddenly, you hear your name mentioned across the room. You weren't consciously listening to anything outside your own conversation. Now, though, you strain to hear what someone might be saying about you, and listen with only half an ear to what your friend says. Chances are you hear neither person very well. This situation illustrates the consequences of divided attention. While you are capable of listening to two or more messages at the same time, the usual result is that you may not completely hear or understand any of them.

Internal and external distractions often divide your attention. *Internal distractions* include anything from hunger to headache to personal worries. Something the speaker says may also trigger a recollection that may cause your mind to drift. In contrast, *external distractions* include noises (whispering, honking horns, screaming sirens) and even excessive heat or cold. It can be hard to listen in an overheated room that is putting you to sleep.

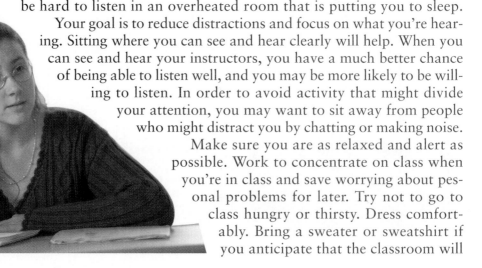

Your goal is to reduce distractions and focus on what you're hearing. Sitting where you can see and hear clearly will help. When you can see and hear your instructors, you have a much better chance of being able to listen well, and you may be more likely to be willing to listen. In order to avoid activity that might divide your attention, you may want to sit away from people who might distract you by chatting or making noise. Make sure you are as relaxed and alert as possible. Work to concentrate on class when you're in class and save worrying about personal problems for later. Try not to go to class hungry or thirsty. Dress comfortably. Bring a sweater or sweatshirt if you anticipate that the classroom will be too cold. If there's a chance you'll be too warm, wear a removable layer of clothing.

Shutting Out the Message

Instead of paying attention to everything the speaker says, many students fall into the trap of focusing on specific points and shutting out the rest of the message. Worse, if you perceive that a subject is too difficult or uninteresting, you may tune out everything. Shutting out the message makes it tough to listen well from that point on, since the information you miss may be the foundation for what goes on in future classes.

Creating a positive listening environment includes accepting responsibility for listening. While the instructor communicates information to you, he or she cannot force you to listen. You are responsible for taking in that information. One important motivator is believing that what your instructors say is valuable. As many students learn the hard way, instructors often cover material from outside the textbook during class and then test on that material. If you work to take in the whole message in class, you will be able to read over your notes later and think critically about what is most important.

The Rush to Judgment

People tend to stop listening when they hear something with which they don't agree. If you rush to judge what you've heard, your focus turns to your personal reaction rather than the content of the speaker's message. Students who disagree during a lecture often spend a lot of thinking time figuring out how to word a question or comment for response.

Judgments also involve reactions to the speakers themselves. If you do not like your instructors or if you have preconceived notions about their ideas or cultural background, you may decide that their words have little value. Anyone whose words have ever been ignored because of race, background, gender, or disability understands how prejudice can interfere with listening (see Chapter 8 for more about how prejudice stifles listening).

Work to recognize and control your judgments. Being aware of what you tend to judge will help you avoid putting up a barrier against incoming messages that clash with your opinions or feelings. Keeping an open mind means being aware of the things you believe in as well as your prejudices. It also means defining education as a continuing search for evidence, regardless of whether it supports or negates your point of view.

Partial Hearing Loss and Learning Disabilities

Good listening techniques don't solve every listening problem. Students who have a partial hearing loss have a physical explanation for why listening is difficult. If you have some level of hearing loss, seek out special services that can help you listen in class. You may require special equipment or may benefit from tutoring. You may be able to arrange to meet with your instructor outside of class to clarify your notes.

Other disabilities, such as Attention Deficit Disorder (ADD) or a problem with processing heard language, can cause difficulties with both focusing on and understanding what is heard. People with such disabilities have varied

Paying Attention in Class
www.iss.stthomas.edu/
studyguides/classr.htm

Learn how to prepare yourself for class and improve your classroom listening skills.

ability to compensate for or overcome them. If you have a disability, don't blame yourself for having trouble listening. Your counselling centre, student health centre, adviser, and instructors should be able to give you particular assistance in working through your challenges.

Become an Active Listener

On the surface, listening seems like a passive activity: You sit back and listen as someone else speaks. Effective listening, however, is really an *active* process that involves setting a purpose for listening, asking questions, and paying attention to verbal signposts.

Set Purposes for Listening

Active listening is difficult if you don't know or care why you are listening. Think through why you listen in any situation. Establish what you want to achieve by listening, such as greater understanding of the material, a more direct connection with your instructor, staying awake in class, or better note taking. When you set a purpose, you have a goal that you can achieve only through active listening. A purpose for listening motivates you to listen.

Ask Questions

Asking questions is not a sign of stupidity or a reason to doubt your intelligence. In fact, a willingness to ask questions shows a desire to learn, and is the mark of an active listener and critical thinker. Some questions are

> "No one cares to speak to an unwilling listener. An arrow never lodges in a stone; often it recoils upon the sender of it."
> St. Jerome

Table 7–2   Paying Attention to Verbal Signposts

Signals Pointing to Key Concepts	Signals of Support
There are two reasons for this…	For example,…
A critical point in the process involves…	Specifically,…
Most importantly,…	For instance,…
The result is…	Similarly,…

Signals Pointing to Differences	Signals That Summarize
On the contrary,…	Finally,…
On the other hand,…	Recapping this idea,…
In contrast,…	In conclusion,…
However,…	As a result,…

Source: Adapted from George M. Usova, *Efficient Study Strategies: Skills for Successful Learning*, Pacific Grove, CA, Brooks/Cole Publishing Company, 1989, p. 69.

informational—seeking information—such as any question beginning with the phrase, "I don't understand…" Other *clarifying* questions state your understanding of what you just heard and ask if that understanding is correct. While some clarifying questions focus on a key concept or theme ("So, some learning disorders can be improved with treatment?"), others highlight specific facts ("Is it true that dyslexia can cause people to reverse letters and words?").

If, for whatever reason, you don't have an opportunity to ask your questions in class, jot them down and ask them during a discussion period or during a talk with your instructor.

Pay Attention to Verbal Signposts

You can identify important facts and ideas and predict test questions by paying attention to the speaker's specific choice of words. *Verbal signposts* often involve transition words and phrases that help organize information, connect ideas, and indicate what is important and what is not. Let phrases like those in Table 7–2 direct your attention to the material that follows.

Effective listening will enable you to acquire knowledge. You also need a good memory, however, so that you can remember what you've heard.

How Does Memory Work?

You need an effective memory in order to use the knowledge you take in throughout your life. Human memory works like a computer. Both have essentially the same purpose: to encode, store, and retrieve information.

Learning to Learn
snow.utoronto.ca/llreadings/

This bibliography, part of the SNOW (Special Needs Opportunity Windows) project, includes a series of articles on how to understand the process of learning. It's an excellent resource.

> During the *encoding stage*, information is changed into usable form. On a computer, this occurs when keyboard entries are transformed into electronic symbols and stored on a disk. In the brain, sensory information becomes impulses that the central nervous system reads and codes. You are encoding, for example, when you study a list of chemistry formulas.

> During the *storage stage*, information is held in memory (the mind's version of a computer hard drive) for later use. In this example, after you complete your studying of the formulas, your mind stores them until you need to use them.

> During the *retrieval stage*, memories are recovered from storage by recall, just as a saved computer file is called up by name and used again. In this example, your mind retrieves the chemistry formulas when you have to take a test or solve a problem.

Memories are stored in three different storage banks. The first, called *sensory memory*, is an exact copy of what you see and hear, and lasts for a second or less. Certain information is then selected from sensory memory and moves into *short-term memory*, a temporary information storehouse where the material stays no more than ten to twenty seconds. You are consciously aware of material in your short-term memory. While unimportant information is quickly dumped, important information is transferred to *long-term memory*—the mind's more permanent storehouse.

Having information in long-term memory does not mean that you will be able to recall it when needed. Particular techniques can help you improve your recall.

How Can You Improve Your Memory?

Your accounting instructor is giving a test tomorrow on the use of bookkeeping programs. You feel confident, since you spent hours last week memorizing the material. Unfortunately, by the time you take the test, you may remember very little. That's because most forgetting occurs within minutes after memorization.

In a classic study conducted in 1885, researcher Herman Ebbinghaus memorized a list of meaningless three-letter words such as CEF and LAZ. Within one short hour he measured that he had forgotten more than 50 per cent of what he learned. After two days, he knew fewer than 30 per cent. Although his recall of the syllables remained fairly stable after that, the experiment shows how fragile memory can be, even when you take the time and energy to memorize information.[4]

People who have superior memories may have an inborn talent for remembering. More often, though, they have mastered techniques for improving recall. Remember that techniques aren't a cure-all for memory difficulties, especially for those who may have disabilities such as ADD. If you have a disability, the following memory techniques may help you but may not be enough. Seek assistance if you consistently have trouble remembering.

THE FAR SIDE   By GARY LARSON

"Mr. Osborne, may I be excused? My brain is full."

Memory Improvement Strategies

As a student, your job is to understand, learn, and remember information, from general concepts to specific details. The following suggestions will help improve your recall.

Develop a Will to Remember

Why can you remember the lyrics to dozens of popular songs but not the functions of the pancreas? Perhaps this is because you want to remember them, you connect them with a visual image, or you have an emotional tie to them. To achieve the same results at school or on the job, tell yourself that what you are learning is important and that you need to remember it. Saying these words out loud can help you begin the active, positive process of memory improvement.

Understand What You Memorize

Make sure that everything you want to remember makes sense. Something that has meaning is easier to recall than something that is gibberish. This basic principle applies to everything you study—from biology and astronomy to history and English literature.

Recite, Rehearse, and Write

When you *recite* material, you repeat it aloud in order to remember it. Reciting helps you retrieve information as you learn it and is a crucial step in studying (see Chapter 5). *Rehearsing* is similar to reciting, but is done in silence, in your mind. It involves the process of repeating, summarizing, and associating information with other information. *Writing* is rehearsing on paper. The act of writing solidifies the information in your memory.

Separate Main Points from Unimportant Details

If you use critical-thinking skills to select and focus on the most important information, you can avoid overloading your mind with extra clutter. To focus on key points, highlight only the most important information in your texts and write notes in the margins about central ideas. When you review your lecture notes, highlight or rewrite the most important information to remember.

Study During Short but Frequent Sessions

If you think you have mastered material after studying it once, you might be shortchanging yourself. Research shows that you can improve your chances of remembering material if you learn it more than once. The more you study, the more you are likely to remember at exam time.

To get the most out of your study sessions, spread them over time. A pattern of short sessions followed by brief periods of rest is more effective than continual studying with little or no rest. Even though you may feel as though you accomplish a lot by studying for an hour without a break, you'll probably remember more from three 20-minute sessions. Try sandwiching study time into breaks in your schedule, such as when you have time between classes.

When studying for several tests at a time, avoid studying two similar subjects back to back. You'll be less confused when you study history after biology rather than, for example, if you study chemistry after biology.

Separate Material into Manageable Sections

When material is short and easy to understand, studying it from beginning to end may work. For longer material, you may benefit from dividing the work into logical sections, mastering each section, putting all the sections together, and then testing your memory of all the material. Actors take this approach when learning the lines of a play, and it can work just as well for students.

Use Visual Aids

Any kind of visual representation of study material can help you remember. You may want to convert material into a think link or outline. Write material in any visual shape that helps you recall it and link it to other information.

Flash cards are a great visual memory tool. They give you short, repeated review sessions that provide immediate feedback. Make them from index cards. Use the front of the card to write a word, idea, or phrase you want to remember. Use the back side for a definition, explanation, and other key facts. Figure 7–2 shows two flash cards for studying psychology.

Here are some additional suggestions for making the most of your flash cards:

- *Use the cards as a self-test.* Divide the cards into two piles: the material you know and the material you are learning. You may want to use rubber bands to separate the piles.
- *Carry the cards with you and review them frequently.* You'll learn more if you start using cards early in the course, well ahead of exam time.
- *Shuffle the cards and learn information in various orders.* This will help avoid putting too much focus on some information and not enough on others.
- *Test yourself in both directions.* First, look at the terms or ideas and provide definitions or explanations. Then turn the cards over and reverse the process.

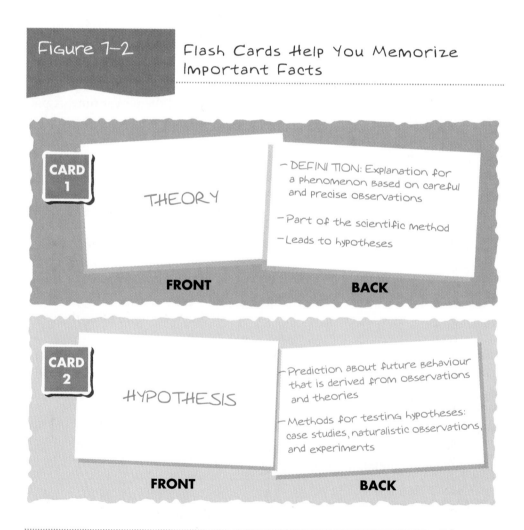

Figure 7–2   Flash Cards Help You Memorize Important Facts

CARD 1

THEORY

– DEFINITION: Explanation for a phenomenon based on careful and precise observations

– Part of the scientific method

– Leads to hypotheses

FRONT   BACK

CARD 2

HYPOTHESIS

– Prediction about future behaviour that is derived from observations and theories

– Methods for testing hypotheses: case studies, naturalistic observations, and experiments

FRONT   BACK

Making the Most of Last-Minute Studying

Last-minute studying, or *cramming*, often results in forgetting much of the material learned. Study conditions, however, aren't always ideal. Sometimes a busy week may leave you only a few hours to prepare for a big exam. Nearly every student crams sometime during his or her post-secondary career. If you end up with a tight schedule, use these hints to make the most of your study time:

- *Go through your flash cards,* if you have them, one last time.

- *Resist going through your notes or textbook page by page.* Focus on crucial concepts; don't sweat the rest.

- *Create a last-minute study sheet with hard-to-remember material.* On a single sheet of paper, write down key facts, definitions, formulas, and so on. Try to keep the material short and simple. If you prefer visual notes, use think links to map out ideas and their supporting examples (see Chapter 6 for information on think links).

- *Arrive at the exam room a few minutes early.* Study the sheet or your flash cards until you are asked to clear your desk.

- *While it is still fresh in your mind, record any helpful information on a piece of scrap paper.* Do this before looking at any test questions.

After your exam, evaluate the effects cramming had on learning the material and what you will do to improve the situation next time. Set a goal and plan ahead.

Mnemonic Devices

Certain performers entertain their audiences by remembering the names of 100 strangers or flawlessly repeating thirty 10-digit phone numbers. These performers probably have superior memories, but genetics alone can't produce these results. These people also rely on memory techniques, known as mnemonic devices (pronounced neh-MAHN-ick) to help them.

Mnemonic devices work by connecting information you are trying to learn with simpler information or information that is familiar. Instead of learning new facts by rote (repetitive practice), associations give you a hook on which to hang these facts and retrieve them. Mnemonic devices make information familiar and meaningful through unusual or unforgettable mental associations and visual pictures.

Here's an example to prove the power of mnemonics. Suppose you want to remember the names of the first six prime ministers of Canada. The first letters of their last names—Macdonald, Mackenzie, Abbott, Thompson, Bowell, and Tupper—together read MMATBT. To remember them, you might add a "y" to the end and create a short nonsense word—"mmatbty"—and remember it as the word "mmat-bity." Since there are two "t's" in your nonsense word, just remember that alphabetically, and historically, Thompson comes before Tupper. To remember their first names—John, Alexander, John, John, Mackenzie, and Charles —you might

mnemonic devices
Memory techniques that involve associating new information with information you already know.

MOM
(More on Mnemonics)
www.demon.co.uk/
mindtool/memory.html

This Web site includes information on how to use mnemonics for studying and for helping you remember names, phone numbers, and dates.

set the names to the tune of "Happy Birthday," or any other musical tune you know.

Visual images, idea chains, and acronyms are a few of the more widely used kinds of mnemonic devices. Apply them to your own memory challenges.

Create Visual Images and Associations

"The true art of memory is the art of attention."
Samuel Johnson

Visual images are easier to remember than images that rely on words alone. In fact, communication through visual images goes back to the prehistoric era, when people made drawings that still exist on cave walls. It's no accident that the phrase "a picture is worth a thousand words" is so familiar. The best mental pictures often involve colours, three-dimensional images, action scenes, and disproportionate, funny, or ridiculous images.

Use an Idea Chain to Remember Items in a List

An *idea chain* is a memory strategy that involves forming exaggerated mental images of a large group of items. The first image is connected to the second image, which is connected to the third image, and so on. Imagine, for example, that you want to remember the seven Thinktrix mind actions that appear in the critical-thinking discussion in Chapter 4: recall, similarity, difference, cause and effect, example to idea, idea to example, and evaluation. You can use the visual icons to form an idea chain that goes like this:

> The other end of a string tied around your finger (*recall*) leads to two pyramids (*similarity*) and ends at a black square office building next to one of the pyramids (*difference*). Inside the building there's a party and people are popping balloons (*cause and effect*). On the wall, a painted "ex" and an arrow direct you to a light bulb (*example to idea*), which points to another "ex" (*idea to example*). Lit by the light bulb above, a set of scales weighs mail (*evaluation*).

Create Acronyms

acronym
A word formed from the first letters or syllables of a series of words, created in order to help you remember the series.

Another helpful association method involves the use of the acronym. The acronym "Roy G. Biv" often helps students remember the colours of the spectrum. Roy G. Biv stands for **R**ed, **O**range, **Y**ellow, **G**reen, **B**lue, **I**ndigo, **V**iolet. In history, you can remember the big-three Allies during World War II—Britain, America, and Russia—with the acronym BAR.

When you can't create a name like Roy G. Biv, create an acronym from an entire sentence, in which the first letter of each word in the sentence stands for the first letter of each memorized term. When science students want to remember the list of planets in order of their distance from the sun, they learn the sentence: <u>M</u>y <u>v</u>ery <u>e</u>legant <u>m</u>other <u>j</u>ust <u>s</u>erved <u>u</u>s <u>n</u>ine <u>p</u>ickles. (Mercury, Venus, Earth, Mars, Jupiter, Saturn, Uranus, Neptune, and Pluto.)

Improving your memory requires energy, time, and work. In school, it also helps to master PQ3R, the textbook study technique that was introduced in Chapter 5. By going through the steps in PQ3R and using the specific memory techniques described in this chapter, you will be able to learn more in less time—and remember what you learn long after exams are over.

How Can Tape Recorders Help You Listen, Remember, and Study?

The selective use of a tape recorder can provide helpful backup to your listening and memory skills and to your study materials. It's important, though, not to let tape recording substitute for active participation. Not all students like to use tape recorders, but if you choose to do so, here are some guidelines and a discussion of potential effects.

Guidelines for Using Tape Recorders

Ask the instructor whether he or she permits tape recorders in class. Some instructors don't mind, while others don't allow students to use them.

Use a small, portable tape recorder. Sit near the front for the best possible recording.

Participate actively in class. Take notes just as you would if the tape recorder were not there.

Use tape recorders to make study tapes. Questions on tape can be like audio flash cards. One way to do it is to record study questions, leaving ten to fifteen seconds between questions for you to answer out loud. Recording the correct answer after the pause will give you immediate feedback. For example, part of a recording for a writing class might be, "The three elements of effective writing are …(ten to fifteen seconds)…topic, audience, and purpose."

Potential Positive Effects of Using Tape Recorders

- You can listen to an important portion of the lecture over and over again.
- You can supplement or clarify sections of the lecture that confused you or that you missed.
- Tape recordings can provide additional study materials to listen to when you drive or exercise.
- Tape recordings can help study groups reconcile conflicting notes.
- If you miss class, you might be able to have a friend record the lecture for you.

Potential Negative Effects of Using Tape Recorders

- You may tend to listen less in class.
- You may take fewer notes, figuring that you will rely on your tape.
- It may be time-consuming. When you attend a lecture in order to record it and then listen to the entire recording, you have taken twice as much time out of your schedule.
- If your tape recorder malfunctions or the recording is hard to hear, you may end up with very little study material, especially if your notes are sparse.

Think critically about whether using a tape recorder is a good idea for you. If you choose to try it, let the tape recorder be an additional resource for you instead of a replacement for your active participation and skills. Tape-recorded lectures and study tapes are just one study resource you can use in preparation for the tests that will often come your way.

How Can Preparation Help Improve Test Scores?

Test-Taking Tips
www.iss.stthomas.edu/
studyguides/tstprp.htm

The University of St. Thomas offers twenty tips on studying for that final. This Web site covers all the bases, from organizing yourself to anticipating test content.

Many people don't look forward to taking tests. If you are one of those people, try thinking of exams as preparation for life. When you volunteer, get a job, or work on your family budget, you'll have to apply what you know. This is exactly what you do when you take a test.

Like a runner who prepares for a marathon by exercising, eating right, taking practice runs, and getting enough sleep, you can take steps to master your exams. Your first step is to study until you understand the material that will be on the test. Your next step is to use the following strategies to become a successful test taker: Identify test type and material covered, use specific study skills, prepare physically, and conquer test anxiety.

Identify Test Type and Material Covered

Before you begin studying, try to determine the type of test you will face and what it will cover:

- Will it be a short-answer test with true/false and multiple-choice questions, an essay test, or a combination?
- Will the test cover everything you studied since the semester began or will it be limited to a narrow topic?
- Will the test be limited to what you learned in class and in the text or will it also cover outside readings?

Your instructors may answer these questions for you. Even though they may not tell you the specific questions that will be on the test, they might let you know what blocks of information will be covered and the question format. Some instructors may even drop hints throughout the semester about possible test questions. While some comments are direct ("I might ask a question on the subject of _____ on your next exam"), other clues are subtle. For example, when instructors repeat an idea or when they express personal interest in a topic ("One of my favourite theories is..."), they are letting you know that the material may be on the test.

Here are a few other strategies for predicting what may be on a test.

Use PQ3R to identify important ideas and facts. Often, the questions you write and ask yourself when you read assigned materials may be part of the test. In addition, any textbook study questions are good candidates for test material.

If you know people who took the instructor's course before, ask them about class tests. Try to find out how difficult the tests are and whether the test focuses more on assigned readings or class notes. Ask about instructor preferences. If you learn that the instructor pays close attention to detail such as facts or grammar, plan your work accordingly.

Examine old tests if instructors make them available in class or on reserve in the library. If you can't get copies of old tests, use clues from the class to predict test questions. After taking the first exam in the course, you will have a lot more information about what to expect in the future.

Use Specific Study Skills

Certain study skills are especially useful for test taking. They include choosing study materials, setting a study schedule, critical thinking, taking a pretest, and becoming organized.

Choose Study Materials

Once you have identified as much as you can about the subject matter of the test, choose the materials that contain the information you need to study. You can save yourself time by making sure that you aren't studying anything you don't need to. Go through your notes, your texts, any primary source materials that were assigned, and any handouts from your instructor. Set aside any materials you don't need so they won't take up your valuable time.

Set a Study Schedule

Use your time-management skills to set a schedule that will help you feel as prepared as you can be. Consider all the relevant factors—the materials you need to study, how many days or weeks until the test date, and how much time you can study each day. If you establish your schedule ahead of time and write it in your date book, you will be much more likely to follow it.

Schedules will vary widely according to situation. For example, if you have only three days before the test and no other obligations during that time, you might set two 2-hour study sessions for yourself during each day. On the other hand, if you have two weeks before a test date, classes during the day, and work three nights a week, you might spread out your study sessions over the nights you have off work during those two weeks.

Prepare Through Critical Thinking

Using the techniques from Chapter 4, approach your test preparation critically, working to understand rather than just to pass the test by repeating facts. As you study, try to connect ideas to examples, analyze causes and effects, establish truth, and look at issues from different perspectives. Although it takes work, critical thinking will promote a greater understanding of the subject and probably a higher grade on the exam. Using critical thinking is especially important for essay tests. Prepare by identifying potential essay questions and writing your responses.

Take a Pre-Test

Use questions from the ends of textbook chapters to create your own pre-test. Choose questions that are likely to be covered on the test, then answer them under testlike conditions—in quiet, with no books or notes to help you, and with a clock telling you when to quit. Try to duplicate the conditions of the actual test. If your course doesn't have an assigned text, develop questions from your notes and from assigned outside readings.

Become Organized

A checklist, like the one in Figure 7–3, will help you get organized and stay on track as you prepare for each test.

Prepare Physically

When taking a test, you often need to work efficiently under time pressure. If your body is tired or under stress, you will probably not think as clearly or perform as well. If you can, avoid working through the night. Get some sleep so that you can wake up rested and alert. If you are someone who presses the snooze button in the morning, try setting two alarm clocks and placing them across the room from your bed. That way, you'll be more likely to get to your test on time.

Eating right is also important. Sugar-laden snacks will bring your energy up only to send it crashing back down much too soon. Similarly, too much caffeine can add to your tension and make it difficult to focus. Eating nothing will leave you drained, but too much food can make you want to take a nap. The best advice is to eat a light, well-balanced meal before a test. When time is short, grab a high-energy snack such as a banana, some orange juice, or a granola bar.

Conquer Test Anxiety

A certain amount of stress can be a good thing. Your body is on alert, and your energy motivates you to do your best. For many students, however, the time before and during an exam brings a feeling of near-panic known as *test anxiety*. Described as a bad case of nerves that makes it hard to think or remember, test anxiety can make your life miserable and affect how you do on tests. When anxiety blocks performance, here are some suggestions:

Prepare so you'll feel in control. The more you know about what to expect on the exam, the better you'll feel. Find out what material will be covered, the format of the questions, the length of the exam, and the percentage of points assigned to each question.

Put the test in perspective. No matter how important it may seem, a test is only a small part of your educational experience and an even smaller part of your life. Your test grade does not reflect the kind of person you are or your ability to succeed in life.

Figure 7-3   Pre-Test Checklist[5]

Course: _____ Instructor: _____

Date, time, and place of test: _____

Type of test (e.g., is it a midterm or a minor quiz?): _____

What the instructor has told you about the test, including the types of test questions, the length of the test, and how much the test counts toward your final grade: _____

_____

_____

_____

_____

Topics to be covered on the test, in order of importance:
1. _____
2. _____
3. _____
4. _____
5. _____

Study schedule, including materials you plan to study (e.g., texts and class notes) and date you plan to complete each source:

Source	Date of Completion
1. _____	_____
2. _____	_____
3. _____	_____
4. _____	_____
5. _____	_____

Materials you are expected to bring to the test (e.g., your textbook, a sourcebook, a calculator): _____

_____

Special study arrangements (e.g., plan study group meetings, ask the instructor for special help, get outside tutoring): _____

_____

_____

Life-management issues (e.g., make child-care arrangements, rearrange work hours): _____

_____

_____

Make a study plan. Divide the plan into a series of small tasks. As you finish each one, you'll feel a sense of accomplishment and control.

Practise relaxation. When you feel test anxiety coming on, take some deep breaths, close your eyes, and visualize positive mental images related to the test, like getting a good grade and finishing confidently with time to spare.

Test Anxiety and the Returning Adult Student

If you're returning to school after a layoff of five, ten, or even twenty years, you may wonder if you can compete with younger students or if your mind is still able to learn new material. To counteract these feelings of inadequacy, focus on how your life experiences have given you skills you can use. For example, managing work and a family requires strong time management, planning, and communication skills that can help you plan your study time, juggle school responsibilities, and interact with students and instructors.

In addition, your life experiences give you examples with which you can understand ideas in your courses. For example, your relationship experiences may help you understand concepts in a psychology course; managing your finances may help you understand economics or accounting practices; and work experience may give you a context for what you learn in a business management course. If you let yourself feel positive about your knowledge and skills, you may improve your ability to achieve your goals.

Coping with Math Anxiety

Help with Math Anxiety
www.woodrow.org/
teachers/math/gender/
03b-tobias.html

If you suffer from math anxiety, read this article by Sheila Tobias, whose research has helped students cope with their fear of numbers.

For many students there is a special anxiety associated with taking a math test. As Sheila Tobias, author of *Overcoming Math Anxiety*[6], explains, *math anxiety* is linked to the feeling that math is impossible:

> The first thing people remember about failing at math is that it felt like sudden death. Whether it happened while learning word problems in sixth grade, coping with equations in high school, or first confronting calculus and statistics in college, failure was instant and frightening. An idea or a new operation was not just difficult, it was impossible! And instead of asking questions or taking the lesson slowly, assuming that in a month or so they would be able to digest it, people remember the feeling as certain as it was sudden, that they would *never* go any further in mathematics.

Students who believe they are no good at math probably won't do well on math tests, even if they study. Their attitude creates a huge problem. If you are one of these students, here are some steps you can take to begin thinking about math—and math tests—in a different way.

See the value in learning to use your mind in a mathematical way. Mathematical thinking is another type of critical thinking. It can help you solve the little and big problems that are part of your world, including how to measure the amount of wallpaper you need in a room, how to compare interest rates on student loans, and even how to analyze the stock market.

Think of math as a tool that will help you land a good job. In fields such as engineering, accounting, and banking, the ability to solve numerical problems

Real World Perspective

How can I prepare for exams?

Jeff Felardeau, Selkirk College, Nelson, B.C., Adult Education

I've been out of school for quite a long time, so when I returned to Selkirk College in Nelson, B.C., and had to memorize material for exams, I just wasn't prepared. The work I was doing didn't require me to use my memorization skills. I had the most difficulty memorizing for classes like biology and any of the sciences where you have to memorize a lot of facts. I'd work hard by repeating the information over and over in my mind, but I'd only be able to recall it for a  short time afterwards—long-term learning wasn't there. Whenever I'd prepare for an exam, I'd find myself in a "cram" mode because I didn't remember any of the material from class. It was like learning the material all over again.

I took a class called College Success, which gave me some good study tips. They taught me things like mind-mapping, listening skills, and note-taking styles. They also taught me to use word associations and visualization to help remember the material. It's helped me improve a lot but still, I get stuck in old habits and patterns and forget to apply the methods that will really help me improve. I know that if I don't change these old study patterns and habits, I'll hit the wall sooner or later. I can't keep using methods that served me in the past but are no longer effective for where I am today. What do you suggest?

Miriam Kapner, Music Major

Even though you have a good understanding of what it takes to prepare for an exam, the key is to remain disciplined. If your mind is wandering in class and you find you're staring out the window looking at the clouds, remember that you have control of your mind. By staying focused in class you will not have to study so much when exam time rolls around. Although we all fall victim to daydreaming, try to gain  control of your mind by thinking of your goals or by using simple mind tricks. Even if the class has a very boring teacher, there are ways to stay focused. One day a friend and I sat down and figured out exactly how much each class was costing us. When we realized the amount of money we were spending for that hour, it was a real eye-opener. If I'm really having a hard time, then I make sure I ask at least two questions per class. This forces me to pay attention.

In order to memorize, you need to be able to find some order. It helps if you have a reference point to begin with and then look for certain patterns or categories. I also use mnemonic devices to help me remember. In fact, I can still remember the ones I learned in elementary school: **G**eneral **E**lectric **L**ights **N**ever **D**im for the first five books of the Bible and of course, **E**very **G**ood **B**oy **D**eserves **F**udge for the lines in the treble clef. But mainly, whatever steps you take to improve your preparation for exams, remember that you are in control of your mind—not the other way around.

is at the heart of the work. In real estate, retail sales, medicine, and publishing, you may use math for tasks such as writing budgets and figuring mortgage rates.

Turn negative self-talk into positive self-talk. Instead of telling yourself that a problem is too hard, tell yourself that if you take small, logical steps, you will succeed. Says Tobias, "If we can talk ourselves into feeling comfortable and secure, we may let in a good idea."[7]

Don't believe that women can't do math. Sheila Tobias says that when male students fail a math quiz, they don't think they worked hard enough; however, when female students fail, they are three times more likely to feel that they just don't have what it takes.[8] Whether you are a man or a woman, work to overcome this stereotype.

Use the people and resources around you. Get to know your math instructor so you're comfortable asking for help. Join a math study group and make building confidence a group goal. Have a pep meeting right before a big test. Look for math-anxiety workshops. Seek out a tutor who can help you improve your skills and build your confidence.

Become comfortable in the world of math. Find a computer program with math games or buy a paperback book with math puzzles. Do percentages and estimations in your head. Have fun with problems and enjoy solving them. Then transfer these feelings to class work and tests.

Understand math's relationship to your life success. Being at ease with numbers can serve you in day-to-day functions. Percentages can help you compare the financial benefits of different loan programs; addition and subtraction will allow you to balance a chequebook, and fractions will help you compare costs at work. Furthermore, working with numbers helps to develop general thinking skills. The precise calculation and problem solving involved in math help you develop precision, a focus on detail, patience, and a sense of order.

When you have prepared using the strategies that work for you, you are ready to take your exam. Focus on methods that can help you succeed when the test begins.

What Strategies Can Help You Succeed on Tests?

Even though every test is different, there are general strategies that will help you handle almost all tests, including short-answer and essay exams.

Write Down Key Facts

Before you even look at the test, write down any key information—including formulas, rules, and definitions—that you studied recently or even right before you entered the test room. Use the back of the question sheet or a piece of scrap paper for your notes (make sure it is clear to your instructor that this scrap paper didn't come into the test room already filled in!). Recording this information right at the start will make forgetting less likely.

Begin with an Overview of the Exam

Even though exam time is precious, spend a few minutes at the start of the test to get a sense of the kinds of questions you'll be answering, what kind of thinking they require, the number of questions in each section, and the point value of each section. Use this information to schedule the time you need to spend on each section. For example, if a two-hour test is divided into two sections of equal point value—an essay section with four questions and a short-answer section with sixty questions—you can spend an hour on the essays (fifteen minutes per question) and an hour on the short-answer section (one minute per question).

As you make your calculations, think about the level of difficulty of each section. If you think you can handle the short-answer questions in less than an hour and that you'll need more time with the essays, rebudget your time in a way that works for you.

Know the Ground Rules

A few basic rules apply to any test. Following them will give you an advantage.

Read test directions. While a test made up of 100 true/false questions and one essay may look straightforward, the directions may tell you to answer eighty, or that the essay is an optional bonus. Some questions or sections may be weighted more heavily than others. Try circling or underlining key words and numbers that remind you of the directions.

Begin with the parts or questions that seem easiest to you. Starting with what you know best can boost your confidence and help you save time to spend on the harder parts.

Watch the clock. Keep track of how much time is left and how you are progressing. You may want to plan your time on a scrap piece of paper, especially if you have one or more essays to write. Wear a watch or bring a small clock with you to the test room. A wall clock may be broken, or there may be no clock at all! Take your time too. Rushing is almost always a mistake, even if you feel you've done well. Stay until the end so you can refine and check your work.

Master the art of intelligent guessing. When you are unsure of an answer, you can leave it blank or you can guess. In most cases, guessing will benefit

qualifier

A word, such as always, never, or often, that changes the meaning of another word or word group.

you. First eliminate all the answers you know—or believe—are wrong. Try to narrow your choices to two possible answers; then, choose the one that makes more sense to you. When you recheck your work, decide if you would make the same guesses again, making sure there isn't a qualifier or fact that you hadn't noticed before.

Follow directions on machine-scored tests. Machine-scored tests require that you use a special pencil to fill in a small box on a computerized answer sheet. Use the right pencil (usually, a number 2) and mark your answer in the correct space. Neatness counts on these tests, because the computer can misread stray pencil marks or partially erased answers. Periodically, check the answer number against the question number to make sure they match. One question skipped can cause every answer following it to be marked as incorrect.

Use Critical Thinking to Avoid Errors

When the pressure of a test makes you nervous, critical thinking can help you work through each question thoroughly and avoid errors. Following are some critical-thinking strategies to use during a test.

Recall facts, procedures, rules, and formulas. You base your answers on the information you recall. Think carefully to make sure you recall it accurately.

Think about similarities. If you don't know how to attack a question or problem, consider any similar questions or problems that you have worked on in class or while studying.

Notice differences. Especially with objective questions, items that seem different from what you have studied may indicate answers you can eliminate.

Think through causes and effects. For a numerical problem, think through how you plan to solve it and see if the answer—the effect of your plan—makes sense. For an essay question that asks you to analyze a condition or situation, consider both what caused it and what effects it has.

Find the best idea to match the example or examples given. For a numerical problem, decide what formula (idea) best applies to the example or examples (the data of the problem). For an essay question, decide what idea applies to, or links, the examples given.

Support ideas with examples. When you put forth an idea in an answer to an essay question, be sure to back up your idea with an adequate number of examples that fit.

Evaluate each test question. In your initial approach to any question, evaluate what kinds of thinking will best help you solve it. For example, essay questions often require cause-and-effect and idea-to-example thinking, while objective questions often benefit from thinking through similarities and differences.

The general strategies you have just explored also can help you address specific types of test questions.

Master Different Types of Test Questions

Although the goal of all test questions is to discover how much you know about a subject, every question type has its own way of asking what you know. Objective questions, such as multiple choice or true/false, test your ability to recall, compare, and contrast information and to choose the right answer from among several choices. Subjective questions, usually essay questions, demand the same information recall but ask that you analyze the mind actions and thinking processes required, then organize, draft, and refine a written response. The following guidelines will help you choose the best answers to both types of questions.

Multiple-Choice Questions

Multiple-choice questions are the most popular type on standardized tests. The following strategies can help you answer these questions:

Read the directions carefully. While most test items ask for a single correct answer, some give you the option of marking several choices that are correct.

Read each question thoroughly. Then look at the choices and try to answer the question.

Underline key words and phrases in the question. If the question is complicated, try to break it down into small sections that are easy to understand.

Pay special attention to qualifiers such as only, except, etc. For example, negative words in a question can confuse your understanding of what the question asks ("Which of the following is *not*...").

If you don't know the answer, eliminate those answers that you know or suspect are wrong. Your goal is to narrow down your choices. Here are some questions to ask:

- ⚙ Is the choice accurate in its own terms? If there's an error in the choice—for example, a term that is incorrectly defined—the answer is wrong.

- ⚙ Is the choice relevant? An answer may be accurate, but it may not relate to the essence of the question.

- ⚙ Are there any qualifiers, such as *always, never, all, none,* or *every*? Qualifiers make it easy to find an exception that makes a choice incorrect. For example, the statement that "children *always* begin talking before the age of two" can be eliminated as an answer to the question, "When do children generally start to talk?"

- ⚙ Do the choices give you any clues? Does a puzzling word remind you of a word you know? If you don't know a word, does any part of the word (prefix, suffix, or root) seem familiar to you?

Look for patterns that may lead to the right answer, then use intelligent guessing. Test-taking experts have found patterns in multiple-choice questions that may help you get a better grade. Here is their advice:

objective questions
Short-answer questions that test your ability to recall, compare, and contrast information and to choose the right answer from a limited number of choices.

subjective questions
Essay questions that require you to express your answer in terms of your own personal knowledge and perspective.

More Hints for Test Taking
www.ursuline.edu/stu_serv/
lrc/hints.htm

No matter what type of test your professors give you, this site offers helpful advice on preparation and writing.

> "A little knowledge that acts is worth infinitely more than much knowledge that is idle."
>
> Kahlil Gibran

- ⊙ Consider the possibility that a choice that is more *general* than the others is the right answer.
- ⊙ Look for a choice that has a middle value in a range (the range can be from small to large, from old to recent). This choice may be the right answer.
- ⊙ Look for two choices with similar meanings. One of these answers is probably correct.

Make sure you read every word of every answer. Instructors have been known to include answers that are correct except for a single word.

When questions are keyed to a long reading passage, read the questions first. This will help you focus on the information you need to answer the questions.

Here are some examples of the kinds of multiple-choice questions you might encounter in an Introduction to Psychology course[9] (the correct answer follows each question):

---

1. Arnold is at the company party and has had too much to drink. He releases all of his pent-up aggression by yelling at his boss, who promptly fires him. Arnold normally would not have yelled at his boss, but after drinking heavily he yelled because_____.

   a. parties are places where employees are supposed to be able to "loosen up"

   b. alcohol is a stimulant

   c. alcohol makes people less concerned with the negative consequences of their behaviour

   d. alcohol inhibits brain centres that control the perception of loudness

   (The correct answer is C)

2. Which of the following has not been shown to be a probable cause of or influence in the development of alcoholism in our society?

   a. intelligence   c. personality

   b. culture   d. genetic vulnerability

   (The correct answer is A)

True/False Questions

True/false questions test your knowledge of facts and concepts. Read them carefully to evaluate what they truly say. Try to take these questions at face value without searching for hidden meaning. If you're really stumped, guess (unless you're penalized for wrong answers).

Look for qualifiers in true/false questions, such as *all, only, always, because, generally, usually*, and *sometimes*, that can turn a statement that would otherwise be true into one that is false, or vice versa. For example, "The grammar rule, 'I before E except after C,' is *always* true" is *false*, whereas "The grammar rule, 'I before E except after C,' is *usually* true," is *true*. The qualifier makes the difference. Here are some examples of the kinds of true/false questions you might encounter in an Introduction to Psychology course.

Are the following questions true or false?

1. Alcohol use is always related to increases in hostility, aggression, violence, and abusive behaviour. (False)
2. Marijuana is harmless. (False)
3. Simply expecting a drug to produce an effect is often enough to produce the effect. (True)

Essay Questions

An essay question allows you to use your writing skills to demonstrate your knowledge and express your views on a topic. Start by reading the questions and deciding which to tackle (sometimes there's a choice). Then focus on what each question is asking, the mind actions you will have to use, and the writing directions. Read the question carefully and do everything you are asked to do. Some essay questions may contain more than one part.

Watch for certain action verbs that can help you figure out what to do. Figure 7–4 explains some words commonly used in essay questions. Underline these words as you read any essay question and use them as a guide.

Next, budget your time and begin to plan. Create an informal outline or think link to map your ideas and indicate examples you plan to cite to support those ideas. Avoid spending too much time on introductions or flowery prose. Start with a thesis idea or statement that states in a broad way what your essay will say (see Chapter 6 for a discussion of thesis statements). As you continue to write your first paragraph, introduce the essay's points, which may be sub-ideas, causes and effects, or examples. Wrap up the essay with a concise conclusion.

Use clear, simple language in your essay. Support your ideas with examples, and look back at your outline to make sure you are covering everything. Try to write legibly: If your instructor can't read your ideas, it doesn't matter how good they are. If your handwriting is messy, try printing, skipping every other line, or writing on only one side of the paper.

Do your best to save time to reread and revise your essay after you finish getting your ideas down on paper. Look for ideas you left out and sentences that might confuse the reader. Check for mistakes in grammar, spelling, punctuation, and usage. No matter what subject you are writing about, having a command of these factors will make your work all the more complete and impressive.

Figure 7-4   Common Action Verbs on Essay Tests

Analyze—Break into parts and discuss each part separately.

Compare—Explain similarities and differences.

Contrast—Distinguish between items being compared by focusing on differences.

Criticize—Evaluate the positive and negative qualities of what is being discussed.

Define—State the essential quality or meaning. Give the common idea.

Describe—Visualize and give information that paints a complete picture.

Discuss—Examine in a complete and detailed way, usually by connecting ideas to examples.

Enumerate/List/Identify—Recall and specify items in the form of a list.

Explain—Make the meaning of something clear, often by making analogies or giving examples.

Evaluate—Give your opinion about the value or worth of something, usually by weighing positive and negative qualities, and justify your conclusion.

Illustrate—Supply examples.

Interpret—Explain your personal view of facts and ideas and how they relate to one another.

Outline—Organize and present the sub-ideas or main examples of an idea.

Prove—Use evidence and argument to show that something is true, usually by showing cause and effect or by giving examples that support the idea to be proven.

Review—Provide an overview of ideas and establish their merits and features.

State—Explain clearly, simply, and concisely, being sure that each word gives the image you want.

Summarize—Give the important ideas in brief.

Trace—Present a history of the way something developed, often by showing cause and effect.

Here are some examples of essay questions you might encounter in your Introduction to Psychology course. In each case, notice the action verbs from Figure 7–4.

1. Summarize the theories and research on the causes and effects of daydreaming. Discuss the possible uses for daydreaming in a healthy individual.
2. Describe the physical and psychological effects of alcohol and the problems associated with its use.

Use Specific Techniques for Math Tests

Mathematical test problems present a special challenge to some students, especially those who suffer from math anxiety. These strategies may help you overcome any difficulties you might have.

Analyze problems carefully. Make sure that you take all the "givens" into account as you begin your calculations. Focus also on what you want to find or prove.

Write down any formulas, theorems, or definitions that apply to the problem. Do this before you begin your calculations.

Estimate before you begin, to come up with a "ballpark" solution. Then work the problem and check the solution against your estimate. The two answers should be close. If they're not, recheck your calculations. You may have made a simple calculation error.

Break the calculation into the smallest possible pieces. Go step by step and don't move on to the next step until you are clear about what you've done so far.

Recall how you solved similar problems. Past experience can give you valuable clues as to how a particular problem should be handled.

Draw a picture to help you see the problem. This can be a diagram, a chart, a probability tree, a geometric figure, or any other visual image that relates to the problem at hand.

Take your time. Precision demands concentration and focus. Also, if you're using a calculator, one wrong keystroke can mean the difference between a right and wrong answer.

Be neat. When it comes to numbers, mistaken identity can mean the difference between a right and a wrong answer. A 4 that looks like a 9 or a 1 that looks like a 7 can make trouble.

Use the opposite operation to check your work. When you come up with an answer, work backwards to see if you are right. Use subtraction to check your addition; use division to check multiplication; and so on. Try to check every problem before you hand in your paper.

Look back at the questions to be sure you did everything that was asked. Did you answer every part of the question? Did you show all the required work? Be as complete as you possibly can.

How Can You Learn from Test Mistakes?

The purpose of a test is to see how much you know, not merely to achieve a grade. The knowledge that comes from attending class and studying should allow you to correctly answer test questions. Knowledge also comes when you learn from your mistakes. If you don't learn from what you get wrong on a test, you are likely to repeat the same mistake again on another test and in life. Learn from test mistakes just as you learn from mistakes in your personal and business life.

Try to identify patterns in your mistakes by looking for:

- *careless errors*—In your rush to complete the exam, did you misread the question or directions, blacken the wrong box, skip a question, or use illegible handwriting?

- *conceptual or factual errors*—Did you misunderstand a concept or never learn it in the first place? Did you fail to master certain facts? Did you skip part of the assigned text or miss important classes in which ideas were covered?

You may want to rework the questions you got wrong. Based on the feedback from your instructor, try rewriting an essay, recalculating a math problem, or redoing the questions that follow a reading selection. As frustrating as they are, remember that mistakes show that you are human, and they can help you learn. If you see patterns of careless errors, promise yourself that next time you'll try to budget enough time to double-check your work. If you pick up conceptual and factual errors, rededicate yourself to better preparation.

When you fail a test, don't throw it away. First, take comfort in the fact that a lot of students have been in your shoes and that you are likely to improve your performance. Then recommit to the process by reviewing and analyzing your errors. Be sure you understand why you failed. You may want to ask for an explanation from your instructor. Finally, develop a plan to really learn the material, if you didn't understand it in the first place.

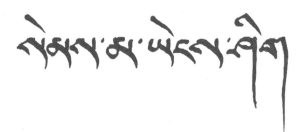

In Sanskrit—the ancient Indo-Aryan language of the Indian subcontinent and source of some of the modern languages of the area, such as Hindi and Bengali—the characters above read *sem ma yeng chik*, meaning "do not be distracted." This advice can refer to focus for a task or job at hand, the concentration required to critically think and talk through a problem, or the mental discipline of meditation.

Think of this concept as you strive to improve your listening and memory techniques. Focus on the task, the person, or the idea at hand. Try not to be distracted by other thoughts, other people's notions of what you should be doing, or any negative messages. Be present in the moment to truly hear and remember what is happening around you. Do not be distracted.

Chapter 7: Applications

Name _____ Date _____

Key into Your Life:
Opportunities to Apply What You Learn

Exercise 1: Optimum Listening Conditions

❂ Describe a recent classroom situation in which you had an easy time listening to the instructor.

Where are you? _____

What is the instructor discussing? _____

Is it a straight lecture or is there give-and-take between instructor and students? _____

_____

What is your state of mind? (List factors that might affect your ability to listen.) _____

_____

_____

_____

Are there any external barriers to communication? If yes, what are they, and how do they affect your concentration? _____

_____

_____

❂ Now describe a situation where you have found it more difficult to listen.

Where are you? _____

What is the instructor discussing? _____

Is it a straight lecture or is there give-and-take between instructor and students? _____

_____

What is your state of mind? (List factors that might affect your ability to listen.) _____

_____

_____

_____

Are there any external barriers to communication? If yes, what are they, and how do they affect your concentration? _____

_____

_____

⊛   Examine the two situations. Based on your descriptions, name three conditions that are crucial for you to listen effectively.

1. _____

2. _____

3. _____

What steps can you take to recreate these conditions in more difficult situations like the second one you described? _____

_____

_____

Exercise 2: Create a Mnemonic Device

Look back at all the memory principles examined in this chapter. Using what you learned about mnemonic devices, create a mnemonic that allows you to remember these memory principles quickly. You can create a mental picture or an acronym. If you are using a mental picture, describe it here; if you are using an acronym, write it and then indicate what each letter stands for.

_____

_____

_____

Think of other situations in which you used a mnemonic device to remember something. What was the device? How effective was it in helping you remember the information?

_____

_____

_____

_____

Exercise 3: Boost Your Memory

What do you have the most trouble remembering? Is it names, historic dates, scientific formulas, the actions in a sequence? Write it here. _____

_____

Now spend a week trying to improve. For example, if you have trouble remembering the battles of the War of 1812 in order, you could recite and rehearse them, then associate each battle with an image and link the images in a chain. Indicate here the techniques that you try:

1. _____

_____

2. _____

_____

3. _____

_____

   Did your skills improve? If so, what technique (or combination of techniques) helped the most? Explain how you think you can apply these techniques to other memory challenges.

_____

_____

_____

_____

Exercise 4: Test Analysis

When you get back your next test, take a detailed look at your performance.

- Start by writing what you think of your test performance and grade. Were you pleased or disappointed? If you made errors, were they careless or due to not knowing facts and concepts?

_____

_____

_____

- Next, list the test-preparation activities that helped you do well on the exam and the activities you wish you had done—and intend to do for the next exam:

Positive actions I took

_____

_____

_____

_____

Positive actions I intend to take next time

_____

_____

_____

_____

⊙ Finally, list the activities you don't intend to repeat when studying
   for the next test.

_____

_____

_____

Exercise 5 : Learning from Your Mistakes

For this exercise, use an exam on which you made one or more mistakes.

⊙ Why do you think you answered the question(s) incorrectly? _____

_____

_____

⊙ Did any qualifying terms, such as *always, sometimes, never, often,
   occasionally, only, no,* and *not,* make the question(s) more difficult or
   confusing? What steps could you have taken to clarify the meaning?

_____

_____

_____

⊙ Did you try to guess the correct answer? If so, why do you think you
   made the wrong choice? _____

_____

_____

_____

⊙ Did you feel rushed? If you had had more time, do you think you
   would have gotten the right answer(s)? What could you have done to
   budget your time more effectively?

⊙ If an essay question was a problem, what do you think went wrong? What will you do differently the next time you face an essay question on a test?

 # Key to Cooperative Learning:
Building Teamwork Skills

Hone Your Listening Skills Improve listening through teamwork. Divide into groups of five to nine to play a game called *Celebrity*. Each group will have two or three teams, each with two or three people (for example, a group of seven will have two teams of two and one of three). Using small slips of paper, each person must write down the names of five well-known people, one on each slip. The people may be living or dead and can have achieved celebrity status in any field—sports, entertainment, politics, arts and literature, science and medicine, and so on. Each scrap of paper should be folded to conceal the name written on it. Put all of the scraps together in one container. The only other equipment you need is a watch with a second hand.

Within each team of two, there is a giver and a receiver (team members switch roles every time they have a new turn). Teams take turns guessing. While a member of a non-guessing team times the pair for one minute, the giver of the guessing team picks a piece of paper and describes the named celebrity to the receiver without saying any part of the person's name. The giver can use words, sounds, motion, singing, anything that will help the receiver. (For Martin Short: "Famous actor, born in Toronto, last name is the opposite of long," etc.) If and when the receiver guesses correctly, the giver keeps that scrap and chooses another, continuing to go through as many names as possible before the minute is up. When time is called, the container of names (minus the names guessed) moves to the next team. (If a name remains unguessed when time is called, that paper has to go back into the container without the giver revealing the name.)

When all the names have been guessed, teams count their papers to learn their scores. Then come together as a class and take some time to exchange views about your experience. How did the time limit, teamwork atmosphere, or noise affect your ability to listen? Which names were you more able to guess? Which gave you trouble, and why? Evaluate your skills.

Key to Self-Expression:
Discovery Through Journal Writing

To record your thoughts, use a separate journal or the lined page at the end of the chapter.

Talk about how you feel about tests and how you generally perform when you take them.

As you walk into a room for a test, does your heart race or your mind go blank? Do you feel apprehensive? Does your performance on tests accurately reflect what you know or do your tests scores fall short of your knowledge? If there is a gap between your knowledge and your scores, why do you think this gap exists? What can you do to work through any test anxiety you have?

Key to Your Personal Portfolio:
Your Paper Trail to Success

Apply Your New Study Skills Combine your study skills to create a study plan that will help you maximize your performance on any test. First, look at your memory skills. Which ones will help you most as you prepare for exams?

- ☺ understanding what you memorize
- ☺ reciting and rehearsing
- ☺ separating main points from unimportant details
- ☺ planning study sessions so that you remember the most from each session
- ☺ separating material into digestible chunks
- ☺ using flash cards
- ☺ using mnemonic devices

Rank the items from most helpful to least helpful. Then, discuss how you will use the five most helpful items.

Next, use the following checklist for any test to make sure that you have covered all your bases.

_____ I asked the instructor what will be covered on the exam and the format of the test questions.

_____ I tried to learn as much as I could about the kinds of tests the instructor gives by talking to former students and getting copies of old exams.

_____ I used critical thinking to explore difficult concepts that might be on the test.

_____ I took a pre-test.

_____ I tried to prepare my body and mind to perform at their best.

_____ I used positive self-talk and other techniques to overcome negative thoughts that might affect my performance.

_____ I have gotten my personal life under control so I can focus on the exam.

_____ I have a plan of action that I will follow when I see the test for the first time. I'll try to get an overview of the test, learn test ground rules, schedule my time, and evaluate questions and choices in case I have to guess.

_____ I reviewed strategies for handling multiple-choice, true/false, and essay questions and feel comfortable with these strategies.

Finally, think back on what you learned in this chapter and in Chapter 5, the reading and studying chapter (you can refer to the material).

Now, develop a plan that shows how you will apply your new knowledge about study skills as you prepare for your next exam. Here are some of the items you can include:

- The specific critical-thinking techniques that will help you master the material

- The memory techniques that work best for you

- What you think about PQ3R as a study technique and whether you will try it

- The test-taking strategies that will help you prepare for and take your exams

- How to overcome what makes you anxious about tests

Using separate sheets of paper, construct your plan, using an outline or a think link.

To make the best plan, you have to know yourself and the techniques that will work best for you. Not every suggestion in this book is right for every person. Choose the skills that will work best for you and then use them to become a better student.

Name _____ Date _____

Journal Entry

_____
_____
_____
_____
_____
_____
_____
_____
_____
_____
_____
_____
_____
_____
_____
_____
_____
_____
_____
_____
_____
_____

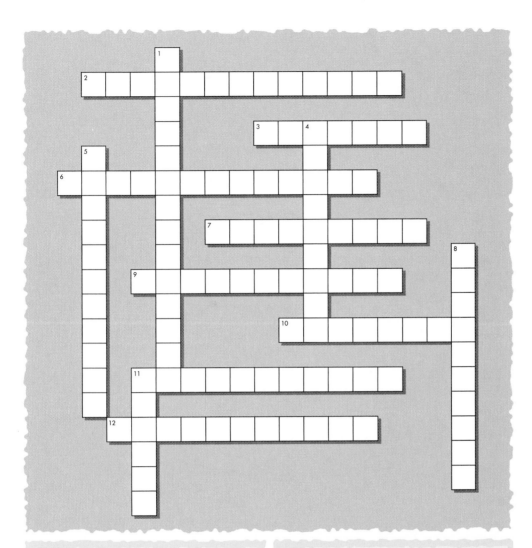

ACROSS

2. a note-taking system that divides a piece of paper into three sections, also called the "T-note" system
3. a system of organizing notes or thoughts that uses line-by-line phrases set off by varying indentations
6. a spontaneous generation of ideas or solutions, often as part of a problem-solving process
7. a system of seven mind actions that represent the ways in which you think
9. a bad case of nerves, occurring in an exam situation, that makes it difficult to think or remember
10. rapid reading of various chapter elements, including introductions, conclusions, and summaries
11. magazines, journals, and newspapers, which are published on a regular basis throughout the year
12. a mental point of view or outlook, based on a cluster of related assumptions, incorporating values, interests, and knowledge

DOWN

1. memory technique that involves associating new information with information you already know; for example, rhymes and acronyms
4. a technique for note-taking or writing down ideas that connects examples and ideas through the use of shapes connected by lines
5. a stream-of-consciousness technique that encourages you to put ideas down on paper as they occur to you, without censoring your ideas or worrying about organization
8. an act or instance of stealing or passing off the ideas or words of another as one's own
11. a word part that is added before the central part of a word

PART 3

Creating
Life Success

8 Relating to Others:
Appreciating Your Multicultural World

In this chapter, you will explore answers to the following questions:

⚬ How can you understand and accept others?

⚬ How can you express yourself effectively?

⚬ How do your personal relationships define you?

⚬ How can you handle conflict and criticism?

⚬ What role do you play in groups?

The greater part of your waking life involves interaction with people—family and friends, fellow students, co-workers, instructors, and many others. When you put energy into relationships and open the lines of communication, you receive much in return. Your relationships can also tell you a lot about the world and yourself. A strong network of diverse relationships can help you grow and progress toward your goals.

In Canada, diversity also means multiculturalism. Students in your class come from various ethnic, religious, and racial backgrounds. This is especially true in major Canadian cities with large immigrant populations such as Toronto, Vancouver, and Montreal. The Canadian Advertising Foundation forecasts that in the new millennium, the top five visible minorities in Canada will be Chinese (23%), Black (19%), South Asian (19%), West Asian/Arab (13%), and Filipino (8%).[1] While some minorities are "visible," others are not. Prejudice and discrimination aren't always visible either. Although Canada's Multiculturalism Act states that each individual is protected from discrimination on the basis of race, national or ethnic origin, or colour, stereotypes may affect how we interact with others.

This chapter will explore the issues of diversity that can hinder or help how you perceive others and relate to them. You will also explore communication styles, personal relationships, and the roles you can play in groups and on teams. Finally, you will read about various kinds of conflict and criticism, examining how to handle them so that they benefit you instead of setting you back.

Thinking It Through

Check those statements that apply to you right now:

☐ When I think of multiculturalism, I think of different races and ethnic groups.

☐ I'm not quite sure why multiculturalism should be important to me.

☐ Sometimes I feel like people don't hear what I'm trying to say.

☐ My personal problems tend to overwhelm me.

☐ I have a difficult time functioning in a group.

☐ I avoid conflict because it makes me uncomfortable.

How Can You Understand and Accept Others?

Human interaction is an essential element of life. In a diverse world, many people are different from what you are familiar with and perceive as "normal." In this section you will explore diversity in your world, the positive effects of accepting diversity, and how to overcome barriers to understanding. The first requirements for dealing with differences are an open mind and a willingness to learn.

Diversity in Your World

For centuries, travel to different countries was seen as part of a complete education. Edith Wharton, a nineteenth-century author, wrote a story called "False Dawn" in which a character named Mr. Raycie recommends travel to his son: "A young man, in my opinion, before setting up for himself, must see the world; form his taste; fortify his judgment. He must study the most famous monuments, examine the organization of foreign societies, and the habits and customs of those older civilizations…I believe he will be able to learn much."[2] When cultures were so separated, learning about differences was best accomplished through travel.

Today, although travelling is still a valuable way to learn, different places and people often come to you. More and more, diversity is part of your community, on your television, on your Internet browser, at your school, in your workplace, and in your family. It used to be that most people lived in societies with others who seemed very similar to them. Now, differences are often woven into everyday life. Canada has been officially multicultural since 1971.

You may encounter examples of diversity such as these:

- Communities with people from different stages of life
- Co-workers who represent a variety of ethnic origins
- Classmates who speak a number of different languages
- Social situations featuring people from various cultures, religions, and sexual orientations
- Individuals who marry a person or adopt a child from a different racial or religious background
- Diverse restaurants, services, and businesses in the community
- Neighbourhoods with immigrants from a variety of backgrounds
- Different lifestyles as reflected in books, magazines and newspapers, television, movies, music, the Internet, and other forms of popular culture
- People in the workplace who have a variety of disabilities—some more obvious than others

Each person has a choice about how to relate to others—or *whether* to relate to them. No one can force you to interact with any other person, or to adopt a particular attitude as being "right." Considering two important responsibilities may help you sort through your options.

diversity

The variety that occurs in every aspect of humanity, including both visible and invisible characteristics.

Encouraging Diversity
www.bby-multicultural.
bc.ca/

The Web site of this Burnaby, British Columbia, organization contains several articles on multiculturalism in Canada. It's an excellent primer on the issues surrounding race and ethnicity in Canada.

Your responsibility to yourself lies in being true to yourself, in taking time to think through your reactions to other people. When you evaluate your thoughts, try to also consider their source: Have you heard these ideas from other people or organizations or the media? Do you agree with them, or does a different approach feel better to you? Through critical thinking you can arrive at decisions about which you feel comfortable and confident.

Your responsibility to others lies in treating people with tolerance and respect. No one will like everyone he or she meets, but acknowledging that others deserve respect and have a right to their opinions will build bridges of communication. The more people accept one another, the more diverse relationships will be able to thrive.

The Positive Effects of Diversity

Accepting diversity has very real benefits to people in all kinds of relationships. Acceptance and respect form the basis of any successful interaction. As more situations bring diverse people into relationships, communication will become more and more dependent upon acceptance and mutual understanding.

Consider how positive relationships with diverse people may contribute to success. Relationships among family, friends, and neighbours affect personal life. Relationships among students, instructors, and other school personnel affect student life. Relationships among co-workers, supervisors, and customers/clients affect work life. Understanding and communication in these relationships can bring positive effects such as satisfying relationships, achievement, and progress. Failure to understand and communicate well can have negative effects.

For example, examine the potential effects of reactions to diversity in the following situations. Although each of these situations focuses on the reaction of only one person, it's important to note that both parties need to work together to establish mutual trust and openness.

A male Italian employee has a female First Nations supervisor. If the employee believes negative stereotypes about women or Native Canadians and resists taking directions from the supervisor, he may lose his job or be viewed as a liability. On the other hand, if the employee can respect the supervisor's authority and consider any different methods or ideas she has, their relationship is more likely to become supportive and productive. He may then be more likely to feel comfortable, perform well, and move up at work.

A student with a learning disability has an Asian instructor. If the student assumes that Asian people are superior and intimidating, and lets that opinion lead her to resist the advice and directions her instructor gives her, she may do poorly in the class or drop the course. On the other hand, if the student stays open to what the instructor has to offer, the instructor may feel respected and may be more encouraging. The student may then be more likely to pay attention in class, work hard, and advance in her education.

A white man has a sister who adopts a biracial child. If the man cuts off contact with his sister because he fears racial differences and doesn't approve of

Canadian Ethnocultural Council
www.ethnocultural.ca/

This Web site contains articles and links promoting multiculturalism as a positive element in Canadian life.

"Minds are like parachutes. They only function when they are open."

Sir James Dewar

racial mixing, he may deny himself her support and create a rift in the family. On the other hand, if the man can accept the new family member and respect his sister's choice, she may feel more supported and continue to support him in turn. The situation may help to build a close and rewarding family relationship.

Accepting others isn't always easy, and it's common to let perceptions about people block your ability to communicate. Following are some barriers that can hinder your ability to accept and understand others, and suggestions for how to overcome them.

Barriers to Understanding

You deserve to feel positive about who you are, where you come from, what you believe, and the others with whom you identify. However, problems arise when people use the power of group identity to put others down or cut themselves off from others. Table 8–1 shows how an open-minded approach can differ from an approach that is characterized by barriers.

Stereotypes, prejudice, discrimination, stereotype vulnerability, and fear of differences all can form barriers to communication.

Table 8–1   A Closed-Minded Approach vs. an Open-Minded Approach

Your Role	Situation	Closed-Minded Approach	Open-Minded Approach
Team member on the job	A co-worker from India observes a Hindu religious ritual at lunchtime.	You stare at the religious ritual, thinking it weird. You feel that this co-worker should just blend in and act like everyone else.	Your observe the ritual, respecting how the person expresses religious beliefs. You study the Hindu faith in your spare time to learn more.
Fellow student	For an assignment, you are paired up with a student old enough to be your mother.	You figure that the student will be closed off to the modern world. You think that she might also act like a parent and preach to you about how to do the assignment.	You avoid thinking that this student will act like your parents and get to know her as an individual. You stay open to what you can learn from her experiences and knowledge.
Friend	You are invited to dinner at a friend's house for the first time. When he introduces you to his partner, you realize that he is gay.	You are turned off by the idea of two men in a relationship and by gay culture in general. You are uncomfortable and make an excuse to leave early. You avoid your friend from then on.	You have dinner with your friend and his partner. You learn that they have a committed, supportive relationship. You take the opportunity to learn more about who they are and what their lives are like.
Employee	Your new boss is Japanese Canadian, hired from a competing company.	You assume that your new boss is very hard-working, expecting unrealistic things from you and your co-workers. You assume she doesn't take time to socialize.	Your rein in your assumptions, knowing they are based on stereotypes, and approach your new boss with an open mind.

Stereotypes

As you learned in Chapter 4, an assumption is an idea that you accept without looking for proof. A stereotype occurs when an assumption is made about a person or group of people, based on one or more characteristics. You may have heard stereotypical assumptions such as these: "Women are too emotional for business." "All Quebeckers want to separate." "All western Canadians are rednecks." "Newfoundlanders like to drink." "First Nations people are lazy." "White people are cold and power-hungry." "Gay people sleep around." "People who are learning-disabled can't hold down jobs." "Older people can't learn new things." "Croatians hate Serbians and vice versa." Stereotypes are as common as they are destructive.

Why might people stereotype? Here are a few reasons:

People seek patterns and logic. Trying to make sense of a complex world is part of human nature. People often try to find order by using the labels and categories that stereotypes provide.

Stereotyping is quick and easy. Making an assumption about a person from observing an external characteristic is easier than working to know a person as a unique individual. Labelling a group of people based on a characteristic they seem to have in common takes less time and energy than exploring the differences and unique qualities within the group.

Movies, magazines, and other media encourage stereotyping. The more people see stereotypical images—the unintelligent blonde, the funny overweight person, the evil white businessman—the easier it is to believe that such stereotypes are universal.

The ease of stereotypes comes at a high price. First and foremost, stereotypes can perpetuate harmful generalizations and falsehoods about others. These false ideas can promote discrimination. For example, if an employer believes that Vietnamese people cannot speak English well, he might not even bother to interview them. Secondly, stereotypes also communicate the message that you don't care about or respect others enough to discover who they really are. And others may not give you a chance if they feel that you haven't given them a chance.

Addressing stereotypes. Recall from the critical-thinking material in Chapter 4 the questions you can ask about an assumption in order to examine its validity. Apply these questions to stereotypes:

1. In what cases is this stereotype true, if ever? In what cases is it not true?

2. Has stereotyping others benefited me? Has it hurt me? In what ways?

3. If someone taught me this stereotype, why? Did that person think it over or just accept it?

4. What harm could be done by always accepting this stereotype as true?

> **stereotype**
> A standardized mental picture that represents an oversimplified opinion or uncritical judgment.

Using these steps, think through the stereotypes you assume are true. When you hear someone else use a stereotype and you know some information that disproves it, volunteer that information. Encourage others to think through stereotypes and to reject them if they don't hold up under examination.

Give others the benefit of the doubt. Thinking beyond stereotypes is an important step toward more open lines of communication.

Prejudice

prejudice

A preconceived judgment or opinion, formed without just grounds or sufficient knowledge.

Basic Rights
www.wwlia.org/
ca-chart.htm

The Canadian Charter of Rights and Freedoms grants everyone the same basic human rights.

Prejudice occurs when people "prejudge," meaning that they make a judgment before they have sufficient knowledge upon which to base that judgment. People often form prejudiced opinions on the basis of a particular characteristic—gender, race, culture, abilities, sexual orientation, religion, and so on. You may be familiar with the labels for particular kinds of prejudice, such as *racism* (prejudice based on race) or *ageism* (prejudice based on age). Any group can be subjected to prejudice, although certain groups have more often been on the receiving end of such closed-minded attitudes. Prejudice can lead people to disrespect, harass, and put down others. In some cases, prejudice may lead to unrealistic expectations of others that aren't necessarily negative, such as if someone were to assume that all Jewish people excel in business.

Prejudice can have one or more causes. Some common causes include the following:

People experience the world through the lens of their own particular identity. You grow up in a particular culture and family and learn their attitudes. When you encounter different ideas and ways of life, you may react by categorizing them. You may also react with ethnocentrism—the idea that your group is better than anyone else's.

When people get hurt, they may dislike or blame anyone who seems similar to the person who hurt them. Judging others based on a bad experience is human nature, especially when a certain characteristic raises strong emotions.

Jealousy and fear of personal failure can lead a person to want to put others down. When people are feeling insecure about their own abilities, they may find it easier to devalue the abilities of others rather than to take risks and try harder themselves.

The many faces of prejudice often show on college and university campuses. A student may not want to work with an in-class group that contains people of another race. Campus clubs may tend to limit their membership to a particular group and exclude others. Religious groups may devalue the beliefs of other religions. Groups that gather based on a common characteristic may be harassed by others. Women or men may find that instructors or fellow students judge their abilities and attitudes based on their gender. All of these attitudes severely block attempts at mutual understanding.

Addressing prejudice. Being critical of people who are different cuts you off from all kinds of perspectives and people that can enhance the quality of your life. Critical thinking is your key to changing prejudicial attitudes. For example, suppose you find yourself thinking that a certain student in your class isn't the type of person you want to get to know. Ask yourself: Where did I get this attitude? Am I accepting someone else's judgment? Am I making judgments based on how this person looks or speaks or behaves? How does having this attitude affect me or others? If you see that your attitude needs to change, have the courage to activate that change by considering the person with an open, accepting mind.

Another tactic, and often an extremely difficult one, is to confront people you know when they display a prejudiced attitude. It can be hard to stand up to someone and risk a relationship or, if the person is your employer, even a job. On the other hand, your silence may imply that you agree. Evaluate the situation and decide what choice is most suitable and is true to your values. Ask yourself if you can associate with a person if he or she thinks or behaves in a way that you do not respect.

You have a range of choices when deciding whether to reveal your feelings about someone's behaviour. You can decide not to address it at all. You may drop a humorous hint and hope that you make your point. You may make a small comment to "test the waters" and see how the person reacts, hoping that later you can have a more complete discussion about it. Whatever you do, express your opinion respectfully. Perhaps the other person will take that chance to rethink the attitude; perhaps he or she will not. Either way, you have taken an important stand.

Discrimination

Discrimination occurs when people deny others opportunities because of their perceived differences. Prejudice often accompanies discrimination. Discrimination can mean being denied jobs or advancement, equal educational opportunities, equal housing opportunities, services, or access to events, people, rights, privileges, or commodities.

Discrimination happens in all kinds of situations, revolving around gender, language, race, culture, and other factors. A 32-year-old married woman may not get a job because the interviewer assumes that she will become pregnant. A Russian person may be fired from a restaurant job because his English is heavily accented. Sheryl McCarthy, an African-American columnist, sees it on the street. "Nothing is quite so basic and clear as having a cab go right past your furiously waving body and pick up the white person next to you," she says in her book, *Why Are the Heroes Always White?*[3] "Sometimes you can debate whether racism was the motivating factor in an act; here there is no doubt whatsoever."

People with disabilities are often targets of discrimination because others may believe that they are depressed and incapacitated. John Hockenberry, a wheelchair-using paraplegic who travels the world in his work as an award-winning journalist, challenges the idea that people with disabilities lead lives of unproductive misery. "My body may have been capable of less, but virtually all of what it could do was suddenly charged with meaning. This feeling was the hardest to translate to the outside, where people wanted to believe that I must have to paint things in this way to keep from killing myself," he says in his memoir *Moving Violations*.[4]

Obesity can invite discrimination as well. People who are overweight may have trouble getting jobs or advancing in their careers. Even shopping for clothing can present limited options. Only recently have certain name-brand designers begun to create clothing in women's sizes above 12, and many designers still discriminate.

Addressing discrimination.   The Canadian Human Rights Act states that it is unlawful to be denied an education, work, or the chance to apply for work, housing, or basic rights based on your race, creed, colour, age, gender, national or ethnic origin, religion, marital status, potential or actual pregnancy, or potential or actual illness or disability. Unfortunately, the law is frequently broken, with the result that incidents go unnoticed. Many times people don't report incidents, fearing repercussions from those they accuse.

There have been several recent cases in which the Canadian Human Rights Commission has ruled that certain hiring practices were discriminatory. Two cases illustrate this point. In the first case, Air Canada agreed to provide more job opportunities for First Nations people after it was found that its hiring practices discriminated against them.[5] Also, the Canadian Armed Forces (CAF) retirement policy was ruled ageist, after nine former members of the CAF were forced to retire in the 1980s.[6]

Sometimes people don't even notice their attitudes seeping through, such as in an interview situation. First and foremost, be responsible for your own behaviour. Never knowingly participate in or encourage discrimination. When you act on prejudicial attitudes by discriminating against someone, the barrier to communication this discrimination causes hurts you as well as anyone else involved. A person who feels denied and shut out may be likely to do the same to you, and may even encourage others to do so.

Second, if you witness a discriminatory act or feel that you have been discriminated against, decide whether you want to approach an authority about it. You may want to begin by talking to the person who can most directly affect the situation—an instructor, your supervisor, a housing authority. Don't assume that people know when they hurt or offend someone. For example, if you have a disability and you find that accommodations haven't been made for you at school, speak up. Meet with an adviser to discuss your needs for transport, equipment, or a particular schedule.

If you don't find satisfaction and change at that level, try the next level of authority (an administrator, your supervisor's boss, a government official). If that doesn't produce results, you can take legal action, although legal struggles can take a lot of time and drain a great deal of money out of your pocket. At each decision stage, weigh all the positive and negative effects and evaluate whether the action is feasible for you. Although keeping quiet may not bring change, you may not be able to act right away. In the long run, if you are able to stand up for what you believe, your actions may be worthwhile.

Stereotype Vulnerability

When people feel that they are part of a certain group, they take pride from what they perceive to be good about that group. On the other hand, they may want to distance themselves from stereotypical qualities associated with that group, such as when a woman in a business situation wants to avoid seeming too emotional. *Stereotype vulnerability* happens when people avoid facing a problem because they think that admitting it will just perpetuate a stereotype.

Canadian Human Rights
Commission
www.chrc.ca

This Canadian government Web site offers information about discrimination and how it can be avoided.

Real World Perspective

How can I adjust to diversity?

Carrie Nelson, Spanish Language Studies

Once I made the decision to study Spanish, the idea of studying abroad in a Spanish-speaking country was simultaneous. I have always been fascinated with learning about other cultures and being introduced to new ideas. Once I started filling out forms for the school in Mexico and buying my plane ticket, however, I began to question my decision. I wondered if I could really handle this big of a change in my life. But in my heart I knew that I had made the right decision.

Now that I am actually studying in Guadalajara, Mexico, I cannot imagine how I could have been nervous. This is one of the best decisions I have ever made, although I have had to adjust to living here. In some aspects the Mexican and North American cultures are very similar but in other regards they can be very different. For example, in Canada and the United States, the customer is considered the most important person and expects to be served very quickly. In Mexico the customer is important but the way of life is much more relaxed. Therefore if a clerk gets a personal phone call they will most likely talk to that person whether there is a customer waiting or not.

Every day I experience something new or begin to better understand the differences in our cultures. By learning about other people, I am learning more about myself and the beauty and complexity of people. Still, I would like to deepen my relationship with the people of Guadalajara. I realize I am just scratching the surface of this experience. Do You have any suggestions?

Kaoruko Kinoshita, Television Broadcasting

I arrived in Canada from Toyama, Japan, in 1996. Toyama is located northwest of Tokyo. I know how you feel as a "stranger in a strange land." It is intense and exciting. I feel that you will benefit from your experiences in Guadalajara. I know I have benefited from my experiences here in Canada.

The main difference I found at school was that here in Canada the classes are very interactive. I guess it is our national character that we don't ask questions during the class. The classroom tends to be quiet the whole time; there are no questions or objections to the professor's lecture. In our culture, an objection is a sign of disrespect and is considered an insult to the teacher.

Your experiences in Guadalajara will be challenging. This is good. I have always felt that you learn by putting yourself in challenging situations. Personally, when I first came here, I decided to be with Canadians all the time, so that I would have to use English as a means of survival. However, it's also important to be proud of your home country and its unique culture, since you do tend to lose or forget some of where you came from while adapting to another culture.

An example of stereotype vulnerability is a Canadian immigrant who resists seeking English tutoring for fear of seeming like just another foreigner. Another example is a person in a wheelchair who avoids asking for help in scheduling class locations for fear of being identified as an angry, demanding, disabled person. Such fears cut people off from communication that could improve their lives.

Another side of stereotype vulnerability occurs when people refuse help because they believe that others want to help them out of pity for their minority status. "She thinks I'm disadvantaged because I'm Black." "He only wants to help because he looks down on my having a learning disability." "They want to give me charity." These refusals are based on assumptions. Sometimes, such assumptions may contain a grain of truth. Frequently, though, the person who offers help just wants to help another human being, and the person who refuses it loses out on what might be valuable assistance.

Addressing stereotype vulnerability. Don't let stereotypes prevent you from getting assistance. If you find yourself avoiding help because you don't want to be labelled, have the courage to overcome your hesitation. Approach someone who can help you and give that person a chance to get to know your individual needs and problems. Perhaps he or she will see you not as a representative of a group but as an individual who needs and deserves specific attention.

Curb your own tendencies to judge according to stereotypes. Even if someone fulfills a stereotype about the group to which he or she belongs, never assume this stereotype is true of everyone else in that group. Approach every person as a unique individual.

If you feel that someone has offered you help out of pity for you, think through your assumption. Consider the possibility that he or she simply wants to help you. You may even want to discuss the situation with the person. Often a person who offers help can offend without meaning to. If you don't need or want that kind of help, or you don't like the way it was offered, say so clearly and respectfully. In addition, if you are the one offering help, be respectful of the fact that others may not want your help.

Fear of Differences

It's human instinct to fear the unknown. Many people stop long before they actually explore anything unfamiliar. They allow their fear to prevent them from finding out anything about what's outside their known world. As cozy as that world may be, it also may be limiting, cutting off communication from people who could enrich that world in many different ways.

The fear of differences has many effects. A young person who fears the elderly may avoid visiting a grandparent in a nursing home. A person of one religion might reject friendships with those of other religions out of a fear of different religious beliefs. Someone in a relationship may fear the commitment of marriage. A person might turn down an offer to buy a house in a neighbourhood that is populated with people from a different ethnic group. In each case, the person has denied himself or herself a chance to learn a new perspective, communicate with new individuals, and grow from new experiences.

"I have a dream that one day on the red hills of Georgia the sons of former slaves and the sons of former slave owners will be able to sit down together at the table of brotherhood."
Martin Luther King, Jr.

Police and Multiculturalism
www.ccprr.com/english.html

Read how police officers are working toward a better understanding of the role of culture in the Canadian justice system.

Addressing your fear of differences. Diversity doesn't mean that you have to feel comfortable with everyone or agree with what everyone else believes. The fear of differences, though, can keep you from discovering anything outside your own world. Challenge yourself by looking for opportunities to expose yourself to differences. Today's world increasingly presents such opportunities. You can choose a study partner in class who has a different ethnic background. You can expand your knowledge with books or magazines. You can visit a museum or part of town that introduces a new culture to you. You can attend an unfamiliar religious service with a friend. Gradually broaden your horizons and consider new ideas.

If you think others are uncomfortable with differences, encourage them to work through their discomfort. Explain the difference so that it doesn't seem so mysterious. Offer to help them learn more in a setting that isn't threatening. Bring your message of the positive effects of diversity to others.

Accepting and Dealing with Differences

Successful interaction with the people around you benefits everyone. The success of that exchange depends upon your ability to accept differences. How open can you be? Your choices range from rejecting all differences to freely celebrating them, with a range of possibilities in between. Ask yourself important questions about what course of action you want to take. Realize that the opinions of family, friends, the media, and any group with which you identify may sometimes lead you into perspectives and actions that you haven't thought through completely. Do your best to sort through outside opinions and make a choice that feels right.

At the forefront of the list of ways to deal with differences is mutual respect. Respect for yourself and others is essential. Admitting that other people's cultures, behaviours, races, religions, appearances, and ideas deserve as much respect as your own promotes communication and learning.

What else can you do to accept and deal with differences?

Avoid judgments based on external characteristics. These include skin colour, weight, facial features, or gender.

Cultivate relationships with people of different cultures, races, perspectives, and ages. Find out how other people live and think, and see what you can learn from them.

Educate yourself and others. "We can empower ourselves to end racism through massive education," say Tamara Trotter and Joycelyn Allen in *Talking Justice: 602 Ways to Build and Promote Racial Harmony.*[7] "Take advantage of books and people to teach you about other cultures. Empowerment comes through education. If you remain ignorant and blind to the critical issues of race and humanity, you will have no power to influence positive change." One source for essays on diversity in Canada is *The Colour of Democracy: Racism in Canadian Society*,[8] by Francis Henry, Carol Tator, Winston Mattis, and Tim Rees, which looks at some subtle forms of institutional racism in Canadian media, education, and history. Meanwhile, the book *Multiculturalism in Canada*,[9] by Augie Fleras and Jean Leonard Elliott, states that while multiculturalism has become a norm in Canadian society, many Canadians "fail to appreciate the complexities and the nuances of multiculturalism." Read about other cultures and people. It can serve to help your communication style.

Be sensitive to the particular needs of others at school and on the job. Think critically about their situations. Try to put yourself in their place by asking yourself questions about what you would feel and do if you were in a similar situation.

Work to listen to people whose perspectives clash with or challenge your own. Acknowledge that everyone has a right to his or her opinion, whether or not you agree with it.

Look for common ground—parenting, classes, personal challenges, interests.

Help other people, no matter how different they may be. Sheryl McCarthy writes about an African-American man who, in the midst of the 1992 Los Angeles riots, saw a man being beaten and helped him to safety. "When asked why he risked grievous harm to save an Asian man he didn't even know, Williams said, 'Because if I'm not there to help someone else, when the mob comes for me, will there be someone there to save me?' "[10] Continue the cycle of kindness.

Explore your own background, beliefs, and identity. Share what you learn with others.

Cultivate your own personal diversity. You may be one of the growing population of people who have two, three, or even ten different cultures in your background. Perhaps your father is Cree and Filipino and Scottish, and your mother is Creole (French, Spanish, and African American). Respect and explore your heritage. Even if you identify only with one group or culture, there are many different sides of you.

Take responsibility for making changes instead of pointing the finger at someone else. Avoid blaming problems in your life on certain groups of people.

Learn from the atrocities of history like slavery and the Holocaust. Cherish the level of freedom you have and seek continual improvement at home and elsewhere in the world.

Teach your children about other cultures. Impress upon them the importance of appreciating differences while accepting that all people have equal rights.

Recognize that people everywhere have the same basic needs. Everyone loves, thinks, hurts, hopes, fears, and plans. People are united through their essential humanity.

Expressing your ideas clearly and interpreting what others believe are crucial keys to communicating within a diverse world. The following section examines how you can communicate most effectively with the people around you.

How Can You Express Yourself Effectively?

The only way for people to know each other's needs is to communicate as clearly and directly as possible. Successful communication promotes successful school, work, and personal relationships. Exploring communication styles, paying attention to body language, addressing specific communication problems, and using specific success strategies will help you express yourself effectively.

Exploring Communication Styles

Communication is an exchange between two or more people. The speaker's goal is for the listener (or listeners) to receive the message exactly as the speaker intended. Different people, however, have different styles of communicating. Problems arise when one person has trouble "translating" a message that comes from someone who uses a different style. There are at least four communication styles into which people tend to fit: the intuitor, the senser, the thinker, and the feeler. Of course, people may shift around or possess characteristics from more than one category, but for most people one or two styles are dominant. Recognizing specific styles in others will help you communicate more clearly.[11]

The Styles

The following are characteristics of each communication style.

A person using the *intuitor* style is interested in ideas more than details, often moves from one concept or generalization to another without referring to examples, values insight and revelations, talks about having a vision, looks toward the future, and can be oriented toward the spiritual.

A person showing the style of *senser* prefers details or concrete examples to ideas and generalizations, is often interested in the parts rather than the whole, prefers the here-and-now to the past or future, is suspicious of sudden insights or revelations, and feels that "seeing is believing."

A person using the *thinker* style prefers to analyze situations, likes to solve problems logically, sees ideas and examples as useful if they help to figure something out, and becomes impatient with emotions or personal stories unless they have a practical purpose.

A person showing the style of *feeler* is concerned with ideas and examples that relate to people, often reacts emotionally, is concerned with values and their effects on people and other living things, and doesn't like "cold logic" or too much detail.

You can benefit from shifting from style to style according to the situation, particularly when trying to communicate with someone who prefers a style different from yours. Shifting, however, is not always easy or possible. The most important task is to try to understand the different styles and to help others understand yours. In general, no one style is any better than another. Each has its own positive effects that enhance communication and negative effects that can hinder it, depending on the situation.

Identifying Your Styles

These four styles are derived from the Myers-Briggs Type Indicator (MBTI). Because the learning style assessments are also in part derived from the MBTI, you will notice similarities between those assessments and these communication styles. Table 8–2 shows how some learning styles may correspond loosely to the communication styles. Not all individual learning styles within the assessments are mentioned, and the styles that are noted may correspond to different styles in different situations, but these matchups depict the most common associations. Finding where your learning styles fit may help you to determine your dominant communication style or styles.

Adjusting to the Listener's Style

When you are the speaker, you will benefit from an understanding of both your own style and the styles of your listeners. It doesn't matter how clear you think you are being if the person you are speaking to can't "translate" your message by understanding your style. Try to take your listener's style into consideration when you communicate.

Following is an example of how adjusting to the listener can aid communication.

An intuitor-dominant instructor to a senser-dominant student: "Your writing isn't clear." The student's reply: "What do you mean?"

- *Without adjustment:* If the intuitor doesn't take note of the senser's need for detail and examples, he or she may continue with a string of big-picture ideas that might further confuse and

Table 8–2 Learning Styles and Communication Styles

Communication Style	Learning-Styles Inventory	Pathways to Learning (Multiple Intelligences)	Personality Spectrum
Intuitor	Theoretical, Holistic	Intrapersonal	Adventurer
Senser	Factual	Bodily-Kinesthetic	Organizer
Thinker	Linear	Logical-Mathematical	Thinker
Feeler	Reflective	Interpersonal	Giver

turn off the senser. "You need to elaborate more. Try writing with your vision in mind. You're not considering your audience."

- ✪ *With adjustment:* If the intuitor shifts toward a focus on detail and away from his or her natural focus on ideas, the senser may begin to understand, and the lines of communication can open. "You introduced your central idea at the beginning but then didn't really support it until the fourth paragraph. You need to connect each paragraph's idea to the central idea. Also, not using a lot of examples for support makes it seem as though you are writing to a very experienced audience."

Adjusting to the Communicator's Style

As a facet of communication, listening is just as important as speaking. When you are the listener, try to stay aware of the communication style of the person who is speaking to you. Observe how that style satisfies or doesn't satisfy what a person of your particular style prefers to hear. Work to understand the speaker in the context of his or her style and translate the message into one that makes sense to you.

Following is an example of how adjusting to the communicator can boost understanding.

A feeler-dominant employee to a thinker-dominant supervisor: "I'm really upset about how you've talked down to me. I don't think you've been fair. I haven't been able to concentrate since our discussion and it's hurting my performance."

- ✪ *Without adjustment.* If the thinker becomes annoyed with the feeler's focus on emotions, he or she may ignore them, putting up an even stronger barrier between the two people. "There's no reason to be upset. I told you clearly and specifically what needs to be done. There's nothing else to discuss."

- ✪ *With adjustment.* If the thinker considers that emotions are dominant in the feeler's perspective, he or she could respond to those emotions in a way that still searches for the explanations and logic the thinker understands best: "Let's talk about how you feel. Please explain to me what has caused you to become upset, and we'll discuss how we can improve the situation."

Words are only one aspect of communication style. People also use their bodies in different ways to communicate messages to one another.

The Power of Body Language

Your actions—not your words—are the most basic form of communication. Even people who cannot speak each other's language can communicate ideas through gestures and facial expressions. Your gestures, eye movement, facial expression, body positioning and posture, touching behaviour, and use of personal space are all types of nonverbal communication, also called *body language.* If you understand how body language works, you can use it to your advantage.

How Body Language Works

Body language can reinforce or contradict verbal statements. For example, if a jittery person on a date says he's nervous, his body language *reinforces* his statement. On the other hand, if he insists that he is relaxed and at ease, his jittery behaviour *contradicts* his statement. When body language contradicts verbal language, the message conveyed by the body language is dominant. Consider, for example, if someone were to ask you how you feel, and you said "fine" although you didn't feel fine at all. In such a case your posture, eye contact, and other body language would convey the real message loud and clear.

Nonverbal cues also colour what you communicate. Consider this statement: "This is the best idea I've heard all day." If you were to say this three different ways—once in a loud voice while standing up, once quietly while sitting with arms and legs crossed and looking away, and once while maintaining eye contact and taking the receiver's hand—you might send three different messages.

Although differences occur from person to person and from culture to culture, some specific types of body language may have particular meanings. For example, a body turned away may signal lack of interest, while an "open" sitting posture with legs uncrossed may show agreement. Crossed arms may show disagreement or a desire to close off. Hands on the hips may show a toughness and readiness, and a firm, brief handshake may radiate capability and friendliness. Good posture and a brisk walking pace may indicate confidence. Eye contact speaks volumes and is often dependent on cultural tradition. In Canada, for example, direct and steady eye contact may show attention and respect, while in Asian countries, respect is often conveyed by avoiding direct eye contact.

Nonverbal communication strongly influences a first impression. First impressions emerge from a combination of nonverbal cues, tone of voice, and words spoken. Usually, nonverbal elements (signals and tone) come across first and strongest. Think about it: When you meet someone, you tend to judge the person before either of you says a word. You make assumptions based on nonverbal behaviour such as posture, eye contact, gestures, and speed and style of movement.

Using Body Language to Your Advantage

The following strategies can help you maximize your awareness and use of body language.

Become aware. Pay attention to what other people communicate nonverbally. If a friend compliments you with strong eye contact and a natural smile, you might feel flattered. If the same friend speaking the same words doesn't look you in the eye and is physically closed off from you, there might be something left unsaid. Also, be aware that your nonverbal communication affects your messages, and try to make sure that what you say nonverbally reinforces your words.

Try not to contradict your words with your body language. A nonverbal message that goes against what you say can cause confusion and perhaps make you appear dishonest. The receiver, unsure of which to believe, may tend to go with the nonverbal message. If you say to your adviser, "That grade is fine with me," with a tense tone of voice and aggressive posture, the adviser may be confused about what you feel. If you tell a friend that he looks nice but you don't look him in the eye, he may think you are lying to make him feel better.

Note cultural differences. In some cultures, casual acquaintances stand close together when speaking; in others, the same distance may be used only in very intimate, personal conversations. Some people shake hands readily and touch others when speaking. Others may feel that touching is invasive and should only be used with intimate friends. Within each conversation you have, you can discover what seems appropriate by paying attention to what the other person does.

Overcoming Communication Problems

Communication problems may occur when information is not clearly presented, or when those who receive information filter it through their own perspectives and interpret it in different ways. Here are some of the most common communication problems, along with strategies to help you combat them.

Problem: Unclear or incomplete explanation
Solution: Support ideas with examples

When you clarify a general idea with supporting examples that illustrate how the idea works and what effects it causes, you will help your receiver understand what you mean and therefore have a better chance to hold his or her attention.

For example, if you tell a friend to take a certain class, that friend might not take you seriously until you explain why. If you then communicate the positive effects of taking that class (progress toward a major, an excellent instructor, friendly study sessions), you may get your message across. The same principle applies to your attitude toward this course. If others communicate to you specific examples of how your work in the course will benefit your education, career, and personal life, you may be more likely to apply yourself.

Work situations benefit from explanation as well. As a supervisor, if you assign a task without explanation, you might get a delayed response or find mistakes in your employee's work. If, however, you explain the possible positive effects of the task, you'll have better results.

Problem: Limited knowledge of audience
Solution: Think about with whom you're communicating

As with writing a paper, considering your audience will improve communication. Ask yourself questions about what is appropriate for your audience. Tailor your words, tone, and level of formality to the person and the situation.

Source: ©Nina Paley.

Even with the same person, your communication style may change from situation to situation. For example, if you have a good relationship with a supervisor, you may have a more informal communication style when the two of you are alone than you have when you are with others in a work setting. People are also in different moods at different times. Be sensitive, stay aware, and make adjustments as necessary.

Problem: Faulty timing
Solution: Choose optimum listening conditions

Even a perfectly worded message won't get through to someone who isn't ready to receive it. If you try to talk to your instructor when she is rushing out the door, coat half on and briefcase in hand, your message probably won't come across too well. If you tell someone to come to your home when you are distracted with work or children, you may not hear them accurately. Pay attention to mood as well. If a friend has had an exhausting and traumatic week, you might not want to choose that time to ask for a favour.

People on both the sending and receiving ends of communication will benefit from good timing. Choose a time to talk or listen according to when you can best focus on your communication.

Problem: Stereotyping
Solution: Look past external appearances

In almost every student's life, there are people of diverse backgrounds—instructors, deans, employers, fellow students, neighbours—who offer helpful and important information. If you want to benefit from what the people around you have to offer, make your best attempt to look past appearance or identification with a group to really hear the words spoken. If your assumptions are affecting your ability to listen, use the methods you explored earlier in this chapter to evaluate their accuracy.

Problem: Attacking the receiver
Solution: Send "I" messages

When a conflict arises, often the first instinct is to pinpoint what someone else did wrong. "You didn't lock the door!" "You never called last night!"

"You left me out!" Making an accusation, especially without proof, puts the other person on the defensive and shuts down the lines of communication.

Using "I" messages will help you communicate your own needs rather than focusing on what you think someone else did wrong or should do differently. "I felt uneasy when I came to work and the door was unlocked." "I became worried about you when I didn't hear from you last night." "I felt disappointed when I realized that I couldn't join the party." "I" statements soften the conflict by highlighting the *effects* that the other person's actions have had on you, rather than the person or the actions themselves. When you focus on your own response and needs, your receiver may feel freer to respond, perhaps offering help and even acknowledging mistakes.

If you often feel dissatisfied and tense after an exchange, you may benefit from focusing more on your own needs when you communicate. Translate your anger into an "I" statement before speaking. Ask the other person, "Can we decide together how to improve this situation? Here's how I feel about what has happened." Using "I" statements will bring better results.

Problem: Passive or aggressive communication styles
Solution: Become assertive

Among the three major communication styles—aggressive, passive, and assertive—the one that conveys a message in the clearest, most productive way is the assertive style. The other two, while commonly used, throw the communication out of balance. An aggressive communicator often denies the receiver a chance to respond, while a passive communicator may have trouble getting the message out. Assertive behaviour strikes a balance between aggression and passivity. If you can be an assertive communicator, you will be more likely to get your message across while assuring that others have a chance to speak as well. Table 8–3 compares some characteristics of each kind of communicator.

assertive
Able to declare and affirm one's own opinions while respecting the rights of others to do the same.

Aggressive communicators focus primarily on their own needs. They can become angry and impatient when those needs are not immediately satisfied. In order to become more assertive, aggressive communicators might try to take time to think before speaking, avoid ordering people around, use "I" statements, and focus on listening to what the other person has to say.

Passive communicators deny themselves the power that aggressive people grab. They focus almost exclusively on the needs of others instead of on their own needs, experiencing frustration and tension that remains unexpressed. In order to become more assertive, passive communicators might try to acknowledge anger or hurt more often, speak up when they feel strongly about something, realize that they have a right to make requests, and know that their ideas and feelings are as important as anyone else's.

Communication Success Strategies

These additional strategies can help improve your communication:

Think before you speak. Spoken too soon, ideas can come out sounding nothing like you intended. Taking time to think, or even rehearsing mentally,

Table 8-3 Aggressive, Passive, and Assertive Styles

Aggressive	Passive	Assertive
Loud, heated arguing	Concealing one's own feelings	Expressing feelings without being nasty or overbearing
Physically violent encounters	Denying one's own anger	Acknowledging emotions but staying open to discussion
Blaming, name-calling, and verbal insults	Feeling that one has no right to express anger	Expressing self and giving others the chance to express themselves equally
Walking out of arguments before they are resolved	Avoiding arguments	Using "I" statements to defuse arguments
Being demanding: "Do this"	Being noncommittal: "You don't have to do this unless you really want to..."	Asking and giving reasons: "I would appreciate it if you would do this, and here's why..."

can help you choose the best combination of words. Think it through and get it right the first time.

Don't withhold your message for too long. One danger of holding back is that a problem or negative feeling may become worse. Speaking promptly has two benefits: (1) you solve the problem sooner; and (2) you are more likely to focus on the problem at hand than to spill over into other issues.

Communicate in a variety of ways, and be sensitive to cultural differences. Remember that words, gestures, and tones mean different things to different people.

Be clear, precise, and to the point. Say exactly what you need to say. Link your ideas to clear examples, avoiding any extra information that can distract.

Communication is extremely important for building and maintaining personal relationships. Explore the role those relationships play in who you are.

How Do Your Personal Relationships Define You?

The relationships you have with friends, family members, and significant others often take centre stage. Jobs and schooling can come and go, but you rely on the people with whom you share your life.

In addition to being part of your life, the people around you help to define who you are. Since birth, you have learned by taking in information from verbal and nonverbal language. The chain of learning stretches back through time, each link formed by an exchange of information between people. Those with whom you live, play, study, and work are primary sources of ideas, beliefs, and ways of living. You grow and change as you have new experiences, evaluate them, and decide what to learn from them.

These influential relationships can affect other areas of your life. You have probably experienced conflict that caused you to be unable to sleep, eat, or get any work done. On the other hand, a successful relationship can have positive effects on your life, increasing your success at work or at school. Following are some strategies for improving your personal relationships.

Relationship Strategies

If you can feel good about your personal relationships, other areas of your life will benefit. Here are some suggestions.

Make personal relationships a high priority. Nurture the ones you have and be open to developing new ones. Life is meant to be shared. In some marriage ceremonies, the bride and groom share a cup of wine that symbolizes life. One of the reasons for this tradition is to double the sweetness of life by tasting it together, and to cut the bitterness in half by sharing it. Any personal relationship can benefit from the experience of this kind of sharing.

Invest time. You devote time to education, work, and the other priorities in your life. Relationships need the same investment. They are like plants in a garden, needing nourishment to grow and thrive. Your attention provides that nourishment. In addition, spending time with people you like can relieve everyday stress and strain. When you make time for others, everyone benefits.

Spend time with people you respect and admire. Life is too short to hang out with people who bring you down, encourage you to participate in activities of which you don't approve, or behave in ways that upset you. Develop relationships with people whom you respect, whose choices you admire, and who inspire you to be all that you can be. This doesn't mean that you have to agree with everything that others do. For example, you may disagree with a friend who lets his child watch a lot of television. However, you may severely disapprove of someone who disciplines a child violently, and you may choose to end your association with that person.

Work through tensions. Negative feelings can multiply when left unspoken. Unexpressed feelings about other issues may cause you to become disproportionately angry over a small issue. A small annoyance over dishes in the sink can turn into a gigantic fight about many unrelated issues. Get to the root of the problem. Discuss it, deal with it, and move on.

Refuse to tolerate violence. It isn't easy to face the problem of violence or to leave a violent relationship. People may tolerate violence out of a belief that it will end, a desire to keep their families together, a self-esteem so low that they believe they deserve what they get, or a fear that trying to leave may lead to greater violence. No level of violence is acceptable. Someone who behaves violently toward you cannot possibly have your best interests at heart. If you find that you are either an aggressor or a victim, do your best to get help. See Chapter 9 for more information on domestic violence.

Show appreciation. In this fast-paced world, people don't thank each other often enough. If you think of something positive, say it. Thank someone for a service, or express your affection with a smile. A little positive reinforcement goes a long way toward nurturing a relationship.

If you want a friend, be a friend. The Golden Rule, "Do unto others as you would have them do unto you," never goes out of style. If you treat a friend with the kind of loyalty and support that you appreciate for yourself, you are more likely to receive the same in return.

Take risks. It can be frightening to reveal your deepest dreams and frustrations, to devote yourself to a friend, or to fall in love. You can choose not to reveal yourself or give yourself to a friendship at all. However, giving is what feeds a relationship, and brings satisfaction and growth. If you take the plunge, you risk disappointment and heartbreak, but you also stand to gain the incredible benefits of companionship, which for most people outweigh the risks.

Keep personal problems in their place. Solve personal problems with the people directly involved and no one else. If possible, try not to bring your emotions into class or work. Doing so may hurt your performance, while doing nothing to help the problem. If you are overwhelmed by a personal problem, try to address it before you go to class or work. If it's impossible to address it at that time, at least make a plan that you can carry out later. Making some step toward resolving the problem will help you concentrate on other things.

If it doesn't work out, find ways to cope. Everyone experiences strain and breakups in intimate relationships, friendships, and family ties. Be kind to yourself and use coping strategies that help you move on. Some people need lots of time alone; others need to spend time with their friends and family. Some seek more formal counselling. Some people throw their energy into a project, a job, a class, a new workout regimen, or anything else that will take their mind off what hurts. Some just need to cry it out and be miserable for a while. Some write in a journal or write letters to the person that they never mail. Do what's right for you, and believe that sooner or later you can emerge from the experience stronger and with a new perspective.

Now and again, your personal relationships will experience conflict. Following are ideas for how to deal with conflict and criticism in a productive and positive way.

How Can You Handle Conflict and Criticism?

Conflict and criticism, as unpleasant as they may often be, are natural elements in the dynamic of getting along with others. It's normal to want to avoid people or situations that cause distress. However, if you can face your fears and think through them critically, you can gain valuable insight into human nature—your own and that of others. You may be able to make important changes in your life based on what you learn.

Conflict Strategies

Conflicts both large and small arise when there is a clash of ideas or interests. You might have small conflicts with a housemate over food left out overnight, a door left unlocked, or a bill that needs paying. On the other end of the spectrum, you might encounter major conflicts with your partner about finances, with an instructor about a failing grade, or with a person who treats you unfairly because of your race, gender, age, or ethnic origin.

Conflict can create anger and frustration, shutting down communication. The two most destructive tendencies are to avoid the conflict altogether (a passive tactic) or to let it escalate into a fight (an aggressive tendency). Avoidance doesn't make the problem go away—in fact, it will probably worsen. If you tend to be passive, assert yourself by acknowledging and expressing your feelings as soon as you can put them into words. On the other hand, a shouting match gives no one an opportunity or desire to listen. If you tend to be aggressive, give yourself time to cool down before you address a conflict. Try to express what you feel without letting your emotions explode.

If calmly and intelligently handled, conflict can shed light on new ideas and help to strengthen bonds between those involved. The primary keys to conflict resolution are calm communication and critical-thinking skills. Think through any conflict using what you know about problem solving.

Identify and analyze the problem. Determine the severity of the problem by looking at its effects on everyone involved. Then, find and analyze the causes of the problem.

Brainstorm possible solutions. Consider as many angles as you can, without making judgments. Explore the ideas you come up with from what you or others have done in a similar situation.

Explore each solution. Evaluate the positive and negative effects of each solution. Why might each work, or not work, or work partially? What would take into account everyone's needs? What would cause the least stress? Make sure everyone has a chance to express an opinion.

Choose, carry out, and evaluate the solution you decide is best. When you have implemented your choice, evaluate its effects. Decide whether you feel it was a good choice.

One more hint: Use "I" statements. Focus on the effects the problem has had on you rather than focusing on someone who caused it. Show that you are taking responsibility for your role in the exchange.

Dealing with Criticism and Feedback

No one gets everything right all the time. People use constructive criticism and feedback to communicate what went wrong and to suggest improvements. Consider any criticism carefully. If you always interpret criticism as a threat, you will close yourself off from learning. Even if you eventually decide that you disagree, you can still learn from exploring the possibility. Know that you are strong enough to embrace criticism and become a better person because of it.

Criticism can be either constructive or unconstructive. Criticism is considered *constructive* when it is offered supportively and contains useful suggestions for improvement. On the other hand, *unconstructive* criticism focuses on what went wrong, doesn't offer alternatives or help, and is often delivered in a negative or harsh manner. Whereas constructive criticism can promote a sense of hope for improvement in the future, unconstructive criticism can create tension, bad feelings, and defensiveness.

Any criticism can be offered constructively or unconstructively. Consider a case in which someone has continually been late to work. A supervisor can offer criticism in either of these ways:

> *Constructive:* The supervisor talks privately with the employee. "I've noticed that you have been late to work a lot. Other people have had to do some of your work. Is there a problem that is keeping you from being on time? Is it something that I or someone else can help you with?"

> *Unconstructive:* The supervisor watches the employee slip into work late. The supervisor says, in front of other employees, "Nice to see you could make it. If you can't start getting here on time, I might look for someone else who can."

If you can learn to give constructive criticism and deal with whatever criticism comes your way from others, you will improve your relationships and your productivity. When offered constructively and considered carefully, criticism can bring about important changes.

Giving Constructive Criticism

When you offer criticism, use the following steps to communicate clearly and effectively:

1. *Criticize the behaviour, rather than the person.* In addition, make sure the behaviour you intend to criticize is changeable. Chronic lateness can be changed; a physical inability to perform a task cannot.
2. *Be strategic and discreet.* Carefully choose a convenient time and a private place to talk.
3. *Define specifically the behaviour you want to change.* Try not to drag any other issues into the conversation.

feedback
Evaluative or corrective information about an action or process.

constructive
Promoting improvement or development.

4. *Limit the behaviours you will criticize to one.* If you have other concerns, discuss them later, one at a time. People can hear criticism better if they are not hit with several issues at once.

5. *Balance criticism with positive words.* Alternate critical comments with praise in other areas.

6. *Stay calm and be brief.* Avoid threats, ultimatums, or accusations. Use "I" messages; choose positive, nonthreatening words, so that the person knows your intentions are positive.

7. *Explain the effects caused by the behaviour that warrants the criticism.* Help the person understand why a change needs to happen, and talk about options in detail. Compare and contrast the effects of the current behaviour with the effects of a potential change.

8. *Offer help in changing the behaviour.* Lead by example.

Receiving Criticism

When you find yourself on the receiving end of criticism, use these coping techniques:

1. *Listen to the criticism before you speak up.* Resist the desire to defend yourself until you've heard all the details. Decide if the criticism is offered in a constructive or unconstructive manner.

2. *Think the criticism through critically.* Evaluate it carefully. While some criticism may come from a desire to help, other comments may have less honourable origins. People often criticize others out of jealousy, anger, frustration, or displaced feelings. In cases like those, it is best (though not always easy) to let the criticism wash right over you.

3. *If the criticism is constructive and you accept it, say so.* If you are unsure, take time to think. You may say, "I would like time to think about that. I'll get back to you." Remember that criticism heard from more than one person is more likely to be valid.

4. *If it is unconstructive, you may not want to respond at that moment.* Unconstructive criticism can inspire anger that might be destructive to express. Wait until you cool down and think about the criticism to see if there is anything important hiding under the way it was presented. Then, tell the person that you see the value of the criticism, but also communicate to him or her how the delivery of the criticism made you feel. If he or she is willing to talk in a more constructive manner, continue with the following steps below. If not, your best bet may be to consider the case closed and move on.

5. *If it is constructive, ask for suggestions on how to change the criticized behaviour.* You could ask, "How would you handle this if you were in my place?"

6. *Before the conversation ends, summarize the criticism and your response to it.* Repeat it back to the person who offered it. Make sure both of you understand the situation in the same way.

"Do not use a hatchet to remove a fly from your friend's forehead."

Chinese proverb

7. *If you feel that the criticism is valid, plan a specific strategy for correcting the behaviour.* Think over what you might learn from changing your behaviour. If you still don't agree with the criticism, explain your behaviour from your point of view.

Remember that the most important feedback you will receive in school is from your instructors, and the most important on-the-job feedback will come from your supervisors, more experienced peers, and occasionally clients. Making a special effort to take in this feedback and to consider it carefully will help you learn many important lessons. Even when the criticism is unwarranted, the way you respond is important. Furthermore, knowing how to handle conflict and criticism will help you define your role and communicate with others when you work in groups.

What Role Do You Play in Groups?

Group interaction is an important part of your educational, personal, and working life. With a team project at work or a cooperative learning exercise in school, for example, being able to work well together is necessary in order to accomplish a goal. If you are comfortable in your designated role and with the different types of people and styles within your group, you will help the group function more effectively because you will be more effective yourself.

A group or team can be co-workers, fellow students, a family, or any other people who need to accomplish a goal together. Everyone in the group has a vested interest in the outcome. Therefore, everyone should have the opportunity to voice opinions and to participate in the activities that the group decides will achieve the goal or goals.

Groups have their own chemistry and structure. The two major roles in the group experience are those of *participant* and *leader*. Any group needs both in order to function successfully. Become aware of the role you tend to play when relating to others. Try different roles to help you decide how you can be most effective. The following strategies (from *Contemporary Business Communication*, by Louis E. Boone, David L. Kurtz, and Judy R. Block) are linked to either participating or leading.[12] Keep in mind that for many groups, the lines may blur—members may perform some leadership tasks and some participant tasks at the same time, or the leadership of the group may shift frequently.

Being an Effective Participant

Some people are happiest when participating in group activities that someone else leads and designs. They don't feel comfortable in a position of control or having the power to set the tone for the group as a whole. They trust others to make those decisions, preferring to help things run smoothly by taking on an assigned role in the project and seeing it through. Participators need to remember that they are "part owners" of the process. Each team member has a responsibility for, and a stake in, the outcome. The following strategies will help a participant to be effective.

Participation Strategies

Get involved. If a decision you don't like is made by a group of which you are a member, and you stayed uninvolved in the decision, you have no one to blame but yourself for not speaking up. Put some energy into your participation and let people know your views. You are as important a team member as anyone else, and your views are likewise valuable.

Be organized. When you participate with the group as a whole, or with any of the team members, stay focused and organized. The more organized your ideas are, the more people will listen, take them into consideration, and be willing to try them.

Be willing to discuss. Everyone has an equal right to express his or her ideas. Even as you enthusiastically present your opinions, be willing to consider those of others. Keep an open mind and think critically about other ideas before you assume that they won't work. If a discussion heats up, take a break or let a more neutral group member mediate.

Keep your word. Make a difference by doing what you say you're going to do. Let people know what you have accomplished. If you bring little or nothing to the process, your team may feel that you weigh them down.

Focus on ideas, not people. One of the easiest ways to start an argument is for participants to attack group members themselves instead of discussing their ideas. Separate the person from the idea, and keep the idea in focus.

Play fairly. Give everyone a chance to participate. Be respectful of other people's ideas. Don't dominate the discussion or try to control or manipulate others.

Being an Effective Leader

Some people prefer to initiate the action, make decisions, and control how things proceed. They have ideas they want to put into practice and enjoy explaining them to others. They are comfortable giving direction to people and guiding group outcomes. Leaders often have a big-picture perspective, which allows them to see how all of the different aspects of a group project can come together. In any group setting the following strategies will help a leader succeed.

Leadership Strategies

Define and limit projects. One of the biggest ways to waste time and energy is to assume that a group will know its purpose and will limit tasks on its own. A group needs a leader who can define the purpose of the gathering and limit tasks so the group doesn't take on too much. Some common purposes are giving/exchanging information, brainstorming, making a decision, delegating tasks, or collaborating on a project.

Map out who will perform which tasks. A group functions best when everyone has a particular contribution to make. You don't often choose who you work with—in school, at work, or in your family—but you can help different personalities work together by exploring who can do what best. Give people specific responsibilities and trust that they will do their jobs.

Set the agenda. The leader is responsible for establishing and communicating the goal of the project and how it will proceed. Without a plan, it's easy to get off track. Having a written agenda to which group members can refer is helpful. A good leader invites advice from others when determining group direction.

Focus on progress. Even when everyone knows the plan, it's still natural to wander off the topic. The leader should try to rein in the discussion when necessary, doing his or her best to keep everyone to the topic at hand. When challenges arise midstream, the leader may need to help the team change direction.

Set the tone. Different group members bring different attitudes and mental states to a gathering. Setting a positive tone helps to bring the group together and to motivate people to peak performance. When a leader values diversity in ideas and backgrounds and sets a tone of fairness, respect, and encouragement, group members may feel more comfortable contributing their ideas.

Evaluate results. The leader should determine whether the team is accomplishing its goals. If the team is not moving ahead, the leader needs to make changes and decisions.

If you don't believe you fit into the traditional definition of a leader, remember that there are other ways to lead that don't involve taking charge of a group. You can lead others by setting an honourable example in your actions, choices, or words. You can lead by putting forth an idea that takes a group in a new direction. You can lead by being the kind of person whom others would like to be.

It takes the equal participation of all group members to achieve a goal. Whatever role works best for you, know that your contribution is essential. You may even play different roles within different groups. You might be a participator at school and a leader in a self-help group. You could enjoy leading a religious group but prefer to take a back seat at work. Finally, stay aware of group dynamics: They can shift quickly and move you into a new position you may or may not like. If you don't feel comfortable, speak up. The happier each group member is, the more effectively the group as a whole will function.

Kente

The African word *kente* means "that which will not tear under any condition." *Kente* cloth is worn by men and women in African countries such as Ghana, Ivory Coast, and Togo. There are many brightly coloured patterns of *kente*, each beautiful, unique, and special.

Think of how this concept applies to being human. Like the cloth, all people are unique, with brilliant and subdued aspects. Despite any mistreatment or misunderstanding by the people you encounter in your life, you need to work to remain strong so that you don't tear and give way to disrespectful behaviour. This strength can help you to endure, stand up against any injustice, and fight peacefully but relentlessly for the rights of all people.

Chapter 8: Applications

<u>Name</u>   <u>Date</u>

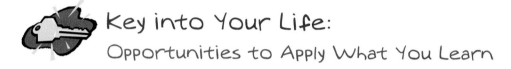

Key into Your Life:
Opportunities to Apply What You Learn

Exercise 1: Diversity Discovery

Express your own personal diversity. Describe yourself in response to the following questions.

What ethnic background(s) do you have?

_____

_____

_____

Name one or more facts about you that someone wouldn't know from simply looking at you.

_____

_____

_____

Name two values or beliefs that govern how you live, what you pursue, and/or with whom you associate.

_____

_____

_____

What other characteristics or choices define your uniqueness?

_____

_____

_____

Now, join with a partner in your class. Try to choose someone you don't know well. Your goal is to communicate what you have written to your partner, and for your partner to communicate to you in the same way. Spend ten minutes talking together and take notes on what the other person says. At the end of that period, join together as a class. Each person will describe his or her partner to the class.

What did you learn about your partner that surprised you? _____

_____

_____

What did you learn that went against any assumptions you may have made about that person based on his or her appearance, background, or behaviour? _____

_____

_____

Has this exercise changed the way you see this person or other people? Why or why not? _____

_____

_____

Exercise 2: Prejudice

Name an incorrect assumption others may have about you. _____

_____

Why would others assume this? How can you help them re-evaluate that assumption? _____

_____

_____

Now, describe one of your prejudices that is directed toward another group. _____

_____

Think critically about this prejudice. In what cases might this not make sense? _____

_____

_____

_____

What might you do to educate yourself about this other group? _____

_____

_____

_____

Exercise 3: The "I"s Have It

In your quest for better communication, rewrite the following sentences so that they are in the less accusatory "I" message style. Check your answers with other students and/or with your instructor.

1. You blew it completely.

    _____

2. Why didn't you tell me the meeting time changed?

    _____

3. You always forget to pick me up.

    _____

4. What does it take for you to understand how this machine works?

    _____

5. Where did you put the stapler? Did you lose it?

    _____

6. You are impossible to understand when you talk like that.

    _____

Exercise 4: Your Communication Style

Look back at the four styles on page 279: intuitor, senser, thinker, and feeler. Which describes you best? Rank the four styles, listing first the one that fits most, and listing last the one that fits least.

1. _____

2. _____

3. _____

4. _____

Of the two styles that best fit you, which one has more positive effects on your ability to communicate? What are those effects?

_____

_____

Which style has more negative effects? What are they?

_____

_____

To determine whether you are primarily passive, aggressive, or assertive, read the following sentences and circle the ones that sound like something you would say to a peer.

1. Get me the keys.
2. Would you mind if I stepped out just for a second?
3. Don't slam the door.
4. I'd appreciate it if you would have this done by two o'clock.
5. I think maybe it needs a little work just at the end, but I'm not sure.
6. Please take this back to the library.
7. You will have a good time if you join us.
8. Your loss.
9. I don't know, if you think so. I'll try it.
10. Let me know what you want me to do.
11. Turn it this way and see what happens.
12. We'll try both our ideas and see what works best.
13. I want it on my desk by the end of the day.
14. Just do what I told you.
15. If this isn't how you wanted it to look, I can change it. Just tell me and I'll do it.

Aggressive communicators would be likely to use sentences 1, 3, 8, 13, and 14.

Passive communicators would probably opt for sentences 2, 5, 9, 10, and 15.

Assertive communicators would probably choose sentences 4, 6, 7, 11, and 12.

In which category did you choose the most sentences? _____

If you scored as an assertive communicator, you are on the right track. If you scored in the aggressive or passive categories, analyze your style. What are the effects? Give an example in your own life of the effects of your style.

_____

_____

Turn back to page 286 to review suggestions for aggressive or passive communicators. What can you do to improve your skills?

_____

_____

Exercise 5: Criticism

Think about any criticism of yourself that you have ignored or rejected. Choose one item of criticism and write it here.

_____

_____

Now, be honest with yourself. Do you agree with this criticism? Why? How did the criticism make you feel? How was it delivered?

_____

_____

_____

Based on what you are learning from exploring this criticism, name a change you plan to make in order to improve what was criticized or how you react to criticism.

_____

_____

Key to Cooperative Learning:
Building Teamwork Skills

Problem Solving Close to Home Divide into small groups of two to five. Assign one group member to take notes. Discuss the following questions, one by one:

1. What are the three largest problems my school faces with regard to how people get along with and accept others?
2. What could my school do to deal with the three problems listed above?
3. What can each individual student do to deal with the three problems listed above? (Talk about what you specifically feel that you can do.)

When you are finished, gather as a class. Each group should share its responses with the class. Observe the variety of problems and solutions. Notice whether more than one group came up with one or more of the same problems. You may want to assign one person in the class to gather all of the responses together. That person, together with your instructor, could put these responses into an organized document that you can share with the upper-level administrators at your school.

Key to Self-Expression:
Discovery Through Journal Writings

To record your thoughts, use a separate journal or the lined page at the end of the chapter.

New Perspective[13] Imagine that you have no choice but to change either your gender (male/female) or your racial/ethnic/religious group. Which

would you change, and why? What do you anticipate would be the positive and negative effects of the change—in your social life, in your family life, on the job, at school? How would what you know and experience before the change affect how you would behave after the change?

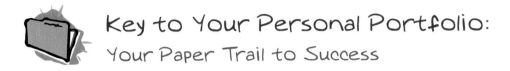

Key to Your Personal Portfolio:
Your Paper Trail to Success

Letters of Recommendation It will be very important to have positive letters of recommendation from people who know and respect you. You can use them when you apply for jobs, internships, scholarships, or academic programs.

First, create a list of people who have served or could serve as references for you. Brainstorm names from all areas of your human resources:

Instructors	Friends	Present/former employers
Administrators	Family members	Mentors
Counsellors	Present/former co-workers	Students

Make a chart that looks like the one that follows. Fill in the information for each reference.

NAME	ADDRESS	PHONE NUMBER	ASSOCIATION
Peter J. Maurin St. Catharines, Ont.	500 Glenridge Ave.	905/688/5550, ext. 4290	Current academic supervisor

Update the information on this chart as you meet potential references or lose touch with old ones. Keep it on hand for the time that you need a new letter or want to cite a reference on a résumé.

Next, decide which three people you would like to approach to write a letter for you. Choose people who know you well and who have seen you in action, either in an academic or work situation. You will want your references to emphasize your strengths and to discuss qualities like open-mindedness, the ability to be a team player, and interpersonal relations. Letters should also contain references to your specific skills, capabilities, and style of working and thinking.

If you have a specific purpose for your letter right now, ask your three references to write letters that suit that purpose. If you don't, keep the information on hand until you do.

When references write letters for you, be sure to thank them right away for their help and to keep them up to date on your activities. Always let a reference know when you have sent a letter out, so that he or she may be prepared to receive a call from the person/company/program to which you have applied.

Name _____ Date _____

Journal Entry

_____
_____
_____
_____
_____
_____
_____
_____
_____
_____
_____
_____
_____
_____
_____
_____
_____
_____
_____
_____
_____
_____

9 Personal Wellness:
Taking Care of Yourself

In this chapter, you will explore answers to the following questions:

❊ How can you maintain a healthy body?

❊ How do you nurture a healthy mind?

❊ How are alcohol, tobacco, and drugs used and abused?

❊ What should you consider when making sexual decisions?

Your mind and body may seem like two independent parts. You go to school for your mind; you exercise for your body. You eat right to improve your body; you read books to improve your mind. Consider, though, that your brain is an organ, and that, just like any other organ, its functioning depends on the health of your body. In this way, a healthy picnic lunch or an afternoon run can improve your mind. The mind influences the body as well—for example, a positive outlook on life can improve your body's ability to handle stress. Your body and mind are intimately connected and affect one another.

Because of the strong mind-body connection, your physical and mental health both affect your ability to succeed in school. It doesn't matter how great your classes are if you aren't physically healthy enough to get to them or mentally healthy enough to focus and learn while you're there. In this chapter you will examine both the physical and mental aspects of wellness, looking at how to maintain your health as well as how to identify and work through particular health problems that many students face. You will also explore substance use and abuse and sexuality as they relate to your personal wellness.

Thinking It Through

Check those statements that apply to you right now:

- ❏ I eat a pretty balanced diet.

- ❏ I'm exhausted a lot of the time.

- ❏ I have too much stress in my life.

- ❏ I am in control when it comes to alcohol and drugs.

- ❏ I don't know much about what it means to be addicted.

- ❏ I've made sexual decisions in the heat of the moment that I've regretted later.

- ❏ I don't always take precautions against sexually transmitted diseases.

How Can You Maintain a Healthy Body?

Your daily schedule may leave you little time to take good care of yourself. As you complete assignments for class, work for your boss, take care of your family, keep up with friends, and do chores, you may find yourself feeling stressed out. It's important to take time to focus on you. The healthier you are, the more energy you'll have both for yourself and for those who share your life. Eating right, exercising, and getting enough sleep will help you maintain a healthy body.

Eating Right

Canada's Food Guide says that the actual amount of food you need each day depends on your age, gender, body size, and how active you are. Pregnant and breast-feeding women also have special dietary needs. However, no matter what category you are in, you still need to eat a balanced diet from each of the four food groups:

Food for Thought
http://www.
hc-sc.gc.ca/hppb/nutrition/

Canada's Food Guide is available online, offering suggestions on eating properly. It includes information about your body mass index (BMI), tips for pregnant mothers, and links to other nutritional information on the Internet.

- grains
- vegetables and fruit
- milk products
- meat and alternatives

You can still eat foods high in fat, carbohydrates, or sugar and drink alcohol, but in moderation. That means knowing what your limits are. Eat more lower-fat foods, and choose whole grains as often as possible.

Maintaining balance and eating in moderation are two important rules to remember. Along with scheduling meals and watching out for potential health hazards, these guidelines can help you maintain a healthy diet.

Maintaining Balance

If you vary your diet with foods from the different food groups—meat and alternatives, milk products, breads and grains, and fruits and vegetables—you are more likely to take in the different nutrients that your body needs. Figure 9–1 shows the types of foods included in each food group that *Canada's Food Guide* recommends. Nutritionists emphasize fruits and vegetables, recommending five to ten servings from that group per day. If that sounds difficult, consider this five-a-day plan: a banana or a glass of juice at breakfast, a salad at lunch (worth two veggies), an apple for a snack, and green beans with dinner. A good food balance will also help you minimize your intake of fat, which is concentrated mostly in the meat and dairy groups.

Eating in Moderation

Your best move is to practise moderation in everything you eat. School, however, doesn't always make moderation easy. You may be taking snack breaks during late-night study sessions. You may frequent a cafeteria where one price buys all you can eat. You may have fast-food options available at all hours of the day or night. Such opportunities can be hard to resist.

| Figure 9-1 | Canada's Food Guide |

Healthy Canada

Health and Welfare Canada   Santé et Bien-être social Canada

CANADA'S Food Guide TO HEALTHY EATING

Enjoy a variety of foods from each group every day.

Choose lower-fat foods more often.

Grain Products
Choose whole grain and enriched products more often.

Vegetables and Fruit
Choose dark green and orange vegetables and orange fruit more often.

Milk Products
Choose lower-fat milk products more often.

Meat and Alternatives
Choose leaner meats, poultry and fish, as well as dried peas, beans and lentils more often.

Canada

Source: *Canada's Food Guide*. Used with permission of Health Canada: Minister of Public Works and Government Services Canada, 2000.

Despite the temptations that may come your way, try to moderate your food intake according to one basic measure: *Don't eat more than your body can use*. Eating too much of even the healthiest food still means taking in more calories than your body needs. Any extra fuel is stored as fat, whether it comes from rice cakes or ice cream. To avoid packing on extra fat, try to sense your body's messages both for hunger and for fullness. Eat slowly so that you don't miss the "stop" message when it arrives.

Scheduling When You Eat

When you're on the move all day and don't eat until the evening, you run a greater risk of overeating when you finally sit down to dinner. In addition, eating full meals shortly before you go to bed can interfere with your sleep. If, however, you schedule your meals so that you spread out your food intake over the day, you'll have more energy and be more satisfied.

Timing your meals isn't easy to do when eating on the run, in a car, between classes, and after a late night at work. You can work toward change by making food scheduling a priority. Look at your day's schedule ahead of time and plan your meals. Consider where you'll be, on campus or off; what's available; how much time you have; and if there's anything you can fix at home to take with you and eat later. Keep a snack with you in case you get tied up and are unable to eat a whole meal.

Watching Out for Potential Health Hazards

An occasional splurge—a piece of cake, a great cup of coffee, or an order of poutine—can add to life's enjoyment. In excess, though, particular substances—sugar, fats, salt, and caffeine—have the potential to damage your health.

- Sugar gives you quick energy but lets you down fast.
- Fats pile on extra pounds that overburden your system.
- Too much salt can raise your blood pressure to dangerous levels.
- Caffeine can irritate your stomach and overstimulate your heart and nervous system.

Many people develop addictive behaviour around these substances—primarily caffeine, which is a drug. If you think you overdo any of these, try cutting back and evaluate how you feel. Give yourself a couple of weeks, because you may actually feel worse for a time. Caffeine withdrawal, for example, can cause severe headaches. If you feel better eventually, continue to limit intake to small, infrequent amounts, or cut out the substance entirely.

withdrawal
The discontinuance of the use of a drug, including attendant side effects.

Watching Your Weight

Weight-control issues have different sources. Some people have inherited genes that predispose them to weight gain. Others suffer from medical conditions that affect their bodies' ability to process food efficiently. Beyond these physical causes, anyone who eats high-fat foods or large amounts of food can gain weight. Being significantly overweight forces your heart, lungs, and other organs to work overtime in order to carry the extra weight around. It can also aggravate ailments and diseases such as digestive problems, arthritis, diabetes, and cancer.

Weight gain isn't always just a medical or chemical issue. Many people eat to find comfort and to escape problems. Judith Linsey Palken, M.S., R.D., suggests that people who seek solace in food try to dig down deep to find the real problem. "If you tend to make poor food choices, try to determine what triggers the problem. Only by understanding the emotions and situations that lead you to overeat can you begin to make changes."[1]

Food cannot fill the gaps that problems in personal life, school, or work can create. When people eat for reasons other than to supply their bodies with adequate fuel, they can become compulsive overeaters. Possible reasons for overeating include:

- ◎ For comfort
- ◎ Out of boredom, frustration, or worry
- ◎ Out of a feeling that a person should finish what's on his or her plate
- ◎ Because it's cheap or free, or because everyone else is eating
- ◎ To please a family member or to fulfill a holiday tradition

If you think you eat for any of these reasons, you may benefit from examining your eating habits. Weight-loss programs and resources are available to you if you decide to lose weight. The best among them combine a balanced, low-fat diet with an increase in exercise. Check out some books on the subject in your library, look in the Yellow Pages under Weight Control Services, surf World Wide Web pages or newsgroups on the Internet, or ask a counsellor for advice. Different programs have different purposes. While a program like Weight Watchers lays out a specific diet plan, Overeaters Anonymous focuses on your mental attitude toward food. Explore all your options and choose one or more that serve your needs. Above all, don't forget to talk to a doctor before starting any weight-loss program.

If you are exhausted, hungry, jittery from sugar or caffeine, or ill from poor nutrition, you may have trouble concentrating. Eating right helps your mind focus on important tasks because it reduces potential distractions and supplies good energy. A well-fed body frees the mind, and so does a physically fit body.

> "To keep the Body in Good health is a duty... Otherwise we shall not Be able to keep our mind strong and clear."
>
> Buddha

Exercising

Good physical fitness increases your energy efficiency. An efficient body system has more energy and more ability to direct that energy toward problem solving and the fulfillment of goals. A fit body also helps the mind handle stress. During physical activity, the brain releases *endorphins*, chemical compounds that have a positive and calming effect on the body.

Like a car, your body's physical power can decrease unless you put it to work. Staying in shape requires discipline. For maximum benefit, make regular exercise a way of life. If you haven't been exercising regularly, start slowly. Walking, for example, is one of the most beneficial, most available, and least stressful forms of exercise. If you exercise frequently and are already relatively fit, you may prefer a more intense or longer workout. Always check with a physician before beginning any exercise program, and adjust your program to your physical type and fitness level.

Types of Exercise

The type of exercise you choose depends on factors such as time available, physical limitations, preferences, available facilities, cost, and level of fitness.

For example, a person with knee problems may choose to swim, thereby avoiding the demands that running places on the knee joint. Someone who wants to lose fat may take long walks, while someone who wants to gain muscle may work out with weights. You might prefer to play basketball with a team, while you can do an aerobics tape on your own.

Types of exercise fall into three main categories.

- *Cardiovascular training* is exercise that strengthens your heart muscle and lung capacity. Examples include running, swimming, in-line skating, aerobic dancing, and cycling.
- *Strength training* is exercise that strengthens any of many different muscle groups. Examples include using weight machines and free weights, or doing pushups and abdominal crunches.
- *Flexibility training* is exercise that maintains and increases muscle flexibility. Examples include various stretches and forms of yoga.

Some exercises, such as lifting weights or cycling, fall primarily into one category. Others combine elements of two or all three, such as astanga yoga, which requires constant movement (cardiovascular), stretching (flexibility), and the support of body weight (strength). For maximum benefit and a comprehensive workout, try alternating your exercise methods through crosstraining. For example, you could build cardiovascular fitness with brisk walking a few times a week and alternate your walking days with yoga or toning exercises for flexibility and strength. If you lift weights, you could use a stationary bike or stair machine on your off days for cardiovascular work.

crosstraining
Alternating types of exercise and combining elements from different types of exercise.

Making Exercise a Priority

Student life in school and out is crammed with responsibilities. You can't always make a nice, neat plan that gets you to the gym three days a week for two hours each time. You also may not have the money for an expensive health club. The following suggestions will help you make exercise a priority, even in the busiest weeks and on the tightest budgets. Be sure to check into your school's fitness opportunities—they may be low-cost or even included in your tuition.

- Walk around campus.
- Take dance, aerobics, martial arts, or yoga classes at a campus fitness centre.
- Choose the stairs rather than the elevator or escalator.
- Purchase exercise tapes for use at home.
- Do strenuous chores, if your doctor approves, such as shovelling snow, raking, or mowing.
- Play team recreational sports with your school's intramural program or at a local YMCA.
- Use home exercise equipment such as weights, an abdominal roller, a treadmill or stair machine, or a mat.

⊙ Work out with a friend or family member to combine socializing and exercise, and to help boost your motivation.

Exercise is a key component of a healthy mind and body, as is adequate rest.

Getting Enough Sleep

No one can function well without adequate sleep. During sleep, your body repairs itself while your mind sorts through problems and questions. A lack of sleep, or poor sleep, causes poor concentration and irritability, which can mean a less-than-ideal performance at school and at work. Irritability can also put a strain on personal relationships. Making up for lost sleep with caffeine may raise your anxiety and stress level and leave you more tired than before.

Sleep expert Gregg D. Jacobs, Ph.D., says that different people need different amounts of sleep. "Adults average about seven to seven-and-one-half hours of sleep per night, and many individuals function effectively with four to six hours of sleep."[2] People in their late teens and early twenties may need eight to nine hours. Gauge your needs by evaluating how you feel. If you aren't fatigued or irritable during the day, you may have slept adequately. On the other hand, if you are groggy in the morning or doze off at various times, you may be sleep-deprived.

Barriers to a Good Night's Sleep

College and university students often get inadequate sleep. Worrying about exams, quizzes, or projects coming due may make you restless. Long study sessions may keep you up late, and early classes may get you up early. Assignments pile up and start to seem more important than a good night's sleep. Socializing, eating, and drinking may make it hard to settle down. Noise can be a problem. If you are a parent, your children may disturb your sleep. Some barriers to sleep are within your control, and some are not.

What is out of your control? Barriers such as outside noise and your children's needs require you to do what you can to address the situation and then try to get as much sleep as possible. Try using earplugs or playing relaxing music in your room to counteract outside noise.

What is within your control? Late nights out, food and drink, and your study schedule are often (although not always) within your power to change. Schedule your studying so that it doesn't all pile up at the last minute. Avoid a late dinner the night before a big test. Respectfully ask the people you live with to keep the noise down when you need to rest. Be willing to do the same for them.

Tips for Quality Sleep

Dr. Jacobs recommends the following steps to better sleep.

Reduce consumption of alcohol and caffeine. Caffeine may keep you awake. Alcohol causes you to sleep more lightly, making you feel less rested and refreshed when you awaken.

Wellness
www.yorku.ca/admin
/wellness/

This York University Web site includes information on how to fine-tune your mind, body, and soul. It also contains a page of wellness links and audio files you can download.

Promoting Health Online
www.hc-sc.gc.ca/hppb/

This government of Canada Web site offers the latest research and data on health and wellness.

Exercise regularly. Studies have shown that regular exercise, especially in the late afternoon or early evening, promotes good sleep because it raises body temperature and then allows it to fall.

Complete tasks an hour or more before you sleep. Getting things done some time before you turn in gives you a chance to wind down and calm your brain activity.

Establish a comfortable sleeping environment. Little or no light usually facilitates sleep. Some people like to have a quiet room, while others prefer the calming, steady noise of a fan or air conditioner.

Sleeping well is one of the most important steps to take toward a healthy body and mind. Following are many other important ways to maintain mental health.

How Do You Nurture a Healthy Mind?

Your success depends on your mental health. Learning some ways to handle stress, and preventing or working through emotional disorders, are two important steps to a healthy mind.

Stress

Stress Relief
www.utexas.edu/student/
lsc/makinggrade/
relaxation.html

If you're having problems dealing with school and life issues, this site at the University of Texas provides information on dealing with stressors. You'll also find a stress test and relaxation exercise.

Hans Selye (1907–1982), a Canadian who was a professor at McGill University in Montreal, is considered by many to be the father of stress research. He once said that "to be totally without stress is to be dead." What Selye meant was that we won't ever be able to eliminate stress from our lives, but we can be taught to manage it effectively. Selye defined stress as our reaction to an outside stimulus. This reaction can be positive (eustress) or negative (distress).[3] Most of the time, when we think of stress we think of the negative *distress*. In a survey commissioned by the Canadian National Mental Health Association, 50 per cent of Canadians felt "really stressed" a few times each week.[4]

When you hear the word "stress," you may think of tension, hardship, problems, anger, and other negative thoughts and emotions. However, stress can have good results as well as bad. Stress is an effect of life change. Remember Selye's definition of stress: It's not the change itself, but our reaction to the change that produces stress. For this reason, even positive events can cause stress. Getting married or moving to a bigger and better home can cause as much stress as trouble with an instructor or a problem at work. Reactions vary with individual people. An event that causes one person great anxiety may cause only a mild reaction in another.

Almost any change in your life can create some level of stress. The Holmes-Rahe "Social Readjustment Scale," developed by two psychologists, assigns to various life changes a number value indicating the capability of causing stress (higher numbers mean higher stress). See Table 9–1 for different changes with their corresponding stress levels. To find your score, add the values of the events that you have experienced in the past year. Scoring over 300 points means that you are at a high risk of illness or injury due to stress.

Event	Value	Event	Value
Death of spouse or partner	100	Son or daughter leaving home	29
Divorce	73	Trouble with in-laws	29
Marital separation	65	Outstanding personal achievement	28
Jail term	63	Spouse begins or stops work	26
Personal injury	53	Starting or finishing school	26
Marriage	50	Change in living conditions	25
Fired from work	47	Revision of personal habits	24
Marital reconciliation	45	Trouble with boss	23
Retirement	45	Change in work hours, conditions	20
Changes in family member's health	44	Change in residence	20
Pregnancy	40	Change in schools	20
Sex difficulties	39	Change in recreational habits	19
Addition to family	39	Change in religious activities	19
Business readjustment	39	Change in social activities	18
Change in financial status	38	Mortgage or loan under $10,000	17
Death of a close friend	37	Change in sleeping habits	16
Change to different line of work	36	Change in # of family gatherings	15
Change in # of marital arguments	35	Change in eating habits	15
Mortgage or loan over $10,000	31	Vacation	13
Foreclosure of mortgage or loan	30	Christmas season	12
Change in work responsibilities	29	Minor violation of the law	11

Table 9–1   The Holmes-Rahe Scale to Measure Stress of Life Events

Source: Reprinted with permission of *Journal of Psychosomatic Research*, 11 (2), T. H. Holmes and R. H. Rahe, "The social readjustment rating scale," Elsevier Science Inc. 1967.

If you score between 150 and 299, your risk is reduced by 30 per cent, and if you score under 150, you have only a very small chance of illness or injury.

Positive Effects of Stress

In a stressful situation, such as during the time before a test, you may feel increased energy and a heightened awareness that may make you feel on edge. Nevertheless, these feelings can have positive effects. Selye would call this positive reaction to stress *eustress*. In fact, moderate levels of stress can actually improve performance and efficiency, while too little stress may result in boredom or inactivity, and too much stress may cause an unproductive anxiety level. Figure 9–2, based on research by Drs. Robert M. Yerkes and John D. Dodson, illustrates this concept.[5]

Figure 9-2   Yerkes-Dodson Law

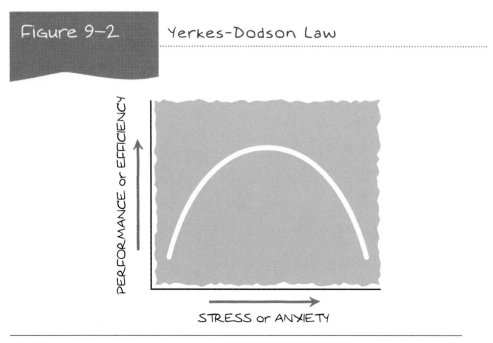

Source: From *Your Maximum Mind* by Herbert Benson, M.D. with William Proctor. Copyright © 1987 by Random House, Inc. Reprinted by permission of Times Books, a division of Random House, Inc.

Control over your responses is essential to maintaining a helpful level of stress. You can exercise some level of control by attempting to respond to stressful situations as positively as possible. Perceiving stress as good encourages you to push the boundaries of your abilities. For example, a student who responds positively to the expectations of instructors might be encouraged to improve study skills and to work on time management in order to have more study time.

Being able to control how you respond will help you deal with the negative effects of stress as well.

Negative Effects of Stress

If you perceive stress as bad, you may pour your energy into unproductive anxiety rather than problem solving. For example, a student who responds negatively to instructor expectations may become distracted and may skip class or avoid studying. Negative stress may have dangerous physical and psychological effects. Physically, you may experience a change in appetite, body aches, or increased vulnerability to illness. Psychologically, you may feel depressed, unable to study or focus in class, unhappy, or anxious. Both kinds of problems may affect your relationships and responsibilities. Selye would call this sort of negative reaction *distress*.

Managing Stress

You can activate your sense of positive control in two ways when you are faced with stressful life changes. You may either adjust whatever is *causing* stress, or use stress management techniques to adjust the *effect* that the change has on you. Start by trying to adjust the cause before you focus on what you can do about the effect. For example, if increased socializing is causing your grades to slip, consider how you can refocus on your school-work and make better decisions about how to manage your time.

If you find that you can adjust the cause, try the following strategies:

Keep your promises to yourself and others. Not doing something you are supposed to do, or not finishing it, can cause internal tension and guilt. In addition, the pressure you put on yourself, or the anger of others who counted on you, can increase the stress. Do what you say you will do.

Set reasonable, manageable goals. Trying to achieve something that is out of your reach will cause more stress than success.

Break jobs into smaller tasks. Goals will appear more manageable when approached as a series of smaller steps. Perform a smaller task well rather than a larger one not so well.

Avoid procrastination. The longer you wait to do something, the more difficulty you may have doing it. However distasteful the task, it will be much worse when time runs short and the expectations of others hang over your head.

Be thorough. Loose ends can be irritating. Many people find that only when they finish something completely can they enjoy a feeling of accomplishment. Finish the job and move on.

Set boundaries and learn to say "no." Don't take responsibility for everyone and everything. Decide what is yours to deal with, then delegate what can or should be taken care of by someone else.

When a cause lies beyond your control, address its effect on you. For example, if a case of the flu keeps you in bed for a week, you can reduce the negative effects of stress by contacting your instructors or classmates to see what schoolwork you can accomplish while you're sick.

The following are techniques that can help you adjust to the effects of a stressful situation.

Exercise, eat right, and get adequate sleep. Physical health promotes clear thinking.

Do something relaxing. Take breaks regularly: Play music, take a nap, read a book, go for a drive, take a walk outside, or see a movie. Recreation restores your mind and body.

Change your surroundings. Getting away from situations and locations you associate with stress can lighten the effect it has on you and help you place problems in perspective.

Think critically. Look at the situation and ask yourself questions about how you can improve it. Work through a problem-solving plan. Brainstorm unusual ideas—something just might work.

Positive thinking and taking action can help you control stress. In some cases, however, an emotional disorder may make stress difficult to handle without special treatment.

Emotional Disorders

Everyone encounters the ups and downs of life. Some people have emotional disorders that interfere with their ability to cope. Following are descriptions of disorders that affect people in all walks of life.

Depression

Dealing with Depression
www.depression.com/

This extensive Web site includes information about the various forms of depression.

Almost everyone has experienced the sadness or melancholy that life's troubles can cause. Many people will experience a major depression at some point in their lives that is more than temporary blues. A depressive disorder is an *illness*, not a sign of weakness or a state that can be escaped by just trying to "snap out of it." This illness requires medical evaluation and is treatable.

A depressive disorder "is a 'whole-body' illness, involving your body, mood, and thoughts."[6] You may feel constantly sad, worried, or anxious. You may lose interest in classes, people, and activities that you normally like. You might be tired all the time, sleep a lot, or have trouble sleeping at all. You could experience a loss of appetite or a desire to eat constantly. You may go to classes and meetings on "autopilot," not participating at all, or you may skip them altogether. You may cry a lot, feel hopeless, and even have thoughts of suicide.

Depression can stem from genetic, psychological, physiological, or environmental causes, or even a combination of different causes. Table 9–2 describes these causes along with depression strategies.

If you recognize yourself anywhere in this discussion of depression, the most important thing to do is to seek help. Start with your school's counselling office or student health program. People at these offices may be able to help or to refer you to someone who can. If you know someone else who suffers from depression, see that the person gets immediate medical attention and evaluation, especially if you sense that he or she is contemplating suicide. The Suicide Information and Education Centre notes that depression is a key warning sign that the person may be suicidal. Over 3 500 people commit suicide in Canada each year.[7]

Clinical depression requires medical treatment. A doctor will help you sort through your symptoms, examine family history, evaluate your situation, and determine the best treatment plan. Treatments range from therapy to medication to a combination of the two. For some people, adequate sleep, a regular exercise program, and a healthier diet may be part of the solution. If you see a doctor and are diagnosed with depression, know that your condition is nothing to be ashamed of, and be proud that you have taken a first step toward recovery.

"God grant me the serenity to accept things I cannot change, courage to change things I can, and wisdom to know the difference."

Reinhold Niebuhr

Post-Traumatic Stress Disorder

Also called "shell shock" and "post-rape syndrome," post-traumatic stress disorder (PTSD) may affect people who have gone through traumatic incidents such as rape, war, domestic violence, child abuse, and natural disasters. PTSD is an illness requiring medical treatment and can include depression or suicidal tendencies. Symptoms include flashbacks (re-experiencing the incident and the emotions), becoming numb and disconnected from others, sudden fear of anything that recalls the incident, irritable behaviour,

Table 9-2 Important Information About Depression

Possible Causes of Depression	Helpful Strategies If You Feel Depressed	Suicide Signs
A genetic trait that makes its carrier more likely to suffer depression	Do the best you can and don't have unreasonable expectations of yourself.	Statements about hopelessness or worthlessness: "The world would be better off without me."
A chemical imbalance in the brain	Try to be with others rather than alone.	Loss of interest in people, things, or activities that the person cares about.
Seasonal Affective Disorder, which occurs when a person becomes depressed in reaction to reduced daylight during autumn and winter	Don't expect your mood to change right away—feeling better will take time.	Preoccupation with suicide or death.
Highly stressful situations such as financial trouble, failing a test or class, a death in the family	Try to avoid making major life decisions until your condition improves.	Making arrangements: visiting or calling close friends and relatives, giving things away.
Illness, injuries, lack of exercise, poor diet	Remember not to blame yourself for your condition.	Sudden sense of happiness or calm. When a person decides to commit suicide, he or she often experiences relief. For this reason others often don't foresee the suicide and may say that the person "seemed to be on an upswing."
Reactions to medications		

Source: National Institutes of Mental Health Publication No. 94-3561, National Institutes of Health, 1994, and Suicide Awareness\Voices of Education (SA\VE) Web site. www.save.org

insomnia, and panic attacks (increased breathing and heart rate, nausea, dizziness).

A psychiatrist or therapist can offer treatment that helps the sufferer restore a sense of safety and control, although the effects of the incident may never completely go away. PTSD sufferers need to confront what happened and learn to accept the trauma as part of the past. Group therapy can also help. If you have experienced a traumatic incident, PTSD could make it difficult for you to deal with school, work, and family issues. Seek medical help immediately so that you can begin to work through the trauma and reclaim control over your life.[8]

Eating Disorders

Millions of people develop serious and sometimes life-threatening eating disorders every year. The most common disorders are anorexia nervosa, bulimia, and binge eating.

Anorexia nervosa. Some people develop such a strong desire to be thin that it creates unnatural self-starvation. This condition—anorexia nervosa—occurs mainly in young women, although men and older women can also be affected. People with anorexia lose an extreme amount of weight and look painfully thin, although they feel that they are overweight. In order to reach their unreasonable weight goals they refuse to eat, exercise constantly, use laxatives, and develop obsessive rituals around food.

The causes of anorexia are not fully known. The desire to emulate an "ideal" body type is one factor, and genetics could be involved (eating disorders tend to run in families). Victims of anorexia are also often perfectionists, critical of themselves, and low in self-esteem. Effects of anorexia-induced starvation include loss of menstrual periods in women, impotence in men, damage to organs, heart failure, and even death.

Bulimia. People who binge on excessive amounts of food, usually sweets and fattening foods, and then purge through self-induced vomiting, have bulimia. They may also use laxatives or exercise obsessively. Bulimia can be hard to notice, because bulimics are often able to maintain a normal appearance. Lee Hoffman of the National Institutes of Mental Health emphasizes, "Because many individuals with bulimia 'binge and purge' in secret and maintain normal or above normal body weight, they can often successfully hide their problem from others for years."[9]

The causes of bulimia, like those of anorexia, can be rooted in a desire to fulfill a body-type ideal or can come from genetically passed-on chemical imbalances. Bulimia patients are also often suffering from depression or other psychiatric illness. Effects of bulimia include damage to the digestive tract, stomach rupture, and even heart failure due to the loss of important minerals.

Binge eating. Like bulimics, people with binge-eating disorder eat large amounts of food and have a hard time stopping. However, they do not purge afterwards. Binge eaters are often overweight and feel that they cannot control their eating. As with bulimia, depression and other psychiatric illness may be partially responsible for binge eating disorder. Effects are similar to the effects of obesity, such as high blood pressure, increased stress on the body, and high cholesterol.

Eating disorders may go untreated for a long time because the sufferer may hide the disease or deny the problem. If you recognize yourself or a friend or relative in these descriptions, know that there are people and resources that can help you. Since eating disorders are a common problem on college and university campuses, most student health centres and campus counselling centres can provide both medical and psychological help. Treatment can involve any combination of psychotherapy, medical treatments, drug therapy, and even hospitalization or residence in a treatment centre.

Food is only one of several possible addictions. Following is an exploration of the use and abuse of other potentially addictive substances.

How Are Alcohol, Tobacco, and Drugs Used and Abused?

Alcohol, tobacco, and drug users include men and women from all socioeconomic levels, racial and cultural groups, and areas of the country. The stereotypical homeless drug or alcohol user actually makes up only a small

Mirror, Mirror
www.mirror-mirror.org/
eatdis.htm

This site is dedicated to the memory of Deborah Simone Fradin, who lost her battle with anorexia. It offers support for those with a variety of eating disorders, from anorexia to compulsive overeating.

percentage of substance users and abusers. Carefully consider the potential positive and negative effects before considering the use of these substances. Although some moderate users are fortunate enough to enjoy long lives, for many others substance abuse can cause financial struggles, emotional traumas, health problems, and even death.

Although the statistics are grim, the user or abuser may ignore them, preferring to think that substances are fun, help them relax, escape problems, or enhance a social occasion. Many people have used a substance, or seen friends use it, and feel that nothing bad happened. Such people may feel that tragedies "will never happen to me." However, the fact remains that the use or abuse of alcohol, tobacco, and drugs can cause problems and even destroy lives. Think critically as you read the following sections and take the time to make decisions that are best for you.

Alcohol

Alcohol is a drug as much as it is a beverage. People receive mixed messages about it as they grow up: "Alcohol is fun." "Alcohol is dangerous." "Alcohol is for adults only." These conflicting ideas can make drinking appear more glamorous, secretive, and exciting than it really is.

When used in moderation, for many people alcohol may not cause a problem. Many people drink only occasionally, and many others choose not to drink at all. The key is to be in control and to ask yourself why you drink. If you drink once in a while at a social gathering or because you like the taste, you are more likely to drink moderately than someone who drinks to escape problems or to fit in with the crowd.

Two recent Canadian reports offer these statistics about alcohol use in Canada:[10]

- The average Canadian drinks 7.6 litres of absolute alcohol per year. Young adults drink more than the average.

- Peer pressure is the key factor in whether or not a young person drinks. If more than half a young person's friends drink, 80% also report drinking.

- First-year students and those living in residence may be the heaviest drinkers.

- Drinking and sex seem to mix. Unplanned sex was reported by most students who drank. Unwanted sexual advances also increase with alcohol consumption.

- Motor vehicle deaths account for the largest number of deaths due to drinking.

- One in ten Canadians reported that they have a drinking problem; almost half of all Canadians said that they had problems because of someone else's drinking.

The bottom line is that heavy drinking causes severe problems. It can damage the liver, digestive system, and brain cells, and impair the central nervous system. Indeed, as *The New Wellness Encyclopedia* states, "chronic, excessive

Canadian Centre on
Substance Abuse
www.ccsa.ca/

Based in Ottawa, this nonprofit organization offers data on tobacco, drugs, and alcohol. This Web site also contains a page of links for help with addictions.

use of alcohol can seriously damage every function and organ of the body."[11] Prolonged use also can cause addiction, making it seem impossibly painful for the user to stop drinking.

Drinking while at school also causes problems. The Addiction Research Foundation's study of 6 000 undergraduates found that some problems associated with drinking included missing classes and lower grades. It also found that the more a student drank, the lower his or her grades tended to be.[12]

The self-test on page 324 will help you determine if your drinking habits may cause problems.

Tobacco

Post-secondary students do more than their share of smoking when compared with national smoking rates. A report issued by the Addiction Research Foundation and the Canadian Centre on Substance Abuse claims that

- 29% of those aged 15 years or older smoke, while 35% of young people aged 20 to 24 smoke.
- Nationally, the smoking rate in Canada is 27%.
- The average Canadian smoker "lights up" a little more than twenty times per day.
- Smokers between the ages of 12 and 19 smoke to "relax"; 31% smoke to keep thin.[13]

When people smoke they inhale nicotine, a highly addictive drug found in all tobacco products. Nicotine's immediate effects may include an increase in blood pressure and heart rate, sweating, and throat irritation. Long-term effects may include high blood pressure, bronchitis, emphysema, stomach ulcers, and heart conditions. Pregnant women who smoke run an increased risk of low birth weight, premature births, or stillbirths.

Inhaling tobacco smoke damages the cells that line the air sacs of the lungs. Smoking has long been thought to cause lung cancer, and in late 1996 researchers found a definitive link. They exposed lung cells to tobacco smoke and saw that the damage done to the genes of the cells mirrors the damage they've seen in lung tumours. Lung cancer causes more deaths in Canada than any other type of cancer. Smoking also increases the risk of mouth, throat, and other cancers.[14]

Smoking also creates a danger to nonsmokers. Environmental tobacco smoke (ETS), also called "secondhand smoke," causes about 3 000 lung cancer deaths per year in nonsmokers.[15] Many workplaces, public buildings, and restaurants have now banned smoking, thereby reducing the problem. However, those rules don't affect private spaces such as homes and cars. ETS is especially harmful to children.

Quitting smoking is extremely difficult and should be attempted gradually. Withdrawal symptoms include insomnia, irritability, depression, difficulty concentrating, and tobacco cravings. Some doctors say that it can be harder to quit smoking than it is to kick a heroin habit. Many lifelong smokers will tell you that the best advice is to never start smoking, because quitting is so difficult. Even so, if you have smoked regularly, you can quit through motivation and perseverance. Half of all people who have ever smoked have quit. Suggestions for quitting include the following:[16]

- ○ Try the nicotine patch or nicotine gum, and be sure to use it consistently.

- ○ Get support and encouragement from a health-care provider, a "quit smoking" program, a support group, and friends and family.

- ○ Avoid situations that cause you to want to smoke, such as being around other smokers, drinking alcohol, and highly stressful encounters or events.

- ○ Find other ways of lowering your stress level, such as exercise or other activities you enjoy.

- ○ Set goals. Set a quit date and tell friends and family. Make and keep medical appointments.

The positive effects of quitting—increased life expectancy, greater lung capacity, and more energy—may inspire any smoker to consider making a lifestyle change. Quitting provides financial benefits as well. If you're a pack-a-day smoker, think about this: If you put three dollars in the bank each day instead of buying a pack of cigarettes, you would have almost $1 100 in your account after a year. That would pay for a nice week at a cottage rented in the Muskokas. If you smoke two packs a day, you would have $2 200 to spend on a new computer or stereo. Now, try to imagine the savings, with interest, you would have over an entire lifetime! Weigh your options and make a responsible choice. In order to evaluate the level of your potential addiction, you may want to take the self-test on page 324, replacing the words "alcohol" or "drugs" with "cigarettes" or "smoking."

addiction
Compulsive physiological need for a habit-forming substance.

Drugs

Although alcohol remains the most abused drug by young people in Canada, use of illicit drugs can also be a problem. Statistics Canada reports that young males are the most likely users of illicit drugs, but it is an issue that affects many young people on Canadian campuses.[17] Drug users rarely think through the possible effects when choosing to take a drug. However, many of the so-called "rewards" of drug abuse are empty. Drug-using peers may accept you for your drug use and not for who you are. Problems and responsibilities may multiply when you emerge from a high. The pain of withdrawal may not compare to the pain of the damage that long-term drug use can do to your body. Table 9–3 shows the most commonly used drugs and their potential effects.

You are responsible for choosing what you want to introduce into your body. If you think critically about drugs and ask important questions, you can draw your own conclusions. Ask questions like the following: Why do I want to do this? What are the positive and negative effects it might have? If others want me to do it, why? Do I respect the people who want me to do this? How does the drug affect other users I know? How would my drug use affect the people in my life? The more informed you are, the better able you will be to make choices that benefit you and avoid choices that harm you.

Table 9-3   How Drugs Affect You

Drug Category	Drug Types	How They make You Feel	Physical Affects	Danger of Physical Dependence	Danger of Psychological Dependence
Stimulants	Cocaine, amphetamines	Alert, stimulated, excited	Nervousness, mood swings, stroke or convulsions, psychoses, paranoia, coma at large doses	Relatively strong	Strong
Depressants	Alcohol, Valium-type drugs	Sedated, tired, high	Cirrhosis, impaired blood production, greater risk of cancer, heart attack, and stroke, impaired brain function	Strong	Strong
Opiates	Heroin, codeine, other pain pills	Drowsy, floating, without pain	Infection of organs, inflammation of the heart, hepatitis	Yes, with high dosage	Yes, with high dosage
Cannabinols	Marijuana, hashish	Euphoria, mellowness, little sensation of time	Impairment of judgment and co-ordination, bronchitis and asthma, lung and throat cancers, anxiety, lack of energy and motivation, reduced ability to produce hormones	Moderate	Relatively strong
Hallucinogens	LSD, mushrooms	Heightened sensual perception, hallucinations, confusion	Impairment of brain function, circulatory problems, agitation and confusion, flashbacks	Insubstantial	Insubstantial
Inhalants	Glue, aerosols	Giddiness, lightheadedness	Damage to brain, heart, liver, and kidneys	Insubstantial	Insubstantial

Source: Adapted from *Educating Yourself about Alcohol and Drugs: A People's Primer* by Marc Alan Schuckit, M.D., New York, Plenum Press, 1995.

You can injure your reputation, your student status, or your employment possibilities if you are caught using drugs or if drug use impairs your performance in school or on the job. These days many companies test both employees and job applicants. Employers don't want to risk hiring a drug user who will have trouble working up to potential. An additional negative effect of drug use is that it violates federal law.

Identifying and Overcoming Addiction

People with addictions have lost their control for any number of reasons, including chemical imbalances in the brain, hereditary tendencies, or stressful life circumstances. When you observe others or yourself and wonder if addiction is a factor, remember that many addicts hide their addictions well. For every loud, obvious alcoholic or drug user, there is someone who abuses substances quietly and secretly, continuing to appear functional and controlled to observers. Women, although they are less likely to be substance abusers, tend to conceal substance problems more carefully than do men.[18]

If you think you may be addicted, look carefully at your situation. Compare the positive and negative effects of your habits and decide if they are worth it. Although others can tell you how they feel and make suggestions, you are the only one who can truly take the initiative to change.

Facing Addiction

Addiction is incredibly hard to face and overcome alone. Because substances often cause physical and chemical changes, quitting often requires guiding your body through a painful withdrawal. Even substances that don't cause chemical changes create psychological dependence that is tough to break. Asking for help isn't an admission of failure, but a courageous move to reclaim a valuable life. Using the self-test on page 324, evaluate your behaviour to see if you may need help.

Even one "yes" answer may indicate that you need to evaluate your alcohol and/or drug use and to monitor it more carefully. If you answered yes to three or more questions, you may benefit from talking to a professional about your use and the problems it may be causing for you.

Working Through Addiction

If you determine that you need to make some changes, there are many resources that can help you along the way. Seek out any combination of the following suggestions.

Counselling and medical care. You can find help from school-based, private, government-sponsored, or workplace-sponsored resources. Check with your school's counselling or health centre, your personal physician, or a local hospital. If you don't find an appropriate program, a medical professional can refer you to one. Check in the Yellow Pages under Addiction—Information and Treatment Centres for services in your area. Some programs are free. Programs that require payment may make allowances for financial limitations, charging you according to what you are able to pay.

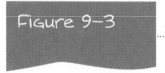

Substance Use and Abuse Self-Test

Even one "yes" answer may indicate a need to evaluate your substance use. Answering "yes" to three or more questions indicates that you may benefit from discussing your use with a counsellor.

Within the last year:

1. Have you tried to stop drinking or taking drugs but found that you couldn't do so for long?

2. Do you get tired of people telling you they're concerned about your drinking or drug use?

3. Have you felt guilty about your drinking or drug use?

4. Have you felt that you needed a drink or drugs in the morning—as an "eye-opener"—in order to improve a hangover?

5. Do you drink or use drugs alone?

6. Do you drink or use drugs every day?

7. Have you found yourself regularly thinking or saying, "I need" a drink or any type of drug?

8. Have you lied about or concealed your drinking or drug use?

9. Do you drink or use drugs to escape worries, problems, mistakes, or shyness?

10. Do you find you need increasingly larger amounts of drugs or alcohol in order to achieve a desired effect?

11. Have you forgotten what happened while drinking or using drugs (had a blackout)?

12. Have you been surprised by how much you were using alcohol or drugs?

13. Have you spent a lot of time, energy, and/or money getting alcohol or drugs?

14. Has your drinking or drug use caused you to neglect friends, your partner, your children, or other family members, or caused other problems at home?

15. Have you gotten into an argument or a fight that was alcohol- or drug-related?

16. Has your drinking or drug use caused you to miss class, fail a test, or ignore schoolwork?

17. Have you rejected planned social events in favour of drinking or using drugs?

18. Have you been choosing to drink or use drugs instead of performing other activities or hobbies you used to enjoy?

19. Has your drinking or drug use affected your efficiency on the job or caused you to fail to show up at work?

20. Have you continued to drink or use drugs despite any physical problems or health risks that your use has caused or made worse?

21. Have you driven a car or performed any other potentially dangerous tasks while under the influence of alcohol or drugs?

22. Have you had a drug- or alcohol-related legal problem or arrest (possession, use, disorderly conduct, driving while intoxicated, etc.)?

Source: Adapted from the Criteria for Substance Dependence and Criteria for Substance Abuse in the *Diagnostic and Statistical Manual of Mental Disorders*, 4th ed., published by the American Psychiatric Association, Washington, D.C., and from materials entitled "Are You An Alcoholic?" developed by Johns Hopkins University.

Real World Perspective

How do I know if I have a substance abuse problem? Where can I go for help?

Anonymous Student

I suppose I was like many boys who grew up in small-town Ontario. We used to drink and smoke in high school to see if we could get away with it. Going to a college in a big city, I was excited and scared. To find friends and fit in, I started to drink. Drinking games in residence were common. Passing joints around at parties was also common and, not wanting to seem like a "farm boy" from Niagara, I began to toke up. The course I am in is very demanding and stressful. We often go out for drinks to discuss the practical aspects of the program. It all seemed like fun at first, but I find myself needing to drink or smoke more often. I'm starting to miss classes and group meetings, and I'm handing in assignments late. Where can I go for help? I'm afraid that I'm becoming addicted.

Laura Brinckerhoff, Program Director— Nonprofit Organization

I started drinking and using drugs when I was in junior high school. It wasn't until my last year of university, though, that I finally got some help. It's amazing that I lasted so long. Part of my cover-up was to give the illusion that everything was fine. If I was in school and doing well, maybe no one would notice 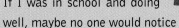 that my life was falling apart. The turning point for me was the realization that I'd die if I continued down the same path. I finally asked for help from my doctor. This was a big step for me because I thought that I was in control. I put my life into his hands and began the journey to recovery. It hasn't been easy though. I've had to let go of unhealthy relationships. I've had to change the way I think about my life. I've had to be humble enough to say, "I need help." But, I'm so glad I did. My life is much more meaningful and rich now.

I believe that most people who are successful at overcoming addictions engage in a regular recovery program. I attend Alcoholics Anonymous (AA) meetings, practise the twelve steps, and lead a spiritually directed life. I don't know of anything that works as well. Another part of staying sober is to serve others who may be struggling with an addiction. That's why I agreed to tell you my story. If you think you're dependent on alcohol or drugs, I recommend you go to an AA meeting right away. By listening to other people's stories, you should be able to tell fairly soon if you have a problem. Try to attend five to ten meetings before you completely make up your mind. Also, if your family or friends have been telling you that you have a problem, then they're probably right. As difficult as it is to hear, listen to them. Their support can help save you a lot of agony. But, regardless of the program you choose, if you're not willing to change the unhealthy patterns in your life or your core beliefs, staying sober will be very difficult. You may end up being a dry drunk—not drinking, but not really happy.

Like me, you may be scared to take the steps to change your life, but it's worth it. I never dreamed that life could be so wonderful and fun. It's the greatest gift God's ever given me.

Detoxification ("detox") centres. If you have a severe addiction, you may need a controlled environment in which to separate yourself completely from the substance that you abuse. Some are outpatient facilities that you visit periodically. Other programs provide a 24-hour home-away-from-home for you until you have gone through the critical period of withdrawal. The life changes required by a live-in or drop-in centre may require that you withdraw from school for a while.

Support groups. You can derive help and comfort from sharing your experiences with others. Alcoholics Anonymous (AA) is the premier support group for alcoholics. Based on a twelve-step recovery program, AA has helped a great number of people over many years. Membership costs little or nothing—members may donate one dollar at meetings if they can afford it. AA has led to many other support groups for addicts such as Overeaters Anonymous (OA) and Narcotics Anonymous (NA). Many schools have AA, NA, or other group sessions on campus. A counsellor may be able to help you decide what is best for your needs.

When people address their problems directly instead of avoiding them through substance abuse, they can begin to grow and improve. Working through substance-abuse problems can lead to a restoration of both health and self-respect.

Substance Abuse Affects Others

The pain and negative effects of substance abuse go beyond the abuser. Those involved in the abuser's life are often drawn into the addiction, becoming codependents. Melody Beattie, in *Codependent No More*, defines codependents as "people whose lives had become unmanageable as a result of living in a committed relationship with an alcoholic." This definition holds true for any kind of addict. You can replace the word *alcoholic* with *drug addict* or *compulsive overeater.*

Codependent spouses, parents, or children of an addict become overwhelmingly preoccupied with the happiness of that person. They expend boundless energy caring for the addict, feeling more and more alone and drained as they wonder why nothing comes back to them in return. They become so involved with the addict's life that they lose sight of their own, resulting in low self-esteem and resentment. They may believe that they have caused the addict to abuse substances. They rescue everyone but themselves.

Codependency prevents change. An addict often will not take responsibility for changing his or her life until a codependent *detaches* from the problem, ending any support actions that prevent the addict from facing his or her problems. Examples of detaching include a husband who stops trying to explain away his alcoholic wife's behaviour, a teenager who stops cooking for and cleaning up after a substance-abusing parent, or a parent who stops making excuses to instructors or employers for an addicted child.

Being a codependent can be almost as painful and harmful as being an addict. If you don't have an abuse problem but have a friend, significant other, child, or parent who does, think about how it affects you. Look into programs, on campus or off, that can help you cope with feelings and change

"Moderation in all things."

Terence

how you react to the abuser in your life. Al-Anon, Ala-Teen, Co-Dependents Anonymous, and Adult Children Of Alcoholics (ACOA), all based on the AA twelve-step model, can help codependents reclaim their own lives.

What Should You Consider When Making Sexual Decisions?

Sexual relationships involve both body and mind on many different levels. Forming your opinions about sexuality takes some thought. In this section, you will explore sexual decision making, birth control options, sexually transmitted diseases (STDs), and sexual harassment and abuse.

Sex and Critical Thinking

What sexuality means to you and the role it plays in your life are your own private business. However, the physical act of sex goes beyond the private realm. Individual sexual conduct can have consequences such as unexpected pregnancy; the spread of the Human Immunodeficiency Virus (HIV), possibly leading to Acquired Immune Deficiency Syndrome (AIDS); and the transmission of other STDs. These consequences affect everyone involved in the sexual act.

Your self-respect depends on making choices that maintain your own health and safety as well as those of any person with whom you are involved. Think critically about sexual issues, asking important questions and weighing the positive and negative effects of any action before you make a decision. Because it can be difficult to think clearly "in the moment," you may want to do some thinking before situations arise, even though it seems unromantic. You may ask yourself questions such as the following:

- Do I feel ready?
- Is this the right person/moment/situation?
- Do I have what I need to prevent pregnancy and exposure to STDs? If not, what may be the consequences? Can I live with those consequences (pregnancy or disease)? Are they worth it?
- Does this person truly care for me and not just for what we might be doing?
- Is this what I really want? Does it fit with my values?
- Will this enhance our emotional relationship or cause problems later?

Critical thinking can help you consider the effects of sexual activity. One of the possible effects is pregnancy. Birth control methods are designed to prevent this particular effect.

Birth Control

Using birth control is a choice, and it is not for everyone. For some, using any kind of birth control is against their religious beliefs. Others may want to have children. Many sexually active people, however, choose one or more methods of birth control.

In addition to preventing pregnancy, some birth control methods also protect against sexually transmitted diseases. Table 9–4 describes the most established methods of birth control, with effectiveness percentages and STD prevention based on proper and regular use.

Evaluate the positive and negative effects of each method for yourself as well as for your partner. Consider cost, ease of use, convenience, reliability, comfort, and protection against STDs. Communicate with your partner and together make a choice that is comfortable for both of you. If a partner refuses to honour your preference, re-evaluate your relationship. A partner who truly cares about you should be concerned about your health and safety. For literature on this subject check your library or bookstore, talk to your doctor, ask a counsellor at your student health centre, or call a helpful organization. Make informed choices.

Sexually Transmitted Diseases

Sexually transmitted diseases cause health problems ranging from the annoying to the life-threatening. Table 9–5 shows some basic information about common STDs. Each one of these diseases is spread through sexual contact—intercourse or other sexual activity that involves contact with the genitals. All are highly contagious. The only birth control methods that protect against them are the methods that prevent skin-to-skin contact—the male and female condoms (latex or polyurethane only). Most of these STDs can also spread to infants of infected mothers during birth, and can cause health problems for the infants. Have a doctor examine any irregularity or discomfort—the sooner you are treated, the less chance you have of suffering permanent damage. Women should have an annual Pap smear to check for diseases or irregularities.

AIDS and HIV

The most serious of the STDs is Acquired Immune Deficiency Syndrome, or AIDS, brought on by the spread of the contagious Human Immunodeficiency Virus (HIV). Not everyone who tests positive for HIV will develop AIDS, but AIDS currently has no cure and results in eventual death. The spread of AIDS has been strong and steady over the last ten years. Recent figures indicate that from 1977 to the end of 1997 more than 40 000 Canadians have tested positive for HIV, and 15 527 have been diagnosed with AIDS.[19] According to *Maclean's* magazine, as we head into the twenty-first

Table 9-4 Methods of Birth Control

Method	Approximate Effectiveness*	Prevents STDs?	Description
Abstinence	100%	Only if no sexual activity occurs	Just saying no. No intercourse means no risk of pregnancy. However, alternative modes of sexual activity can still spread STDs.
Condom (male)	94%	Yes, if made of latex	A sheath that fits over the penis and prevents sperm from entering the vagina.
Condom (female)	90%	Yes	A sheath that fits inside the vagina, held in place by two rings, one of which hangs outside. Can be awkward. It is relatively new and may not be widely available.
Diaphragm or cervical cap	85%	No	A bendable rubber cap that fits over the cervix and pelvic bone inside the vagina (the cervical cap is smaller and fits over the cervix only). Both must be fitted initially by a gynecologist and used with a spermicide.
Oral contraceptives (the Pill)	97%	No	A dosage of hormones taken daily by a woman, preventing the ovaries from releasing eggs. Side effects can include headaches, weight gain, and increased chances of blood clotting. Various brands and dosages; must be prescribed by a gynecologist.
Spermicidal foams, jellies, inserts	84% if used alone	No	Usually used with diaphragms or condoms to enhance effectiveness, they have an ingredient that kills sperm cells (but not STDs). They stay effective for a limited period of time after insertion.
Intrauterine device (IUD)	94%	No	A small coil of wire inserted into the uterus by a gynecologist (who must also remove it). Prevents fertilized eggs from implanting in the uterine wall. Possible side effects include bleeding.
Norplant	Nearly 100%	No	A series of up to five small tubes implanted by a gynecologist into a woman's upper arm, preventing pregnancy for up to five years. Can be tough to remove. Possible side effects may resemble those of oral contraceptives. Must be removed by a doctor.
Depo-Provera®	Nearly 100%	No	An injection that a woman must receive from a doctor every few months. Possible side effects may resemble those of oral contraceptives.
Tubal ligation	Nearly 100%	No	Surgery for women that cuts and ties the fallopian tubes, preventing eggs from travelling to the uterus. Difficult and expensive to reverse. Recommended for those who do not want any more children.
Vasectomy	Nearly 100%	No	Surgery for men that blocks the tube that delivers sperm to the penis. Like tubal ligation, difficult to reverse and only recommended for those who don't want children.
Rhythm method	Variable	No	Abstaining from intercourse during the ovulation segment of the woman's menstrual cycle. Can be difficult to time and may not account for cycle irregularities.
Withdrawal	Variable	No	Pulling the penis out of the vagina before ejaculation. Unreliable, because some sperm can escape in the fluid released prior to ejaculation. Dependent on a controlled partner.

*This effectiveness rating applies if directions are followed carefully. Actual effectiveness may vary.

Table 9-5 Sexually Transmitted Diseases

Disease	Symptoms	Health problems if untreated	Treatments
Chlamydia	Discharge, painful urination, swollen or painful joints, change in menstrual periods for women	Can cause pelvic inflammatory disease (PID) in women, which can lead to sterility or ectopic pregnancies; infection; miscarriage or premature birth.	Curable with full course of antibiotics; avoid sex until treatment is complete.
Gonorrhea	Discharge, burning while urinating	Can cause PID, swelling of testicles and penis, arthritis, skin problems, infections.	Usually curable with antibiotics; however, certain strains are becoming resistant to medication.
Genital herpes	Blisterlike itchy sores in the genital area, headache, fever, chills	Symptoms may subside and then recur, often in response to high stress levels; carriers can transmit the virus even when it is dormant.	No cure; some medications such as Acyclovir reduce and help heal the sores and may shorten recurring outbreaks.
Syphilis	A genital sore lasting one to five weeks, followed by a rash, fatigue, fever, sore throat, headaches, swollen glands	If it lasts over four years, it can cause blindness, destruction of bone, insanity, or heart failure; can cause death or deformity of a child born to an infected woman.	Curable with full course of antibiotics.
Human Papilloma Virus (HPV, or genital warts)	Genital itching and irritation, small clusters of warts	Can increase risk of cervical cancer in women; virus may remain in body even when warts are removed and cause recurrences.	Treatable with drugs applied to warts or various kinds of wart-removal surgery.
Hepatitis B	Fatigue, poor appetite, vomiting, jaundice, hives	Some carriers will have few symptoms; others may develop chronic liver disease that can lead to other diseases of the liver.	No cure; some will recover, some will not. Bed rest may help ease symptoms.

century, Vancouver is Canada's AIDS death "hot spot," with nineteen AIDS-related deaths per 100 000. In comparison, Montreal has fourteen AIDS deaths per 100 000, while Toronto has eleven.[20]

AIDS disarms the body's immune system, making it unable to fight viruses that it normally would kill. HIV can lie undetected in the body for up to ten years before surfacing, and a carrier can spread it during that time. Although AIDS was at first associated with male homosexuals, anyone who is sexually active can contract it. AIDS is growing fastest among heterosexual populations, especially women and children. Medical science continues to develop drugs to combat AIDS and its related illnesses. However, the drugs can cause severe side effects, many have not been thoroughly tested, and none is a proven cure.

HIV is transmitted through two types of bodily fluids: fluids associated with sex (semen and vaginal fluids) and blood. People have been known to acquire HIV through sexual relations, by sharing hypodermic needles for drug use, and by receiving tainted blood transfusions. You cannot become infected with the virus unless one of those fluids is involved. Therefore, it is unlikely you would contract HIV from toilet seats, hugging, kissing, or sharing a glass.

The best defence against AIDS is not having sex. Most experts believe, however, that the risk of getting AIDS and other sexually transmitted diseases can be greatly reduced if a condom is used properly. Always use a latex condom, because natural skin condoms may let the virus pass through. Use K-Y® Jelly or a spermicide as a lubricant, because petroleum jelly can destroy the latex in condoms and diaphragms. Although some people dislike using condoms, it's a small price to pay for preserving your life.

To be safe, have an HIV test done at your doctor's office. Your school's health department may also administer HIV tests. If you are infected, first inform any recent sexual partners and seek medical assistance. Then contact support organizations in your area. Check in the Yellow Pages under AIDS—Information and Support Services.

AIDS Awareness
www.aidsfoundation.ca/

The latest information on AIDS, including support group information, is available online from the AIDS Foundation of Canada.

Sexual Harassment and Abuse

Your sexuality is a private matter for you to express when, where, and to whom you choose. Sexual abuse occurs when someone violates that privacy or tries to interfere with or take away your choices. It can range from an offensive sexual comment or display to spousal abuse and rape. This section describes different types of sexual abuse and offers strategies for coping and prevention.

Sexual Harassment

The facts. Sexual harassment covers a wide range of behaviour that has been divided into two types. The first, *quid pro quo harassment*, refers to a request for some kind of sexual favour or activity in exchange for something else. It is a kind of bribe or threat ("If you don't do X for me, I will fail you/fire you/make your life miserable."). The second, *hostile environment harassment*, indicates any situation in which sexually charged remarks, behaviour, or displayed items cause discomfort. Harassment of this type ranges from lewd conversation or jokes to display of pornography.

Both men and women can be victims of sexual harassment, although the more common situation involves a woman subjected to harassment by a man. Unfortunately, even as women continue to gain equality, sexism remains alive. Sexist attitudes can create an environment in which men feel they have the right to use words, ideas, and attitudes that degrade women. Even though physical violence is not involved, the fear and mental trauma that such harassment can cause is extremely harmful.

How to cope. Sexual harassment can be difficult to identify and monitor because what offends one person may seem acceptable to another. If you take offence or feel degraded by anything that goes on at school or work, you have a

sexism
Behaviour or attitudes, especially against women, that promote gender-based stereotypes or that discriminate based on sex.

right to address it. Start with the person who you believe is harassing you, or, if that makes you uncomfortable, speak to another authority. Try to uncover the truth and avoid assumptions. Perhaps the person simply had no idea that his or her behaviour could be perceived as offensive. On the other hand, the person may have dishonourable intentions toward you. Either way, you are entitled to request that the person put an end to what has offended you. Most Canadian colleges and universities have a sexual harassment policy. Check your student handbook for information about your school's policy.

Rape and Date Rape

The facts. Rape is an all-too-common occurrence, both in the community and on campus. Any sexual act (intercourse or anal/oral penetration) by a person against another person's will is defined as rape. Consent for sex must be freely and clearly given. Under Canadian law, "no means no." Rape is primarily a violent act, not a sexual one. It is an expression of power and control.

Rape is a problem on many campuses, especially *acquaintance rape*, also called date rape. Any sexual activity during a date that is against one partner's will constitutes date rape, including situations in which one partner is too drunk or drugged to give consent. Most date rape victims do not report the incidents. Victims may believe that they can't prove it, that they might have asked for it, that they should be ashamed if drugs or alcohol were involved, or that their assailants may seek revenge if accused.

Beyond the physical harm from the rape itself and any accompanying violence, rape has serious effects on mental health. Campus Advocates for Rape Education (C.A.R.E.), an organization at Wheaton College in Massachusetts, describes the specific harms of date rape. "One's trust in a friend, date, or acquaintance is also violated. As a result, a victim's fear, self-blame, guilt, and shame are magnified because the assailant is known."[21] Many rape victims develop rape-related post-traumatic stress disorder, an emotional disorder requiring medical evaluation and therapy (see page 316).

Most schools have a sexual harassment officer on campus. Check your student handbook or institution's calendar for his or her phone number, e-mail address, or office location.

How to cope. Rape victims often neglect to report the incident. Remember, says C.A.R.E, "No matter how stupid you feel...if you knew the person...if you were high on drugs/alcohol...if you originally said yes, then said no...if you've had sex with that person before...if no one believes you...if you choose not to report it...*it's not your fault!*"[22] No kind of rape is deserved or permissible.

If you are the victim of a rape, get medical attention immediately. Try not to shower or change your clothing, because doing so will destroy evidence that you may need. Next, find someone you can talk to. A close friend is good, and a trained counsellor is even better. Consider reporting the incident to the police or to campus officials if it occurred on campus. Finally, consider pressing charges if you know your assailant or if there is a chance the police can find the person. Whether or not you press charges or report the incident, don't stop getting help. Continue counselling, join a rape survivor group, or use a hotline.

date rape
Sexual assault perpetrated by the victim's escort during an arranged social encounter.

Date Rape Drug Information

www.ucalgary.ca/UofC/ departments/SHO/daterap.htm

www.sfu.ca/student-services/ residences/rohypnol.html

Information on rohypnol, a drug often used in rapes and date rapes is available online. These Canadian sites also include details on what to do if you suspect you may have been a victim.

Domestic Abuse

The facts. The abuse of a spouse or partner isn't always of a sexual nature. However, it occurs within the context of a relationship that may have a sexual dimension, such as a married or closely involved couple. Although men may sometimes experience abuse, women are the primary victims.

Domestic abuse is a real problem in many households. Because victims often hide the effects, abuse is more common than people might think. Very few victims want anyone to know that the partner they have chosen is subjecting them to abuse, especially if they love or have loved the abuser. They may also believe that they have done something wrong and deserve the abuse in return. Therefore they may try to endure it alone, hoping that it will end if they can give more to the relationship.

How to cope. Domestic abuse is an extremely touchy situation because the abuser is often very close to the victim. If you are being abused, your safety and sanity depend on your seeking help. Take one step at a time. When you are alone, call a shelter or abuse hotline and talk to someone who understands what you are going through. Seek counselling at your school or at a centre in your community. If you can, see if your abuser will consent to counselling as well.

Sometimes abuse becomes life-threatening. If you need medical attention, get to a clinic or hospital. Your doctor may be able to help you or refer you to someone who can. If you feel that your life is in danger, get out and take any children with you. Through your local police department, you can get a restraining order that will require your abuser to stay away from you. Bringing charges against an abuser isn't easy, but it is your right if you feel you can. No matter how difficult a relationship may be, no one deserves to be abused.

Reasons to Take Action

Rape, domestic abuse, and sexual harassment are crimes punishable by law. If you are a victim of sexual or domestic abuse, you must make a decision about how to act. Evaluate the positive and negative effects of your options. Some people fear that speaking up may cause them to lose their jobs or fail their classes. Some think no one will believe them. These are very real fears. However, remaining silent may have more profound negative consequences. When you neglect to stand up for your rights, you may be sending yourself a subtle message that you aren't worth the trouble. Staying in a relationship, class, or job in which you feel threatened may have long-lasting effects on your mental stability.

Making the decision is a delicate and personal process. If you do report an incident or take legal action, gather as many supportive people around you as you can. Remind yourself that no matter how difficult the road may be, you are worth the trouble.

Preventing Sexual Abuse

Both potential players in the drama of sexual abuse—potential abusers and potential victims—can take steps to prevent incidents from occurring. Table 9–6 shows suggestions for both potential victims and potential abusers.

Table 9–6   Ways to Avoid Sexual Abuse

Potential Victims	Potential Abusers
Avoid situations that present clear dangers. Don't walk alone at night in neglected areas, don't park far away at night, don't do anything that makes you nervous.	Become aware of your tendencies. If you have a hot temper, avoid acting impulsively on your anger. Take a breather, take a walk, do whatever helps you calm down so that you and your partner can resolve the problem without violence.
Avoid use of drugs or overuse of alcohol. Anything that reduces or obliterates your judgment will make you more vulnerable to any kind of assault.	Communicate. Be clear about what you feel and why. Be honest. If you have a request, make it respectfully and invite your partner to express a reaction to the request.
When you have a date with someone you don't know well, don't go far off. Make plans to stay in a familiar and populated area.	Listen. Hear your partner out just as you expect to be heard. If he or she says no, take it seriously. Listen for hints concerning your partner's limits.
When anger is brewing in your relationship, don't bury or ignore it. Take the time to talk through it as calmly as possible. Identify the problems and work through them together.	Pay attention to body language. Even if your partner doesn't express feelings verbally, body language may be telling you to slow down or stop. Honour that as much as you would a verbal request.
When you perceive a situation as truly threatening, don't hesitate to get out. Leave your house, take a cab home from a date, call a friend to pick you up. Don't wait to find out whether your instincts are right—you may put yourself in a dangerous situation.	Don't make assumptions. Don't assume that your partner wants everything you want. Don't assume your partner *knows* what you want. Don't assume that a "no" to a particular sexual activity means a "no" to who you are or to the relationship. Ask, ask, always ask.

Joie de vivre

There is a phrase in French that has become commonly used in the English language as well: *joie de vivre*, which literally means "joy of living." A person with *joie de vivre* is one who finds joy and optimism in all parts of life, who is able to enjoy life's pleasures and find something positive in its struggles. Without experiencing difficult and sometimes painful challenges, people might have a hard time recognizing and experiencing happiness and satisfaction.

Think of this concept as you examine your level of personal wellness. If you focus on what is positive about yourself, that attitude can affect all other areas of your life. Give yourself the gift of self-respect so that you can nourish your body and mind every day, in every situation. Through both stressful obstacles and happy successes, you can find the joy of living.

Chapter 9: Applications

Name _____   Date _____

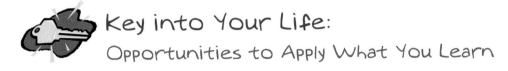 Key into Your Life:
Opportunities to Apply What You Learn

Exercise 1: Food Log

Examine your eating habits by keeping track of what you eat for three typical midweek days. In order to be as accurate as possible, try not to change your normal eating habits. On a separate sheet of paper, write in detail the names and amounts of each food that you eat. Then, on the following chart, tally how many servings you eat each day from the four food groups (breads/cereals, dairy, meats, fruits and vegetables), and indicate any sweets, caffeine, or high-fat foods you eat. In the last column, indicate the times when you ate a meal or snack.

	BREADS	DAIRY	MEATS	FRUITS/ VEG	SWEETS	CAFFEINE	HIGH-FAT FOODS	TIMES OF MEALS/ SNACKS
Day 1								
Day 2								
Day 3								

Did you overdo it anywhere? If so, name the category: _____

Did you not eat enough of any of the four groups? If so, which one?

_____

Evaluate your eating times. Did your eating schedule have positive or negative effects? Describe the effects. Indicate any changes you want to make and their predicted effects.

_____

_____

_____

Name one change that you want to make in your food choices. Describe the positive effects you expect to gain from this change.

_____

_____

_____

Using your problem-solving skills, come up with a plan to address this change and illustrate it with a think link on a separate piece of paper (you may want to use a copy of the problem-solving plan in Chapter 4).

Exercise 2: Exercise Log

Log your exercise over a two-week period. Don't forget to include exercise such as climbing stairs, walking when your ride didn't show up, or cleaning your floors. For each entry, indicate the type of exercise you did and for how long a period of time you exercised (duration).

DAY	TYPES OF EXERCISE	DURATION OF EACH TYPE OF EXERCISE
1		
2		
3		
4		
5		
6		
7		
8		
9		
10		
11		
12		
13		
14		

From a look at this table, evaluate your fitness profile. Are you more or less active than you need to be? Do you need to crosstrain? If you could make one change in your physical activity, what would it be?

_____

_____

_____

Work to make that change during one week. Evaluate the change. How did it make you feel? Do you sense any change in your energy level or strength?

Exercise 3: Sleep Log

For a week, log exactly how many hours you sleep. Indicate exactly when you slept. Include naps and note any waking periods during sleep. Check the appropriate column on days when you felt well rested or run-down.

Day	Major Period of Sleep	Waking Periods	Naps	Well rested?	Run-down?
1					
2					
3					
4					
5					
6					
7					

When you felt well rested, what effects did your sleeping pattern have on your day?

When you felt run-down, did a different sleeping pattern that day affect you negatively?

Judging from the information in the table, what seems to be the ideal sleep schedule for you? Describe it here, including number of hours, where you sleep, and when you sleep.

Exercise 4: Early Warning Signs of Stress

Step 1   Check any items that you have experienced at least once in the last three months. Under the Behavioural column, "compulsive behaviours" are behaviours that are repeated excessively, such as constant handwashing.

PHYSICAL	PSYCHOLOGICAL	BEHAVIOURAL
[ ] Indigestion	[ ] Irritability	[ ] Forgetfulness
[ ] Diarrhea/constipation	[ ] Excessive anger	[ ] Poor concentration
[ ] Nausea or vomiting	[ ] Worry	[ ] Distorted perception
[ ] Appetite problems	[ ] Depression	[ ] Compulsive behaviours
[ ] Headaches	[ ] Excessive crying	[ ] Decrease in productivity
[ ] Neck or back pain	[ ] Aggressiveness	[ ] Decrease in creativity
[ ] Allergies	[ ] Isolation	[ ] Living in the past
[ ] Hair loss	[ ] Boredom	[ ] Drinking more
[ ] Colds, flu, cold sore	[ ] Decreased sense of humour	[ ] Smoking more
[ ] Teeth grinding	[ ] Critical of self/others	[ ] Decreased sex drive
[ ] Problems sleeping	[ ] Decreased motivation	[ ] Acting "antsy"
[ ] Fatigue	[ ] Decreased self-esteem	[ ] Accident prone

Step 2   Circle the three items that usually occur as early warning signs of stress for you.

Step 3   From what you know about relieving stress, describe the steps you plan to take when you experience any of the three items you circled as early warning signs.

_____

_____

_____

Note: Discuss any early warning signs you are experiencing with a doctor. Some of the symptoms listed above could also signify a condition that requires medical treatment.

Exercise 5: Sexual Abuse Prevention

Imagine that you are on a second date with someone you know casually. The first time you went out, either you or your date (choose which role you want to play) wanted to take things much farther than the other person. Describe the setting and what tactics you would use to prevent trouble. Consider where you would go on the date, what you would do, how you would get around, what you would eat or drink, what time of day or night you would leave and return, and what you would say to your date.

_____

_____

_____

_____

_____

_____

_____

 ## Key to Cooperative Learning:
Building Teamwork Skills

Think Critically About Stress By yourself, make a list of stressors—whatever events or factors cause you stress. As a class, discuss the stressors you have listed and see what causes are the most common. Choose the five most common. Divide the class into five groups according to who would choose what stressor as his or her number one (redistribute some people if the group sizes are unbalanced). Each group should discuss its assigned stressor, and brainstorm solutions and strategies. Make up a list of your best coping strategies and present it to the class. You may want to make copies of the lists so that every member of the class has five, one for each stressor.

 ## Key to Self-Expression:
Discovery through Journal Writing

To record your thoughts, use a separate journal or the lined pages at the end of the chapter.

Substance Use and Abuse Describe what role alcohol, drugs, and/or cigarettes play in your life. How much do you drink or smoke, if at all? If you don't, why? If you have used or currently use a drug, why do you think you do it? What positive and negative effects do your alcohol, smoking, or drug use have on your life? If you want to make a change, describe the change and how you plan to do it. If you do not drink, smoke, or take drugs, discuss how these substances affect your life in a different way, perhaps by your interaction with friends and family who do use them.

Key to Your Personal Portfolio:
Your Paper Trail to Success

Your Health Record On a separate sheet of paper, draw up a "medical record" for yourself. Include the following:

- Health insurance plan and policy numbers
- Phone numbers of physicians and clinics; phone numbers of other important people to call in a medical emergency
- Immunizations: ones you have completed, and any you have yet to receive
- Surgeries you have had (include reason for surgery)
- Hospital stays (include reason for stay)
- Illnesses and/or diseases
- Family health history (parents, grandparents, siblings)
- Chronic health problems (arthritis, tendinitis, ulcer, etc.)
- Vision and/or hearing statistics, if applicable
- Prescriptions used regularly and why
- Other

Highlight any conditions you feel you could improve with work or treatment. Choose one and draw up a problem-solving plan for making that improvement a reality.

Look again at the self-test on page 324. Make a copy of the questions and answer them on a separate sheet that you keep with your portfolio. If you feel that your score indicates a problem, write on the sheet what steps you intend to take, and get help.

Consider the positive side of your health as well. Make a list of the areas in which you enjoy very good health. For each, describe briefly how you maintain it.

Keep these lists up to date so you can monitor your health. You'll have many opportunities to refer to this information. If you change health plans or apply for a new job, for example, you may need to furnish information about your health record.

Name _____ Date _____

Journal Entry

_____

_____

_____

_____

_____

_____

_____

_____

_____

_____

_____

_____

_____

_____

_____

_____

_____

_____

_____

_____

10 Managing Career and Money:

Reality Resources

In this chapter, you will explore answers to the following questions:

⊛ How can you plan your career?

⊛ How can you juggle work and school?

⊛ What should you know about the Canada Student Loan Program?

⊛ How can strategic planning help you manage money?

⊛ How can you create a budget that works?

⊛ What should you know about banking and credit cards?

There are four possible "categories" for any career. Many people have a job in one of the two middle categories—either they love their jobs but don't make much money, or dislike their jobs but are paid well. Still other people have jobs in the most problematic category—they have neither job satisfaction nor a good paycheque to show for their work. A career in the ideal category interests and challenges you *and* pays you enough to live comfortably.

Career exploration, job-hunting strategy, and money management can work together to help you find that ideal fourth-category career. In this chapter, you will first look at career exploration and how to balance work and school. Then you will explore how to bring in money with financial aid and how to manage the money you have. Managing your resources and investigating career options can help you develop skills and insights that will serve you throughout your life.

Thinking It Through

Check those statements that apply to you right now:

☐ I have no idea what I want to do for a career.

☐ I don't know how to be marketable in the workplace if I don't have experience.

☐ I have a job and it's tough to fit everything in with my classes.

☐ I can't pay for my education on my own.

☐ It's a drag to save money for the future when I need it now.

☐ I don't need to budget because the bank keeps track of my money.

☐ I've run into trouble with credit cards, but I need them.

How Can You Plan Your Career?

College or university is an ideal time to investigate careers, because so many different resources are available to you. Students are in all different stages of thought when it comes to careers. You may not have thought too much about it yet. You may have already had a career for years and are looking for a change. You may have been set on a particular career but are now having second thoughts. Regardless of your starting point, now is the time to make progress.

Even outside this particular chapter, everything you read and work on in this book is geared toward workplace success. As you work on the exercises, you think critically, become a team player, hone writing skills, and develop long-term planning, all of which prepare you to thrive in any career.

Define a Career Path

Career Tips
www.careertips.com

This Web resource will help you to investigate your skills and interests and match your strengths to careers.

Youth Resource Network of Canada
www.youth.gc.ca/servprog/intrex_e.shtml

This extensive site provides information to help you understand more about yourself and what kinds of opportunities lie ahead for you. It includes everything from aptitude tests to job search strategies.

Aiming for a job in a particular career area requires planning the steps that can get you there. Whether these steps take months or years, they help you focus your energies on your goal. Defining a career path involves investigating yourself, exploring potential careers, and building knowledge and experience.

Investigate Yourself

When you explore your learning style in Chapter 2, evaluate your ideal note-taking system in Chapter 6, or look at how you relate to others in Chapter 8, you build self-knowledge. Gather everything that you know about yourself, from this class or from any of your other life experiences, and investigate. What do you know or do best? Of the jobs you've had, what did you like and not like to do? How would you describe your personality? And finally, what kinds of careers make the best use of everything you are?

Don't feel as though you should automatically know what you want to do. Most students who have not been in the workplace don't know what career they want to pursue. Students who have been working often return to school to explore other careers that they might prefer. More and more, people are changing careers many times in their lives instead of sticking with one choice. This discovery is a lifelong process.

The potential for change applies to majors as well. If you declare a major and decide later that you don't like it, feel glad that you were able to discover that fact about yourself.

Explore Potential Careers

Career possibilities extend far beyond what you can imagine. Brainstorm about career areas. Ask instructors, relatives, and fellow students about careers that they have or know about. Check your library for books on careers or biographies of people who worked in fields that interest you. Explore careers you discover through reading the newspaper, novels, or nonfiction. If a character in your favourite movie has a job you think you'd like, see what you can find out about it.

Your school's career centre is an important resource in your investigation. The career centre may offer job listings, occupation lists, assessments of skills and personality types, questionnaires to help you pinpoint career areas that may suit you, informational material about different career areas, and material about various companies. The people who work at the centre can help you sort through the material.

Use your critical-thinking skills to broaden your question-asking beyond just what tasks you perform for any given job. Many other factors will be important to you. Look at Table 10–1 for some of the kinds of questions you might ask as you talk to people or investigate materials.

Within every career field, a wide array of job possibilities exists that you might not see right away. For example, the medical world involves more than just doctors and nurses. Emergency medical technicians respond to emergencies, administrators run hospitals, researchers test new drugs, lab technicians administer specific procedures such as X-rays, pharmacists administer prescriptions, retirement community employees work with the elderly, and so on.

Within each job there is also a variety of tasks and skills that often go beyond what you know. You may know that an instructor teaches, but you may not see that instructors also often write, research, study, create course outlines, create strategy with other instructors, give presentations, and counsel students. Push past your first impression of any career and explore what else it entails. Expand your choices as much as you can using thorough investigation and an open mind.

Build Knowledge and Experience

Having knowledge and experience specific to the career area you want to pursue will be valuable in your job hunt. Courses, internships, jobs, and volunteering are four great ways to build both.

Table 10–1 Critical-Thinking Questions for Career Investigation

What can I do in this area that I like/am good at?	Do I respect the company and/or the industry?
What are the educational requirements (certificates or degrees, courses)?	Do companies in this industry generally accommodate special needs (child care, sick days, "flex time," or working at home)?
What skills are necessary?	Will I belong to a union?
What wage or salary is normal for an entry-level position, and what benefits can I expect?	Are there opportunities in this industry within a reasonable distance from where I live?
What kinds of personalities are best suited to this kind of work?	What other expectations are there beyond the regular workday (travel, overtime, etc.)?
What are the prospects for moving up to higher-level positions?	Do I prefer a service or manufacturing industry?

Career Edge
www.careeredge.org/

This Web site provides information and links on internships and co-ops across Canada.

internship
A temporary work program in which a student can gain supervised practical experience in a particular professional field.

Courses. After you've narrowed your career exploration to a couple of areas that interest you, look through your school course calendar and take a course or two in those fields. How you react to these courses will give you important clues about how you feel about the area in general. Be careful to evaluate your experience based on how you feel about the subject matter and not other factors. Think critically. If you didn't like a course, what was the cause: an instructor you didn't like, a time of day when you tend to lose energy, or truly a lack of interest in the material?

In addition, interview an instructor who teaches a subject related to a career field that interests you. Find out what courses you have to take to major in the field, what jobs are available in the field, what credentials (degrees and/or training) you need for particular jobs, and so on.

Internships. Sometimes known as a "co-op," an internship may or may not offer pay. While this may be a financial drawback, the experience you can gather and contacts you can make may be worth the work. Many internships take place during the summer, but some part-time internships are also available during the school year. Companies that offer internships are looking for people who will work hard in exchange for experience they can't get in the classroom.

Your career centre, or even some of your instructors, may be able to help you explore internship opportunities. Since money isn't the draw, stick to areas that interest you. Look for an internship that you can handle while still being able to fulfill your financial obligations. Absorb all the knowledge you can while working as an intern. If you discover a career worth pursuing, you'll have the internship experience behind you when you go job hunting. Internships are one of the best ways to show a prospective employer some "real world" experience and initiative.

Jobs. No matter what you do for money while you are in school, whether it is in your area of interest or not, you may discover career opportunities that appeal to you. Someone who takes a third-shift legal proofreading job to make extra cash might discover an interest in the law. Someone who answers phones for a newspaper company might be drawn into journalism. Stay aware of the possibilities around you.

Volunteering. Offering your services in the community or at your school can introduce you to career areas and increase your experience. Some schools have programs that can help you find opportunities to work as an aid on campus or volunteer off campus. Volunteer activities are important to note on your résumé. Many employers seek candidates who have shown commitment through volunteering.

Map Out Your Strategy

After you've gathered enough information to narrow your career goals, plan strategically to achieve them. Make a career time line that illustrates the steps toward your goal, as shown in Figure 10–1. Mark years and half-year points (and months for the first year), and write in the steps where you think they should take place. If your plan is five years long, indicate what you plan to do by the fourth, third, and second years, and then the first year, including a six-

Figure 10-1   Career Time Line

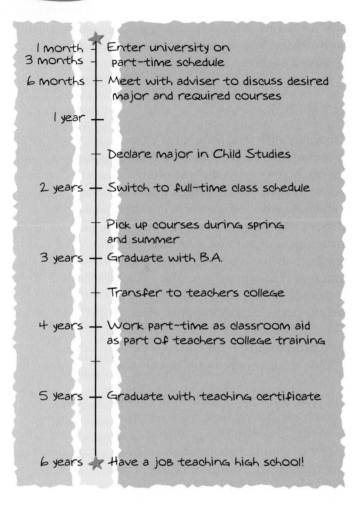

1 month	Enter university on
3 months	part-time schedule
6 months	Meet with adviser to discuss desired major and required courses
1 year	
	Declare major in Child Studies
2 years	Switch to full-time class schedule
	Pick up courses during spring and summer
3 years	Graduate with B.A.
	Transfer to teachers college
4 years	Work part-time as classroom aid as part of teachers college training
5 years	Graduate with teaching certificate
6 years	Have a job teaching high school!

month goal and a one-month goal for that first year. Set goals that establish to whom you will talk, what courses you will take, what skills you will work on, what jobs or internships you will investigate, and any other research you need to do. Your path may change, of course—use your time line as a guide rather than as a rigid plan.

The road to a truly satisfying career can be long. Although changing careers used to be a risky and rare practice, now people commonly have as many as five careers over the course of their lives, and this number may continue to rise. Seek support as you work toward your goals. Confide in supportive people, talk positively to yourself, and read inspiring books. Two helpful books are *What Color Is Your Parachute?* by Richard Nelson Bolles, and *Zen and the Art of Making a Living: A Practical Guide to Creative Career Design* by Laurence G. Boldt.

Finally, learn from surprises and misfortune. Life's sudden changes can open doors for you that you never even imagined were there. Susan Davenny

Parachute the Web
www.parachute.net/

Richard Bolles, author of *What Color is Your Parachute?*, has a Web site with information on career planning.

Wyner, for example, was a classical singer who had appeared at the Metropolitan Opera in New York. One day, at the height of her career, a car hit her while she was cycling, knocking her on her face and damaging her vocal cords so badly that they have never healed. After some time she discovered that conducting, which she didn't really enjoy in her student years, held an opportunity for her to express herself musically in a way she didn't think she could ever do again. Stay open to what can come out of changes, and you will find new ways to achieve.

Seek Mentors

mentor
A person of knowledge or authority who becomes a trusted counsellor or guide.

You may go to many different people for career advice, but if you are lucky, you may find among them a true mentor. A mentor takes a special interest in helping you to reach your goals. People often seek a mentor who has excelled in a career area or specific skill in which they also wish to excel. You may also be drawn to a person who, no matter what their skills or specialty, has ideas and makes choices that you admire and want to emulate.

Because it requires depth and devotion on both sides, a mentoring relationship often evolves from a special personal relationship. A relative, instructor, friend, supervisor, or anyone else whom you admire and respect may become your mentor. Think about whom you go to when you are confused, troubled, need guidance, or seek support. Also, consider who may know a lot about a skill or career area you want to pursue. Some schools have faculty or peer mentoring programs to help match students with people who can help them. Check your student handbook or ask your adviser if this is offered at your school.

Mentoring relationships demand time and energy on both sides. A mentor can give you a private audience for questions and problems, advice tailored to your needs, a wealth of experience, support, guidance, and trust. A mentor cares about you deeply enough to be devoted to your success and growth, taking pleasure in your development. You owe it to your mentor to be open to his or her ideas and to respectfully take his or her advice into consideration. You and your mentor can learn from each other, receive positive energy from your relationship, and grow and develop together.

Know What Employers Want

Revisiting the Conference Board of Canada
www.conferenceboard.ca

This site was listed and discussed earlier in the book. Now you may want to go back to the site to review some of the skills Canadian employers are looking for.

Certain basic skills will make you an excellent job candidate no matter what career you decide to pursue. Employers look for particular skills and qualities that signify an efficient and effective employee. You can continue to develop these skills as you work in current and future jobs—and you will, if you always strive to improve. In Chapter 1, you were introduced to the Conference Board of Canada's Employability Skills Profile. Now that you've worked through the book, it might be a good idea to go back and review the skills that Canadian employers desire. What skills do you possess that are in demand? What skills still need some work?

These employability skills appear throughout this book, and they are as much a part of your school success as they are of your work success. The more you develop them now, the more employable and promotable you will prove yourself to be. You may already use them on the job if you are a student who works.

Many students need to work and take classes at the same time in order to fund the education that they hope will move them into better careers. While you may not necessarily work in a career area that interests you, you can hold a job that helps you pay the bills and still make the most of your school time.

How Can You Juggle Work and School?

What you are studying today can prepare you to find a job when you graduate that suits your abilities and brings in enough money to support your needs and lifestyle choices. In the meantime, though, you can make work a part of your student life in order to make money, explore a career, and/or increase your future employability through contacts or résumé building.

As the cost of education continues to rise, more and more students are working and taking classes at the same time. Being an employed student isn't for everyone, although many students don't have a choice. Adding a job to the list of demands on your time and energy may create problems if it sharply reduces study time or family time. However, many people want to work and many need to work in order to pay for school. Ask yourself important questions about why or why not to work. Weigh the potential positive and negative effects of working. From those answers you can make a choice that you feel benefits you most.

> "Whatever you think you can do or believe you can do, begin it. Action has magic, grace, and power in it."
>
> Johann Wolfgang von Goethe

Effects of Working While in School

Working while in school has many different positive and negative effects, depending on the situation. Evaluate any job opportunity by looking at these effects. Following are some that might come into play.

Potential Positive Effects

Money for essentials. A job can provide crucial income to pay for rent, transportation, food, and important bills.

Money for unexpected expenses. Even if you have enough to live on, it's nice to have extra cash to provide a buffer zone. A small financial cushion can help you be prepared. Many financial planners say that an ideal cushion consists of enough money to pay for three months' worth of living expenses.

General and career-specific experience. Important learning comes from hands-on work. Your education "in the trenches" can complement your classroom experience. Even if you don't work in your chosen field, you can improve universal skills such as teamwork and communication.

Being able to keep a job you currently hold. If you leave a job temporarily, your company might not be able to hold your position open until you come back. New mothers who want to take a longer maternity leave than company policy permits may run into this problem. Consider adjusting your responsibilities or hours while still holding down your job.

Keeping busy. Work can provide a stimulating break from studying. In fact, working up to fifteen hours a week may actually enhance academic performance, because working students often manage their time more efficiently and may gain confidence from their successes in the workplace. Working on campus may help you manage your time and connect to your school experience.

Establishing and maintaining connections. If you don't maintain relationships formed at work, people may lose track of you. Maintaining your network of contacts by continuing to work may help you avoid losing ground. If you work for your educational institution, you may be able to develop beneficial relationships with instructors and administrators.

Potential Negative Effects

Time commitment. Whereas a nonworking student splits time between academic and personal life, a working student must add a third, time-consuming factor. More responsibilities and less time to fulfill them demand more efficient time management. Many schools recommend that students not work more than twenty hours a week while taking a full course load.

Adjusting priorities. The priority level of your job may vary. For a student who depends on the income, work may take priority over study time. Evaluate priorities carefully. Realize that you may have to reduce social activities, exercise at home, cut back on nonacademic activities, or lighten your course load in order to maintain a job and still get studying done. Your job is important, but if you are also committed to school, earning a good average may be just as crucial.

Shifting gears. Unless your job meshes with your classroom curriculum, it may take some effort to shift gears mentally as you move back and forth between academia and the workplace. Each environment has its own set of people, responsibilities, joys, and problems. Establish mental boundaries that can help you shake off academic stress while at work, and vice versa.

If you consider the positive and negative effects and decide that working will benefit you, you should establish what you need in a job.

Establishing Your Needs

Think about what you need in a job before you begin your job hunt. Table 10–2 shows factors you may want to consider. Evaluate any potential job in terms of these needs.

Sources of Job Information

Many different routes can lead to satisfying jobs. Use your school's career planning and placement office, networking skills, classified ads, employment agencies, and online services to help you explore.

	Table 10-2 What You May Need in a Job	

Need	Description
Salary/wage level	Consider how much money you need to make month by month and annually. You may need to make a certain amount for the year as a whole, but you may need to earn more of that total amount during the months when you are paying tuition. Consider also the amount that justifies taking the time to work. If a job pays well but takes extra hours that should go toward studying or classes, it might not be worth it. Take time to compare the positive effects with the negative effects of any job's pay structure.
Time of day	When you can work depends on your school schedule. For example, if you take classes Monday, Tuesday, and Thursday during the day, you could look for a job with weekend or evening hours. If you attend evening classes, a daytime job could work fine.
Hours per week (part time vs. full time)	If you take classes part time, you may choose to work a full-time job. If you are a full-time student, it may be best to work part time. Balance your priorities so that you can accomplish your schoolwork and still make the money you need.
Duties performed	If you want hands-on experience in your chosen field, narrow your search to jobs that can provide it. On the other hand, if a regular paycheque is your priority, you might not care as much about what you do. Consider if there is anything you absolutely hate to do. Working somewhere and/or doing something that makes you miserable may not be worth any amount of money.
Location	Weigh the effects of how long it takes to get to a job against what you are getting out of it, and decide whether it is worth your while. A job at or near your school may give unparalleled convenience. When you know you can get to work quickly, you can schedule your day more tightly and get more done.
Flexibility	Even if your classes are at regular times, you might have other projects and meetings at various times. Do you need a job that offers flexibility, allowing you to shift your working time when you have to attend to an academic or family responsibility that takes priority? Choose according to the flexibility you require.
Accommodation of special needs	If you have a hearing or vision impairment, reduced mobility, children for whom you need daycare, or other special needs, you may want to find an employer who can and will accommodate them.

Your School's Career Planning and Placement Offices

Generally, the career planning and placement office deals with post-graduation job placements, while the student employment office, along with the financial aid office, has more information about working while in school. At either location you might find general workplace information, listings of job opportunities, sign-ups for interviews, and contact information for companies. The career office may hold frequent informational sessions on different topics. Your school may also sponsor job or career fairs that give you a chance to explore job opportunities.

Many students, because they don't seek job information until they're about to graduate, miss out on much of what the career office can do. Don't wait until the last minute. Start exploring your school's career office early in your academic life. The people and resources there can help you at every stage of your career and job exploration process.

Networking

networking

The exchange of information and/or services among individuals, groups, or institutions.

Networking is one of the most important job-hunting strategies. With each person you get to know, you build your network and tap into someone else's. Imagine a giant think link connecting you to a web of people just a couple of phone calls away. Of course, not everyone with whom you network will come through for you. Keep in contact with as many people as possible in the hope that someone will. You never know who that person might be.

With whom can you network? Friends and family members may know of jobs or other people who can help you. At your school, instructors, administrators, or counsellors may give you job or contact information. People at school employment or career offices can help you locate work. Some schools even have opportunities for students to interact with alumni. Look to your present and past work experience for more leads. Employers or co-workers may know someone who needs new employees. A former employer might even hire you back with similar or adjusted hours, if you left on good terms.

contact

A person who serves as a carrier or source of information.

The contacts with whom you network aren't just sources of job opportunities. They are people with whom you can develop lasting, valuable relationships. They may be willing to talk to you about how to get established, the challenges on the job, what they do each day, how much you can expect to make, or any other questions you have similar to those in Table 10–1. Thank your contacts for their help and don't forget them. Networking is a two-way street. Even as you receive help, be ready to extend yourself to others who may need help and advice from you.

Classified Ads

Some of the best job listings are in daily or periodic newspapers. Most papers print help-wanted sections in each issue, organized according to career categories. At the beginning of most help-wanted sections you will find an index that tells you the categories and on what pages they begin in the listings. Individual ads describe the kind of position available and will give a telephone number or address for you to contact. Some ads will include additional information such as job requirements, a contact person, and the salary or wages offered.

You can run your own classified ads if you have a skill you want to advertise. Many students make extra money by doing specific tasks for campus employees or other students, such as typing, editing, cleaning, tutoring, or baby-sitting. You may want to advertise your particular job skills in your school or local paper.

Online Services

The Internet is growing as a source of job listings. Through it you can access job-search databases such as the National Job Bank maintained by Human Resources Development Canada. Individual associations and companies may also post job listings and descriptions, often as part of their World Wide Web pages. For example, Petro-Canada includes job openings on its Web page.

Employment Agencies

Employment agencies are organizations that help people find work. Most employment agencies will put you through a screening process that consists of an interview and one or more tests in your area of expertise. For example, someone looking for secretarial work may take a word-processing test and a spelling test, while someone looking for accounting work may take accounting and math tests. If you pass the tests and interview well, they will try to place you in a job.

Most employment agencies specialize in particular career or skill areas, such as accounting, medicine, legal, computer operation, graphic arts, child care, and food services. Agencies may place job seekers in either part-time or full-time employment. Many agencies also place people in temporary jobs, which can work well for students who are available from time to time. Such agencies may have you call in whenever you are free and will see if anything is available that day or week.

Employment agencies are a great way to hook into job networks. However, they usually require a fee that either you or the employer has to pay. Investigate any agency before signing on. See if your school's career counsellors know anything about the agency, or if any fellow students have used it successfully. Ask questions so that you know as much as possible about how the agency operates.

Making a Strategic Job Search Plan

When you have gathered information on the jobs you want, formulate a plan for pursuing them. Organize your approach according to what you need to do and how much time you have to devote to your search. Do you plan to make three phone calls per day? Will you fill out three job applications a week for a month? Keep a record—on index cards, a computer file, or in a notebook—of the following:

- People you contact
- Companies to which you apply
- Jobs you rule out (for example, jobs that become unavailable or that you find don't suit your needs)
- Response from your inquiries (phone calls to you, interviews, written communications) and the information on whoever contacted you (names, titles, times, and dates)

Keeping accurate records will enable you to both chart your progress and maintain a clear picture of the process. You never know when information might come in handy again. If you don't get a job now, another one could open up at the same company in a couple of months. In that case, well-kept

records would enable you to contact key personnel quickly and efficiently. See Figure 10–2 for a sample file card.

Your Résumé and Interview

Information on résumés and interviews fills many books. Therefore, your best bet is to consult some that will go into more detail, such as *The Resume Kit* by Richard Beatty, or *Job Interviews for Dummies* by Joyce Lain Kennedy (don't be insulted by the title—it has lots of terrific information). Here are a few basic tips to get you started on giving yourself the best possible chance at a job.

Résumé. Your résumé should always be typed or printed from a computer. Design your résumé neatly, using an acceptable format (books or

"And all that rubbish about placing the interviewee on a lower chair to make him feel inferior ... quite the opposite is true..."

Source: Cartoon by Bill Stott, from *The Crazy World of the Office*. Reprinted with permission of Exley Publications Ltd., Watford, U.K.

Figure 10–2   Sample File Card

Job/company: Child-care worker at Morningside Day Care

Contact: Kim McKay, Morningside Day Care, 136 Rockwood Avenue, St. Catharines, Ontario L2P 3R8

Phone/fax/e-mail: (905) 555-3353 phone, (905) 555-3354 fax, no e-mail

Communication: Saw ad in paper, sent résumé and cover letter on October 7

Response: Call from Kim to set up interview

— Interview on Oct. 15 at 2 p.m., seemed to get a positive response, she said she would contact me again by the end of the week

Follow-up: Sent thank-you note on October 16

your career office can show you some standard formats). Proofread it for errors, and have someone else proofread it as well. Type or print it on a heavier bond paper than is used for ordinary copies. Use white or off-white paper and black ink.

Interview. Pay attention to your appearance. Be clean, neat, and appropriately dressed. Don't forget to choose a nice pair of shoes—people notice. Bring an extra copy of your résumé with you, and any other materials that you want to show the interviewer, even if you have already sent a copy ahead of time. Avoid chewing gum or smoking. Offer a confident handshake. Make eye contact. Show your integrity by speaking honestly about yourself. After the interview is over, no matter what the outcome, send a formal but pleasant thank-you note right away as a follow-up.

Earning the money you need is hard, especially if you work part time in order to have time for school. Financial aid can take some of the burden off your shoulders. If you can gather one or more loans, grants, or scholarships, they may help make up for what you don't have time to earn.

What Should You Know About Financial Aid?

Seeking help from various sources of financial aid has become a way of life for much of the student population. Education is an important but often expensive investment. The cost of a post-secondary education in Canada depends on the length of the program and whether you attend a college or university. Human Resources Development Canada offers the following as a guide to the high cost of education in Canada.[1] The cost includes tuition, books, and room and board:

- One-year college program: $ 9 800
- Two-year college program: $19 600
- Three-year college program: $29 400
- Three-year university degree: $34 800
- Four-year university degree: $46 400
- Master's Degree: $58 000
- Doctoral Degree (Ph.D.): $92 800

Very few people can pay for tuition in full without some sort of financial aid. In fact, some graduates, particularly those with university degrees, finish school with a debt load of $30 000 to $40 000. That's according to the Ontario Confederation of University Faculty Associations.[2]

Most sources of financial aid don't seek out recipients. Take the initiative to learn how you (or you and your parents, if they currently help to support you) can finance your education. Find the people on campus who can help you with your finances. Do some research to find out what's available, weigh the pros and cons of each option, and decide what would work best for you.

Try to apply as early as you can. The types of financial aid available to you are loans, grants, and scholarships.

Canada Student Loans

Canada Student Loans
Program
www.hrdc-drhc.gc.ca/
student_loans/

All of the latest information from
the Canada Student Loans
Program, including an online
assessment, is available on the
Internet.

Because of the high cost of post-secondary education, chances are good that you will need some sort of assistance. Each province has its own form of student financial aid—check with your school's financial aid office for more information. Besides provincial initiatives, the Canada Student Loans Program offers loans to needy post-secondary students. It can provide up to $165 per week (interest-free while you are in school) to help you meet your academic expenses. Provincial aid is used to supplement the Canada Student Loan. To be eligible for a Canada Student Loan,[3] you must:

- Be a Canadian citizen or permanent resident of Canada

- Be a resident of a province or territory that participates in the Canada Student Loans Program. The province of Quebec and the Northwest Territories operate their own student assistance plans.

- Satisfy the appropriate provincial or territorial student assistance office that financial resources available to you are not enough to cover your educational costs

- Enroll, or be qualified to enroll, in at least 60 per cent of a full-time course load at a designated post-secondary educational institution. Students with permanent disabilities are required to enroll in at least 40 per cent of a full-time course load.

- Enroll, or be qualified to enroll, in a program leading to a degree, diploma, or certificate. The program must be at least twelve weeks in length, and taken within a period of fifteen consecutive weeks.

If you are applying for a Canada Student Loan for the first time and are over 22 years old, the loan will be contingent on a credit check.

To continue to be eligible for full-time Canada Student Loans in subsequent years:

- You must successfully complete at least 60 per cent of a full-time post-secondary course load for which you have received a Canada Student Loan. This means, for example, passing three out of five courses.

- You can't receive assistance for more than 520 weeks of study if you received your first student loan before August 1, 1995 under the Canada Student Loans Act, or for more than 340 weeks of study if you received your first student loan on or after August 1, 1995 under the Canada Student Financial Assistance Act. Students enrolled in doctoral programs are exempt—they are eligible for up to 400 weeks of assistance.

- You must complete the program within the number of periods of study normally specified by the school for completion of that program, plus one additional period. For example, for a program that normally takes four years to complete, loans may be available for the first four years of the program, plus one extra year.

- You can't have been denied further assistance for reasons such as failing to make payments on your Canada Student Loan for sixty days or more, or because your previous Canada Student Loan was included in bankruptcy proceedings.

Recent changes have affected the way the more than 350 000 student loans are processed each year. In the past, student loans were negotiated with banks. Now, student loans are handled by the government through Human Resources Development Canada. The Canadian Association of University Teachers feels that the change from banks to government control over student loans may make accessibility to student loans easier.

Once you've been out of school for six months, you have to begin to pay back your student loans in full, with interest, whether you're working or not. This is when the full costs of taking out a student loan are felt. Table 10–3 shows what your monthly payment (over ten years at 12 per cent interest) might be.

If you're really in dire financial straits, the Canada Student Loans program does offer an interest relief program. Ask your bank or your financial aid officer for information.

Grants and Scholarships

Both grants and scholarships require no repayment, and therefore give your finances a terrific boost. Grants, funded by the government, are awarded to students who show financial need. Scholarships are awarded to students who show talent or ability in the area specified by the scholarship. They may be financed by government or private organizations, schools, or individuals. Check your school's calendar for information.

Repaying Your Loan
www.hrdc-drhc.gc.ca/
student_loans/entext/
y232074.html#interest

Information on repaying your student loan and possible interest relief is available online.

Grants
www.hrdc-drhc.gc.ca/
student_loans/entext/
y232073.html#200

This site provides information on Canada Study Grants, which do not need to be repaid.

Table 10–3 The Cost of Borrowing	
Amount of Loan ($)	Monthly Payment ($)
5 000	72
10 000	143
15 000	215
20 000	287
25 000	359
30 000	430
40 000	574

Source: Taken from *Canada Prospects, 1999–2000*, Student Loan Estimate.

How Can Strategic Planning Help You Manage Money?

So you work hard to earn your wages and study hard to hold on to your grants and loans. What do you do with that money? Popular culture tells you to buy. You are surrounded by commercials, magazine ads, and notices in the mail that tell you how wonderful you'll feel if you indulge in some serious spending. On the other hand, there are some definite advantages to not taking that advice. Making some short-term sacrifices in order to save money can help you a great deal in the long run.

Short-Term Sacrifices Can Create Long-Term Gain

When you think about your money, take your values and your ability to plan strategically into account. Ask yourself what goals you value most and what steps you will have to take over time to achieve those goals. You are already planning ahead by being in school and committing to paying for tuition. You may be scrimping now, but you are planning for a career that may reward you with job security and financial stability. Sometimes the most important goals are also the ones that require a long-term commitment. If you can make that commitment, the rewards will be worth the short-term sacrifices.

Table 10–4 shows some potential effects of spending. Some effects are negative, some positive, and some more positive than others. Evaluate which you would prefer in the long run. You may find that the pleasure luxuries provide isn't worth the stress created by debt.

Critical thinking is the key to smart money planning. Impulsive spending usually happens when you don't take time to think through your decision before you buy. To use your hard-earned money to your greatest benefit, take time to think critically about your finances. First, establish your needs, and be honest about what you truly need and what you just want. Second, brainstorm available options of what to do with your money—evaluate the positive and negative effects of each. Third, choose an option and carry it out. Finally, evaluate the result.

This section doesn't imply that you should never spend money on things that won't bring you any long-term satisfaction. The goal is to make choices that give short-term satisfaction while still providing for long-term money growth. If you need a vacation, drive to another city or province to visit friends instead of buying an expensive package deal at a resort. Buy a less expensive sound system instead of a state-of-the-art one that will test the limits of your credit card. Buy clothes at an outlet and choose pieces that you can mix and match. You will appreciate it later when you spend wisely.

Table 10-4 Potential Effects of Spending

Option	Potential Short-Term Effects	Potential Long-Term Effects
Purchase new sound system	High-quality sound	If paid on credit, a credit card debt, with finance charges, that requires monthly payment; if paid in cash, a loss of benefits that could have come from saving that money
Reduce or pay off credit card debt	Less money for day-to-day expenses; reduction of monthly bills	Improved credit rating and credit history; increased ability to be approved for loans and mortgages; less money charged in interest and fees
Take a week's vacation	Fun and relaxation; stress reduction	Credit card debt or less money saved for future needs
Invest in mutual fund	Less money on hand; more money earning interest	More money earned, due to an interest rate higher than banks can offer
Buy a car	Transportation and independence; gas, maintenance, parking fees	Debt in the form of a car loan; monthly payments for a few years; gradual decrease in car value
Pay health insurance bills	Health insurance coverage; a tighter monthly budget	The safety and security of knowing that your health and that of your family is protected beyond what provincial health plans cover
Invest in your family business	Commitment to family; less money to spend on extras	Involvement in a family business that can earn you money and provide solid employment for you and other family members
Put money toward tuition	Having to scrimp while in school due to less money on hand; fewer loans and debts	Less money to pay off later in student loans, which means less money charged in interest; more freedom to spend your money on getting settled after you graduate; shorter period of debt

Develop a Financial Philosophy

You can develop your own personal philosophy about spending, saving, and planning. Following are a couple of strategies that you might want to incorporate into that philosophy.

Live beneath your means. Spend less than you make. This strategy helps you create savings, no matter how much or how little. Any amount of savings will give you a buffer zone that can help with emergencies or bigger expenditures. Sometimes your basic needs will cost more than you make, in which case living beneath your means becomes very difficult. If you find, however, that extras are putting your spending over your earnings, cut back.

Pay yourself. After you pay your monthly bills, put whatever you can save from your monthly earnings in an investment account where it can grow. Paying yourself helps you store money in your savings where it can grow.

"It is thrifty to prepare today for the wants of tomorrow."
Aesop

That savings could become security when you grow older, financing for your children's college or university education, help with a financial crisis, or a down payment on a large purchase. Don't think of the money left after paying bills as automatically available for spending. Make your payment to yourself a high priority so that you honour it as you do your other bills.

How Can You Create a Budget That Works?

budgeting

Making a plan for the coordination of resources and expenditures; setting goals with regards to money.

Every time you have some money in your pocket and have to figure out whether it will pay for what you want at that moment, you are budgeting your money. It takes some thought and energy to budget efficiently. The more money you can save each month, the more you will thank yourself later when you need it. Consider your resources (money coming in) and expenditures (money flowing out). A smart budget adjusts the money flow for the best possible chance that what comes in will be more than what goes out. Smart budgeting is a worthwhile investment in your future.

The Art of Budgeting

Budgeting involves following a few basic steps, in order. These steps are: determining how much money you make, determining how much money you spend, subtracting the second number (what you spend) from the first number (what you make), evaluating the result, and making decisions about how to adjust your spending or earning based on that result. Budgeting regularly is easiest. Use a specified time frame, such as a week or month. Most people budget on a month-by-month basis.

Determine How Much You Will Make

Do this by adding up all your money receipts from the month. If you currently have a regular full-time or part-time job, add your pay stubs. If you have received any financial aid, loans, or scholarship money, determine how much of that you can allow for each month's income and add it to your total. For example, if you received a $1 200 grant for the year, each month you would have an income of $100. Be sure, when you are figuring your income, to use the amounts that remain *after* taxes have been taken out.

Figure Out How Much You Spend

You may or may not have a handle on your spending. Many people don't take the time to keep track. If you have never before paid much attention to how you spend money, examine your spending patterns (you will have an opportunity to do this in the Applications for this chapter). Over a month's time, record expenditures in a small notebook or on a piece of paper on a home bulletin board. You don't have to list everything down to the penny. Just indicate expenditures over five dollars, making sure to count smaller expenditures if they are frequent (bus tickets for the month, drink or newspaper purchases per week). In your list, include an estimate of the following:

- Rent/mortgage/residence fees
- Tuition or educational loan payments (divide your annual total by 12 to arrive at a monthly figure)
- Books, lab fees, and other educational expenses
- Regular bills (heat, gas, electric, phone, car payment, water)
- Credit card or other payments on credit
- Food, clothing, toiletries, and household supplies
- Child care
- Entertainment and related items (meals out, books and other publications, movies)
- Health, automobile, and home/tenant insurance
- Transportation and car expenses

Subtract what you spend from what you make. Ideally, you will have a positive number. You may end up with a negative number, however, especially if you haven't made a habit of keeping track of your spending. This indicates that you are spending more than you make, which over a long period of time can create a nasty debt.

Evaluate the Result

After you arrive at your number, determine what it tells you. If you have a positive number, decide how to save it if you can. If you end up with a negative number, ask yourself questions about what is causing the deficit—where you are spending too much or earning too little. Of course, surprise expenses during some months may cause you to spend more than usual, such as if you have to replace your refrigerator or pay equipment fees for a particular course. However, when a negative number comes up for what seems to be a typical month, you may need to adjust your budget over the long term.

Make Decisions About How to Adjust Spending or Earning

Looking at what may cause you to overspend, brainstorm possible solutions that address those causes. Solutions can involve either increasing resources or decreasing spending. To deal with spending, prioritize your expenditures and trim the ones you really don't need to make. Do you eat out too much? Can you live without cable, a beeper, a cellular phone? Be smart. Cut out unaffordable extras. As for resources, investigate ways to take in more money. Taking a part-time job, hunting down scholarships or grants, or increasing hours at a current job may help.

A Sample Budget

Table 10–5 shows a sample budget of an unmarried student living with two other students. It will give you an idea of how to budget (all expenditures are general estimates, based on averages).

Table 10-5 A Student's Sample Budget

Part-time salary: $10 an hour, 20 hours a week. 10 × 20 = $200 a week, × 4 1/3 weeks (one month) = $866. Student loan from school's financial aid office: $2 000 divided by 12 months = $166. Total income per month: $1 032.

Monthly Expenditures	Amount
Tuition ($3 500 per year)	$ 291
Public transportation	$ 90
Phone	$ 51
Food	$ 140
Books and magazines	$ 200
Rent (including utilities)	$ 350
Entertainment/miscellaneous	$ 100
Total spending	$1 222

$1 032 (income) − $1 222 (spending) = $-190 ($190 over budget)

To make up the $190 that this student went over budget, he can adjust his spending. He could rent movies or check them out of the library instead of going to the theatre. He could socialize with friends at someone's apartment instead of paying high prices and tips at a bar or restaurant. Instead of buying compact discs and tapes, he could borrow them. He could also shop for specials and bargains in the grocery store or go to a warehouse supermarket to stock up on staples at discount prices. He could make his lunch instead of buying it and walk instead of taking public transportation.

Not everyone likes the work involved in keeping a budget. While linear, factual, reflective, and verbal learners may take to it more easily, active, holistic, theoretical, and visual learners may resist the structure and detail (see Chapter 2). Visual learners may want to create a budget chart like the one shown in the example or construct a think link that shows the connections between all the month's expenditures. Use images to clarify ideas, such as picturing a bathtub you are filling that is draining at the same time. Use strategies that make budgeting more tangible, such as dumping all of your receipts into a big jar and tallying them at the end of the month. Even if you have to force yourself to do it, you will discover that budgeting can reduce stress and help you take control of your finances and your life.

Savings Strategies

You can save money and still enjoy life. Make your fun less-expensive fun— or save up for a while to splurge on a really special occasion. Here are some suggestions for saving a little bit of money here and there. Small amounts can add up to big savings after a while.

- Rent movies or attend bargain matinees.
- When safe for the fabric, hand-wash items you ordinarily dry-clean.
- Check movies, compact discs, tapes, and books out of your library.
- Make popcorn instead of buying bags of chips.
- Walk instead of paying for public transportation.
- If you have storage space, buy detergent, paper products, toiletries, and other staples in bulk.
- Shop in second-hand stores.
- Keep your possessions neat, clean, and properly maintained—they will last longer.
- Take advantage of weekly supermarket specials and bring coupons when you shop.
- Reuse grocery bags for food storage and garbage instead of buying bags.
- Return bottles and cans for deposits if you live in a city that accepts them.
- Trade clothing with friends and barter services (plumbing for baby-sitting, for example).
- Buy display models of appliances or electronics (stereo equipment, TVs, VCRs).
- Take your lunch instead of buying it.
- Find a low-rate long distance calling plan, use e-mail, or write letters.
- Save on heat by dressing warmly and using blankets; save on air conditioning by using fans.
- Have pot-luck parties; ask people to bring dinner foods or munchies.

Add your own suggestions here!

_____

_____

_____

_____

You can also maximize savings and minimize spending by using bank accounts and credit cards wisely.

What Should You Know About Banking and Credit Cards?

Banks and credit unions are probably the two most common financial institutions that people use. The more you know about how to use them, the more they can help you manage money and spending.

Bank Accounts

Choose a bank with convenient locations, hours that fit your schedule, account fees that aren't too high, and a convenient network of ATMs (automatic teller machines). Banks also issue debit cards that take money directly out of your chequing account the way a cheque does. Many banks now have phone or online payment services that let you bank from your home, as well as services that allow you to set up automatic payment of bills directly from your account each month. Different accounts have features that serve different needs. Decide which are important to you.

Chequing Accounts

Most banks offer more than one type of chequing plan. Some accounts include cheque-writing fees, a small charge on every cheque you write or on any cheques above a certain number per month. Some accounts have free chequing, meaning unlimited cheque writing without extra fees—but you will often have to maintain a minimum balance in your account to qualify. Some accounts charge a monthly fee that is standard or varies according to your balance. *Interest chequing* pays you a low rate of interest, although you may have to keep a certain balance or have a savings account at the same bank.

Savings Accounts

The most basic account, the *interest savings account*, pays a rate of interest to you determined by the bank. Many interest savings accounts do not have a required balance, but the interest rate they pay is very low. A *guaranteed investment certificate* (GIC) pays greater interest, but your money is "locked in" for a specific period of time—often six months or a year. There is also a penalty if you withdraw part or all of your money.

Credit Cards

Credit can be an incredible lifesaver or a black hole of debt. As Eric Clapton says in one of his songs, "It's in the way that you use it!"

Most credit comes in the form of a powerful little plastic card. Credit card companies often solicit students on campus or through the mail. When choosing a card, pay attention to the *annual fee* and *interest rates*, the two ways in which a credit card company makes money from you. Some cards have no annual fee; others may charge an annual flat rate fee. Interest rates can be fixed or variable. A variable rate of 12 per cent may shoot up to 18 per cent when the economy slows down. You might be better off with a mid-range fixed rate that will always stay the same.

Following are some potential effects of using credit.

Positive Effects

Establishing a good credit history. If you use your credit card moderately and pay your bills on time, you will make a positive impression on your creditors. Your *credit history* (the record of your credit use, including positive actions such as paying on time and negative actions such as going over your credit limit) and *credit rating* (the score you are given based on your history) can make or break your ability to take out a loan or mortgage. How promptly you make loan payments and pay mortgage and utility bills affects your credit rating as well. Certain companies track your credit history and give you a credit rating. Banks or potential employers will contact these companies to see if you are a good credit risk.

Emergencies. Few people carry enough cash to handle unexpected expenses. Your credit card can help you in emergency situations, such as when you need towing.

Record of purchases. Credit card statements give you a monthly record of purchases made, where they were made, and exactly how much was paid. Using your credit card for purchases that you want to track, such as work expenses, can help you keep records for tax purposes.

Negative Effects

Credit can be addictive. Credit can be like a drug, seeming fun because the pain of paying is put off until later. If you get hooked, though, you can wind up thousands of dollars in debt to creditors. The high interest will enlarge your debt; your credit rating may fall, potentially hurting your eligibility for loans and mortgages; and you may lose your credit cards altogether.

Credit spending can be hard to monitor. Paying by credit can seem so easy that you don't realize how much you are spending. When the bill comes at the end of the month, the total can hit you hard.

You are spending someone else's money. The money you spend belongs to the credit card company. The company then pays the retailer, counting on you to pay later. It can be tempting to overspend when the money isn't really yours and you don't have to face up to paying it right away. That can lead to trouble if you find you are unable to make your monthly payments.

You are taking out a high-interest loan. Buying on credit is similar to taking out a loan—you are using money with the promise to pay it back. Loan rates, however, especially on fixed-interest loans, are often much lower than the 11 to 23 per cent on credit card debt. Fifteen per cent interest per year on a credit card debt averaging $2 000 is approximately $300; 5 per cent interest per year on a loan in the same amount is $100. You lose money if you pay more interest on your credit card debt than you earn on your savings. If you can't pay off your credit card every month, try to keep the debt lower than the amount of money you have saved.

creditors
People to whom debts are owed, usually money.

"Put not your trust in money, But put your money in trust."
Oliver Wendell Holmes

Real World Perspective

What should I do about all these credit card offers?

Brett Cross, Engineering Student

Recently, I have been receiving a number of credit card applications offering a low interest rate. In fact, I get at least one offer a week. I've been thinking it would be nice to establish credit, but I'm not sure if getting a credit card right now is a good idea. Even though I have a part-time job hauling and I have financial aid, it seems like there's never enough to make it to the end of the semester. Should I apply for one of these credit cards? It would be really great to have some extra cash every now and then.

Tim Short, Graduating Student

Dealing with financial hardships while in school is a part of life for many students these days. Credit card offers are in abundance for college and university students, and for good reason. Credit companies know that most students won't be able to pay off their cards until after they graduate, and that they tend to carry balances and pay interest and hefty fees until they are solvent. Believe me, I know. Throughout my past four years at university, I have acquired several credit cards. On them I have charged things such as books, car repairs and insurance, and other personal items. I am still paying interest on these cards monthly and will not be able to pay them off until after I graduate.

My suggestion to you is this: Don't take out a credit card unless you absolutely have to. If you can take out student loans or borrow from your parents, do that instead. Most academic loans have a lower rate than most credit cards. Don't be fooled by offers for a card with a low rate. These invariably expire after one year and then the rate jumps up. If you miss a payment during that year, some companies will raise your rates immediately. Rationalizing that you will pay the card off before that time frame is up is also not a good idea. Unless you are on the verge of graduation, you will probably not have any more cash in a year than you do now. Overall, my advice is this: If you can avoid borrowing from credit card companies, do so! You will be a lot happier in the long run.

Bad credit ratings can haunt you. Any time you are late with a payment, default on a payment, or in any way misuse your card, a record of that occurrence will be entered on your credit history, lowering your credit rating. If a prospective employer or loan officer discovers a low rating, you will seem less trustworthy and may lose the chance at a job or a loan.

Managing Credit Card Debt

There are ways to manage credit card debt so that it doesn't get worse. Stay in control by having only one or two cards and paying bills regularly and on time. Try to pay in full each month. If you can't, at least pay the minimum. Make as much of a dent in the bill as you can.

If you get into trouble, three steps will help you deal with the situation. First, *admit* that you made a mistake, even though you may be embarrassed. Then, *address* the problem immediately and honestly in order to minimize the damages. Call the bank or credit card company to talk to someone about the problem. He or she may draw up a payment plan that allows you to pay your debt gradually, in amounts that your budget can manage. Creditors would rather accept small payments than nothing at all.

Finally, *prevent* this problem from happening again. Figure out what got you into trouble and take steps to avoid it in the future if you can. Some financial disasters, such as medical emergencies, may be beyond your control. Overspending on luxuries, however, is something you have the power to avoid. Make a habit of balancing your chequebook. Cut up a credit card or two if you have too many. Don't let a high credit limit tempt you to spend. Pay every month, even if you pay only the minimum. If you work to clean up your act, your credit history will gradually clean up as well.

Sacrifici

In Italy, parents often use the term *sacrifici*, meaning "sacrifices," to refer to tough choices that they make in order to improve the lives of their children and family members. They may sacrifice a larger home so that they can afford to pay for their children's sports and after-school activities. They may sacrifice a higher-paying job so that they can live close to where they work. They give up something in exchange for something else that they have decided is more important to them.

Think of the concept of *sacrifici* as you analyze the sacrifices you can make in order to get out of debt, reach your savings goals, and prepare for a career that you find satisfying. Many of the short-term sacrifices you are making today will help you do and have what you want in the future. Keep that notion as a light to guide you through the ups and downs of student life.

Chapter 10: Applications

Name   Date

Key into Your Life:
Opportunities to Apply What You Learn

Exercise 1: Career Possibilities

Establish career possibilities for yourself by investigating some career areas. Consider what you know about yourself, and consult others if you want additional opinions. Write two career areas here that you would like to investigate.

1. _____   2. _____

Investigate both areas. You may want to talk to people in those fields, do research at the library, meet with someone at your career planning and placement office, or talk to someone who teaches in those fields. Make notes in a separate notebook as you investigate. Then, summarize your impressions here. What do you like or dislike? What suits your needs? What would be difficult to handle? Do you plan to keep these areas as possibilities or discard them?

1. _____

_____

_____

2. _____

_____

_____

Exercise 2: Mentors

First, consider the people you go to with problems and questions, people whom you trust and with whom you share a lot of yourself. Name up to three—don't fill the list unless you can really think of three people you trust.

1. _____

2. _____

3. _____

Evaluate your list according to the description of mentoring that you read in the chapter. With which of those people do you feel you could have a mentoring relationship? Name up to two; for each, name two steps you can take to invest even further in your relationship.

1. _____

_____

2. _____

_____

Exercise 3: Your Job Priorities

What kind of a job could you manage while you're in school? How would you want a job to benefit you? Discuss your requirements in each of the following areas.

Salary/wage level _____

Time of day _____

Hours per week (part time vs. full time) _____

Duties _____

Location _____

Flexibility _____

Affiliation with school _____

What kind of job might fit all or most of your requirements? List two possibilities here.

1. _____

2. _____

Exercise 4: Following Your Job Leads

Choose one of the job possibilities you listed and follow up on it using the following leads. Describe the results of your research from each of the following.

Help-wanted listings in newspapers, magazines, or Internet databases

_____

_____

Listings of job opportunities/company contact information at your career centre, student employment office, or independent employment agency

_____

_____

Contacts from friends or family members

_____

_____

Contacts from instructors, administrators, or counsellors

_____

_____

Current or former employers or co-workers

_____

_____

Exercise 5: Where Your Money Goes

Estimate your current expenses in dollars per month, using the table below. This may require tracking expenses for a month, if you don't already keep a record of your spending.

EXPENSE	AMOUNT SPENT
Rent/mortgage or residence fees	$
Utilities (electric, heat, gas, water)	$
Food (shopping and eating out)	$
Telephone	$
Tuition	$
Books, lab fees, or other educational expenses	$
Loan payments (educational or bank loans)	$
Car expenses (repairs, insurance, monthly payments)	$
Gasoline/public transportation	$
Clothing/personal items	$
Entertainment	$
Child care (caregivers, clothing and supplies, other fees)	$
Medical care/insurance	$
Miscellaneous/unexpected	$
	$
GRAND TOTAL:	$

The total is your total monthly expenses.

Exercise 6: Where Your Money Comes From

Calculate the money you take in each month. Divide any annual payments by 12 to derive the monthly figure.

INCOME SOURCE	AMOUNT EARNED
Regular work salary/wages (full time or part time)	$
Grants or work-study payments	$
Scholarships	$
Monthly assistance you may receive from family members	$
Any independent contracting work or private sale of items	$
Other	$
GRAND TOTAL	$

Now, subtract the grand total of your monthly expenses (Exercise 5) from the grand total of your monthly income (Exercise 6).

My income is $ _____ per month $ _____

My expenses are $ _____ per month   − $ _____

                    CASH FLOW $ _____

Choose one: I have $ + _____

               I have $ − _____

               I pretty much break even.

Exercise 7: Adjusting Your Budget

If you have a negative cash flow, you can increase your income, decrease your spending, or do both. Go back to your list of current expenses to determine where you may be able to save. Look also at your list of income sources to determine what you can increase.

My current expenses $ _____ per month

I want to spend $ _____ less per month

My current income $ _____ per month

I want to earn $ _____ more per month

Evaluating your situation, describe here your ideas about how you can adjust your budget.

_____

_____

_____

_____

Exercise 8: Your Financial Planning Philosophy

Look again at what you read about how short-term sacrifices can have positive effects in the long term. Think about how smart money decisions can help you achieve your long-term goals. Here, write two long-term goals that will cost money to fulfill.

1. _____

2. _____

For each, briefly describe a couple of steps you can take now that will enable you to stay on course toward those goals and have the money you need when you need it.

1. _____

_____

_____

2. _____

_____

_____

 # Key to Cooperative Learning:
Building Teamwork Skills

Savings Brainstorm As a class, brainstorm areas that require financial management (such as funding an education, running a household, or putting savings away for the future) and write them on the board. Divide into small groups. Each group should choose one area to discuss (make sure all areas are chosen). In your group, brainstorm strategies that can help with the area you have chosen. Think of savings ideas, ways to control spending, ways to earn more money, and any other methods of relieving financial stress. Agree on a list of possible ideas for your area and share it with the class.

Key to Self-Expression:
Discovery Through Journal Writing

To record your thoughts, use a separate journal or the lined page at the end of the chapter.

Credit Cards Describe how you use credit cards. Are you conservative, overindulgent, or in between? Do you pay on time, and do you pay the full balance of the card, or not? How does using a credit card make you feel—powerful, excited, apprehensive, or nervous? For what sort of purchases do you use credit cards? If you would like to change how you use credit, discuss any changes you want to make and how they would help you.

Key to Your Personal Portfolio:
Your Paper Trail to Success

Financial and Career History Create for yourself a detailed picture of your finances and work history. First, put your budget exercises, or copies of them, in your portfolio so that you have a record of your spending habits. Then answer these questions on a separate sheet and keep your work on file. Keeping accurate financial records is vital to being able to make intelligent financial decisions. Including your work record will help you maintain an accurate résumé and update it as needed.

In addition, you should always have a copy of important account and credit card numbers separate from your wallet or purse. That way, should you lose your cards, you have records of all of your credit card numbers and can cancel them immediately. Note: Do not include any PINs (personal identification numbers) anywhere in your portfolio. For your protection, any record of PINs should be kept separate from credit cards or credit card numbers.

1. What sources make up your financial aid package? List school/provincial/federal/personal loans, scholarship funds, grants, and the amount that you pay out of pocket. Indicate all account numbers, payment plans, and records of payment, including dates and cheque numbers if applicable.

2. List bank accounts to which you have access, including all names on the accounts, bank names, type of accounts, and account numbers. Include any restrictions on the accounts such as minimum balances or time frames during which you will receive a penalty for removing funds.

3. List any nonacademic loans you are currently repaying, noting the purpose of the loan, repayment schedule, loan payment amounts and dates of payments made, bank names and loan account numbers, and loan types.

4. List credit cards you use. Include major credit cards (American Express, Visa, MasterCard, etc.) as well as specific cards, such as cards for gas stations or department stores. For each card, include:

   ⚙ Name on the card
   ⚙ Card number
   ⚙ Expiration date
   ⚙ Date you got the card
   ⚙ Payment style (pay in full, pay minimum each month, etc.)
   ⚙ Problems (late payments, lost cards, card fraud, etc.)
   ⚙ Current balance and date

5. Detail your current job history. List the jobs you have had or currently have. Include the following information for each:

   ⚙ Name of the company/business
   ⚙ Job title
   ⚙ Wages or salary
   ⚙ Job descriptions (your duties and responsibilities)
   ⚙ The dates of your employment there
   ⚙ Personal contacts you made and have maintained (possible sources of references)

After you have completed this information, store it in your portfolio. Be sure to update it whenever there are changes.

Name _____ Date _____

Journal Entry

11 Moving Ahead:
Building a Flexible Future

In this chapter, you will explore answers to the following questions:

⊛ How can you live with change?

⊛ What will help you handle success and failure?

⊛ Why give back to the community and the world?

⊛ Why is school just the beginning of lifelong learning?

⊛ How can you live your mission?

The end of one path can be the beginning of another. For example, graduation is often referred to as *commencement*, because the end of your student career is the beginning or renewal of your life as a working citizen. As you come to the end of your work in this course, you have built up a wealth of knowledge. Now you have more power to make decisions about what directions you want your studies, your career, and your personal growth to take. Change will be one of the few constants in your life; the average Canadian will make several career choices in the course of his or her lifetime.

This chapter will explore how to manage the constant change you will encounter. Developing your flexibility will enable you to re-evaluate and modify goals, make the most of successes, and work through failures. You will consider what is important about giving back to your community and continuing to learn throughout your life. Finally, you will revisit your personal mission, exploring how to revise it as you encounter changes in the future. "A positive attitude toward change" is an important job skill for Canadians, according to the Conference Board of Canada.[1]

Thinking It Through

Check those statements that apply to you right now:

❏ Every time I think I've got my life under control, something new happens.

❏ I have a hard time shifting gears when I can't achieve my goals.

❏ When I fail or have a setback, I can't keep it in perspective.

❏ I try to find time to help others.

❏ I want to keep learning even after I graduate.

❏ I tend to lose sight of my mission in life.

How Can You Live with Change?

Even the most carefully constructed plans can be turned upside down by change. In this section, you will explore some ways to make change a manageable part of your life: accepting the reality of change, maintaining flexibility, re-evaluating and modifying your goals, and being open to unpredictability.

Accept the Reality of Change

As Russian-born author Isaac Asimov once said, "It is change, continuing change, inevitable change, that is the dominant factor in society today. No sensible decision can be made any longer without taking into account not only the world as it is, but the world as it will be."[2] Change is a sure thing. Two significant causes of change on a global level are technology and the economy.

Technological Growth

Today's technology has spurred change. Tasks that people have performed for years are now taken care of by computers in a fraction of the time and for a fraction of the price. Advances in technology come into being daily: Computer companies update programs, new models of cars and machines appear, and scientists discover new possibilities in medicine and other areas. People make changes in the workplace, school, and home to keep up with the new systems and products that technology constantly offers. People and cultures are linked around the world through the Internet and World Wide Web.

The dominance of the media, brought on by technological growth, has increased the likelihood of change. A few hundred years ago, no television or magazines or Internet existed to show people what was happening elsewhere in the world. A village could operate in the same way for years with very little change, because there would be little or no contact with anyone from the outside who could introduce new ideas, methods, or plans. Now, the media constantly present people with new ways of doing things. When people can see the possibilities around them, they are more likely to want to find out whether the grass is truly greener on the other side of the fence.

Economic Instability

The unpredictable economy is the second factor in this age of constant change. Businesses have had to cut costs in order to survive, which has affected many people's jobs and careers. Some businesses discovered the speed and cost-effectiveness of computers and used them to replace workers. Some businesses have had to downsize and have laid off people to save money. Some businesses have merged with others, and people in duplicate jobs were let go. The difficult economy has also had an effect on personal finances. Many people face money problems at home that force them to make changes in how much they work, how they pursue an education, and how they live.

downsize
To reduce in size; streamline.

Maintain Flexibility

The fear of change is as inevitable as change itself. When you become comfortable with something, you tend to want it to stay the way it is, whether it is a relationship, a place you live, a job, a schedule, or the racial/cultural mix of people with whom you interact. Change may seem to have only negative effects, and consistency only positive effects. Think about your life right now. What do you wish would always stay the same? What changes have upset you and thrown you off balance?

You may have encountered any number of changes in your life to date, many of them unexpected. You may have experienced ups and downs in relationships, perhaps marriage or divorce. You may have changed schools, changed jobs, or moved to a new home. You may have shifted your course of study. You may have added to your family or lost family members. Financial shifts may have caused you to change the way you live. All of these changes, whether you perceive them as good or bad, cause a certain level of stress. They also cause a shift in your personal needs, which may lead to changing priorities.

Change Brings Different Needs

Your needs can change from day to day, year to year, and situation to situation. Although you may know about some changes ahead of time, such as when you plan to attend school or move in with a partner, others may take you completely by surprise, such as losing a job, illness, or an unexpected pregnancy. Even the different times of year bring different needs, such as a need for extra cash around the holidays or a need for additional child care when your children are home for the summer.

Some changes that shift your needs will occur within a week or even a day. For example, an instructor may inform you that you have a quiz or extra assignment at the end of the week, or your supervisor at work may give you an additional goal for the week. During the course of a day, your daughter might tell you that she needs you to drive her somewhere that evening, or a friend may call and need your help with something that has come up suddenly. Table 11–1 shows how the effects of certain changes can lead to new priorities.

Flexibility vs. Inflexibility

When change affects your needs, *flexibility* will help you shift your priorities so that you address those needs. You can react to change with either inflexibility or flexibility, each with its resulting effects.

Inflexibility. Not acknowledging a shift in needs can cause trouble. For example, if you lose your job and continue to spend as much money as you did before, ignoring your need to live more modestly, you can drive yourself into debt and make the situation worse. Or if you continue to spend little time with a partner who has expressed a need for more contact, you may lose your relationship.

Table 11-1 Change Produces New Priorities		
Change	Effects and Changed Needs	New Priorities
Lost job	Loss of income; need for others in your household to contribute more income	Job hunting; reduction in your spending; additional training or education in order to qualify for a different job
New job	Change in daily/weekly schedule; need for increased contribution of household help from others	Time and energy commitment to new job, maintaining confidence, learning new skills
Started school	Fewer hours for work, family, and personal time; responsibility for classwork; need to plan semesters ahead of time	Careful scheduling; making sure you have time to attend class and study adequately; strategic planning of classes and of career goals
Relationship/marriage	Responsibility toward your partner; merging of your schedules and perhaps your finances and belongings	Time and energy commitment to relationship
Breakup/divorce	Change in responsibility for any children; increased responsibility for your own finances; possibly a need to relocate; increased independence	Making time for yourself, gathering support from friends and family, securing your finances, making sure you have your own income
Bought car	Responsibility for monthly payment; responsibility for upkeep	Regular income so that you can make payments on time; time and money for upkeep
New baby	Increased parenting responsibility; need money to pay for baby's needs or if you had to stop working; need help with other children	Child care, flexible employment, increased commitment from a partner or other supporter
New cultural environment (from new home, job, or school)	Exposure to unfamiliar people and traditions; tendency to keep to yourself	Learning about the culture with which you are now interacting; openness to new relationships

Flexibility. Being flexible means acknowledging the change, examining your different needs, and addressing them in any way you can. As frightening as it can be, being flexible can help you move ahead. Discovering what change brings may help you uncover positive effects that you had no idea were there. For example, a painful breakup or divorce can lead you to discover greater capability and independence. A loss of a job can give you a chance to re-evaluate your abilities and look for another job in an area that suits you better. An illness can give you perspective on what you truly value in life. In other words, a crisis can spur opportunity—you may learn that you want to adjust your goals in order to pursue that opportunity.

Sometimes you may need to resist for a while, until you are ready to face an important change. When you do decide you are ready, being flexible will help you cope with the negative effects and benefit from the positive effects.

Re-Evaluate and Modify Your Goals

Your changing life will often result in the need to adjust goals accordingly. A goal to finish school in four years may not be reasonable if an illness, increased job and/or family responsibilities, or economic constraints take you out of school for a while. A goal to stay married forever might not be safe if you are in an abusive relationship. Sometimes goals must change because they weren't appropriate in the first place. People don't always set the best goals for themselves. Some turn out to be unreachable; some may not pose enough of a challenge; others may be unhealthy for the goal-setter or harmful to others.

"Risk! Risk anything! Care no more for the opinion of others, for those voices. Do the hardest thing on earth for you. Act for yourself. Face the truth."

Katherine Mansfield

Step One: Re-Evaluate

Before making adjustments in response to change, take time to *re-evaluate* both the goals themselves and your progress toward them.

The goals. First, determine whether your goals still fit the person you have become in the past week, month, or year. Circumstances can change quickly. An unexpected pregnancy might cause a female student to rethink her educational goals. A couple in the market for a used car may discover their combined income enables them to buy a new car. Sometimes, your goals conflict with someone else's goals. For example, one spouse may want to move to a larger apartment, but the additional work hours needed to pay for the rent increase would prevent the other spouse from finishing required course work.

Your progress. If you feel you haven't come very far, determine whether the goal is out of your range or simply requires more stamina than you had anticipated. Don't rush to let yourself off the hook—you may risk letting an important goal slip away. As you work toward any goal you will experience alternating periods of progress and stagnation; the ability to follow through will keep you on target. Sticking with a tough goal may be the hardest thing you'll ever do, but the payoff may be worth it. You may want to seek the support and perspective of a friend or counsellor as you evaluate your progress.

Step Two: Modify

If after your best efforts it becomes clear that a goal is out of reach, don't feel you have failed. *Modifying* your goal may bring success. Perhaps the goal doesn't suit you. For example, an active, interpersonal learner might become frustrated while pursuing a detail-oriented, sedentary career such as computer programming.

Based on your re-evaluation, you can modify a goal in two ways:

1. Adjust the existing goal. To adjust a goal, change one or more aspects that define that goal—for example, the time frame, the due dates, or the specifics of the expectations. For example, a woman with an unexpected pregnancy could adjust her educational due

date, taking an extra year or two to complete her course work. She could also adjust the time frame, taking classes at night if she had to care for her child during the day.

2. Replace it with a different, more compatible goal. If you find that you just can't handle a particular goal, try to find another that makes more sense for you at this time. For example, a couple who wants to buy a home but just can't afford it can choose to work toward the goal of making improvements to their current living space. Because you and your circumstances never stop changing, your goals should keep up with those changes.

Be Open to Unpredictability

Life is by nature unpredictable. If you ask people whether ten years ago they would have been able to predict their current life, most will say they would have had absolutely no idea. Think about how much of your life matches what you had envisioned. Chances are that not much of what you do and who you are is exactly as you may have planned.

In their article "A Simpler Way," Margaret J. Wheatley and Myron Kellner-Rogers discuss how the unpredictability of life can be in fact a gift that opens up new horizons. "We often look at this unpredictability with resentment, but it's important to notice that such unpredictability gives us the freedom to experiment. It is this unpredictability that welcomes our creativity."[3] Wheatley and Kellner-Rogers offer these suggestions for being open to unpredictability:

Look for what happens when you meet someone or something new. Be aware of the new feelings or insights that arise when you interact with a new person, class, project, or event. Instead of accepting or rejecting them based on whether they fit into your idea of how life should be, follow them a bit. See where they lead you.

Be willing to be surprised. Great creative energies can come from the force of a surprise. Instead of turning back to familiar patterns after a surprise throws you off balance, see what you can discover.

Use your planning as a guide rather than a hard-and-fast rule. As so much of this book discusses, planning—from daily goals to strategic, long-term planning—is an important tool that helps you focus your efforts, shape your path, and gain a measure of control over your world. Life, however, won't always go along with your plan. If you see your plans as a guide, allowing yourself to adjust those plans and follow new paths when changes come your way, you will be able to grow from what life gives you instead of using your old plan as a way to hide and shut down.

Focus on what is, rather than what is supposed to be. Often people are unable to see what's happening because they are too focused on what they feel *should* be happening. When you put all your energy into thinking about your plan for where you will be five years from now, you may miss out on some incredible occurrences happening right in front of you. Planning for the future is extremely important, but it works best as a guide when combined with an awareness of the changes that the present brings.

When you stay open to unpredictability, you will be more aware of life's moments as they go by. You will become an explorer, experiencing everything that comes across your path. Having this awareness and flexibility will help you understand that both successes and failures are a natural part of your exploration.

What Will Help You Handle Success and Failure?

The perfect, trouble-free life is a myth. The most wonderful, challenging, fulfilling life is full of problems to be solved and difficult decisions to be made. If you want to handle the bumps and bruises without losing your self-esteem, you should prepare to encounter setbacks along with your successes.

Dealing with Failure

Things don't always go the way you want them to go. Sometimes you may come up against obstacles that are difficult to overcome. Sometimes you will let yourself down or disappoint others. You may make mistakes or lose your motivation. All people do, no matter who they are or how smart or accomplished they may be. What is important is how you choose to deal with what goes wrong. If you can arrive at reasonable definitions of failure and success, accept failure as part of being human, and examine failure so that you can learn from it, you will have the confidence to pick yourself up and keep improving.

Measuring Failure and Success

Most people measure failure by comparing where they are to where they believe they should be. Since individual circumstances vary widely, so do definitions of failure. What you consider a failure may seem like a positive step for someone else. Here are some examples:

- Imagine that your native language is Vietnamese. You have learned to speak English well, but you still have trouble writing it. Making writing mistakes may seem like failure to you, but to a recent immigrant from Yugoslavia who knows limited

English, your command of the language will seem like a success story.

- If two people apply for internships, one may see failure as receiving some offers but not the favourite one, while someone who was turned down may see any offer as a success.

- Having a job that doesn't pay you as much as you want may seem like a failure, but to someone who is having trouble finding any job, your job is a definite success.

Accepting Failure

"The word impossible is not in my dictionary."
Napoleon

No one escapes failure, no matter how hard he or she may try (or how successful he or she may be at hiding mistakes). The most successful people and organizations have experienced failures and mistakes. For example, the producers of the film *Waterworld* spent over $198 million on a film that made only a fraction of that cost at the box office. America Online miscalculated customer use and offered a flat rate per month, resulting in thousands of customers having trouble logging onto the service. Many an otherwise successful individual has had a problematic relationship, a substance-abuse problem, or a failing grade in a course.

You have choices when deciding how to view a failure or mistake. You can pretend it never happened, blame it on someone or something else, blame yourself, or forgive yourself.

Pretending it didn't happen. Avoiding the pain of dealing with a failure can deny you valuable lessons and could even create more serious problems. HIV is one example of this. Imagine that a person has unprotected sex with a potentially HIV-infected partner and then denies it ever happened. If that person later discovers that he or she has contracted HIV from that partner, the deadly virus may have been passed on to any subsequent partners.

Blaming others. Putting the responsibility on someone else stifles opportunities to learn and grow. For example, imagine that an unprepared and inappropriately dressed person interviews for a job and is not hired. If he or she decides that the interviewer is biased, the interviewee won't learn to improve preparation or interview strategies. Evaluate causes carefully and try not to assign blame.

Blaming yourself. Getting angry at yourself for failing, or believing that you should be perfect, can only result in your feeling incapable of success and perhaps becoming afraid to try. Negative self-talk can become self-fulfilling.

Forgiving yourself. This is by far the best way to cope. First, although you should always strive for your best, don't expect perfection of yourself or anyone else. Expect that you will do the best that you can within the circumstances of your life. Just getting through another day as a student, employee, and/or parent is an important success. Second, forgive yourself when you fail. Your value as a human being does not diminish when you make a mistake. Forgiving yourself will give you more strength to learn from the experience, move on, and try again.

Once you are able to approach failure and mistakes in a productive way, you can explore what you can learn from them.

Learning from Failure

Learning from your failures and mistakes involves thinking critically through what happened. The first step is to evaluate what happened and decide if it was within your control. It could have had nothing to do with you at all. You could have failed to win a job because someone else with equal qualifications was in line for it ahead of you. A family crisis that disrupted your sleep could have affected your studying, resulting in a failing grade on a test. These are unfortunate circumstances, but they are not failures. On the other hand, something you did or didn't do may have contributed to the failure.

If you decide that you have made a mistake, your next steps are to analyze the causes and effects of what happened, make any improvements that you can, and decide how to change your action or approach in the future.

For example, imagine that after a long night of studying you forgot your part-time work-study commitment the next day.

Analyze causes and effects. *Causes:* Your exhaustion and your concern about your test caused you to forget to check on your work schedule. *Effects:* Because you weren't there, a crucial curriculum project wasn't completed. An entire class and instructor who needed the project have been affected by your mistake.

Make any possible improvements on the situation. You could apologize to the instructor and see if there was still a chance to finish up part of the work that day.

Make changes for the future. You could set a goal to note your work schedule regularly in your date book—maybe in a bright colour—and to check it more often. You could also arrange your future study schedule so that you would be less exhausted.

Think about the people you consider to be exceptionally successful. They didn't rise to the top without taking risks and making their share of mistakes. They have built much of their success upon their willingness to recognize and learn from their shortfalls. You too can benefit from staying open to this kind of active, demanding, hard-won education. Learning involves change and growth. Let what you learn from falling short of your goals inspire new and better ideas.

Think Positively About Failure

When you feel you have failed, how can you boost your outlook?

Stay aware of the fact that you are a capable, valuable person. People often react to failure by becoming convinced that they are incapable and incompetent. Fight that tendency by reminding yourself of your successes, focusing your energy on your best abilities, and knowing that you have the strength to try again. Realize that your failure isn't a setback as long as you learn from it and rededicate yourself to excellence. Remember that the energy you might expend on talking down to yourself would be better spent on trying again and moving ahead.

Share your thoughts and disappointment with others. Everybody fails. Trading stories will help you realize you're not alone. People refrain from talking about failures out of embarrassment, often feeling as though no one else could have made as big a mistake as they did. When you open up, though, you may be surprised to hear others exchange stories that rival your own. Be careful not to get caught in a destructive cycle of complaining, however. Instead, focus on the kind of creative energy that can help you find ways to learn from your failures.

Look on the bright side. At worst, you at least have learned a lesson that will help you avoid similar situations in the future. At best, there may be some positive results of what happened. If your romance flounders, the extra study time you suddenly have may help you boost your grades. If you fail a class, you may discover that you need to focus on a different subject that suits you better. What you learn from a failure may, in an unexpected way, bring you around to where you want to be.

Dealing with Success

Success isn't reserved for the wealthy, famous people you see glamourized in magazines and newspapers. Success isn't money or fame, although it can bring such things. Success is being who you want to be and doing what you want to do. Success is within your reach.

Pay attention to the small things when measuring success. You may not feel successful until you reach an important goal you have set for yourself. However, along the way each step is a success. When you are trying to drop a harmful habit, each time you stay on course is a success. When you are juggling work, school, and a personal life, just coping with what every new day brings equals success. If you received a C on a paper and then earned a B on the next one, your advancement is successful.

Remember that success is a process. If you deny yourself the label of "success" until you reach the top of where you want to be, you will have a much harder time getting there. Just moving ahead toward improvement and growth, however fast or slow the movement, equals success.

Here are some techniques to handle your successes.

First, appreciate yourself. You deserve it. Take time to congratulate yourself for a job well done—whether it be a good grade, an important step in learning a new language, a job offer, a promotion or graduation, or a personal victory over substance abuse. Bask in the glow a bit. Everybody hears about his or her mistakes, but people don't praise themselves (or each other) enough when success happens. Praise can give you a terrific vote of confidence.

Take that confidence on the road. This victory can lead to others. Based on this success, you may be expected to prove to yourself and others that you are capable of growth and of continuing your successes and building upon them. Show yourself and others that the confidence is well-founded.

Stay sensitive to others. There could be people around you who may not have been so successful. Remember that you have been in their place, and they in yours, and the positions may change many times over in the future. Enjoy what you have, work to build on it and not to take it for granted, and support others as they need it.

Staying sensitive to others is an important goal always, whether you are feeling successful or less than successful. Giving what you can of your time, energy, and resources to the community and the world is part of being aware of what others need. Your contributions can help to bring success to others.

Why Give Back to the Community and the World?

Everyday life is demanding. You can become so caught up in the issues of your own life that you neglect to look outside your immediate needs. However, from time to time you may feel that your mission extends beyond your personal life. You have spent time in this course working to improve yourself. Now that you've come so far, why not extend some of that energy and effort to the world outside? With all that you have to offer, you have the power to make positive differences in the lives of others. Every effort you make, no matter how small, improves the world.

Your Imprint on the World

As difficult as your life can sometimes seem, looking outside yourself and into the lives of others can help put everything in perspective. Sometimes you can evaluate your own hardships more reasonably when you look at them in light of what is happening elsewhere in the world. There are always many people in the world in great need. You have something to give to others. Making a lasting difference in the lives of others is something to be proud of.

Your perspective may change after volunteering at a soup kitchen. Your appreciation of those close to you may increase after you spend time with cancer patients at the local hospice. Your perspective on your living situation may change after you help people improve their housing conditions.

If you could eavesdrop on someone *talking about you* to another person, what do you think you would hear? How would you like to hear yourself described? What you do for others makes an imprint that can have far more impact than you may imagine. Giving one person hope, comfort, or help can improve his or her ability to cope with life's changes. That person in turn may be able to offer help to someone else. As each person makes a contribution, a cycle of positive effects is generated. For example, Helen Keller, blind and deaf from the age of two, was educated through the help of her teacher Annie Sullivan, and then spent much of her life lecturing to raise money for the teaching of the blind and deaf. Another example is Betty Ford, who was helped in her struggle with alcoholism and founded the Betty Ford Center to help others with addiction problems. Canadian Norman Jewison, who

Community Organizations Online

Big Brothers and Big Sisters
www.bbsc.ca

Canadian Red Cross
www.redcross.ca

Daily Bread Food Bank
www.dailybread.ca

YMCA
www.ymca.ca

If you're thinking about how you can make a difference in the lives of others, you can find out what these nonprofit organizations do in your community.

achieved success in Hollywood with films like *In the Heat of the Night* and *Moonstruck*, came back to Canada and founded the Canadian Film Institute to help the Canadian film industry. CFL superstar Mike "Pinball" Clemons donates a great deal of his spare time to charities in Ontario.

How can you make a difference? Many schools and companies are realizing the importance of community involvement and have appointed committees to find and organize volunteering opportunities. Make some kind of volunteering activity a priority on your schedule. Join a group from your company that tutors at a school. Organize a group of students to clean, repair, or entertain at a nursing home or shelter. Look for what's available to you or create opportunities on your own. Table 11–2 lists organizations that provide volunteer opportunities; you might also look into more local efforts or private clearinghouses that set up a number of different smaller projects.

Sometimes it's hard to find time to volunteer when so many responsibilities compete for your attention. One solution is to combine other activities with volunteer work. Get exercise while cleaning a park or your yard or bring the whole family to sing at a nursing home on a weekend afternoon. Whatever you do, your actions will have a ripple effect, creating a positive impact for those you help and those they encounter in turn. The strength often found in people surviving difficult circumstances can strengthen you as well.

Valuing Your Environment

Your environment is your home. When you value it, you help to maintain a clean, safe, and healthy place to live. What you do every day has an impact on others around you and on the future. One famous slogan says that if you are not part of the solution, you are part of the problem. Every saved bottle, environmentally aware child, and reused bag is part of the solution. Take re-

Table 11–2 Organizations That Can Use Your Help

AIDS-related organizations	Amnesty International	Canadian Red Cross
Audubon Society	Battered women shelters	Big Brothers and Big Sisters
Churches, synagogues, temples, and affiliated organizations such as the YM/WCA	Educational support organizations	Environmental awareness/support organizations such as Greenpeace
Daily Bread Food Bank/other food donation organizations	Shelters and organizations supporting the homeless	World Wildlife Fund
Hospitals	Hotlines	Kiwanis/Knights of Columbus/ Lions Club/Rotary
Libraries	Meals on Wheels	Nursing homes
Planned Parenthood	School districts	Scouting organizations

sponsibility for what you can control—your own habits—and develop sound practices that contribute to the health of the environment.

Recycle anything that you can. What can be recycled varies with the system set up in your area. You may be able to recycle any combination of plastics, aluminum, glass, newspapers, and magazines. Products that make use of recycled materials are often more expensive, but if they are within your price range, try to reward the company's dedication by purchasing the products.

Trade and reuse items. When your children have grown too old for the crib, baby clothes, and toys, give away whatever is still usable. Give clothing you don't wear to others who can use it. Organizations like the Salvation Army may pick up used items in your neighbourhood on certain days or if you make arrangements with them. Rinse out the clear produce bags you get at the supermarket and use them as sandwich bags. Wrap presents in plain newsprint and decorate with markers. Use your imagination—there are many, many items that you can reuse, all around you.

Respect the outdoors. Participate in maintaining a healthy environment. Use products that reduce chemical waste. Pick up after yourself. Through volunteering, voicing your opinion, or making monetary donations, support the maintenance of parks and the preservation of natural, undeveloped land. Be creative. One young woman planned a cleanup of a local lakeside area as the main group activity for the guests at her birthday party (she joined them, of course). Everyone benefits when each person takes responsibility for maintaining the fragile earth.

Remember that valuing yourself is the basis for valuing all other things. Improving the earth is difficult unless you value yourself and think you deserve the best living environment possible. Valuing yourself will also help you understand why you deserve to enjoy the benefits of learning throughout your life.

Why Are College and University Just the Beginning of Lifelong Learning?

Although it may sometimes feel more like a burden, being a student is a golden opportunity. As a student, you are able to focus on learning for a period of time, and your school focuses on you in return, helping you gain access to knowledge, resources, and experiences. Take advantage of the academic atmosphere by developing a habit of seeking out new learning opportunities. That habit will encourage you to continue your learning long after you have graduated, even in the face of the pressures of everyday life.

Learning brings change, and change causes growth. If you confine your learning to your time as a student, you will make it difficult to improve and move ahead, both on the job and in your personal life. On the other hand, if you take advantage of the chances to learn that can come your way, you will continue to move ahead. As you change and the world changes, new knowledge and ideas continually emerge. Absorb them so that you can propel yourself into the future. Visualize yourself as a student of life who learns something new every single day.

Here are some lifelong learning strategies that can encourage you to continually ask questions and explore new ideas.

Investigate new interests. When information and events catch your attention, take your interest one step further and find out more. If you are fascinated by politics on television, find out if your school has political clubs that you can explore. If a friend of yours starts to take yoga, try out a class with him. If you really like one portion of a particular class, see if there are other classes that focus on that specific topic. Turn the regretful, "I wish I had tried that," into the purposeful, "I'm going to do it."

Read books, newspapers, magazines, and other writings. Reading opens a world of new perspectives. Check out what's on the bestseller list at your bookstore. Ask your friends about books that have changed their lives. Stay on top of current change in your community, your province, your country, and the world by reading newspapers and magazines. A newspaper or magazine that has a broad scope, such as *The Toronto Star* or *Maclean's*, can be an education in itself. Explore family letters and Internet news groups and Web pages. Keep something with you to read for those moments when you have nothing to do.

Spend time with interesting people. When you meet someone new who inspires you and makes you think, keep in touch. Have a potluck dinner party and invite one person or couple from each corner of your life—your family, your work, your school, a club to which you belong, your neighbourhood. Sometimes, meet for reasons beyond just being social. Start a book club, a home-repair group, a play-reading club, a hiking group, or an investing group. Learn something new from each other.

continuing education
Courses that students can take without having to be part of a degree program.

Pursue improvement in your studies and in your career. When at school, take classes outside of your major if you have time. After graduation, continue your education both in your field and in the realm of general knowledge. Stay on top of ideas, developments, structural changes, and new technology in your field by seeking out continuing education courses. Sign up for career-related seminars. Take single courses at a local college or community learning centre. Some companies offer additional on-the-job training or will pay for their employees to take courses or seminars that improve their knowledge and skills. If your company doesn't, you may want to set a small part of your income aside as a "learning budget." When you apply for jobs, you may want to ask about what kind of training or education the company offers or supports.

Talk to people of different generations than yours. Younger people can learn from the experienced, broad perspective of those belonging to older generations; older people can learn from the fresh and often radical perspective of those younger than themselves. Even beyond the benefits of new knowledge, there is much to be gained from developing mutual respect among generations.

Delve into other cultures. Given Canada's multiculturalism, this is not hard to do. Visit the home of a friend who has grown up in a culture entirely different from your own. Then, invite him or her to your home. Eat at a restaurant that serves food from a country you've never seen. Initiate conversations with people of different races, religions, values, and ethnic backgrounds, asking them about their experiences. Travel to different countries. Travel nearby to different neighbourhoods or cities near you—they may seem as foreign as another country. Take a course that deals with some aspect of cultural diversity.

Nurture a spiritual life. You can find spirituality in many places. You don't have to regularly attend a house of worship to be spiritual, although that may be an important part of your spiritual life. "A spiritual life of some kind is absolutely necessary for psychological 'health,'" says psychologist and author Thomas Moore in his book *The Care of the Soul*. "We live in a time of deep division, in which mind is separated from body and spirituality is at odds with materialism."[4] The words *soul* and *spirituality* hold different meaning for each individual. Decide what they mean to you. Whether you discover them in music, organized religion, friendship, nature, cooking, sports, or anything else, making them a priority in your life will help you find a greater sense of balance and meaning.

Experience what others create. Art is "an adventure of the mind" (Eugene Ionesco, playwright); "a means of knowing the world" (Angela Carter, author); something that "does not reproduce the visible; rather, it makes visible" (Paul Klee, painter); "a lie that makes us realize truth" (Pablo Picasso, painter); a revealer of "our most secret self" (Jean-Luc Godard, filmmaker). Through art you can discover new ideas and shed new light on old ones. Explore all kinds of art and focus on any forms that hold your interest. Seek out whatever moves you—music, visual arts, theatre, photography, dance, domestic arts, performance art, film and television, poetry, prose, and more.

Make your own creations. Bring out the creative artist in you. Take a class in drawing, in pottery, or in quilting. Learn to play an instrument that you have always wanted to master. Write poems for your favourite people or stories to read to your kids. Invent a recipe. Design and build a set of shelves for your home. Create a memoir of your life. You are a creative being. Express yourself, and learn more about yourself, through art.

Lifelong learning is the master key that unlocks every door you will encounter on your journey. If you keep it firmly in your hand, you will discover worlds of knowledge—and a place for yourself within them.

How Can You Live Your Mission?

As you learn and change, so may your life's mission. Whatever changes occur, your continued learning will give you a greater sense of security in your choices. Recall your mission statement from Chapter 3. Think about how it is changing as you learn and develop. It will continue to reflect your goals, values, and strength if you live with integrity, roll with the changes that come your way, continue to observe the role models in your life, and work to achieve your personal best in all that you do.

Live with Integrity

integrity
Adherence to a code of moral values; incorruptibility, honesty.

You've spent a lot of time exploring who you are, how you learn, and what you value. Integrity is about being true to that picture you have drawn of yourself while also considering the needs of others. Living with integrity will bring you great personal and professional rewards.

Honesty and sincerity are at the heart of integrity. Many of the decisions you make and act upon in your life are based on your underlying sense of what is "the right thing to do." Having integrity puts that sense into day-to-day action.

The Marks of Integrity

A person of integrity lives by the following principles:

1. *Honest representation of himself or herself, and his or her thoughts.* For example, you tell your partner when you are upset about something that he or she did or didn't do.

2. *Sincerity in word and action.* You do what you say you will do. For example, you tell a co-worker that you will finish a project when she has to leave early, and you follow through by completing the work.

3. *Consideration of the needs of others.* When making decisions, you take both your needs and the needs of others into account. You also avoid hurting others for the sake of your personal goals. For example, your sister cares for your elderly father in her home where he lives with her. You spend three nights a week with him so that she can take a course toward her degree.

The Benefits of Integrity

When you act with integrity, you earn trust and respect from yourself and from others. If people can trust you to be honest, to be sincere in what you say and do, and to consider the needs of others, they will be more likely to encourage you, support your goals, and reward your hard work. Integrity is a must for workplace success. To earn promotions, it helps to show that you have integrity in a variety of situations.

Think of situations in which a decision made with integrity has had a positive effect. Have you ever confessed to an instructor that your paper was late without a good excuse, only to find that despite your mistake you have earned the instructor's respect? Have extra efforts in the workplace ever helped you gain a promotion or a raise? Have your kindnesses toward a friend or spouse moved the relationship to a deeper level? When you decide to act with integrity, you can improve your life and the lives of others.

Most importantly, living with integrity helps you believe in yourself and in your ability to make good choices. A person of integrity isn't a perfect person, but one who makes the effort to live according to values and principles, continually striving to learn from mistakes and to improve. One way of judging the integrity of your decisions is to examine your willingness to discuss a decision with someone you respect. If revealing your choice would make you feel deeply uncomfortable or ashamed—if you wouldn't be proud to defend your choice—chances are you haven't honoured your sense of integrity. Take responsibility for making the right moves, and you will follow your mission with strength and conviction.

Roll with the Changes

Think again about yourself. How has your idea of where you want to be changed since you first opened this book? How has your self-image changed? What have you learned about your values, your goals, and your styles of communication and learning? Consider how your goals in the five life areas from Chapter 3—personal, family, career, financial, and lifestyle—have changed. As you continue to grow and develop, keep adjusting your goals to your changes and discoveries.

Stephen Covey says in *The Seven Habits of Highly Effective People*, "Change—real change—comes from the inside out. It doesn't come from hacking at the leaves of attitude and behaviour with quick fix personality ethic techniques. It comes from striking at the root—the fabric of our thought, the fundamental essential paradigms which give definition to our character and create the lens through which we see the world."[5]

Examining yourself deeply in that way is a real risk. Most of all, it demands courage and strength of will. Questioning your established beliefs and facing the unknown are much more difficult than staying with the way things are. When you have the courage to face the consequences of trying something unfamiliar, admitting failure, or challenging what you thought you knew, you open yourself to growth and learning opportunities. You can make your way through changes you never anticipated if you make the effort to live your mission—in whatever forms it takes as it changes—each day, each week, each month, and for years to come.

paradigm
An especially clear pattern or typical example.

Learn from Role Models

People often derive the highest level of motivation and inspiration from learning how others have struggled through the ups and downs of life and achieved their goals. Somehow, seeing how someone else went through difficult situations can give you hope for your own struggles. The positive effects of being true to one's self become more real when an actual person has earned them.

Learning about the lives of people who have achieved their own version of success can teach you what you can do in your own life. Bessie and Sadie Delany, sisters and accomplished African-American women born in the late 1800s, are two valuable role models. They took risks, becoming professionals

role model
A person whose behaviour in a particular role is imitated by others.

in dentistry and teaching at a time when women and minorities were often denied both respect and opportunity. They worked hard to fight racial division and prejudice and taught others what they learned. They believed in their intelligence, beauty, and ability to give, and lived without regrets. Says Sadie in their *Book of Everyday Wisdom*, "If there's anything I've learned in all these years, it's that life is too good to waste a day. It's up to you to make it sweet."[6]

Aim for Your Personal Best

Your personal best is simply the best that you can do, in any situation. It may not be the best you have ever done. It may include mistakes, for nothing significant is ever accomplished without making mistakes and taking risks. It may shift from situation to situation. As long as you aim to do your best, though, you are inviting growth and success.

Aim for your personal best in everything you do. As a lifelong learner, you will always have a new direction in which to grow and a new challenge to face. Seek constant improvement in your personal, educational, and professional life, knowing that you are capable of that improvement. Enjoy the richness of life by living each day to the fullest, developing your talents and potential into the achievement of your most valued goals.

Kaizen is the Japanese word for "continual improvement." Striving for excellence, always finding ways to improve on what already exists, and believing that you can have an impact, is at the heart of the Japanese spirit. The drive to improve who you are and what you do will help to provide the foundation of a successful future.

Think of this concept as you reflect on yourself, your goals, your lifelong education, your career, and your personal pursuits. Create excellence and quality by continually asking yourself, "How can I improve?" Living by *kaizen* will help you to be a respected friend and family member, a productive and valued employee, and a truly contributing member of society. You *can* change the world.

Chapter 11: Applications

Name _____   Date _____

 Key into Your Life:
Opportunities to Apply What You Learn

Exercise 1: Changes in Goals

Have you experienced any shifts in your goals? Think about what may have changed since you began this course. List three major goals for each of the five goal areas. In each area, highlight or circle the goal that has changed the most and discuss why the change occurred.

Personal

1. _____

2. _____

3. _____

Discuss changes:

_____

_____

Family

1. _____

2. _____

3. _____

Discuss changes:

_____

_____

Lifestyle

1. _____

2. _____

3. _____

Discuss changes:

_____

_____

Career

1. _____

2. _____

3. _____

Discuss changes:

_____

_____

Financial

1. _____

2. _____

3. _____

Discuss changes:

_____

_____

Exercise 2: Looking at Change, Failure, and Success

Life can go by so quickly that you don't take time to evaluate what changes have taken place, what failures you could learn from, and what successes you have experienced. Take a moment now and answer the following questions for yourself.

What are the three biggest changes that have occurred in your life this year?

1. _____

2. _____

3. _____

Choose one that you feel you handled well. What shifts in priorities or goals did you make?

_____

_____

_____

Choose one that you could have handled better. What happened? What do you think you should have done?

_____

_____

_____

Now name a personal experience, occurring this year, that you would consider a failure. What happened?

_____

_____

How did you handle it—did you ignore it, blame it on someone else, or admit and explore it?

_____

_____

What did you learn from experiencing this failure?

_____

_____

Finally, describe a recent success of which you are the most proud.

_____

_____

How did this success give you confidence in other areas of your life?

_____

_____

Exercise 3: Volunteering

Research volunteering opportunities in your community. What are the organizations? What are their needs? Do any volunteer positions require an application, letters of reference, or background checks? List three possibilities for which you have an interest or a passion.

1. _____

2. _____

3. _____

Of these three, choose one that you feel you will have the time and ability to try next semester. Suggestions that don't take up too much time include spending an evening serving in a soup kitchen, or driving for Meals on

Wheels during a lunch or dinner shift. Name your choice here and tell why you selected it.

_____

_____

Research the suggestion you have chosen. Describe the activity. What is the time commitment? Is there any special training involved? Are there any problematic or difficult elements to this experience?

_____

_____

_____

_____

_____

_____

Exercise 4: Lifelong Learning

Review the strategies for lifelong learning in this chapter. Which ones mean something to you? Which do you think you can do, or plan to do, in your life now and when you are out of school? Name them and briefly discuss the role they play in your life.

_____

_____

_____

_____

_____

 ## Key to Cooperative Learning:
Building Teamwork Skills

Support and Affirmation Gather in groups of three to five, and make sure that in each group the students are as familiar as possible with one another. Each member of the group should independently write two things on a piece of paper: one specific goal that he or she has attained, and one specific goal that he or she wants to work harder to achieve. When all are ready, sit in a small circle. Each member should first take turns sharing details and thoughts about the successful goal. Show your support and encouragement. If you know a group member well and have seen the difference hard work has made, say so. Then, go around the group again, giving each member a chance to bring up the goal that needs work. Offer suggestions and ideas. Boost each other's motivation by discussing the positive effects that can result from working on the goal.

Key to Self-Expression:
Discovery Through Journal Writing

To record your thoughts, use a separate journal or the lined page at the end of the chapter.

One Hundred Positive Thoughts Make a list for yourself. The first fifty items in the list should be things you like about yourself. You can name anything—things you can do, things you think, things you've accomplished, things you like about your physical self, and so on. The second fifty items should be things you'd like to do in your life. These can be of any magnitude—anything from trying Vietnamese food to travelling to the Grand Canyon to keeping your room neat to getting to know someone. They can be things you'd like to do tomorrow or things that you plan to do in twenty years. Be creative. Let everything be possible.

Key to Your Personal Portfolio:
Your Paper Trail to Success

Revised Mission Statement Retrieve the mission statement you wrote at the end of Chapter 3. Give yourself a day or so to read it over and think about it. Then, revise it according to the changes that have occurred in you. Add new priorities and goals and delete those that are no longer valid. Continue to update your mission statement so that it reflects your growth and development, helping to guide you through the changes that await you in the future.

Name _____ Date _____

Journal Entry

_____
_____
_____
_____
_____
_____
_____
_____
_____
_____
_____
_____
_____
_____
_____
_____
_____
_____
_____
_____

ENDNOTES

Chapter 1

[1] Study in Canada: Community Colleges and Technical Institutes Web site. http://www.studyincanada.com/english/edsys/comcoll.htm

[2] Statistics Canada, "Education in Canada, 1996"; and *The Daily*, September 29, 1999.

[3] Association of Canadian Comunity Colleges Web Site. http://www.accc.ca/english/forum/publications/CollegeCanada/9899-4-1/learningbank.htm

[4] *TheDaily*, Statistics Canada, December 22, 1998.

[5] Conference Board of Canada, "Employability Skills Profile: The Critical Skills Required of the Canadian Workforce." http://www.conferenceboard.ca/nbec/pdf/empskill.pdf

[6] Human Resources Development Canada, *Canada Prospects: Canada's Guide to Career Planning* (Ottawa: 1997),16.

[7] David K. Foot and Daniel Stoffman, *Boom, Bust and Echo 2000: Profiting from the Demographic Shift in the New Millennium* (Toronto: Macfarlane, Walter and Ross, 1998).

[8] John Robert Colombo, *The 1997 Canadian Global Almanac* (Toronto: Macmillan Canada, 1997).

[9] Rhonda Montgomery, Patricia Moody, Robert M Sherfield, Lisa Fraser, and Don Fraser, *Cornerstones: Building On Being Your Best, Canadian Edition* (Toronto: Allyn and Bacon Canada, 1997), 11.

Chapter 2

[1] Barbara Soloman, North Carolina State University.

[2] Howard Gardner, *Multiple Intelligences: The Theory in Practice* (New York: HarperCollins, 1993), 5–49.

[3] Joyce Bishop, Ph.D., Psychology faculty, Golden West College, Huntington Beach, CA.

Chapter 3

[1] Paul R. Timm, Ph.D., *Successful Self-Management: A Psychologically Sound Approach to Personal Effectiveness* (Los Altos, CA: Crisp Publications, Inc., 1987), 22–41.

[2] Stephen Covey, *The Seven Habits of Highly Effective People* (New York: Simon & Schuster, 1989), 70–144, 309–318.

Chapter 4

[1] Conference Board of Canada, "Employability Skills Profile: The Critical Skills Required of the Canadian Workforce." http://www.conferenceboard.ca/nbec/pdf/empskill.pdf

[2] Frank T. Lyman, Jr., Ph.D., "Think-Pair-Share, Thinktrix, Thinklinks, and Weird Facts: An Interactive System for Cooperative Thinking." In *Enhancing Thinking Through Cooperative Learning*, ed. Neil Davidson and Toni Worsham (New York: Teachers College Press, 1992), 169–181.

[3] Sylvan Barnet and Hugo Bedau, *Critical Thinking, Reading, and Writing: A Brief Guide to Argument*, 2nd ed. (Boston: Bedford Books of St. Martin's Press, 1996), 43.

[4] Roger von Oech, *A Kick in the Seat of the Pants* (New York: Harper & Row Publishers, 1986), 5–21.

[5] T. Z. Tardif and R. J. Sternberg, "What do we know about creativity?" In *The Nature of Creativity*, ed. R. J. Sternberg (Cambridge, MA: Cambridge University Press, 1988).

[6] J. R. Hayes, *Cognitive Psychology: Thinking and Creating* (Homewood, IL: Dorsey, 1978).

[7] T. M. Amabile, *The Social Psychology of Creativity* (New York: Springer-Verlag, 1983).

[8] Roger von Oech, *A Whack on the Side of the Head* (New York: Warner Books, 1990), 11–168.

[9] Dennis Coon, *Introduction to Psychology: Exploration and Application*, 6th ed. (St. Paul: West Publishing Company, 1992), 295.

Chapter 5

[1] Conference Board of Canada, "Employability Skills Profile: The Critical Skills Required of the Canadian Workforce." http://www.conferenceboard.ca/nbec/pdf/empskill.pdf

[2] Sherwood Harris, *The New York Public Library Book of How and Where to Look It Up* (Englewood Cliffs, NJ: Prentice Hall, 1991), 13.

[3] George M. Usova, *Efficient Study Strategies: Skills for Successful Learning* (Pacific Grove, CA: Brooks/Cole Publishing Company, 1989), 45.

[4] Francis P. Robinson, *Effective Behavior* (New York: Harper & Row, 1941).

[5] Karl E. Case, Ray C. Fair, J. Frank Strain, and Michael R. Veall, *Principles of Microeconomics, First Canadian Edition* (Scarborough: Prentice Hall Canada, 1998), 72–73.

[6] Sylvan Barnet and Hugo Bedau, *Critical Thinking, Reading, and Writing: A Brief Guide to Argument*, 2nd ed. (Boston: Bedford Books of St. Martin's Press, 1996), 15–21.

[7] John J. Macionis, Juanne Nancarrow Clarke, and Linda M. Gerber, *Sociology*, 3rd Canadian Edition (Prentice Hall Canada, 1999), 170–171.

[8] Teresa Audesirk and Gerald Audesirk, *Life on Earth* (Upper Saddle River, NJ: Prentice Hall, 1997), 55–56.

Chapter 6

[1] Conference Board of Canada, "Employability Skills Profile: The Critical Skills Required of the Canadian Workforce." http://www.conferenceboard.ca/nbec/pdf/empskill.pdf

[2] William Strunk, Jr., and E. B. White, *The Elements of Style*, 3rd ed. (Boston: Allyn & Bacon, 1979).

[3] Walter Pauk, *How to Study in College*, 5th ed. (Boston: Houghton Mifflin Company, 1993), 110–114.2

[4] Analysis based on Lynn Quitman Troyka, *Simon & Schuster Handbook for Writers* (Upper Saddle River, NJ: Prentice Hall, 1996), 22–23.

[5] Anne Lamott, *Bird by Bird: Instructions on Writing and Life* (New York: Pantheon Books, 1994).

[6] Troyka, 22–23.

[7] Philip R. Harris and Robert T. Moran, *Managing Cultural Differences*, 3rd ed. (Houston, TX: Gulf Publishing Company, 1991), 59.

[8] Joseph Gibaldi, *MLA Handbook for Writers of Research Papers* (New York: Modern Language Association of America, 1995).

[9] Natalie Goldberg, *Writing Down the Bones: Freeing the Writer Within* (Boston: Shambhala Publications, 1986).

[10] Alfred Rosa, Paul Eschholz, and John Roberts, *The Writer's Brief Handbook* (Toronto: Allyn and Bacon Canada, 1996).

Chapter 7

[1] Conference Board of Canada, "Employability Skills Profile: The Critical Skills Required of the Canadian Workforce." http://www.conferenceboard.ca/nbec/pdf/empskill.pdf

[2] Ralph G. Nichols, "Do We Know How to Listen? Practical Helps in a Modern Age," *Speech Teacher* (March 1961), 118–124.

[3] Ibid.

[4] Herman Ebbinghaus, *Memory: A Contribution to Experimental Psychology*, trans. H. A. Ruger and C. E. Bussenius (New York: New York Teacher's College, Columbia University, 1885).

[5] Adapted from Ron Fry, *"Ace"Any Test*, 3rd ed. (Franklin Lakes, NJ: Career Press, 1996), 123–124.

[6] Sheila Tobias, *Overcoming Math Anxiety* (New York: W.W. Norton & Company, 1993), 50.

[7] Ibid., 69.

[8] Ibid., 63.

[9] Many of the examples of objective questions used in this chapter are from Gary W. Piggrem, Test Item File for Charles G. Morris, *Understanding Psychology*, 3rd ed. (Upper Saddle River, NJ: Prentice Hall, 1996).

Chapter 8

[1] T. J. Samuals, *Visible Minorities in Canada: A Projection* (Toronto: Race Relations Advisory Council on Advertising, Canadian Advertising Foundation, 1992).

[2] Edith Wharton, "False Dawn," In *Old New York* (New York: Simon & Schuster, 1951), 18–19.

[3] Sheryl McCarthy, *Why Are the Heroes Always White?* (Kansas City, MO: Andrews and McMeel, 1995), 188.

[4] John Hockenberry, *Moving Violations* (New York: Hyperion, 1995), 78.

[5] Lise Dessaint, "Air Canada to Provide More Work Opportunities for Aboriginal Peoples." http://www.chrc.ca/frames/news/june20e.html and http://www.chrc-ccdp.ca/issues/aboriginal.asp

[6] Lise Dessaint, "Tribunal Upholds Age Discrimination Complaint Against CAF." http://www.chrc.ca/frames/news/jan14e.html and http://www.chrc-ccdp.ca/news-comm/1999/Oct19.oct.asp

[7] Tamara Trotter and Joycelyn Allen, *Talking Justice: 602 Ways to Build and Promote Racial Harmony* (Saratoga, CA: R & E Publishers, 1993), 51.

[8] Frances Henry, Carol Tator, Winston Mattis, and Tim Rees, *The Colour of Democracy: Racism in Canadian Society* (Toronto: Harcourt Brace, 1995).

[9] Augie Fleras and Jean Leonard Elliott, *Multiculturalism in Canada* (Scarborough: Nelson Canada, 1992).

[10] McCarthy, 137.

[11] Adapted from an interpretation of the Myers-Briggs Type Indicator by Margaret Keys.

[12] Louis E. Boone, David L. Kurtz, and Judy R. Block, *Contemporary Business Communication* (Englewood Cliffs, NJ: Prentice Hall, 1994), 49–54.

[13] Adapted by Richard Bucher, Professor of Sociology, Baltimore City Community College, from Paula Rothenberg, William Paterson College of New Jersey.

Chapter 9

[1] Herbert Benson and Eileen Stuart, et al., *The Wellness Book* (New York: Simon & Schuster, 1992), 160.

[2] Ibid., 292.

[3] Hans Selye, *The Stress of Life* (New York: McGraw-Hill, 1976).

[4] Patricia Chisholm, "Coping with Stress." In *Maclean's*, January 8, 1996, 33–36.

[5] Benson and Stuart, 178.

[6] National Institutes of Mental Health Publication No. 94-3561, National Institutes of Mental Health, 1994.

[7] The Suicide Information and Education Centre, "Frequently Asked Questions." http://siec.ca/faq.htm.

[8] American Psychiatric Association, "Let's Talk Facts About Post-Traumatic Stress Disorder," Copyright APA, all rights reserved.

[9] National Institutes of Mental Health Publication No. 93-3477, National Institutes of Mental Health, 1993. Rewritten by Lee Hoffman, Office of Scientific Information (OSI), National Institutes of Mental Health.

[10] Diane McKenzie and Eric Single, "Canadian Profile 1997: Alcohol." http://www.ccsa.ca/cp97alc.htm#alcohol and http://www.ccsa.ca/cp99alc.htm

[11] The Editors of the University of California at Berkeley Wellness Letter, *The New Wellness Encyclopedia* (Boston: Houghton Mifflin Company, 1995), 72.

[12] Addiction Research Foundation, "Alcohol Use Among University Students by Selected Characteristics, 1993." http://www.arf.org/isd/stats/univalc.html

[13] Diane McKenzie, Eric Single, Minh Van Truong, and Gary Timoshenko, Canadian Centre on Substance Abuse. "Canadian Profile 1997: Tobacco." http://www.ccsa.ca/cp97tob.htm#tobacco and http://www.ccsa.ca/cp99tob.htm

[14] David Stout, "Direct Link Found Between Smoking And Lung Cancer," *New York Times*, October 18, 1996, A1, A19.

[15] *Chicago Tribune*, February 26, 1997, "Secondhand Smoke Blamed in 3,000 Yearly Cancer Deaths." http://archives.chicago.tribune.com

[16] National Institutes of Health, Agency for Health Care Policy and Research, "Nicotine: A Powerful Addiction."

[17] Eric Single, Joan Brewster, Patricia MacNeil, Jefferey Hatcher, and Catherine Trainer, *Alcohol and Drug Use: Results from the 1993 General Social Survey*. A report prepared for the Studies Unit, Health Promotion Directorate (Health Canada, January 1995).

[18] Kim Painter, "Drinking: Loving and Leaving It," *USA Today*, June 4, 1996, D1.

[19] Diane Riley and Diane McKenzie, Canadian Centre on Substance Abuse, "Canadian Profile 1997: AIDS and Drug Use." http://www.ccsa.ca/cp99aids.htm

[20] www.macleans.ca/pub-doc/1999/10/25/cover/24536.shtml. October 18, 1999.

[21] Parker Corwin and Amanda Haskell (September 1996). Campus Advocates for Rape Education at Wheaton College. http://gossamer.wheatonma.edu/groups/care/WebPage.HTML

[22] Esta Soler, Family Violence Prevention Fund: The Facts. http://www.fvpf.org/facts

Chapter 10

[1] Human Resources Development Canada, *Canada Prospects: Canada's Guide to Career Planning* (Ottawa, 1999), 18.

[2] Elaine Carey, "Fees create U of Elite," *Toronto Star*, August 30, 1997, and *Maclean's*, November 15, 1999, 84.

[3] Canada Student Loans Program. http://www.hrdc-drhc.gc.ca/student_loans/engraph/index.html

Chapter 11

[1] Conference Board of Canada, "Employability Skills Profile: The Critical Skills Required of the Canadian Workforce." http://www.conferenceboard.ca/nbec/pdf/empskill.pdf

[2] Isaac Asimov, "My Own View." In *The Encyclopedia of Science Fiction*, ed. Robert Holdstock (London: Octopus Books, 1978).

[3] Margaret J. Wheatley and Myron Kellner-Rogers, "A Simpler Way," *Weight Watchers Magazine* 30.3, (1997), 42–44.

[4] Thomas Moore, *The Care of the Soul* (New York: Harper Perennial, 1992), xi–xx.

[5] Stephen Covey, *The Seven Habits of Highly Effective People* (New York: Simon & Schuster, 1989), 70–144, 309–318.

[6] Sarah Delany and Elizabeth Delany with Amy Hill Hearth, *Book of Everyday Wisdom* (New York: Kodansha International, 1994), 123.

INDEX

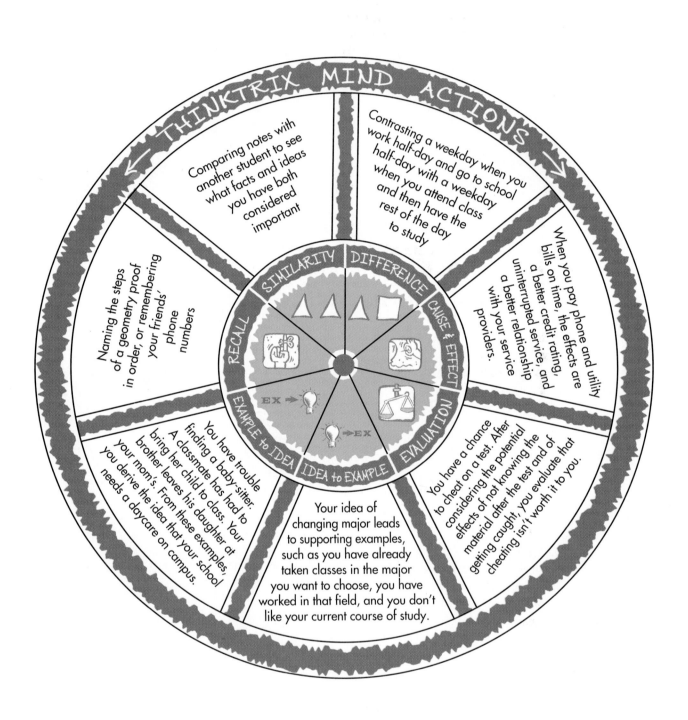